LYNNE PALMER'S

ASTROLOGICAL ALMANAC

FOR 2019

ISBN 978-726129992

First Printing 2018

Published by:

Lynne Palmer
Phone: (702) 894-4196
Fax: (702) 894-9918
Toll Free: (866)721-1871
Web Site: www.lynnepalmer.com
Email: lynnepalmer@lynnepalmer.com

Printed and bound in the United States of America

BOOKS BY LYNNE PALMER

- Astrological Compatibility
- Prosperity
- Is Your Name Lucky For You?
- ABC Basic Chart Reading
- Horoscope of Billy Rose
- Horoscope of Richard Nixon
- Your Lucky Days And Numbers
- Bet To Win
- Money Magic
- Astro-Guide To Nutrition And Vitamins
- Gambling To Win
- Be Your Own Astrologer
- Astrological Potpourri
- Illness: Planetary Rulerships--
  Medical Astrological
- Are You Compatible With Your Boss,
  Partner, Coworker,
  Clients, Employees?

LYNNE PALMER

ACTIVITIES IN THE ASTROLOGICAL FIELD: Professional astrologer since 1957, international consultant, writer, lecturer, teacher, columnist, researcher. First to initiate Marathon crash courses.

Recipient of Professional Astrologers, Inc. annual award "For Outstanding Contribution to the Art and Science of Astrology". Biographical sketch in Who's Who of American Women, The Directory of Distinguished Americans and Contemporary Personalities of the World, Who's Who in the West, Who's Who in the World, Who's Who in America.

COLUMNIST: Formerly for Self, Diet and Exercise and House Beautiful magazines, and Keyhole and Lottery Advantage newspapers.

RECORD ALBUM: Cast and Read Your Horoscope (2 LP's and booklet).

NATIONAL TELEVISION APPEARANCES: The Johnny Carson "Tonight Show", "Good Morning America", "60 Minutes", "Geraldo", "What's My Line?", "The Young Set", "The Alan Burke Show", "For Women Only" and "The Joe Franklin Show".

INTERNATIONAL TELEVISION SHOWS: Cosmos on BBC TV (England), Science Series, Italian TV (Italy); Fantastico, Brazilian TV (Brazil); Japanese TV (three shows on three stations).

RADIO SHOWS: Numerous appearances on many shows throughout the United States and Canada.

SPEAKER: Women's Clubs, Industrial and Trade Shows, Astrological Organizations.

PUBLICITY: Interviews in the New York Post and many other newspapers and magazines, including The New York Times, Boston Sunday Globe, Wall Street Journal, London Sunday Mirror, The National Observer, People, World Journal Tribune, The Herald News, The Atlanta Journal, Mobile Register, Tulsa World, The Chronicle, Las Vegas Review Journal, Life, Forbes, Newsweek, and international publications such as Oggi (Italian magazine) and Veja ((Brazilian magazine).

NEWSPAPER AND MAGAZINE A R T I C L E S : New York magazine, Horoscope, Astrology Your Daily Guide, Enquirer, Globe.

CONTENTS

Calendar 2019 9

Preface... 10

Foreword 12

PART ONE — SUN SIGNS

Introduction... 16

Rising Sign Table... 17

Chapter One - Aries 18

Chapter Two - Taurus.. 24

Chapter Three - Gemini 30

Chapter Four - Cancer... 36

Chapter Five - Leo 43

Chapter Six - Virgo 50

Chapter Seven - Libra 56

Chapter Eight - Scorpio 62

Chapter Nine - Sagittarius... 69

Chapter Ten - Capricorn.. 76

Chapter Eleven - Aquarius 83

Chapter Twelve - Pisces.. 90

PART TWO — BEST DAYS GUIDE FOR DAILY ACTIVITIES

Introduction... 97

A 105

Acquisitions, acupuncture, advertising, affectional interests, agents, (literary, screen, television, theatrical), alcohol, amusements, animals, apologizing, applications (I.D. card, permit, passport, visa), appraisals, architectural plans, assessments, art, auctions, auditions (actors, actresses, clowns, comedians, dancers, musicians, singers), authorities; avoid: accidents, anger, animals (birth, breed, neuter, spay or train), blind dates, buying or wearing shoes, boots, slippers, sneakers or clothing, contracts, cutting cloth or timber, danger, debts, dental cleaning, extraction, surgery or dental work, ear piercing, eating sugars and starches, falls, fires, gossip, hair transplants, harvesting, hiring employees, making important decisions, manicures, moving, nuclear power areas, pedicures, schemes, strikes, surgery, terrorist attacks, theft, and travel by air, land or water.

B 119

Baking, balloons (hot air), bankers, barbecue (clambake, luau), beauty appointments, beer (brewing), body piercing, bosses (good will), budgets, building, building (construction, demolition), bunion removal, business (commence, deals, expansion, open), bust development, buying; air conditioners, antiques, artistic objects, attaché case, automobiles, balloons, bargains, beepers, binoculars, boots, briefcase, cameras, cassette tapes, C-D ROM's, clocks, clothes, compact disk/

players, computers, cosmetics, curios, cutlery, DVD's, dolls, drinking vessels, electrical appliances/equipment, electronic equipment, exercise equipment, eye glasses, fax machine, flooring, flowers, franchise, furniture, games, glass, hats, head-gear (helmets), hi-fi sets, home furnishings/accessories, horses, implements, ipods, jewelry, knives, machinery, laser printer, lens, lenses, linen (bedding, towels), luggage, machinery, medical instruments, microscopes, microwave ovens, mirrors, modems, motorcycles, musical instruments, optical equipment, ornaments, pagers, perfume, pets, pewter, phonograph machines/records, photocopier, plastics, podcasts. portfolio case, pottery, radar detector, radios, real estate, recorders (mixers), religious items, retread tires, robots, satellite dish, scanners, scarves, scissors, shoes, silver, slippers, sneakers, software (for computers), sports equipment, stained glass, stereo systems, surveillance systems, synthetic fabrics/ materials, telephones, telescopes, television sets, thrift shop items, tires, tools, toys, trailers, transistors, trucks, tuxedo, tweezers, uniforms, vans, VCR's, video tapes/discs/games, watches, watercraft, water filters, wheelchair, wigs/toupees/hair pieces, wood.

C 134
Calluses (removal), campaigns (commencing), canning, canvassing, carpet (shampooing), cement pouring, charity (donations, fund raising, solicit), check gimmick, chemistry, chiropractic treatments, cigarettes, classes (astrology, cooking, meditation, modeling), cleaning, cloth (cut/dye), clubs (join), colonic irrigation, comic (books, strips), commercials (infomercials; radio/television), committees, computer (e-mail, fraud, games, internet, online, programming, secret code, web site), contracts, corns (removal), courage, credit (application, purchase), crusades (commencing).

D 142
Dating, debates (controversies), debts (collecting), decorating, dental work (braces, bonding, caps, cleaning, extraction, fillings, plate impressions, reconstruction and root canal), designing, diet (to gain or lose weight), dining, distribution (books, magazines, products), dramatic expression, drugs, dude-ranch.

E 145
Ears (piercing, plate impressions), eggs (set to hatch, quick maturity, for size), electrolysis, employment agency, encouragement, engagements, engraving, entertainment, errands, ESP (psychic endeavors), exams, excursions, exercising, exhibits, exploration (geographical, medical, search), eye tests.

F 149
Fabrics, (bleaching, dying, tinting), fads, fasting, favor, fertilizing, filibustering, fingernails (false), fireworks (make, shoot), fishing (other than for shellfish), fishing (shellfish), foods, (dehydrated/dry/freezing), foot treatments, foreclosure, fruit, furniture.

G 152
    Gambling, games (toys; create), gas station (open), gifts, government, grafting (pollinating), grain (harvesting/planting), grass (cutting), group activities.

H 155
    Hair (coloring, cutting, for beauty, quick/slow/luxuriant growth, thickness, extensions, permanents, straightening, transplants, treatments, weaving), harvesting, hay (cutting), healing (mental, physical, rehabilitation), hedges, helicopter, hiding, hire (consultant, security), hobbies, house (remodel, repair), hypnosis.

I 160
    Ideas (expressing, new/radical/utopian), illumination, installation (answering machine, elevator, fax machine, flooring, signs, telephones, surveillance systems), insurance, inventing (marketing), inventions, investigation, irrigation.

J 163
    Job (apply for work, hiring employees, interviews, permanency, promotions, temporary).

K 164
    Knitting.

L 164
    Land (develop properties, subdivide), landscaping, lecturing, legal actions, lending, licenses (broker, business, driver's), limousine service, lessons (acting, aviation, clowning, dancing, driving, horseback riding, musical instruments, singing, skiing, swimming, tennis, trapeze), livestock, lobbying.

M 169
    Magic, magnetizing objects, mail, makeup (permanent, tattoo), manicures (and pedicures), manuscripts (outlines/proposals), marriage (proposals, wedding dates), massage, mediation, meditation, men, mental deductions, menus (plan), Mercury retrograde, mergers, military (enlist), mining, mirrors, moles, (removal), money (borrowing, economizing, lending, saving), movies, moving (long/short stay), muscle development, museum, mushrooms.

N 175
    Networking

O 175
    Oil (drilling, lubricants), originality.

P 176
    Packing, painting, parties, pawning, pet (grooming, kennels), petitions, photography, physical therapy, pickling (beets, cucumbers, herring), plans, planting (bulbs, evergreens, flowers, lawn, plants, shrubs, trees, vegetables), poles, posts, pottery (making), pregnancy, printing, projects (pitch, sell), promoting, propositions, proposals, prosthesis (artificial limbs), psychic (development, endeavors, readings), psychoanalysis, psychotherapy, publicity, public relations, publishing, puzzles (crossword, jigsaw).

R 183
Reconciliations, recording (audio, disc or video tape), recreation, reforms, regulations, rehearsals, renovating, renting (boat, watercraft; for beauty, neatness, comfort; costumes, equipment, furniture; fast results; horse; inexpensive, permanent, temporary, to others; theatre; tuxedo; wheel chair; yacht), reorganizing, repair (audio tapes, automobiles, boots, cassette tapes, clocks, compact disc players, computers, electrical appliances and products, electronic equipment, furniture, jewelry, machinery, mechanical devices, phonographs, plumbing, radios, recorders, shoes, silver, stereos, tape players, television sets, tools, transistors, video cassettes and games, watches), research, reservations (airplane, cruise ship, hotel, inn, lodge, motel, train), returning items, reunions, rodeo (perform), romance, roof (installation, repair).

S 191
Sauerkraut, sculpting, secrets, self-discipline, selling (franchise), sewing, sex (boldness, endurance, passion), sheep, shingling, shipping, shoes (boots, slippers, sneakers), shows, skin care, skydiving (bungee jumping, hang gliding, paragliding), socializing (enjoyment, meeting new people), social security, sodding, speculating, spirituality, sports activities(competitive, non-competitive, training, water), spraying, stone (cut, polish), storage, strikes, subscriptions (magazine, newspaper, newsletter, periodical, tabloid), surgery, sweets (cook: make).

T 203
Tailoring, tattoo (body removal), taxes (audit, calculate, installment agreement, quick action), teaching, terrorist, timber, tinting (car windows), trading, training, travel (by land, water; city, country, island hop; enjoyment, plans).

U 206
Upholstery

V 206
Vaccinations, voice mail, volunteer work.

W 206
Warts (removal), weaning (animals, human babies), weaving (basket, cloth), weeds, wells (to dig/drill), wheat, wine (make), women, writing (commencement, correspondence).

X 208
X-Rays.

Y 208
Yoga (learn).

2019

January

S	M	T	W	T	F	S
		1	2	3	4	5
6	7	8	9	10	11	12
13	14	15	16	17	18	19
20	21	22	23	24	25	26
27	28	29	30	31		

February

S	M	T	W	T	F	S
					1	2
3	4	5	6	7	8	9
10	11	12	13	14	15	16
17	18	19	20	21	22	23
24	25	26	27	28		

March

S	M	T	W	T	F	S
					1	2
3	4	5	6	7	8	9
10	11	12	13	14	15	16
17	18	19	20	21	22	23
24	25	26	27	28	29	30
31						

April

S	M	T	W	T	F	S
	1	2	3	4	5	6
7	8	9	10	11	12	13
14	15	16	17	18	19	20
21	22	23	24	25	26	27
28	29	30				

May

S	M	T	W	T	F	S
			1	2	3	4
5	6	7	8	9	10	11
12	13	14	15	16	17	18
19	20	21	22	23	24	25
26	27	28	29	30	31	

June

S	M	T	W	T	F	S
						1
2	3	4	5	6	7	8
9	10	11	12	13	14	15
16	17	18	19	20	21	22
23	24	25	26	27	28	29
30						

July

S	M	T	W	T	F	S
	1	2	3	4	5	6
7	8	9	10	11	12	13
14	15	16	17	18	19	20
21	22	23	24	25	26	27
28	29	30	31			

August

S	M	T	W	T	F	S
				1	2	3
4	5	6	7	8	9	10
11	12	13	14	15	16	17
18	19	20	21	22	23	24
25	26	27	28	29	30	31

September

S	M	T	W	T	F	S
1	2	3	4	5	6	7
8	9	10	11	12	13	14
15	16	17	18	19	20	21
22	23	24	25	26	27	28
29	30	31				

October

S	M	T	W	T	F	S
		1	2	3	4	5
6	7	8	9	10	11	12
13	14	15	16	17	18	19
20	21	22	23	24	25	26
27	28	29	30	31		

November

S	M	T	W	T	F	S
					1	2
3	4	5	6	7	8	9
10	11	12	13	14	15	16
17	18	19	20	21	22	23
24	25	26	27	28	29	30

December

S	M	T	W	T	F	S
1	2	3	4	5	6	7
8	9	10	11	12	13	14
15	16	17	18	19	20	21
22	23	24	25	26	27	28
29	30	31				

PREFACE

A horoscope is based upon a person's day, month, year, time and place of birth. Once a chart has been cast, it indicates an individual's attitude toward everything in life. A horoscope contain 12 houses (each representing a different part of life), 10 planets and 12 signs of the Zodiac. The Rising Sign is based upon the time a person is born. (Refer to pages 16 and 17).

The time of birth is usually recorded on a birth certificate, in a baby book, family Bible or at the Registrar's Office. Without the time of birth, an accurate horoscope cannot be cast. However, the Astrological Almanac can be used by those who know, and those who do not know, their exact time of birth.

Everyone can benefit with this Astrological Almanac! It can be used by people in all age brackets, of both sexes, professionals and non-professionals, and from all walks of life. There is something for everyone in this book: a complete Sun sign synopsis, as well as information to determine the best time to undertake or fulfill any venture.

Why is this book unique? A general Sun sign book does not give the information contained in this Astrological Almanac, especially as provided in Part One — Sun Signs; your color, gem, stone, number, day, city, state, country, healthful herb teas for the zone of the body ruled by your sign, cell salts, books, music and fashion ruled by your sign, the kinds of flowers, gifts and perfumes to give as presents for each sign and compatibility (or how you get along sexually) with everyone, as well as the best days for sex.

Another unique feature is the Best Days Guide for Daily Activities (Part Two), which gives dates to enable you to determine the right time to do whatever you wish in order to obtain the best results and quickest action possible.

Thus, you can consult this Astrological Almanac for information to apply to your daily life (altogether, there are 500 categories), enabling you to make advance plans concerning a specific activity or venture. For instance: What is a good date to start a legal action? Open a business? Advertise? Get hired for a job? Give a party? Go on a diet? Go on a trip? Have your hair cut? Have dental work? Have surgery? Plant crops? Can food?

Have you ever wondered why a restaurant opened and then folded even though the food was tasty, the decor charming and the service good? Because it was opened, astrologically, at the wrong time. "Everything in life is in the timing" is a well-known adage that has been expressed over and over by countless thousands of people.

In this Astrological Almanac you will be able to determine when to do something to attain the most propitious results. To use this information you do not need your horoscope, nor do you need to know your Sun sign. Just look for the activity you are interested in (all are listed alphabetically), find the favorable dates to take action throughout the year and plan accordingly. This applies to everyone, regardless of your Sun sign.

Most astrologers charge from five to ten dollars to answer their clients' questions along these lines. In order to determine the answers, mathematical calculations are necessary and this takes time. Many professional astrologers do not have the requisite knowledge to answer any and all questions they may be asked. With the Astrological Almanac they will be better equipped to fulfill this obligation to their clients and do so with greater efficiency. In addition, the client can also use the Astrological Almanac.

People are interested in knowing what is going to happen, especially in troubled times. Many turn to Sun sign books or professional astrologers for guidance. Or they turn to the Astrological Almanac, which tells them the best time to participate in a certain activity or venture and, thus, they plan their day-to-day life around these dates. In this book, answers are given that are needed by millions of people who are searching for the right time to take action. Thus a person is able to enrich his/her life by using astrological principles and knowledge.

One friend wrote, "My household runs smoother since I have been using your Astrological Almanac."

And that is what this book is all about — it is designed to save lives, to help you avoid pitfalls, injury, eliminate needless problems, to make everything you do easier, therefore bringing you success, happiness, wealth and a life filled with everything you desire.

FOREWORD

I have been a professional astrologer since 1957. More than 10,000 people have been referred to me as clients. Many more thousands have used my services, although I have never cast their horoscopes or met them personally. Yet, without having a horoscope for each person, I was able to help each one through applying the principles as set forth in this book. My Astrological Almanac has been published every year since 1978.

Part One of the Astrological Almanac contains the compatibility between Sun signs, which do not need explaining. However, the Sun sign rulership may be new to some of you with regard to: climate, part of land, music, fashion, color, stone, metallic element, senses (physical or non-physical), Talismanic gem, flower, lucky number/day, cell salts, herbs, zones of the body, cities, states, countries, books, gifts and perfumes.

Centuries ago, ancient civilizations discovered that each sign and planet corresponded to a distinct part of nature; thus, everything in life is governed (ruled) by a particular sign and its corresponding planet, including your thoughts and actions and the events which you attract. Based upon these observations and my experiences, I have updated and added in modern day products, conveniences, and daily activities.

Also, I would like to add that man is comprised of 70% water and the Moon moves great bodies of water. Science is beginning to recognize that man is pulled by flows of human energy and emotional cycles which are governed by planetary forces. The calculations provided in this book are the planetary vibrations active during certain time periods and influence the way you may be pulled, especially if you plan your daily activities by them.

Do you want to purchase a present for someone you do not know very well? Are you buying a gift for a person who is fussy or seems to have everything? Or are you just indecisive about selecting a present for a friend, loved one, co-worker, boss, relative or child? Do you know that astrology can help solve your problems?

Now you can send flowers or give a book, video game, video or audio tape or other gift according to a person/s Sun sign. And why not give your sweetheart something she/he will cherish and find attractive? And why not give a friend a present he or she can use or really likes? Now you can avoid the embarrassing moment of having your gift returned, exchanged for something else, given away or hidden in a closet. Take the guesswork out of giving — let astrology help answer your question, "What present should I buy for _____?" It is all here in the Astrological Almanac.

Do you want to move to another city, state or country? Does the place where you now live lack the lifestyle you yearn for? Do you feel isolated — a buried feeling in this locality? Have you been unlucky here? Ever since you moved to this place, does it seem as though you cannot get ahead financially or advance on a job? Is it difficult to make friends in this town, yet when you travel to other places it is a different story? Are you weary of a small municipality and want the bright lights and the hustle and bustle of a metropolis? Or do you want to leave the big city and just do not know where to go? Are you aware that astrology can help you relocate to a place that is best suited for you?

Every city has a horoscope which is based upon the day, month, year and place of birth when it was founded, a charter was signed or the incorporation occurred. In most instances, it is impossible to obtain the time that this took place; therefore, the sign the Sun was in at that time will suffice as being the ruler of the city. In this book, I have taken into consideration the Sun sign, the dominant sign (many planets in a sign) and the Ascendant (rising sign), therefore some places may have more than one sign ruling them. When the time of birth is known of a city or country, I list the Ascendant sign. In some instances, there is more than one horoscope used for a locale and there is some doubt as to which is the correct one; in this situation, I give you both of them.

If your town is not listed under any of the Sun signs in this book, check with the library, city clerk or chamber of commerce for the date (day, month, year) the city was incorporated. Then locate the sign that rules it (the sign the Sun is in), using the following as a guide:

Aries:	March 21 - April 19	Libra:	September 23 - October 22
Taurus:	April 20 - May 20	Scorpio:	October 23 - November 21
Gemini:	May 21 - June 20	Sagittarius:	November 22 - December 21
Cancer:	June 21 - July 22	Capricorn:	December 22 - January 19
Leo:	July 21 - August 22	Aquarius:	January 20 - February 18
Virgo:	August 23 - September 22	Pisces:	February 19 - March 20

SIGNS AND CITIES

In the Sun sign section of Part One of this book, read the sign descriptions and discover which town, state or country interest you the most. Find out how that place may influence your life if you live there at the present time or how it may affect you if later you move there.

HARMONY AND DISCORD

If you reside in a city, state or country that is ruled by your Sun sign and you are unlucky there, it is because your Sun or a planet in the Sun sign of that city, state or country's sign is afflicted. If your Sun, or a planet in that sign in your horoscope, is harmonious, you are lucky there. You may fare very well in a place that is not under your Sun sign, because that sign's city, state or country is a fortunate influence in your horoscope. You have ten planets in various signs in your horoscope. Therefore, when a planet in a particular sign is well aspected (harmonious), fortunate events are attracted and your attitude is positive in that environment. When a planet in a particular sign is not well aspected (discordant), unfortunate events are attracted and your attitude is negative in that environment.

Mary Q. is a Libra Sun sign who lived in a Capricorn town. A planet in Capricorn in her horoscope is afflicted. She was always pessimistic, broke, worked hard, and did not have the energy or the desire to socialize; she was lonely. Mary consulted me and moved to a Sagittarius (planets in this sign are harmonious in her horoscope) city and now she is optimistic, has a good job, money in the bank, a boyfriend and having lots of fun.

For the greatest harmony, choose a place that is in your Sun sign category or your own Sun sign if you have been lucky when expressing the traits ruled by it. Same Sun Sign Category: Aries, Gemini, Leo, Sagittarius and Aquarius are harmonious for you if you were born under any one of those signs and if it is not afflicted in your horoscope.

Same Sun Sign Category: Taurus, Cancer, Virgo, Scorpio, Capricorn and Pisces are harmonious for those born under any of these signs and if it is not afflicted in your horoscope.

BEFORE YOU MOVE

Do your homework before you make any major move. Write to the Chamber of Commerce about the town's industry, taxes, climate, population, etc. Buy newspapers from that city; scrutinize the want ads in order to obtain a general outlook on the employment situation, including salaries and job openings. Look at the real estate section for the price range of rental and sale properties. Read all the pages in the newspaper and you will be well informed as to the town's politics, entertainment, crime, social life, sports activities, etc.

Once you have decided that this place sounds like it is for you, visit the city. Talk with the local inhabitants; inquire about clubs, schools, playgrounds, and artistic culture programs. What kind of night life does it have? Are the streets well protected? Are the people's needs taken care of, that is, from the standpoint of what the city is supposed to do for its citizens? Is the town getting run down? Is it well kept? Is it a growing city? Are people and industry moving in or out, and what is drawing them in or driving them away? Do not be afraid to ask questions of everyone you meet — shop owners, strangers (especially those who look friendly); the answers received may be your final deciding factor.

WHEN SHOULD YOU MOVE?

Now that you have come to the conclusion that this is the metropolis you want to live in, when should you move? The following "do not's" imply that you have one or more planets afflicted in your horoscope, and thus may later regret the move:

Do not move if you have been procrastinating more than usual or you have become absentminded or forgetful, or are in a fog and confused. (Neptune negative aspects in a horoscope.).

Do not move if you have been behaving impulsively or are abrupt, erratic, jittery or high strung. This indicates you are not analyzing everything carefully and that, most likely, negative Uranus aspects are influencing your horoscope.

Do not move if you are depressed, full of negative energy, have thoughts of self pity, are fearful of making the change, or you are worried and insecure. (Saturn negative aspects in a horoscope.).

The best time to move is \Vhen your spirits are up, when your are happy, bubbly, enthusiastic, laughing, confident and positive that you are doing the right thing. This implies that you are under the influence of Jupiter and you will benefit from the change. You will enjoy and make the most out of your new home because Lady Luck smiles on you. And that is what you want, isn't it?

PART ONE — SUN SIGNS
INTRODUCTION

The Sun sign is the sign that the Sun was in at the moment you were born. And at that same hour and minute of birth, there were nine other planets in various signs of the Zodiac, as well as a sign that was rising on the Ascendant (appearing in view on the horizon of the celestial equator as the earth turned on its axis), which is called the Rising Sign as well as the Ascendant sign.

If you know what your rising sign is, you have additional information to get a more in-depth reading from any magazine, newspaper, periodical or book that deals with Sun sign astrology. You can combine your Sun sign qualities with those of your rising sign. In other words, if you are a Cancer Sun sign and Virgo rising sign, you read the Cancer Sun sign and the Virgo rising (or Sun Sign). After reading them, you will realize that the traits of both fit you.

If you are going to give someone flowers or a gift, etc., or take someone out and if you know that person's rising sign as well as the Sun sign, you will have a wider choice of flowers and presents to give and a better understanding of the individual.

FINDING THE RISING SIGN

If you wish to know your rising sign, the following table on page 17 will give you a general idea of what your rising sign is. However, your latitude of birth and whether you were born during Daylight Savings or War Time could make a difference. If they were in effect, subtract one hour from the birth time (if Double Summer Time was in effect, subtract two hours from the birth time) and use that new Standard Time when you read the table on page 17 to locate your rising sign.

If your time falls near the first hour given, your rising sign may be the one before that given on the table. Or if your time falls near the last hour given, your rising sign could be the following sign. For example: If you were born at 6 a.m. (and your Sun sign is Aries), you could be Aries rising, or possibly Pisces rising (which is the sign before Aries). Or if you were born at 8 a.m. (and your Sun sign is Aries), you could be Taurus rising instead of Aries rising.

— TIME —

SIGN	6:00 AM - 8:00 AM	8:00 AM - 10:00 AM	10:00 AM - 12:00 PM	12:00 PM - 2:00 PM	2:00 PM - 4:00 PM	4:00 PM - 6:00 PM
Aries	Aries	Taurus	Gemini	Cancer	Leo	Virgo
Taurus	Taurus	Gemini	Cancer	Leo	Virgo	Libra
Gemini	Gemini	Cancer	Leo	Virgo	Libra	Scorpio
Cancer	Cancer	Leo	Virgo	Libra	Scorpio	Sagittarius
Leo	Leo	Virgo	Libra	Scorpio	Sagittarius	Capricorn
Virgo	Virgo	Libra	Scorpio	Sagittarius	Capricorn	Aquarius
Libra	Libra	Scorpio	Sagittarius	Capricorn	Aquarius	Pisces
Scorpio	Scorpio	Sagittarius	Capricorn	Aquarius	Pisces	Aries
Sagittarius	Sagittarius	Capricorn	Aquarius	Pisces	Aries	Taurus
Capricorn	Capricorn	Aquarius	Pisces	Aries	Taurus	Gemini
Aquarius	Aquarius	Pisces	Aries	Taurus	Gemini	Cancer
Pisces	Pisces	Aries	Taurus	Gemini	Cancer	Leo

— TIME —

SIGN	6:00 PM - 8:00 PM	8:00 PM - 10:00 PM	10:00 PM - 12:00 AM	12:00 AM - 2:00 AM	2:00 AM - 4:00 AM	4:00 AM - 6:00 AM
Aries	Libra	Scorpio	Sagittarius	Capricorn	Aquarius	Pisces
Taurus	Scorpio	Sagittarius	Capricorn	Aquarius	Pisces	Aries
Gemini	Sagittarius	Capricorn	Aquarius	Pisces	Aries	Taurus
Cancer	Capricorn	Aquarius	Pisces	Aries	Taurus	Gemini
Leo	Aquarius	Pisces	Aries	Taurus	Gemini	Cancer
Virgo	Pisces	Aries	Taurus	Gemini	Cancer	Leo
Libra	Aries	Taurus	Gemini	Cancer	Leo	Virgo
Scorpio	Taurus	Gemini	Cancer	Leo	Virgo	Libra
Sagittarius	Gemini	Cancer	Leo	Virgo	Libra	Scorpio
Capricorn	Cancer	Leo	Virgo	Libra	Scorpio	Sagittarius
Aquarius	Leo	Virgo	Libra	Scorpio	Sagittarius	Capricorn
Pisces	Virgo	Libra	Scorpio	Sagittarius	Capricorn	Aquarius

CHAPTER ONE
ARIES: THE RAM... MARCH 21 — APRIL 20

To understand this chapter, read the Preface and Foreword. If you know your rising sign, read the advice given for that sign, as well as for your Sun sign. The combination of these two will give you even more information than could be gained by simply reading only the Sun sign. Refer to pages 16 and 17 if you do not know what your rising sign is.

The following descriptions are typical for those born under the Sun sign Aries. However, your own horoscope may contradict some of this, depending upon your rising sign and the signs occupied by the other planets in your horoscope.

Aries is a fire, masculine and barren sign. Mars is the planetary ruler. Each of the signs and/or planets has rulership over certain phases of life; the following are ruled by Aries or Mars.

COLORS
You may want to enhance your living quarters or wardrobe in these shades:

Mars: Bright red.

Aries: Light (pale) red; such hues as red coral, strawberry. Pink shades, such as coral rose, dark, hot and shocking pink.

TALISMANIC GEMS
Amethyst, carnelian, rose quartz, red opal, red spinal. You may want to magnetize the gem for good luck and/or to protect you from harm. Refer to Part Two under Magnetizing Objects for auspicious dates to magnetize a talismanic gem.

STONES
Brimstone, ocher, iron pyrite, and all kinds of red stones. You may accent your abode with these stones as accessories or wear them as jewelry. You may find that you have good luck when wearing or owning one of these stones.

METALLIC ELEMENT

Mars: Iron

NUMBER
Number 13; You may want to bet with this number, or perhaps favorable events will occur on this date. If you want to plan ahead for certain activities you could use this date for something important, especially if it coincides with a date for that event in the Best Days section in Part Two.

DAY
Tuesday: You may want to plan important activities for Tuesday. Your energy is at its height on Tuesdays.

SENSES: PHYSICAL OR NON-PHYSICAL

Physical Sense: Taste

Physical Organs: Mouth and tongue

Psychic Sense: Tasting food that is non-physical (not there in reality)

MUSIC

You are a peppy Aries and will really come to life with a snappy beat — jazz, swing, funk, ragtime, heavy metal, African rhythms (including Afro-Caribbean), Samba, Tumba, rock and roll, punk rock, martial, march, and all rhythmic tunes.

PERFUMES

These fragrances bring out your impetuousness, sportiness and pioneering spirit. Because you're always ready for action, and require lots of activity, a taste of adventure will follow when you wear these essences. Your bubbly and vivacious personality will surface. These scents will remind you of the great outdoors. Be ready to explore new realms and conquer your secret ambitions.

For the Female: Amazone by Hermès, Aphrodisia, Calandre, Charlie Red by Revlon, CK One by Calvin Klein, Concrete de Parfum by L'Occitane, Emprise, Frederique by Zenue, Givenchy II, Givenchy III, Le de Givenchy, Ma Liberte by Jean Patou, Masumi, Norell, Ormolu by Penhaligon, Spa by Alfred Sung, Weil de Weil.

For the Male: Clairborne's Men's Perfume, Grass Oil, Gucci Pour Homme, Halston's 1-12, Halston Limited, Lagerfeld, Monsieur Rochas, Paco Rabanne Pour Homme, Red for Men by Giorgio.

FLOWERS

Flowers and flowering plants that are from light (pale) to bright red hues, such as Aloe, amaryllis, aptenia (red hearts), astilbe, bergamot, blomeliad, camellia, carnation, clematis, columbine, field poppy, freesia, gentian, gladiolus, hollyhock, oriental lily, panda, peony, ragged robin, ranunculus, tulip, verbena.

Flowers and flowering plants that are shades of pink or rose, such as: African violet, amaryllis, anemone, astilbe, azalea, baby's breath, camellia, carnation, chrysanthemum, clematis, clove pink, coresposis rosea, cornflowers, crocus (autumn), cyclamen, daisy (English), daylily, dianthus, digitalis (foxglove), dog rose, echinacea (coneflower), erodium, freesia, geranium, gladiolus, gloxinia (pink beauty), hibiscus, hollyhock, hyacinth, hydrangea, iris, Lady's thumb, larkspur, lenten rose, lily (oriental trumpet), lonicera (honeysuckle), Lycoris, magnolia, moccasin, moss pink, mountain laurel, Newport pink, nosegays, passionflower, petunia, phlox paniculata, pink scabiosa, poinsettia, ragged robin, ranunculus, rhododendron (California), rosebay, rosebud, rose mallow, rose moss, rose-of-Sharon, rose oxalis, rose peony, roses, sweet pea, tea rose, tulip, verbena, wake-robin, wild pink, wood hyacinth and zinnia.

BOOKS

Those that contain a lot of sex and plenty of action; adventure, camping, hiking, sports, westerns, novels and sagas. Also books about legendary figures, mechanics, repairing, mending and do-it-yourself.

FASHION

Your clothes must be comfortable, light-weight and made so you can move about freely. Nothing cumbersome for you. Soft and light fabrics such as polyester for the women and gaberdine for the men. Cashmere, wool and cotton are also in for Aries. Clothes and materials that are heat-free are a necessity. Styles that give the impression of adventure are your favorite. You like all shades of red — either in the fabrics of your clothes or used as part of your accessories. When you wear red, you sparkle and feel full of pep and vigor because it acts as a tonic.

GIFTS

See preceding sections for type of books, flowers, music or perfume that may appeal to an Arien. Buy her something personal with her name or initials engraved on it such as an I.D. bracelet. Romantic novels appeal to her sensuous side. The latest time-saving appliances (microwave), devices, gadgets and equipment fascinates this gal.

An Arien guy is mechanical and likes to putter around with saws, tools, hammers, wrenches, engines, and likes cutting equipment: penknife, Swiss Army knife, lawnmower or sharpening device. Both Sexes may be pleased with a knife sharpener, or an electric carving knife, or cutlery, scissors or a butcher block cutting board. They like items made of steel, such as stainless steel cookware. An Arien is attracted to mobiles or modern sculpture especially if it is made of steel, iron or heavy metal.

Aries is active, impulsive, energetic, dynamic, and always on the go. Give them a ticket to a super event such as their favorite sporting event. They also enjoy tickets for the movies, theatre or balloon flights, or airplane lessons and a moonlight sail may appeal to them. The male and female Aries love a challenge and are extremely competitive; thus, give an Aries sports equipment, a volleyball, or badminton set, tennis or racquetball racquet, golf club set. Anything that appeals to outdoor games or sports; rollerskates, water holder for the bicycle, a tent, a sleeping bag, backpack, picnic basket, camping, hiking or climbing gear. Sports clothing: stylish sweats, tennis or jogging outfit. To satisfy an Arien's love of activity: exercise equipment (including weight lifts). Games: darts, slot car racer, hand-held computer, monopoly (or other board games) or a video game machine.

Other Aries-ruled Gifts: a bicycle, motor scooter, motorcycle, tennis ball pump, shaving set, blow or hair dryer, leather goods, artistic carvings of wood or copper or any hardware store item. Bottle of wine or liquor. Amethyst (geode, stone or jewelry). Bowling ball. Pepper mill, wood cheese tray, fondue set, iron cooking pot, griddle, waffle or crepe maker, pressure cooker, electric frying pan or a coffee mug, pot or grinder. Or an ideal gift may be gourmet treats in a basket—ham, cheese, fruit, assorted jams, jellies, or biscuits. Or a hat, cap or t-shirt with the Arien's name or monogram inscribed on it.

For the Young: A bicycle, tricycle, wagon, scooter, mini-auto (walk ride), fire truck (ride), pony (wood, rocker, ride on), 4-wheel rider, row cart, helmets (bike), a pair of skates (roller or ice), or bag for ice skates. They enjoy mechanical toys such as a truck that scoops and dumps. Action toys keep them happy: model cars, railroad cars and tracks, speed cars, fire rescue set (with fire engine). Or give an Aries a mini-golf set, football, baseball and bat, boxing play set, soccer game (gear driven) or toys for warfare (toy guns, missiles, soldiers, tanks), cowboy or military outfit, video game, mini pinball machine. Aries also likes bendable construction sets, a carpenter box (pre-cut wood tools), tool box or wood blocks which are building sets. Aries is the sign of construction and destruction so toys along this line suit them fine. Mini ramp and cars, motorcycles and drivers, cranes, garage with cars, keys, mini-car wash and gas pumps, micro and mini-cars, vans and carrier trucks.

Wood garage set, truck, blocks, and frontier set — all made of wood. Dolls that talk and are moveable.

Note: FOR ALL ARIES OF ALL AGES: Aries moves fast; therefore, do not give them anything that can be easily broken. Also, Aries does not like to acquire many possessions (the adults), because if they get a sudden urge to move—they want it to be a quick move without being tied down to material possessions. When something is no longer of use to them, they give it away without a second thought.

CELL SALTS

Kali, phosphoricum or phosphate of potash.

ZONES OF THE BODY

The brain (upper hemisphere), brow, cerebrum, cheeks, eyelids, eyes, face, forehead, gums, head, jaw (upper), lips, mouth, nose, teeth (upper). Thus you could be subject to brain problems, cerebral disorders, eye problems, headaches, rhinitis, sinus infections, teeth difficulties (gum disease, tooth decay).

HERBS

Effective herbs and plants for the Aries afflicted body zones are: Bayberry, bark, bilberry (American blueberry), black or blue cohosh, bloodroot, blue violet, broom, buchu, calamint, camomile, catnip, coltsfoot, comfrey, dock, elder, fern, fringe tree, garlic, ginkgo biloba, golden seal, gold thread root, holly, holy thistle, hyssop, Indian hemp, lungwort, marjoram, masterwort, mountain balm, mullein, mustard, myrrh, nettles, onions, pennyroyal, peppermint, peppers (bell, sweet, cayenne, capsicum, chili), poppies, radishes, red root, rhubarb, rosemary, rue, sanicle, sarsaparilla, saw palmetto berries, skullcap, skunk cabbage, sumach berries, sweet balm, tansy, thistle, thyme, vervain, violet, white pine, white pond lily, wild alum root, wood betony, yerba santa.

CLIMATE

Hot and dry. Therefore, you may want to live in a hot or dry climate. However, many Ariens can not take the heat and would rather live in a colder area.

PART OF LAND AND COUNTRY

Plowed fields, plenty of pebbles and boulders on the land, and a countryside which is high and rugged. Thus, as an Arien, this sort of land and/or country might appeal to you.

U.S. Cities: Phoenix and Yuma, AZ; Berkeley, Indio, Palm Springs, Sacramento, San Diego, San Francisco, Santa Barbara and Stockton, CA; Pueblo and Greeley, CO; Stamford, CT; Newark, DE; Flagler Beach, Ft. Lauderdale Miami Beach and Palm Beach, FL; Honolulu, HI; Twin Falls, ID; Dubuque, IA; Moline, Springfield and Urbania, IL; Wichita, KS; Shreveport, LA; Brockton, MA; Ann Arbor, Dalton, Dearborn, Grand Rapids, Holton and Sullivan, MI; Mankato and St. Paul, MN; Joplin and Kansas City, MO; Great Falls and Helena, MT; Henderson, NV; Concord and Manchester, NH; Elizabeth and Paterson, NJ; Albuquerque, NM; Binghampton, Ithaca, Niagara Falls, Schenectady, Syracuse, and Utica, NY; Chapel Hill, Durham and Winston-Salem, NC; Grand Forks, ND; Erie and Harrisburg, PA; Chattanooga, TN; Corpus Christi, Lubbock and Odessa, TX; Provo and Salt Lake City, UT; Oshkosh, WI.

U.S. States: None.

Islands: Ireland, Japan.

Countries: Andorra, Cambodia, Ethiopia, Guatemala, Liberia, Luxembourg, Spain, Zimbabwe.

Province: Newfoundland (Canada).

Cities (Other than U.S.): Brunswick and Cracoq (Queensland), Australia; Phnom Penh, Cambodia; Copenhagen, Denmark; Ashton-under-Lyne, Blackburn, Leicaster and Oldham, England; Addis-Ababa, Ethiopia; Marseilles, France; Guatemala City, Guatemala; Utrecht, Holland; Dublin, Ireland, Florence, Naples and Verona, Italy; Tokyo, Japan; Monrovia, Liberia; Lexembourg City, Lexembourg; Madrid, Spain; Salisbury, Zimbabwe.

IN AN ARIES VIBRATION

You are creative, generous, aggressive, temperamental and impatient — even your sex drive is given a boost! In this environment, you are assertive, physically active and constantly on the go; perhaps you exercise a lot, are a member of a health club or play competitive sports. You are daring, gutsy and nervy, and may start a new and risky enterprise. The place and its activities are a challenge and you have the strength and courage to overcome all obstacles thrown in your direction. You may be a leader in the community or an enthusiastic activist in civic or personal areas — like fire or law enforcement issues, or fighting city hall about a zoning law which affects your home or business.

ARIES TRAITS

You are an activist and will also pioneer in adventuresome enterprises that require lots of nerve and stamina; it's the challenge on which you thrive. Your dauntless courage is shown constantly and is admired by others. You'll speak up or tell it like it is, thereby getting into plenty of hot water. By nature, you are sexy, fiery and impulsive. You don't take "no" for an answer. You will go where angels fear to tread. Your best trait is leadership. Your downfall is impatience and selfishness.

ARIES COMPATIBILITY

With Leo: The two of you are compatible because you are both doers. However, the Leo ego and the Aries selfishness could spell trouble. Both are fiery and risk takers. Anything goes with making love. With Sagittarius: The both of you are candid and don't hold back with the words. It's a great relationship; honesty reigns. Besides, you both like to live it up and have a ball. Sex is stimulating and exciting; there are not any dull moments. With Aries: You may battle and constantly challenge one another. Two selfish people who both want the limelight could be a problem. However, lovemaking is wild, abandoned and thrilling.

With Gemini: This person will keep you on your toes. You'll never know which Twin is emerging; and you'll therefore find the Gemini's dual personalities fascinating. Mental stimulation and challenges will be constant. In the bedroom, sexual experimentation occurs; the frenzied states that are reached are enjoyed to the utmost. With Aquarius: Each of you gives the other freedom. Spur-of-the-moment activities and surprises will keep you spellbound. Lovemaking is indescribably fascinating and experimentation is enjoyed. With Taurus: If you want someone who is practical (and I doubt that you do), this person could suit you. Taurus may move and think too slowly for you, which could bring out your wrath and impatience. This individual is sensuous but takes a while to be aroused sexually, but once warmed up, the two of you are overwhelmed with passion. With Libra: This one's charm appeals to you. You are opposites, but opposites attract. Libra can calm you down and teach you how to relax. Problems could occur if you are too animalistic for this person who likes tenderness and romance. With Virgo: This individual is too fussy for you. You won't like being nagged or criticized. Virgo is more mental than physical — the opposite of you. In the bedroom Virgo is curious and likes to experience various forms of lovemaking which you find challenging and right up your alley. With Capricorn: This one's cheapness could turn you off. Both of you are selfish. Your fiery nature could be cooled off by Capricorn's coldness; however, you may find it stimulating because you enjoy conquering others. New techniques in the bedroom may be a turnoff for Capricorn, which won't be to your liking.

With Scorpio: This person's possessiveness bugs you. You fight and challenge each other constantly. It's deadly passion and a very dangerous relationship. In the boudoir, both are like dynamite — you could blow up at any minute. With Pisces: This person may be too sensitive and clinging for you. The Piscean's desire to relax and your drive to keep busy may cause problems. But the bedroom scene is filled with carnal ecstasy which never seems to end. With Cancer: You hurt this individual's feelings constantly and don't want to "baby" your mate. This is not a good twosome. However, both of you are captivated by eroticism in its most enticing and rapturous state.

ARIES 2019 FORECAST

From January 1st to March 6th, obstacles between your personal life and career creating disruptions, cancellations of plans, upheavals, delays and drastic changes. It is one shock after another making you erratic, abrupt. It is best to avoid temper tantrums and be diplomatic with a boss, people in your personal life and those in authority. Lots of red tape to get plans approved. If possible wait until after March 5th to speak up or make important career decisions--everything is too topsy-turvy with terminations and changes. However overseas travel, lectures, taking classes, publishing and advertising are favored. You will have a ball by going on a quick journey to another country and hopping from one place to another. The only problem could be with long distance trips being a disappointment if plans are made, broken and you don't get to go on your dream journey.

From March 7th to December 31st, wonderful surprises with finances, a raise, promotion, honors bestowed upon you. It is a great time to be in the limelight and get publicity or be well thought of by people above you in position. You will, during that time, swing from wild, spur of the moment, compulsive spending sprees to being frugal and conservative. Ambition and persistence brings success. You may deal with secret deals, go to special hush-hush meetings and get involved in making new rules, regulations and/or branch out with large companies, corporations or mass production.

From January 1st to December 3rd, your personality will impress others because you'll be smiling, happy, have a good sense of humor and be ever so friendly. Your philosophy will be to enjoy life, make the most of all situations and believe that everything happens for the best. No wonder you are so popular whether you are in a classroom or traveling abroad.

Best Period for Romance... July 23 — August 22
Best Dates For Sex

Jan: 1, 3, 8, 13, 17, 28, 30; Feb: 9, 14, 18, 24, 26, 27; Mar: 3, 4,8, 9, 13, 17, 23, 24, 26, 30, 31; Apr: 4, 9, 14, 20, 22, 27; May: 2, 6, 7, 11, 17, 19, 20, 24, 25, 29, 30; Jun: 7, 14, 16, 20, 21, 25, 26, 30; Jul: 4, 5, 11, 13, 18, 23, 28; Aug: 1, 7, 9, 10, 14, 19, 21, 24, 30; Sep: 3, 5, 6, 10, 11, 15, 16, 20, 21, 25; Oct: 1, 3, 7, 8, 12, 17, 18, 22, 28, 30; Nov: 4, 9. 14, 18, 24, 25, 27; Dec: 1, 2, 6, 9, 11, 15, 16, 22, 24, 29.

CHAPTER TWO
TAURUS: THE BULL ... APRIL 20 — MAY 20

To understand this chapter, read the Preface and Foreword. If you, know your rising sun, read the advice given for that sign as well as for your Sun sign. The combination of these two will give you more information than could be gained by simply reading only the Sun sign. Refer to pages 16 and 17 if you do not know what your rising sign is.

The following descriptions are typical for those born under the sign Taurus. However, your own horoscope may contradict some of this, depending upon your rising sign and the signs occupied by the planets in your horoscope.

Taurus is an earth sign and is feminine and semi-fruitful. Venus is the planetary ruler. Each of the signs and/or planets has rulership over certain phases of life; the following are ruled by Taurus and Venus:

COLORS
You may want to enhance your living quarters or wardrobe in these shades:

Venus: Bright yellow and such shades as butter, ripe lemon, the Sun or yolk of an egg.

Taurus: Dark yellow and such shades as buttercup, caliopsia or the oxeye daisy flower.

TALISMANIC GEMS
Moss agate and yellow opal; thus, you may want to magnetize either, or both, of these gems for good luck and/or to protect you from harm. Refer to Part Two under Magnetizing Objects for auspicious dates to magnetize a talismanic gem.

STONES
Alabaster, amber, white coral and white opaque; therefore, you may accent your abode with these stone as accessories or wear them as jewelry. You may find that you have good luck when wearing or owning one of these stones.

METALLIC ELEMENT
Venus: Copper

NUMBER
Number 14; You may want to bet with this number, or perhaps favorable events will occur on this date. If you want to plan ahead for certain activities, you could use this date for something important, especially if it coincides with a date for that event in the Best Days section in Part Two.

DAY
Friday: You may want to plan important activities for Friday. Your energy is at its height on Fridays.

SENSES: PHYSICAL OR NON-PHYSICAL
Physical Sense: Hearing
Physical Organs: Ears
Psychic Sense: Clairaudience

MUSIC

Pastoral, big band, contemporary, instrumental, love themes, and light and dreamy tunes to stir your soul and put you in a romantic mood. Classical sounds relax you, especially when you get all jumbled up.

PERFUMES

Bring all your earthiness to the surface when you wear these scents — their message is soft and intimate. They bring out your enchanting ways, love of flowers, rolling hills and the need to enjoy a quiet countryside and romantic nights. Wear them when you want to marvel at the beauties of nature. Be irresistible and allure your lover with these fragrances. Become gloriously alive while relaxing with a loving companion.

For the Female: Armasi, Arpege by Lanvin, Beautiful by Esteé Lauder, Blue Grass, Casaque, Catalyst by Halston, C'est Moll by Avon, Chanel #5, Chanel #19, Ciara, Diamonds and Sapphires by Elizabeth Taylor, Diorissimo, Ecusson, Emeraude, Eternity by Calvin Klein, Flore by Carolina Herrera, Interlude, J. Pavlova, Le Jardin de Max Factor, Madame Rochas, Narcisse Noir by Canon, Nicole Miller Fragrance, Ombre Rose by Jean-Charles Brosseau, Paloma Picasso, Passion by Elizabeth Taylor, Quelques Fleurs L'Original by Houbigant, Red by Geoffrey Beane, Regency Elegence by Lauren, Sand & Sable, Snob, Sortilege, Tatiana by Diane von Furstenberg, White Diamonds by Elizabeth Taylor, Wings by Georgio Beverly Hills, Worth by Je Revien, Zen.

For the Male: Armani for Men, Aston, Bogart, Chanel Pour Monsieur, Dunhill, Givenchy Gentlemen, Starring by Avon, Verbena.

FLOWERS

Flowers and flowering plants that are shades of dark yellow such as Aaron's rod, agrimony, Alexanders, Alyssum, buttercup, chrysanthus, clover (hop), columbine, cow slip, crocus, daisy (oxeye), freesia, gentian, iris, jonquil, Lady's Slipper, lily (daylily, trumpet, lily-flowered tulip), loosestrife, magnolia, moneywort, pansy, ranunculus, rose, spearwort, stonecrop, toadflax, tulip and zinnia.

BOOKS

Those that deal with art, beauty, music, planting, gardening, cooking, finance and success — especially regarding famous financiers and those who have made fortunes.

FASHION

Your clothes must give the impression of status and respectability; thus your apparel will be somewhat conservative and casual with a tailored look. Your way of dressing reflects your refinement. However, single gals often dress in a sexy and sensuous fashion to allure guys.

Good quality in a fabric is a necessity. The seams must be straight. Lined clothing is preferred. You are a practical shopper and wash and wear clothes are favored. Wearing apparel must be open-necked; thus, a blouse or shirt that closes in on your throat is a no-no unless you are attending a very important affair.

Linens, gabardines, polyester and light-weight wools make up the main part of your wardrobe. Skirts, blouses, sweaters, suits and dresses appeal to the Taurean woman; and for the man, open-necked shirts, sweaters, trousers and jackets. The opposite sex seems to be around more when a Taurus female wears dark yellow or a Taurean male dons a dark yellow scarf, handkerchief or other accessory. However, one must not overlook the Taurean charm which draws others like a magnet.

GIFTS

See preceding sections for type of books, flowers, music or perfume that may appeal to a Taurean. Buy her a bauble or jewelry such as something with an opal or agate or earrings or a necklace. Taurus likes to be pampered and to fuss with herself and look good; thus, give her a gift certificate for a spa message or a day at a full-body beauty salon (facial, manicure, pedicure, hair styling, and set, etc.). She's sensuous and into beauty and fashion — give her a basket of bath luxuries, bubble bath, or aromatherapy gels, perfume, cosmetics, cosmetic make-up kit, body lotions; a scarf, v-necked blouse (to show off her neck — Taurus rules the neck) or collar. Appeal to her love of luxury; give her a photograph framed in Sterling silver. A purse or a tote bag can keep her smiling. Clothing, fabrics or a sewing machine (she likes homemade items).

Buy him something practical, useful and valuable. Give that guy a necktie, v-necked shirt, money clip, billfold, wallet, fishing (rod, box), or golfing equipment (golf balls, clubs). Both sexes have a green thumb and enjoy landscaping. Thus give them a plant, decorative pot (for the plant), filigree plant stand, hanging basket (with, or for plants and flowers), seeds, bulbs, gardening tools, lawnmower, garden journal, video or subscription to a gardening magazine or book about planting.

Taurean's enjoy a comfortable home; thus, gifts for their abode are enjoyed or give them a gift certificate so they can shop in their favorite store, and perhaps, they'll purchase a piece of furniture or accessory for their living quarters — time saving kitchen appliances appeal to them. A cutting board, embroidered bath towel set (especially with their initials — monogrammed), needlepoint items (pillows), tapestries, prints, paintings, engravings, art objects, figurines, porcelain, curios, pottery, miniature antiques or old world sculpture with a classic look. Or an appeal to their sweet tooth; candy such as a box of chocolates, bon-bons, fruit cake. Appeal to their desire for food (they enjoy eating): baskets (seasonal fruits, breakfast foods, cheese and gourmet food). Or give them wine or liquor bottles/baskets.

A Taurean loves pleasure and a life that is quiet and well cushioned. This guy and gal like to relax and listen to music (the ears are ruled by Taurus). Thus, give them CD's, records, tapes, a CD or digital player, portable compact disc player, or sound equipment. They'll be happy with a ticket to the opera, concert (classical or the latest "in" performer), ballet or sporting event. Both sexes love money, so actual cash, money market or stock certificates, Series E bonds, or a miniature bank (with money in it) will make them glow.

For the Young: Taurus children love cuddly, soft and tactile toys: furry stuffed animals, especially a teddy bear, ragdolls in ruffles and bows. They tend toward the artistic; thus, give them an artist's kit (art paper, paint, crayons), wax sculpting set, basket weaving kit, peg art screen board, coloring books, or beautifully illustrated books. Appeal to their love of music: give a guitar, xylophone, mini-keyboard, rhythm band instrument (tambourine, drum set) or any other musical instrument. A portable CD player and headset, boom box, tape player, tote bag for cassettes or CD's or shelves and cabinets to store them. Other Suggested Gifts: an ink blot set, fishing rod outfit or a savings bank (piggy, jar, bottle, mechanical), cash register, or calculator.

CELL SALTS
Natrum sulphurica or sulphate of soda.

ZONES OF THE BODY
The blood vessels (of the carotid arteries), brain (base, lower lobes), cerebellum, ears, jaw (lower), larynx, neck (and its bony structure), occipital region (bone), palate, pharynx, teeth (lower), throat, thyroid gland, tonsils, vein (jugular), vocal cords. Thus you could be subject to ear infections, goiter, hearing problems, injuries to the cleft, jaw, neck or throat, laryngitis, mastoiditis, mumps, pharyngitis, thyroid problems, tonsillitis, growths such as polyps on the vocal cords.

HERBS
Effective herbs and plants for the Taurus afflicted body zones are: Bayberry bark, bistort root, bloodroot, blue cohosh, blue violet, borage (bugloss), buchu, burnet, cayenne, chickweed, coltsfoot, comfrey, daisy, dandelion, echinacea, ele-campane, fenugreek, flax, fringe tree, gentian, ginger, ginkgo biloba, golden seal, gold thread root, hops, horehound, hyssop, Indian hemp, larkspur, lily, lobelia, lungwort, marshmallow, moss, mullein (pimpernel), myrrh, myrtle, origanum, peach leaves, red clover, red root, red sage, rock rose, sage, sanicle, sarsaparilla, sassafras, saw palmetto berries, self-heal, skunk cabbage, slippery elm, spinach, twinleaf, vervain, white oak bark, white pine, white pond lily, wild alum root, wild cherry, wintergreen, wood sage and wood sanicle.

CLIMATE
Cold, dry; you may therefore want to live in a cold or dry climate.

PART OF LAND AND COUNTRY
Rolling hills with low and level ground devoid of woods or too much brush. If seed has been planted on the land, so much the better.

U.S. Cities: Berkeley, Indio, Oakland, Palm Springs and Vallejo, CA; Waterbury, CT; Ft. Myers and Miami Beach, FL; Honolulu, HI; Pocatello and Twin Falls, ID; Moline, IL; South Bend, IN; Des Moines, IA; Lexington, KY; Boston and Springfield, MA; Dalton, MI; Duluth, MN; Greenville, Hattiesburg and Jackson, MS; Missoula, MT; Hastings and Omaha, NE; Atlantic City, Elizabeth, Secaucus and Vineland, NJ; Buffalo, Long Island City and Rochester, NY; Greensboro and Winston-Salem, NC; Warwick, RI; Hilton Head, SC; Rapid City and Sioux Falls, SD; Abilene and Wichita Falls, TX; Portsmouth, VA; Spokane, WA; Oshkosh, WI.

U.S. States: Louisiana, Maryland, Minnesota.

Countries: Austria, Ecuador, Israel, Paraguay, Sierra Leone, Tanzania, Togo.
Island: New Zealand
Constituent Countries: Scotland (the U.K.).

Cities (other than U.S.): Vienna, Austria; Quito, Ecuador; Leipzig, Germany; Rhodes, Greece; Tel Aviv, Israel; Mantova (Mantua), Palermo and Parma, Italy; Tokyo, Japan; Auckland, New Zealand; Olso, Norway; Asuncion, Paraguay; Freetown, Sierra Leone; Dar-es-Salaam, Tanzania; Lome, Togo.

IN A TAURUS VIBRATION

You are quiet, conservative, industrious, patient, persistent and stubborn. In this environment, you may become a gardening enthusiast or take up music, oil painting or the ballet. Community projects such as beautifying the city parks, streets and starting a botanical garden may appeal to your aesthetic senses. Cultural and art programs may keep you busy. This is a socially active locale; however, if you do not get out often enough you will get into a rut very quickly. Money can become a goal here — you may pile up a sizable bank account and also become involved in city or state fund-raising projects. Your drive to be successful makes you push yourself to the point of overworking; however, you can handle it very well.

TAURUS TRAITS

You love beauty, comfort and quiet moments. You are romantic, sensual and possessive. You tend to be fixed on ideas; obstinacy can be a problem. You are even-tempered; your persistence pays off time and again. By nature, you are practical and can save money. You want a sure thing and quality in the merchandise you buy. You have a horror of being in debt. You are calm, cool and collected when making business decisions. Your best trait is stability. Your downfall is your desire to control everyone.

TAURUS COMPATIBILITY

With Capricorn: Both are ambitious and persistent. Because you're both conscious of money, you're compatible. Sex starts slowly, but, once aroused, unforgettable states of sensuality are reached. With Virgo: You appreciate his practicality; it matches your own. Both are neat and tidy. Lovemaking starts calmly but is heightened with the passage of time — neither of you wants to rush. With Taurus: You understand each other's drive for success. Both can be stubborn and reach stalemate conditions. Too many quiet moments may shut out a chance for communication. You complement one another when your strong hunger for sexual pleasure is satisfied.

With Cancer: Date this person if you want someone who is protective. You like to eat and Cancer likes to cook, so it's a great match. The two of you are easily intoxicated by each other's embrace, kiss and deep-moving lust. With Pisces: You like this person's subserviency and clinging ways. The flexibility of Pisces is perfect for the inflexible Taurus. Pisces is receptive to your desires; once the two of you are in the bedroom, it'll never be the same — wow! With Scorpio: Both are fixed; thus problems could easily be attracted, especially when two immovable people get together. You two are possessive and oversexed — steamy moments of bliss. Your insatiable sexual appetites can be gratified by lasciviousness.

With Aries: This individual is adventuresome and takes you out of your rut. Risk-taking moments in business will turn you off, but in lovemaking you'll be fearful when you dive in. Both are ravished by fleshly desires. With Gemini: This person's non-stop talking may bug you but it'll pep up your many dull moments. Gemini's changeableness upsets you to no end. With this individual, you will learn why variety (with sex and everything else) is the spice of life (that is, if you are not too stubborn to try some new techniques). With Libra: This one's charming (like you). The arts are your common interest. Libra's indecisiveness disturbs decisive you. The social scene attracts both of you. Lovemaking is beautifully tender and soul-stirring.

With Aquarius: Both are too obstinate and contrary. This person's too unreasonable and unpredictable for you. New areas of sex could be explored and enjoyed if the two of you refrain from being so stubborn. With Leo: This individual's ego and wanting to be the boss will be a sore spot. Leo is just as fixed as you; neither one of you will give an inch, so it is not a good match. However, carnal pleasure is a real experience in eroticism; therefore, you are happy when the two of you are indulging in passionate lovemaking. With Sagittarius: You will not like this person's restlessness and wanting to be on the go constantly. Sagittarius is too blunt and outspoken for you. You may have fun in bed, but could be displeased when Sagittarius rushes the sex act.

TAURUS 2019 FORECAST

From January 1st to March 6th, you will be amazed at the unexpected sums of money coming through either investments, backers, investors, clients, legal matters, insurance or an inheritance. This is a great time to apply for a loan or buy a car. However, do not lend money to a friend or anyone, regardless of the sob story you are told. Promises made are broken. Lies and deception prevail. Do not listen or invest in anything that a pal recommends. Phony deals and schemes can be attracted from January 1st to December 2nd. Nothing is as it seems, everything mentioned can fall through and bring a huge disappointment and put you in debt-- something you abhor. Actually, you are very alert and smart when it comes to get -rich-quick schemes; therefore don't change your nature now.

From March 7th to December 31st, many changes occur in your personality and personal life. You will be very charismatic, independent, intuitive, and be interested in the latest in technology or New Age areas. It is like you have awakened and are more willing to make changes involving the latest fad, invention, social media or being more modern in your views. However, you will still think things through in a diplomatic fashion and will not break rules or tradition. Your approach is combining seriousness and old methods with new and different techniques and ideas. You may be flabbergasted with the new you--reinventing yourself! You may attend classes or lectures in these various areas that arouse your curiosity. To know more about, and be enlightened, could keep you preoccupied.

This is a year to make plans or go, on the spur of the moment, overseas--the journey will be even greater than anticipated. You may find everything mind-boggling. You could travel with pals or make friends in foreign lands. It seems like you are crawling out of a shell and experiencing life as you never expected it to be. So, let your hair down and enjoy every fun-filled moment.

Best Period For Romance... August 23 — September 22
Best Dates For Sex

Jan: 1, 10, 11, 12, 13, 14, 15, 19, 28; Feb: 6, 7, 8, 9, 10, 11, 12, 16, 24; Mar: 8, 9, 10, 11, 15, 23, 24; Apr: 2, 4, 5, 6, 7, 11, 12, 20, 29, 30; May: 2, 9, 17, 27, 28, 29, 30, 31; Jun: 1, 5, 14, 20, 25, 26, 27, 28; Jul: 11, 20, 21, 22, 23, 24, 25, 26, 30; Aug: 7, 16, 17, 19, 20, 21, 22, 26; Sep: 3, 13, 14, 15, 16, 17, 18, 23; Oct: 1, 10, 11, 12, 13, 14, 15, 20, 28; Nov: 6, 7, 8, 9, 10, 11, 16, 24, 25; Dec: 4, 5, 6, 7, 8, 9, 13, 22, 31.

CHAPTER THREE
GEMINI: THE TWINS... MAY 21 — JUNE 21

To understand this chapter, read the Preface and Foreword. If you, know your rising sign, read the advice given for that sign as well as for your Sun sign. The combination of these two will give you more information than could be gained by simply reading only the Sun sign. Refer to pages 16 and 17 if you do not know what your rising sign is.

The following descriptions are typical for those born under the sign Gemini. However, your own horoscope may contradict some of this, depending upon your rising sign and the signs occupied by the planets in your horoscope.

Gemini is an air sign and is masculine and barren. Mercury is the planetary ruler. Each of the signs and/or planets has rulership over certain phases of life. The following are ruled by Gemini or Mercury:

COLORS

You may want to enhance your living quarters or wardrobe in these shades:

Mercury: Bright violet; such hues as a deep reddish-bluish purple like mauve or heliotrope.

Gemini: Light (pale) violet, such as lavender. Also bicolors, mixed colors, two-toned, striped and variegated.

TALISMANIC GEMS

Beryl, Alexandrite, chrysoberyl, aquamarine, agate. You may want to magnetize either, or both, of these gems for good luck and/or to protect you from harm. Refer to Part Two under Magnetizing Objects for auspicious dates to magnetize a talismanic gem.

STONES

Striped, Cinnabar, Vermilion. Therefore, you may accent your abode with striped stones as accessories or wear them as jewelry. You may find that you have good luck when wearing or owning one of these stones.

METALLIC ELEMENT

Mercury: Quicksilver.

NUMBER

Number 17; You may want to bet with this number, or perhaps favorable events will occur on this date. If you want to plan ahead for certain activities, you could use this date for something important, especially if it coincides with a date for that event in the Best Days section in Part Two.

DAY

Wednesday: You may want to plan important activities for Wednesday. Your energy is at its height on Wednesdays.

SENSES: PHYSICAL OR NON-PHYSICAL

Physical Sense: Sight
Physical Organs: Eyes
Psychic Sense: Psychometry

MUSIC

All types from rock, jazz, pop, Celtic, fusion, Calypso, vocals and religious to heavy classical are enjoyed, depending upon your momentary whim — you are changeable and volatile. Dance rhythms make you feel like making whoopee — all your nervous energy gets unwound when your feet start to move.

PERFUMES

These fragrances bring out your wit, versatility and adaptability. Wear these scents and you'll sparkle by expressing your complex whims, dual nature and many personalities. Your flirty ways and naughtier side will show. Thus, sprinkle them on and you will be ready for anything...and everything.

For the Female: Amarige de Givenchy, Anne Klein, Breezy, Charlie Naturals by Revlon, Donna Karan New York, Fleurs de Rocaille, French Vanilla by Parfums Parquets, Glorious, Head-Over-Heels by Ultima II, Heavenly Sent, Laughter, Patches, Rive Gauche, Starry by Avon, Vanilla Field's by Coty, Vanilla Musk by Coty, Wind Song.

For the Male: Braggi, Chaz by Aramis, Clint, Eau de Revillon, Nomade, Perry Ellis for Men, Xeryus by Parfums Givenchy.

FLOWERS

Flowers and flowering plants that are shades of light (pale) violet, such as: Bee orchid, lavender, lungwort, pansy and African violets.

Flowers and flowering plants that are striped, two-toned or variegated)bicolors and mixed colors), such as: Amaryllis (butterfly, starry-eyed), camellia, clematis, columbine, corydalis, crocus, daffodil (split-corona and others), digitalis (foxglove). Dutchman's-breeches, gladiolus, iris, Johnny-jump-up, lilac, lily (oriental, polka-dot, trumpet) oxalis, candycane, passionflower, scabiosa, spotted jewelweed, tulip (lily-flowered and mixed), verbena and windflower (wood anemone).

BOOKS

Those that contain lots of activity, information, news, education, travel, cross-word puzzles, five-minute mysteries, tests for twosome books and biographies that satisfy your love of gossip and to know the real dirt. However, you are interested in any subject from soup to nuts.

FASHION

You are an impulsive buyer and a big spender. You grab whatever pleases you, regardless of price, material or quality. Wearing apparel must give you freedom to fly about. You like material that feels airy and gives a lightness to your skin. Polyester, jersey, silk, or chiffon may be among your favorites if you are a Gemini woman. Polyester fabrics may appeal to you Gemini men.

You have an outfit for every occasion. Colors and styles are diverse. You mix and match or have unusual combinations. You go along with the times and enjoy the latest fads. For women: Stripes, checks and floral prints, or gypsy dresses may be donned more than anything else. For men: Pin striped suits, Hawaiian shirts, western garb, or any type of outfit depending on a momentary whim.

Your closet is full of all types of clothing. You like to change your outfit as many times during the day or evening as is convenient. When you wear light violet, shades of light violet or accessories, you sparkle and bubble. You feel like painting the town red. And you very well might!

GIFTS

See preceding section for type of books, flowers, music or perfume that may appeal to a Geminian. Any type of present that deals with communication is "in" with a Gemini of any age: beeper, cellular phone, fax, answering machine, antique or novel telephone, phone shoulder-holder, headphone, radio, video tape, recorders, CD's, TV or a computer. Gifts that come in pairs (Gemini is a dual sign): Two-way radios, walkie-talkies, shoes, socks, bookends, gloves or earrings. Keep those Gemini fingers busy and appeal to his/her love of writing: stationary, diary, daily journal, rubber stamp, address and appointment book, memo pads, post-it notes. Or how about a copy machine?

Gemini's mind is always racing and needs a mental challenge; thus, he/she is always happy with a crossword or jigsaw puzzle. You can't go wrong with a game: a chess set, monopoly kit, pin ball machine, or video TV/computer game. The twins (Gemini is represented by the twins) are clever, versatile, restless and mentally alert; thus, things that exercise their brilliant minds can be appealing: register him/her in a creative writing or language course or give tape or video lessons. A sleep-learning record or tape might appeal to this guys/gals curious nature. Or why not gift them with an enrollment in an art or computer class?

Gemini is always busy and on the go. The twins make quick changes, enjoy meeting and conversing with new people and love it when they make interesting discoveries. You can't go wrong when you appeal to their quizzical mind, adoration of transportation and travel. Thus, appeal to his/her jet-setting nature with: luggage, a tote bag, travel ticket, portable iron, travel clock radio, mini cassette recorder or carrying case for CD's or cassette tapes; guidebook for foreign locales, a magazine subscription, (travel — best subject matter); a book-of-the-month subscription. Books are intriguing to Gemini.

Other suggested items: jogger's cap, buckskin jacket, wind chimes, cigarette lighter, key chain or case, wristwatch, bracelet, ring, jewelry (with a beryl stone), manicure set, nail polish/various colors to satisfy this gals desire for change and variety, biorhythm set, gadgets, fun fads, novelties, ice bucket, wine glasses, coasters, or cheese board. Note: Gemini likes to change residences frequently thus does not like to get bogged down with possessions. Also, this guy/gal bores easily and is impatient; therefore, buy a gift that will keep Gemini intrigued.

For the Young: Tin whistle, musical instrument (keyboard, drums, xylophone, maracas, tambourine, castanets) play melody phone, bike, radio, yo-yo, stencil set, pens (ballpoint, doodle-writer), drawing pencils, chalk, crayons, talking doll, robot (voice activated), sled, trampoline, rocking horse, pogo stick, bicycle, scooter, skateboard, rollerskates, soft-sided bowling set, magic tricks kit, spinning top, bean bag toss, Jack-in-the-Box, balls (tumble, rubber), marbles, baseball card set, cordless phone holder, play phone or answering machine, walkie talkie, mini-electronic play typewriter, play set (airport or credit card), puzzle box, radio-controlled racer, electronic powered road race set, railroad engine, electronic car and tracks. Lip and nail color kit, basic language course for kids or keep their hands busy with a model kit. Due to getting bored easily, Gemini can go through toys and games so fast you'd have to be a millionaire to keep up with them.

CELL SALTS
Kali muriaticum or chloride of potash.

ZONES OF THE BODY
The arms, bronchi (bronchial tubes), clavicle (collarbone), fingers, hands, lungs (upper lobes), nervous system (central), respiratory system (upper), ribs, shoulders and shoulder blades, windpipe, wrists. Thus you could be subject to asthma, bronchitis, bursitis, emphysema, injury to the arms, hands, rib cage, wrists, shoulders, neuritis in the arms and shoulders, pleurisy, pneumonia, respiratory afflictions, tuberculosis.

HERBS
Effective herbs and plants for the Gemini afflicted body zones are: Angelica, balm of Gilead, bayberry bark, bethroot, black cohosh, bloodroot, blue violet, boneset, borage (bugloss), burnet (pimpernel), camomile, cayenne, cedron, celery root/seed, chickweed, chicory (endive), colombo, coltsfoot, comfrey, coral, cubeb berries, doggrass, elder, elecampane root, fireweed, fit root, flax seed, ginger, ginkgo biloba, ginseng, golden seal, henbane, holy thistle, hops, horehound, hyssop, Indian hemp, lobelia, lungwort, madder, marjoram, marshmallow, masterwort, meadowsweet, milkwood root, mistletoe, motherwort, mullein, myrrh, nettle, pennyroyal, Peruvian bark, plantain, pleurisy root, prickly ash, provet, Queen of the Meadow, red clover, red root, red sage, rosemary, rue, sage, sanicle, sassafras, saw palmetto berries, skullcap, shepherd's purse, skunk cabbage, slippery elm, Solomon's Seal, speedwell, spikenard, St. John's wort, tansy, thyme, twinleaf, valerian, vervain, wahoo, water pepper, white pine, white pond lily, wild cherry, wild yam, wintergreen, witch hazel bark/leaves, wood betony, woodbine, wood sanicle, yarrow, yerba santa.

CLIMATE
Temperature — where the wind blows; thus, you may want to live atop a mountain or in a windy city.

PART OF LAND AND COUNTRY
Rather billowy and covered with small shrubs, trees and grass.

U.S. Cities: Anchorage and Juneau, AK; Flagstaff, AZ; Hot Springs, AR; Indio and San Francisco, CA; Hartford, CT; Naples, FL; Gary and South Bend, IN; Springfield and Worcester, MA; Rochester, MN; Greenville, MS; Kansas City, MO; Reno, NV; Secaucus and Vineland, NJ; Santa Fe, NM; Fayetteville and Winston-Salem, NC; Cranston and Newport, RI; Nashville, TN; El Paso and Houston, TX; Tacoma, WA; Casper and Sheridan, WY.

U.S. States: Arkansas, Kentucky, Rhode Island, South Carolina, Tennessee, West Virginia and Wisconsin.

Countries: Afghanistan, Croatia, Denmark, Eritrea, Egypt, Guyana, Iraq, Jordan, Kuwait, Lebanon, Montenegro, Norway, Sweden, and the U.S.A.

Islands: Iceland, Sardinia (Italy), Tonga.

Cities (other than U.S.): Brabant Island, Antarctica; Vienna, Austria; Bruges and Leuven, Belgium; Copenhagen, Denmark; Cairo, Egypt; London, Plymouth, Wales, Wednesbury and Wolverhampton, England; Metz and Versailles, France; Nuremberg, Germany; Georgetown, Guyana; Reykjavik, Iceland; Rome and Sardinia, Italy; Amman, Jordan; Kuwait, Kuwait; Beirut, Lebanon; Oslo, Norway; Cordoba, Spain; Stockholm, Sweden; Nuku' Alofy, Tonga.

IN A GEMINI VIBRATION

You are curious, restless, changeable and versatile. It is difficult for you to settle down to a quiet lifestyle — you are not home much. The town and its various activities keep you on the go constantly; you are interested in the numerous calendar events offered here. You might find yourself busily engaged in youth programs, a save-the-library crusade, bond issue, community project involving education, transportation, or an election campaign. This is a locality where communication plays the major role in one's daily affairs. You may be caught up in it through expressing brilliant ideas verbally or in written form; or perhaps you yak so much you have become the town gossip.

GEMINI TRAITS

You are the go - go - go sign. Your nerves can't stand sitting still. You are an intellectual and can talk about any subject, often lacking continuity and jumping from topic to topic. You like to pick people's brains, asking the "how" and "why" of everything. Your ideas can be brilliant. It's easy for you to adapt to your surroundings or to people. You have multiple personalities and can go through life leading many different lives (isn't it fun, though?). Your best trait is versatility. Your downfall is changeableness.

GEMINI COMPATIBILITY

With Aquarius: This is a great match — both are interested in many things. Endless and fascinating conversations keep you both mentally alert. Sex is spur-of-the-moment and full of surprises — experimentation is a must for you two! With Libra: You adore talking to Libra, who enjoys listening to your every word. You are challenged by Libra's indecisiveness. Lovemaking is romantic and mentally stimulating. With Gemini: You will not be bored with each other. You'll feed off of each other's restlessness and the desire for new adventures mentally and physically. If the two of you can stop talking long enough, sex will be great because anything goes.

With Taurus: You might find Taurus dull and an old stick-in-the-mud type. However, you're just the one to liven up the life of this person. Date Taurus if you want stability. Lovemaking can be exhilarating if you can get Taurus to adapt to new techniques. With Aries: Your life is filled with fun and adventure together. Non-stop yakking will keep you both busy when you indulge in sports or attend the movies or other forms of entertainment. Both can dance up a storm. Sex has the two of you inflamed in a sea of passion. With Cancer: You will never know where you stand with this person, but you'll love every wondering moment. You're mentally changeable and Cancer is emotionally changeable — have fun! The two of you make fervent love when the mood strikes, which fulfills all of your wildest fantasies.

With Leo: This is a great match. Leo makes you feel like talking more, especially when Leo shows you off to everyone. You are a challenge to Leo's ego and you enjoy the chase — you like to keep Leo guessing. Both of you are consumed by a raging sexual desire which leads to carnal ecstasy. With Sagittarius: This person can adapt to your changes, but could tire of them eventually. However, both of you are restless and continually on the go; these similarities are a plus for this relationship. You are both game for anything, especially in the sexual arena; the moments spent together are astonishing and joyous with many new discoveries. With Capricorn: This person is too dull for you. Capricorn sticks with the old, tried and true, whereas you are interested in the new, different and experimentation. Conversations may lack responses from Capricorn, who doesn't like to waste time talking about trivialities. Sexually, this individual's too inhibited for you.

With Virgo: There's a good mental rapport with plenty of yakking about everything from A to Z. However, you won't like Virgo's nagging or nitpicking. If Virgo is a prude and won't try new sexual pleasures, you'll be turned off. However, if you get a curious Virgo who wants to experience everything in the sexual arena, you've got it made. With Pisces: This person is too sensitive to your words and will try to tie you down. You shun clinging vines and overly emotional people. However, in the bedroom both are dazzled to states of delirium. With Scorpio: This person is too jealous and possessive for you. You'll be bored staying home most of the time and being interrogated over your every moment outside the house. Scorpio's passion shakes you up, but after awhile constant sex may be tiresome to you.

GEMINI 2019 FORECAST

Your career dreams can come true. It is an excellent year to promote projects; follow your psychic impressions. Honors, awards, recognition and raises in pay may give a secure feeling. People above you in position think highly of you. Express your concrete views for cost-saving methods and reorganization in a business at meetings or on a one -on-one basis with a boss. From March 7th to December 31, amazing surprises may make your head reel, especially with publicity and those in superior positions who favor you. Grasp every opportunity even though it may interfere with taking time out with a spouse. However, if you are single, that is not an issue.

Do not lend money to pals from January 1st to March 6th. Ignore their advice on investments. Be ready for shocks with the debts of your buddies. However, during this time, you could have wonderful fun-loving times with friends but let them do their share with paying for meals and in recreational areas. You will increase your acquaintances and make friends easily due to your jolly, friendly and confident personality. Your inspirational messages are filled with encouragement. You are understanding of the pitfalls and tolerant of the shortcomings of others. You are well liked by strangers, clients, pals and/or partners.

This year is beneficial for making serious plans involving saving money, retirement, pension funds and taking out insurance policies or annuities. Fund-raising is helpful to various charity institutions and gives you a sense of usefulness that you are contributing your utmost to universal welfare. If you own a business, mergers may be contemplated and discussed--go for the propositions that are sincere, frugal and have long-term arrangements and pay-offs. it is the time to turn your eyes and ears to money ventures that involve future years. You are a good negotiator with buying products or in deals involving backers, investors or large corporations. People like your sound judgment and will cooperate with your plans.

Best Period For Romance... September 23 — October 22
Best Dates For Sex

Jan: 1, 8, 13, 14, 15, 28; Feb: 9, 10, 11, 12, 18, 24; Mar: 3, 4, 8, 9, 10, 11, 17, 23, 24, 30, 31; Apr: 4, 5, 6, 7, 14, 20, 27; May: 2, 11, 17, 24, 25, 29, 30, 31; Jun: 1, 7, 14, 20, 21, 25, 26, 27, 28; Jul: 4, 5, 11, 18, 23, 24, 25, 26; Aug: 1, 7, 14, 19, 20, 21, 22, 28; Sep: 3, 10, 11, 15, 16, 17, 18, 25; Oct: 1, 7, 8, 12,13, 14, 15, 22, 28; Nov: 4, 9, 10, 11, 18, 24, 25; Dec: 1, 2, 6, 7, 8, 9, 15, 16, 22, 29.

CHAPTER FOUR
CANCER: THE CRAB... JUNE 21 — JULY 22

To understand this chapter, read the Preface and Foreword. If you, know your rising sign, read the advice given for that sign as well as for your Sun sign. The combination of these two will give you more information than could be gained by simply reading only the Sun sign. Refer to pages 16 and 17 if you do not know what your rising sign is.

The following descriptions are typical for those born under the sign Cancer. However, your own horoscope may contradict some of this, depending upon your rising sign and the signs occupied by the planets in your horoscope.

Cancer is a water sign and is feminine and fruitful. The Moon is the planetary ruler. Each of the signs and/or planets has rulership over certain phases of life. The following are ruled by Cancer or the Moon:

COLORS

You may want to enhance your living quarters or wardrobe in these shades:

Moon: Bright and dark shades of green, such as mint, emerald, forest, jungle green, grass, plants, leaves. Silver, such as pewter (silver-gray) and shining metallic silver.

Cancer: Light (pale) green, such hues as green grapes. Yellow-green — such shades as chartreuse, olive, avocado, lime, asparagus, olive, moss and sea-green.

TALISMANIC GEMS

Emerald, Moonstone, green tourmaline. Note: In folklore, it is said that the Moonstone has magic properties that change with the phases of the Moon; during a waxing Moon, it is an aid to clairvoyance.

You may want to magnetize either, or both, of these gems for good luck and/or to protect you from harm. Refer to Part Two under Magnetizing Objects for auspicious dates to magnetize a talismanic gem.

STONES

Soft and white, including selenite and chalk. Therefore, you may accent your abode with striped stones as accessories or wear them as jewelry. You may find that you have good luck when wearing or owning one of these stones.

METALLIC ELEMENT

Moon: Silver.

NUMBER

Number 18; You may want to bet with this number, or perhaps favorable events will occur on this date. If you want to plan ahead for certain activities, you could use this date for something important, especially if it coincides with a date for that event in the Best Days section in Part Two.

DAY

Monday: You may want to plan important activities for Monday. Your energy is at its height on Mondays.

SENSES: PHYSICAL OR NON-PHYSICAL

Physical Sense: Feeling
Physical Organ: The gut (stomach, solar plexus)
Psychic Sense: Spirit Communion

MUSIC

Romantic, sentimental, sleepy-time melodies — soft, quiet and dreamy sounds. Soul music, the blues and torch songs, especially if you are suffering from a lost love and a broken heart.

PERFUMES

These scents bring out your passions, whimsicality, flirtatiousness and love of nostalgia. Wear these fragrances and you'll create an illusion, feel romantic, uplifted and invigorated, while capturing a loved one.

For the Female: #22 by Chanel, 360° by Perry Ellis, 1000 by Patou, Antonias' Flowers, Black Pearls by Elizabeth Taylor, Carnations by Bellodgia, Charles of the Ritz, Chloe Narcisse by Karl Lagerfeld, Destiny by Marilyn Miglin, Eve, Fidji, Fracas, Freesia by Crabtree and Evelyn, Gardenia by Bellodgia, Gardenia Passion by Annick Goutal, Jasmine, Jontue, Jungle Gardenia, La Rose de Rosine, Magnolia by Diane von Furstenberg, Nature's One Gardenia by Perfumers Workshop, Paris by Yves Saint Laurent, Rose by Madame Rochas, White Shoulders, Youth Dew by Esteé Lauder.

For the Male: Acqua De Fresca, Acqua di Colonia, Bill Blass, Cool Water by Davidoff, Mon Triomphe, Polo Sport, Royal Lyme by Prince Matchabelli, Royal Pub.

FLOWERS

Flowers and flowering plants that are light (pale) green or yellowish green, such as: Figwort, iris, mignonette, rose root, African violets.

Flowers and flowering plants that are white, such as: Achillea (yarrow), althea, amaryllis, anemone, aster, azalea, Baby's breath, bladder campion, camellia, clematis, clover (Dutch), cuckooflower, daisy (Shasta), digitalis (foxglove), echinacea (coneflower), edelweiss, eyebright, feverfew, forget-me-not, freesia, fuchsia, geranium, gladiolus, grass-of-parnassus, hibiscus, honey-lotus, honeysuckle, hydrangea, iris, jasmine, jonquil, Lady's smock, larkspur, lead-wort, lilac, lilies-of-the-Valley, lily (calla, trumpet), lotus, magnolia, moon-flower, mullein, narcissus, orchid, oxalis, peony, persicaria, petunia, pimpernel, poinsettia, poppy, ranunculus, rhododendron, rose (Burnet), snapdragon, tulip (including the lily-flowered), rose mallow, shepherds'-purse, snowball, snowbell, snow lily, Star-of-Bethlehem, sweet pea, sweet William, trillium, tulip, vervain, viburnum, white daisy, white water lily and yucca.

BOOKS

Those that are about romance, the sea, cooking, wine making, the home, family sagas, sewing, knitting, music, mysticism and restaurant guides. Also memoirs and sensationalism involving current celebrities.

FASHION

You are a practical shopper, except when you are in one of your whimsical moods. The attire you wear is to please yourself and not because it is the latest fashion. A closet full of all types of clothes makes you feel secure; thus, you have an outfit for every occasion and role which you play. Loose garments are preferable because they give comfort and do not show your stomach, thus allowing you to eat plenty.

If you are a Cancer Woman, you are equally at ease in old-fashioned attire, chic suits, elegant dresses, frocks or jeans. You are like an actress and can be the country girl, a sophisticated lady of the city or a femme fatale. You are partial to eyelet, lace, ruffles, frills and embroidered raiments. You like chiffon and satin for evening wear. Cottons and polyesters are the favorites of both sexes.

If you are a Cancer Man, vests may appeal to you when you wear a suit. You enjoy the comfort of denim jeans but need room to breathe (especially in the tummy area); thus, tight-fitting clothes are not for you. All shades of green — chartreuse, emerald, olive and sea green appeal to you. When you don clothes or accessories in these colors, you feel calm, relaxed and uninhibited. You could come out of your shell and be the life of the party.

GIFTS

See preceding section for types of books, flowers, music or perfume that may appeal to a Cancerian. Because Cancerian's love home-sweet-home, purchase gifts for their living quarters: fluffy pillows, quilts (soft down, patched), doilies, candles, plants, ceramics, figurines, lead-crystal, vase/bowl or a chair, table or lamp. A way to your cancer guy's/gal's heart is through the tummy; thus, a basketful of cheeses, preserves, canned meats, fruit or a picnic basket, should be considered. Or how about a gift certificate to a restaurant or supermarket? Also, appealing are home baked goods (cookies, fruitcake) packed in attractive canisters or stored in beautifully decorated baskets.

Cancer's favorite hangout is in the kitchen. Buy cooking gadgets or appliances: a blender, juicer, mixer, toaster, electric can opener, dishes, tablecloth, kitchen towel set, wine rack, decanter, personalized coffee mug, gourmet food accessories (crepe-maker, fondue set, shrimp cocktail dishes), salt-and-pepper shakers or anything silver (flatware, serving tray, tea set, dishes, for serving). Keep in mind that if you want Cancer to be happy, give presents that make him/her feel cozy and secure. A Cancerian never tires of cook books, or anything that appeals to his/her domestic urges.

Other Cancerian gifts: items connected with the sea, river or lake: ocean scenes in paintings, a boat, fishing equipment, bathing suit, sea shell, aquarium or a ticket on a cruise ship. Or how about a bottle with a ship inside? A Cancerian gal often enjoys sewing, knitting or doing needlepoint. Thus, a sewing machine, embroidery fabrics, yarn, crewel, needles or hand-decorated porcelain thimbles might make her smile. Cancer is nostalgic, sentimental, romantic, easily moved and sensitive. Give a keepsake, souvenir, antique curio or other antique items such as a pen, locket, frame for a photo. Give jewelry (with an emerald). For the Cancerian's various mood swings: stamps, coins, backgammon or bridge game, bath salts, blouse, shirt, vest. Those Cancerian's of all ages might enjoy a pet; a pet brings out their caring motherly/fatherly and nurturing side.

For the Young: Appeal to their imagination and let them play out their fantasies; perhaps, pretending to be Mommy/Daddy; doll, baby doll carrier, doll house, mini-furniture or food/kitchen items, play washer and dryer combo, cooking kit with junior pot and pan set, miniature playhouse, compact play kitchen, table and chair or stool set. Or a play picnic set with plastic or polyester food, utensils and place settings. A snack vending machine with coins or a supermarket checkout shelves; a food set may be just what a Cancerian child craves. Make-believe can be put to use with a doctor or nurse set.

Other suggested items for kids: a sewing kit, mini-tea set, play stove, pegloom weaving loom with knitting case/kit. Nursery rhymes in books and/or puzzles. Or moon shoes may be what they fancy. Water toys such as a boat (for bath with paddle wheel and fish), rubber raft or swimsuit. Rubber ducks for the bath fascinate a Cancerian baby.

CELL SALTS
Calcarea fluorica or fluoride of lime.

ZONES OF THE BODY
The breasts, diaphragm, digestive organs, lacteals (lymph carrying vessels), lungs (lower lobes), respiratory system, stomach, womb (belly). Thus you could be subject to breast problems, colitis, food digestion, gastritis, stomach ailments, ulcers.

HERBS
Effective herbs and plants for the Cancer afflicted body zones are: Angelica, anise, balmony, blue violet, borage, (bugloss), buckbean, burnet (pimpernel), calamus (sweet myrtle), camomile, caraway, catnip, cedron, chickweed. Chicory (endive), colombo, comfrey, coriander seed, cucumbers, dandelion, dill, echinacea (corn-flower), fennel, fenugreek, fleabane, gentian root, giant Solomon Seal, ginseng, golden seal, gold thread root, hyssop, magnolia bark, marjoram, marshmallow, melons, myrrh, parsley, peach, bark/kernels/leaves/twigs, pennyroyal, peppermint, Peruvian bark, pilewort, poke root, psylla, red clover, red root, red sage, rhubarb, rue, rushes, sage, sanicle, sassafras, senna, sorrel, spearmint, squashes, St. John's wort, strawberry leaves, sweet balm, tansy, thyme, tormentil, twinleaf, uva ursi, valerian, violet, water plants, white willow, wild alum root, wild cherry, wintergreen, witch hazel bark/leaves, wood betony, and wormwood.

CLIMATE
Wet and cool; thus, you may want to live where it rains heavily, or near water.

PART OF LAND AND COUNTRY
Near the ocean, river, lake or creek, or where any small active streams of water flow. A rich soil compounded of sand, clay or organic matter, usually found in creeks, river bottoms or near the ocean.

U.S. Cities: Juneau, AK; Fayetteville, AR; Stockton, and Newport Beach, CA; Bunnel, Naples, Orlando and St. Petersburg, FL; Honolulu, HI; Chicago and Peoria, IL; Gary, IN; Burlington, IA; Baton Rouge, LA; Portland, ME; Baltimore, MD; Worcester, MA; Egelson, MI; Greenville, MS; St. Joseph, MO; Concord, NH; Edgewood and Santa Fe, NM; New York City and Niagara Falls, NY; Norman and Oklahoma City, OK; Watertown, SD; Wichita Falls, TX; Casper and Sheridan, WY.

U.S. States: Idaho, New Hampshire, Virginia, Wyoming.

Countries: Afghanistan, Algeria, Argentina, Burundi, Canada, Djibouti, Egypt, Iraq, Israel, Italy, Malawi, Mozambique, Nepal, Oman, Rwanda, Slovenia, Somalia, Thailand, U.S.A., Vietnam and Zaire.

Islands: Bahamas, Cape Verde, Comoros, Kiribati, Madagascar, New Zealand, Phillippines, São Tomé e Principé, Seychelles, Solomon Islands.

Cities (other than U.S.): Kabul, Afghanistan; Algiers, Algeria; Tucuman, Argentina; Lubeck (Victoria), Australia; Nassau, Bahamas; Bujumbura, Burundi; Ottawa, Canada; Praia, Cape Verde; Hong Kong, China; Moronia, Comoros; Djibouti, Djibouti; Cairo, Egypt; Deptford, Manchester and Rochdale, England; Magdeburg, Germany; Amsterdam, Holland; Genoa, Milan, Rome and Venice, Italy; Bairiki, Kiribati; Antananarivo, Madagascar; Blantyre, Malawi; Maputo, Mozambique; Auckland, New Zealand; Muscat, Oman; Kigali, Rwanda; São Tomé, São Tomé; Victoria, Seychelles; Honiara, Guadacanal, Solomon Islands; Mogadishu, Somalia; Cadiz, Spain; Bangkok, Thailand; Hanoi, Vietnam; Kinshasa, Zaire.

IN A CANCER VIBRATION

You are mediumistic, follow your gut feelings and help others; perhaps you aid a wounded cat or disabled person, or baby sit for a working mother. Variety is desired and satisfied when you attend numerous affairs. All forms of music are enjoyed. Your moods fluctuate rapidly in this environment; money is spent on a whim. In this locale, domesticity plays a major role — food gets top priority. Needlepoint, sewing, knitting and crocheting keep you occupied. Your super-sensitivity shows when your emotions have been tampered with — buckets of tears flow. You are drawn to issues which affect the common classes, land development, housing, the waterworks, and nursing homes.

CANCER TRAITS

You are constantly helping others, satisfying your desire to be needed. By nature, you are timid, caring, nurturing, sympathetic and protective. Your maternal/paternal instincts are strong. You are domestically inclined, especially when it comes to cooking food. Overeating due to frustrations causes weight gain, which could be a major problem. You are sensitive and overly emotional. Your moods change within seconds. You have a lively imagination which should be put to creative endeavors rather than emotional upsets. Your best trait is tenacity. Your downfall is touchiness.

CANCER COMPATIBILITY

With Cancer: You understand each other's mood shifts. Both are sensitive; thus, you take care not to hurt each other's feelings. It is a warm and loving relationship which is a good match. Lovemaking is gentle, emotionally moving and filled with passion — you can't keep you hands off each other. With Scorpio: You'll enjoy clinging to this possessive mate. Scorpio gives you the attention you crave and loves to control you. Sex is a breathtaking and electrifying experience which could keep you both in the bedroom for hours or all day and night! With Pisces: You like the way this person understands you. Both are changeable and quiet. Sentimentality is shared. Enraptured states of carnal joy are experienced by both of you.

With Taurus: You feel needed by this person because Taurus protects and cares for you. Your mood swings don't disturb steady Taurus; in fact, Taurus tries to stabilize you. Taurus stirs your heartstrings and makes you feel as if you are on Cloud Nine while making love. With Gemini: He/she keeps your curiosity aroused; you will never have a dull moment. Both of you like variety. You'll learn plenty from Gemini. New sex techniques gratify both of your dreams, which can become a reality. With Leo: You feel safe and secure and don't mind Leo being the boss or on center stage; you feel better when the spotlight is not shining in your direction. Your carnal appetites are quenched when the two of you make ardent and soul-stirring love.

With Virgo: You are happy with this one because Virgo analyzes your moods and actions and thus comprehends the real you. However, your feelings are hurt when Virgo criticizes you. The two of you are slowly aroused to sensual states of exaltation, which results in complete gratification of the physical senses. With Sagittarius: This person can hurt you emotionally with bluntness. Lots of tears are shed in this relationship, especially when Sagittarius wants to be out all the time and you want to stay home. Sex may be too quick and not have the emotional impact that you need. With Aquarius: This person is too independent for you. You'll cry a bucketful of tears when Aquarius is unreliable and comes home late or suddenly decides to socialize with pals. However, while indulging in erotic delights, you might feel as if you were under a hypnotic spell.

With Aries: This individual is so self-centered that you could be ignored and you will not like that. You'll be hurt and upset when Aries tells you like it is — words are cutting. But lovemaking thrills you beyond your wildest imagination. With Capricorn: Opposites attract, and what one lacks the other has. However, Capricorn can be cold and indifferent to your needs. This person is more interested in satisfying career goals than in indulging in personal concerns; it could mean loneliness for you. Once Capricorn is aroused sexually, carnal pleasures are deeply felt and enjoyed. With Libra: Both of you are indecisive, so who is going to make the decisions? You'll like Libra's kindness and desire to balance everything in life. Erotic desires are satisfied when you both pour your hearts and souls into making love.

CANCER 2019 FORECAST

From January 1st to March 6th, there are upheavals with your career which could lead to your getting fired, laid off, quitting or a decrease in your salary. Do not be late to work, erratic, or abrupt with a boss. Be calm, cool, diplomatic and go about your duties obediently, seriously and work hard keeping your nose to the grindstone. If you tell superiors like it is, you are facing a change or termination. Your personal life could make you so emotional that you become too sensitive and unpredictable, especially if you are married. Partnerships and clients could bring topsy-turvey conditions, especially if you are self-employed. With the ups and downs that are taking place, do not despair. Be confident; take on added work, responsibility with a cheerful attitude. Make the best of all situations and issues; the result will be success and could be a promotion or raise; therefore, by taking care of your feelings and actions, you can counteract any disruptive influence and will come out on top.

From March 7th to December 31st, you can make wonderful new friends--old pals could pop back into your life and bring stability and lasting friendships. It is a favorable time to join forces with your buddies such as forming a corporation. Group activity is wonderful, regardless of whether it is through being a member of a club or going into business. After March 7th, overseas trips with friends, or a spouse, can bring happy moments---it is an ideal time to travel to exotic locales and experience a cultural awakening that has you fascinated, especially with your pals and foreigners. Your philosophy for an ideal world where people are free from hunger may appeal to you. It is a great time to go to lectures or take a course that will be mind-boggling. Watch TV travel shows or discs on exotic locales. You may discover utopia and want to journey to a place that could make you believe you are in shangri-la. If you travel with a partner, it may be a trip of a lifetime. Therefore, try to make plans for a getaway sometime before the year ends. If your job involves trade with other countries, success and fun-filled moments with blend into one fantastic trip. Or try to get work in a foreign country or that involves business trips with exotic locales.

Best Period For Romance... October 23 — November 21
Best Dates For Sex

Jan: 1, 10, 11, 15, 19, 28; Feb: 6, 7, 11, 12, 16, 24; Mar: 11, 15, 23, 24; Apr: 2, 7, 11, 12, 20, 29, 30; May: 9, 17, 27, 31; Jun: 1, 5, 14, 20, 25, 26, 28; Jul: 11, 20, 21, 30; Aug: 7, 16, 17, 21, 22, 26; Sep: 3, 13, 18, 23; Oct 1, 10, 11, 15, 20, 28; Nov: 6, 7, 11, 16, 24, 25; Dec: 4, 9, 13, 22, 31.

CHAPTER FIVE
LEO: THE LION... JULY 23 — AUGUST 23

To understand this chapter, read the Preface and Foreword. If you, know your rising sign, read the advice given for that sign as well as for your Sun sign. The combination of these two will give you more information than could be gained by simply reading only the Sun sign. Refer to pages 16 and 17 if you do not know what your rising sign is.

The following descriptions are typical for those born under the sign Leo. However, your own horoscope may contradict some of this, depending upon your rising sign and the signs occupied by the planets in your horoscope.

Leo is a fire sign and is masculine and barren. The Sun is the planetary ruler. Each of the signs and/or planets has rulership over certain phases of life. The following are ruled by Leo or the Sun:

COLORS
You may want to enhance your living quarters or wardrobe in these shades:

Sun: Bright orange, such as mandarin orange, tangerine or carrot. Gold.

Leo: Light (pale) orange. Shades of the sunset, such as sun-glow, peach, apricot. Shades of orange-yellow and/or brownish, such as tan, tawny, tiger, leopard, amber, coral, sunflower, rust, burnt orange, burnt copper, salmon-orange. Coreopsis.

TALISMANIC GEMS
Ruby, amber, cat's eye, chrysolite, girasol (fire opal), hyacinth, ruby spinel, sun-stone (adventurine). You may want to magnetize one, or more, of these gems for good luck and/or to protect you from harm. Refer to Part Two under Magnetizing Objects for auspicious dates to magnetize a talismanic gem.

STONES
Chrysolite, hyacinth and soft yellow minerals. Therefore, you may accent your abode with striped stones as accessories or wear them as jewelry. You may find that you have good luck when wearing or owning one of these stones.

METALLIC ELEMENT
Sun: Gold.

NUMBER
Number 19; You may want to bet with this number, or perhaps favorable events will occur on this date. If you want to plan ahead for certain activities, you could use this date for something important, especially if it coincides with a date for that event in the Best Days section in Part Two.

DAY
Sunday: You may want to plan mportant activities for Sunday. Your energy is at its height on Sundays.

SENSES: PHYSICAL OR NON-PHYSICAL
Physical Sense: Energy absorption, thus giving vitality
Physical Organ: The heart
Psychic Sense: Inspiration

MUSIC

Ballads, rock concerts, opera, classical, ceremonial, love songs, traditional jazz, pomp and ceremony, soundtracks (movies, Broadways shows). The romantic composers of the 19th Century.

PERFUMES

These magical scents provide a smooth diffusing of warmth and sensuality. Because you like to be the center of attention, wear these fragrances and you'll bask in the limelight. Dab these essences on when you want to be a bit of a tease; you'll be irresistible.

For the Female: 212 by Carolina Herrera, Anaís, Anaís by Cacharel, II Bacio (The Kiss) by Princess Marcella Borghese, Blazer by Anne Klein, Calache by Hermès, Calyx by Prescriptives, Cavale de Fabergé, Champagne by Yves Saint Laurent, Chloe by Karl Lagerfeld, Colonia's No. 4711, Cristalle by Chanel, Delicious by Gale Hayman, Diorella, Eau de Patou, Eau d' Hadrien by Annick Goutal, Eau de Sud by Annick Goutal, Eau Dynamisante, Eau Savage, Elysium by Clarins, Fleur d' Interdit by Givenchy, Gio de Giorgio Armani, La Nuit de Rabanne by Paco Rabanne, L' Eau d' Issey by Issey Miyake, L'Effleur by Coty, Love's Fresh Lemon, Mariel Parfums by H20 Plus, Molinard, Nectar by Goodebodies, Ô de Lancôme, Sheherazade by Jean Desprez, Sunflowers by Elizabeth Arden, Tigress, Trésor by Lancôme, Trouble by Revlon, Tuxedo by Ralph Lauren.

For the Male: Bel Ami by Hermès, Chand, Chaps, Eau de Cologne Imperiale, Eau Savage, First Pour Homme, Nomande, Oleg Cassini, Serrano.

FLOWERS

Flowers and flowering plants that are coral, gold, peach, apricot, tangerine, yellow-red, rust, golden yellow and orange, and all the colors of the Sun and sunset, such as: Amaryllis, azalea, Bird of Paradise, Black-eyed Stella, Black-eyed Susan, butterfly flower, Cat's Ear, Chrysanthemum, chrysogoneum, clivia, crocus. Crown Imperiale, daffodil, flamboyant (Poinciana), fothergilla, gaillardia, gladiola, goldenrod, hawkweed, Impatiens (touch-me-not), iris, lily (daylily, foxtail, leopard, oriental, tiger, trumpet), lycoris, marigold, miniata, morning glory, narcissus, peony, poppy (Orange, California), sunflower (helianthus), sunray, tormentil, trollius and tulip (including the lily-flowered).

BOOKS

Those that are about art, power, wealth, prestige, success, royalty, politics, love, and the opera, ballet, movie-making, show business and theatre. Also epics that deal with heroism and illustrated "coffee" table books.

FASHION

You like to buy everything at once for the forthcoming season. Money is spent quickly without counting the cost of anything. Expensive clothes are desired, designer ones are favored; but if you can not afford them you will buy quality outfits at the better shops. You love furs and real fabrics and frown upon imitations.

Your wardrobe is chic; elegance is a must. It is important for you to be perfectly groomed from head to toe at all times; thus, your clothes are in immaculate condition. You dress for the occasion. When you walk into a room, you want everyone to notice you and compliment you on your outfit. You carry yourself with such dignity that everyone believes you have paid plenty for whatever you are wearing.

If you are a Leo woman: An evening gown in velvet, brocade, chiffon, crepe de chine, gold lame, and raw or French silk appeal to you. The classic styles, such as Empire, make you feel like a true Leo Queen. Your wardrobe consists of knits, culottes (for day or night), satin, silk, sportswear and dresses for any affair. The fabrics preferred are suede, rayon, lambs wool, polyester, wool nylon or fleece.

If you are a Leo man: A blazer, flannel trousers, yachting outfit or tuxedo makes you feel like a true Leo King. You also enjoy wearing a velour vest, V-neck, or turtleneck shirt or sweater of acrylic or lambs wool. The fabrics preferred are silk, flannel, suede, polyester, acrylic and lambs wool.

All the shades of the sun or sunset-gold, yellow, orange, tangerine, coral and burnt copper appeals to you. When you don your clothes or accessories in any of these colors, you will feel vibrant and alive, especially when all heads turn your way, approvingly.

GIFTS

See preceding sections for type of books, flowers, music or perfume that may appeal to a Leonine. Purchase Leo something expensive (if you can afford it; if not then make sure it looks like it cost a lot). A Leonine likes quality, luxury and the best and finest that money can buy. Leo is the royal sign of the Zodiac and wants to be treated like a King/Queen. Leo's like to shine and be on center stage; thus, don't buy a gift that is drab or looks cheap — the gifts that glitter, sparkle or show brilliant jewel tones are pleasing to a Leonine. Sweaters (jeweled or embroidered lavishly), silk scarves (preferably designer), blouses or an ascot.

Leo glows when the clothes are bright, colorful, elegant, flashy (but in good taste). Items that are made exclusively for Leo will make the Leonine feel important and prestigious. You can't go wrong when your gifts are monogrammed; so have their initials put on such items as sweaters, shirts, clothes, linens (sheet, pillow cases, towels for the bath), handkerchiefs, jewelry (bracelet, pendant, gold watch). Leo basks in showing off his/her possessions or self; the more ostentatious, the better.

A Leo knows how to enjoy life; entertaining is done in lavish style. Gifts they would be proud of (if they don't already own) are: gold napkin rings, gold tableware, glasses and plates with gold trimming (china preferred), ashtray or wine bottle holder (especially in gold); candelabra, champagne cooler (or magnum of the finest bubbly you can afford), crystal decanter or stemware or fancy gourmet food such as caviar.

A Leonine loves to look at himself/herself; thus, an ornate mirror or a gold frame dressing table with a mirror (and brush set) could satisfy Leo. Other items for Leo: gold lion doorbell cover, oil painting framed in gold, antiques, perfume, collector books (gold on the edges of the pages), bath oil, satin sheets, padded hangers, hair dryer, belt (suede or leather), expensive desk set (suede or leather), a gift certificate to an expensive department store, furs, sable-lined raincoat, designer clothes, gold jewelry box, a tiara (for her queenly head) or genuine jewelry (ruby or gold).

Leo enjoys the theatre; thus a ticket to a movie, play, musical, opera, ballet, or concert would be ideal. Or opera glasses. A ticket to a sporting event (ice skating or regular sports). Leo would be elated with a soundtrack of his/her favorite film or musical. Since he/she enjoys gambling: a deck of cards, mini-video poker, slot or roulette game. Or how about a deluxe cabin on a cruise ship that stops in exotic ports? Or an airline ticket to romantic locales.

For the Young: Huge stuffed animals, fashion dolls with changeable clothes, a vanity kit with mirror accessories. Leo kids love to play dress up and make up; party clothes, feather boas, velvet hats, gowns, tuxedos, costumes, a tutu, tap shoes, ballet slippers, a tiara. Or a castle playhouse, puppets with a theatre, microphone, tape player, sing-a-long cassette player, videocassette movie or give them ballet or tap lessons, or acting classes.

CELL SALTS

Magnesia phosphoricum or phosphate of magnesia.

ZONES OF THE BODY

The aorta, back, heart, spine (and the marrow and nerves of the spine), spleen. Thus you could be subject to back disorders/problems (backaches), carditis, heart problems (aneurysm, angina pectoris, attacks, ballooning of the aorta, enlargement, impeded heart beat, narrowing of the arteries, palpitations, congestive heart failure), spinal problems such as curvature of the spine.

HERBS

Effective herbs and plants for the Leo afflicted body zones are: Angelica, anise, bloodroot, borage (bugloss), camomile, coriander seed, cowslip, dandelion, dill, eglantine, eyebright, fennel, garden mint, golden seal, holy thistle, laudanum, lavender, lily of the valley, lobelia, marigold, mistletoe, motherwort, parsley, peppermint, pimpernel, poppy, sorrel, St. John's wort, valerian, vervain, wintergreen, wood betony, yellow lily and zinnia.

CLIMATE

Dry and hot; thus, you may want to live in the desert, or in a place that is dry and hot. However, most Leos can not stand the heat.

PART OF LAND AND COUNTRY

Ruled low countryside, with smooth or level surfaces tending to be similar to desert or having desert conditions. Land which is barren, waste, wild or which is kept for sports (hunting, shooting, rodeo, horseback riding, etc.), or entertainment, recreation or amusement.

U.S. Cities: Newport Beach and San Bernardino, CA; Colorado Springs, CO; Miami, FL; Chicago, IL; Hutchinson, KS; Baltimore, MD; Rochester, MN; St. Joseph, MO; Concord, NH; Minot, OK; Cranston, RI; Charleston, SC.

U.S. States: Colorado, Hawaii, Missouri, New York.

U.S. Territories: Guam, Puerto Rico.

Countries: Algeria, Bhutan, Bolivia, Central African Republic, Chad, Colombia, Congo, Croatia, Gabon, India, Ivory Coast, Korea (North), Korea (South), Kuwait, Liberia, Niger, Pakistan, Peru, Romania, Senegal, Slovenia, Sudan, Tunisia, Upper Volta.

Islands: Bahrain, Cyprus, Iceland, Jamaica, Maldives, Phillippines, Singapore, Solomon Islands, Vanuatu.

British Crown Colony: Gibraltar.

Provinces: Benin, Sicily (Italy).

Cities (other than U.S.): Algiers, Algeria; Manama, Bahrain; Porto Nova, Benin; Thimpu, Bhutan; La Paz, Bolivia; Bangui, Central African Republic; N'djamena, Chad (Africa); Bogota, Columbia; Brazzaville, Congo, (Africa); Nicosia, Cyprus; Bath, Blackpool, Bristol, Portsmouth and Taunton, England; Libreville, Gabon; Reykjavik, Iceland; New Delhi, India; Tel Aviv, Israel; Abidjan, Ivory Coast; Kingston, Jamaica; Pyongyang, North Korea; Seoul, South Korea; Kuwait, Kuwait; Monrovia, Liberia; Niamey, Niger; Karachi, Pakistan; Lima, Peru; Manila, Phillipines; Bucharest, Romania; Dakar, Senegal; Singapore, Singapore; Honiara, Gudalcanal, Solomon Islands; Khartoum, Sudan; Tunis, Tunisia; Ouagadougou, Upper Volta; Vila, Vanuatu.

IN A LEO VIBRATION

Your ideas are large and majestic. In this environment, you are determined to rise and strive to rule through strength and stability. You want to be the boss, a leader, an official, or on center stage with your friends. You could over-reach your mark if you aim too high. The respect, dignity and admiration hungered for is received when you are praised for your part in a community project. Your actions show a flair for the dramatic. You may be drawn to entertainment establishments — arenas, stadiums, theatres, fairs, exhibition halls. For ego purposes, you may support a local or state athletic team, public school or playground issue, solar energy and power plant movement, or a campaign to legalize gambling in your municipality.

LEO TRAITS

You are generous to friends and loved ones. Others can see that you are warm, devoted and loyal. Attention is a necessity...it is your food. You enjoy impressing others with wealth, power, prestige and often hold a high position — in business or politics. You tend to be egotistical. Once aroused emotionally, you forget the cost — your heart rules. You are industrious and must be at the top; you'll take risks to get ahead. You frown upon petty things; large scale operations are for you. You possess a strong and unbending will. To lead, rule the roost and be in the spotlight are cravings that must be satisfied. You demand from others love or praise. Your best trait is kindness. Your downfall is flattery.

LEO COMPATIBILITY

With Libra: Both love luxury and go first class. Libra's charm has you entranced. Both enjoy entertaining in grand style. You two are romantic. When in one another's company, you both feel as if you had taken an aphrodisiac; sex is sensational. With Aries: The two of you enjoy spending money and are great risk takers in business and in the sexual arena. Generosity abounds in this match. Violent passion rages when making love — eroticism prevails. With Sagittarius: You love the attention your Sagittarius mate bestows, especially when this person encourages you to be successful and important. It's a fiery duo who are inflamed with desire and consumed by carnal pleasure.

With Gemini: This person's wit and intelligence fascinates you. Gemini's mercurial personality lightens your day. This individual's adaptability is to your liking. Sexually, you are thrilled over the diversity Gemini brings into your life. With Cancer: You enjoy this person's domesticity, protectiveness and caring nature. Cancer gives you the attention you crave. Lovemaking is full of tenderness and emanates from the bottom of each other's heart. With Virgo: The two of you stimulate each other's mind. However, you dislike Virgo's nit-picking, criticism and nagging. In the bedroom you are ecstatic when you bring Virgo's sensuality to the surface.

With Pisces: You'll have this one clinging and adoring you — satisfying your hunger to be worshiped. Pisces will wait on you and make you feel like royalty. When you two have sex, it is as if you have found paradise. With Capricorn: Capricorn's practicality will turn you off and interfere with your desire to live "high on the hog." Both are ambitious and could be too competitive for the top spot on the ladder of success. This person is too inhibited for your fiery nature; however, once Capricorn trusts you, you'll be in for a great carnal surprise! With Taurus: Both of you are stubborn and refuse to back down from fixed opinions. However, Taurus won't steal center stage which is to your liking. Lovemaking tends toward passionate lasciviousness.

With Scorpio: Jealousy and possessiveness could make you break the relationship. You both want to control and two chiefs make for a bad match. But your sexual appetites are completely consumed and satisfied by excessive eroticism that is almost non-stop. With Aquarius: This person's independent and free-spirit ways will disturb you, especially if Aquarius doesn't let you be the boss. However, opposites attract and you are drawn to this individual's magnetism. The Aquarian's desire to experiment with sex attracts and mesmerizes you, but, in the long run, Aquarius is too cool for your fiery nature. With Leo: Your egos clash. Who's going to be the boss? Center stage is up for grabs with each trying to steal the spotlight. In the bedroom, fire meets fire — fervent and fleshly appetites lead to ecstasy.

LEO 2019 FORECAST

This is a fantastic year for you--all of your dreams could come true. After March 7th to December 31st, your fame, career, job, vocation or business soars to dizzying heights of success. You'll be flabbergasted at the good luck that knocks on your door. It may seem like you can do no wrong and that everything you touch turns to golden success. Unpredictable events could bring earth-shattering overnight results that could blow your mind. You will not believe that this is all happening to you. You are a true entrepreneur, executive, administrator who can see the overall view and organize all of your business ideas through being extremely ambitious and finishing all projects. Publicity, awards, honors and recognition for your talents bring you to the top of your profession. You can wheel and deal by promoting all projects and easily get backers and investors to put their money in your plans and get-rich-quick schemes. However, avoid getting involved in any stock options--go after money. Form corporations. Chain stores or business done on a show-string basis could bring prosperity. Mass production is favored. You know how to convince people at meetings to go along with you. Do not hesitate to push your ambitious plans all the way to the top. Persistence and diplomacy are the keys to achievement. If you are employed, put your best foot forward by working hard and long hours--it will pay off now.

If you travel overseas, try to take a quick trip from January 1st to March 6th. Go with a loved one--kick up your heels and have the time of your life--laughing, frolicking and living it up as if there is no tomorrow. Or, during this time, go to lectures. You may meet a person that fascinates you. Both of you may be mesmerized by each other and experience a spellbound relationship. It may not last but it will be unforgettable. Go to amusement centers, theme parks, arenas, and sporting events or take up New Age studies. It is a great time to be philosophical and make the best of all that life has to offer. You may feel like a new and different person.

Best Period For Romance... November 22 — December 21
Best Dates For Sex

Jan: 3, 10, 11, 12, 13, 17, 30; Feb: 6, 7, 8, 9, 14, 18, 26, 27; Mar: 6, 7, 8, 9, 13, 19, 26; Apr: 2, 3, 4, 9, 14, 22, 29, 30; May: 1, 2, 6, 7, 11, 19, 20, 27, 28, 29, 30; Jun: 7, 16, 23, 24, 25, 26, 30; Jul: 4, 5, 13, 20, 21, 22, 23, 28; Aug: 1, 9, 10, 16, 17, 18, 19, 21, 24, 30; Sep: 5, 6, 13, 14, 15, 16, 20, 21, 25; Oct: 3, 10, 11, 12, 17, 18, 30; Nov: 6, 7, 8, 9, 14, 18. 27; Dec: 4, 5, 6, 9, 11, 15, 16, 24, 31.

CHAPTER SIX
VIRGO: THE VIRGIN... AUGUST 23 — SEPTEMBER 22

To understand this chapter, read the Preface and Foreword. If you, know your rising sign, read the advice given for that sign as well as for your Sun sign. The combination of these two will give you more information than could be gained by simply reading only the Sun sign. Refer to pages 16 and 17 if you do not know what your rising sign is.

The following descriptions are typical for those born under the sign Virgo. However, your own horoscope may contradict some of this, depending upon your rising sign and the signs occupied by the planets in your horoscope.

Virgo is an earth sign and is feminine and barren. Mercury is the planetary ruler. Each of the signs and/or planets has rulership over certain phases of life. The following are ruled by Virgo or Mercury:

COLORS
You may want to enhance your living quarters or wardrobe in these shades:

Mercury: Bright violet; such shades as a deep reddish-bluish purple, i.e. mauve or heliotrope.

Virgo: Dark violet; such hues as grape. Earthy Virgo, the sign of the harvester and grains, you may be attracted to the earth colors represented by your sign, such as the lighter hues of brown: beige, wheat, sand, camel and caramel.

TALISMANIC GEMS
Jasper. You may want to magnetize the jasper for good luck and/or to protect you from harm. Refer to Part Two under Magnetizing Objects for auspicious dates to magnetize a talismanic gem.

STONES
Flint, pyrites. Therefore, you may accent your abode with pyrites as accessories. You may find that your luck is enhanced when owning a flint stone or pyrite.

METALLIC ELEMENT
Mercury: Quicksilver.

NUMBER
Number 2; You may want to bet with this number, or perhaps favorable events will occur on this date. If you want to plan ahead for certain activities you could use this date for something important, especially if it coincides with a date for that event in the Best Days section in Part Two.

DAY
Wednesday: You may want to plan important activities for Wednesday. Your energy is at its height on Wednesdays.

SENSES: PHYSICAL OR NON-PHYSICAL
Physical Sense: Inner Sight
Physical Organ: Pineal Gland, also called the "third eye"
Psychic Sense: Clairvoyance

MUSIC

Country, instrumental, and serious heavy but earthy sounds. Old favorites preferable over new hits. Classical and Baroque helps you relax and encourages your analytical mind to start working. Often, you like quiet background music while conversing on intellectual subjects.

PERFUMES

These scents bring out your neat, cool-clean-crisp look and down-to-earth sensuality. You'll find them refreshingly vital. A smoldering sexuality lies behind that prim facade when you wear these fragrances. Sprinkle them on and you'll be effervescent and ready for romance.

For the Female: Aramis, Babe, Belle de Jovan, Bouquet de Provence by Frédéric Fekkai, Cobochard, Feminité du Bois by Shiseido, Infini by Caron, Kenzo Parfum d'ete, Knowing by Esteé Lauder, Laura Ashley No. 1, Lutece, Maja, Memoire Cherie, Must de Cartier, Raffini, Sinan by Jean-Marc Sinan, Sweet Earth, Woodhue.

For the Male: Brut, English Leather, Joop! Homme, Kanøn, Polo by Ralph Lauren, Royal Copenhagen, Wood Grains, Sandalwood.

FLOWERS

Flowers and flowering plants that are dark violet, such as: Ageratum, allium, anemone, aubrietia, bird's nest orchid, chrysanthus, crocus, friesland, giganteum, hearts-ease, heliotrope, iris, jasmine, mazus reptans's, pansy, pasque flower, poppy, violet (including African).

BOOKS

Those that are educational or give information: Almanacs, thesaurus, dictionaries, encyclopedias, biographies, how-to and fix-it books. Also statistical, factual, geography, travel, nutrition, health, medical, exercise, catalogs (mail order), and books that explain the mysteries behind amazing origins, quotes and clichés.

FASHION

You have an eye for value; fabrics are analyzed — good texture and craftsmanship are musts. You are a practical shopper and only buy what you need and will wear. You mix and match skirts, blouses and sweaters, thus, giving variety to your wardrobe at little expense.

You are picky with clothes. Your wearing apparel has a tailored look; you like simple lines and dress conservatively and in good taste. Your favorite fabrics are wools and tweeds, especially wool herringbone tweed and machine washable polyester/wool. You also like rayon, and raw and French silks.

If you are a Virgo woman, you are drawn to shirtwaist or piped pocket dresses, knits, tweed suits or tailored pantsuits. If you are a Virgo man, you enjoy wearing wool blazers, jackets, or suits with vests, tweed sports coats, worsted wool trousers and sweaters.

All shades of earth and sand tones — beige, wheat, flaxen, caramel and brown appeal to you. Navy and grey are colors you also enjoy wearing. When you don clothes or accessories in the earth and sand tones, you feel a strong affinity with nature. You should add a dash of dark violet or green accessories to your wardrobe; you will thus brighten your personality and have more fun.

GIFTS

See preceding sections for type of books, flowers, music or perfume that may appeal to a Virgoan. Virgo isn't picky or critical but likes practical gifts. If he/she doesn't like your present don't be surprised if you're told, "You wasted your money." Buy the Virgoan something that is utilitarian (food processor), functional (home furnishings designed and made by artisans and craftsman), sturdy (chef's knives), durable, gives good service (a serving tray or cart). Virgo appreciates anything that educates the mind: non-fiction books, catalogs, encyclopedias, dictionaries, how-to-books, rare and leather bound "first editions" or magazine subscriptions. Or a bedtime book light.

The Virgo guy/gal likes to stay on time and live on a schedule; therefore, buy an alarm clock, old or antique model clock, electronic timer, date or appointment book. Virgo is neat, tidy, clean, meticulous and well organized; therefore, give a present that caters to these needs: record keeping book, stationary set, pen and pencil set, storage bins, filing cabinet, wastepaper basket, office supplies, attaché case, pocket calculator, ash tray, cleaning materials, products or equipment. Organizers: desk set for the office: (for the gal that travels — cosmetics, hose or lingerie bags; for the guy — leather bags (small) with compartments for toothbrush, shaving, etc. Virgo's enjoy a manicure and grooming kit.

For the health-nut Virgoan, give something related to diet, health, medicine, fitness; loofah back scrubber, soaps made of natural herbs, fruit package, health food basket, a pillbox, subscription to a health magazine, gift certificate for a fruit-of-the-month club, or a class devoted to exercise, a nutrition or health food cooking class. For the Virgo who loves to garden: a plant, seeds, exotic flower bulbs, sun hat, gloves, clippers, vitamins for plants or gardening equipment.

Virgo is exact, efficient and a perfectionist; thus, tools or equipment that will help his/her love of precision will be appreciated. Give items that allow them to exercise their minds or brain teasers such as puzzles and trivia games. Or a Virgo will be happy with a tape recorder, stereo headphones, CD's, tapes or video's that teach or inform. Other suggestions are: a diary, afghan wrap, dress pattern, print, lithograph, woven leather belt, sweater, tailored tie, shirt, dress, wool socks or garment made from wool and tweed. A basket of cheeses could make a serious Virgo smile.

For the Young: A Virgo kid loves to play school, especially teacher. Give a desk (pegboard for younger children), bulletin board, toy calculator or drafting set, fraction teaching board, paper well and dispenser, rubber stamp kit, folding bookcase, school days scrap book, school (play set, playground kit, mini-school house). To aid their desire to learn: print books, spelling books, stacking blocks, alphabet and number learning puzzles. These intelligent kids are book worms and enjoy reading books and magazines that appeal to a hobby or special interest. A model kit (for assembling things), colorful stickers they can put in an album, a stamp collecting kit, or index cards to put things in order. A Virgo child likes to play doctor; thus, buy a toy medical bag, first aid or nurse kit. They'll adore a small pet (cat, dog, bird, frog, hamster, turtle) or a farm play set, wood animal puzzle, or plastic farm animals.

CELL SALTS
Kali sulphuricum or sulphate of potash.

ZONES OF THE BODY
The abdominal region, appendix, bowels, chyle, colon, duodenum, gastro-intestinal system, intestinal canal tract, mesenteric glands, navel, peristaltic action of the bowels, pyloris glands, small intestines. Thus you could be subject to appendicitis, colon irregularities, constipation, diverticulitis, hernia obstruction in the bowel, ileitis, intestinal problems, peritonitis, tapeworm.

HERBS
Effective herbs and plants for the Virgo afflicted body zones are: Aloes, angelica, balm, balmony, barley, bayberry bark, beech, bethroot, birch, bistort, bitterroot, bloodroot, blue cohosh, blue violet, buckthorn bark, butternut bark, calamus, camomile, caraway seed, carrot root/seed, cascara sagrada, catnip, cayenne, chickweed, colombo, comfrey, coriander, cubeb berries, dandelion, dill, echinacea, endive, fennel, fenugreek, fireweed, flaxseed, fleabane, fringe tree, gentian root, geranium, giant Solomon's Seal, ginger, ginseng, golden seal, gold thread, gum arabic, horehound, hyssop, Lady's slipper, magnolia, mandrake, marshmallow, milkweed root, masterwort, millet, mint, motherwort, mugwort, mullein, myrrh, nettle, oats, origanum, peach leaves, pennyroyal, peppermint, Peruvian bark, pilewort, plantain, pleurisy root, prickly ash, privet, rue, rye, sage, sanicle, sassafras, senna, skullcap, skunk cabbage, slippery elm bark, spearmint, St. John's wort, strawberry leaves, succory, sumach berries, summer savory, tansy, thyme, uva ursi, valerian, vervain, wahoo, water pepper, wheat, white oak bark, white pond lily, wild alum root, wild cherry, wintergreen, witch hazel bark/leaves, wood betony, woodbine, yarrow and yellow dock.

CLIMATE
Cold with mild rainfall; thus, you may want to live in a place where rainfall is moderate and the climate cold.

PART OF LAND AND COUNTRY
Slightly elevated with grass or with tracts of land where there are corn or wheat fields, orchards or agricultural crops.

U.S. Cities: Anchorage, AK; Fayetteville, AR; Desert Hot Springs, Newport Beach and Los Angeles, CA; Colorado Springs, CO; Chicago, IL; Des Moines, IA; Rockville, MD; Boston, MA; Manchester, NH; Fairview Forest, NC; Minot, ND; Reading, PA.

U.S. State: California.

Countries: Belize, Botswana, Bulgaria, Chile, Guinea-Bissau, Korea (North), Malaysia, Mali, Mexico, Qatar, Saudi Arabia, Swaziland, Switzerland, Uruguay, Venda, Yemen Arab Republic and Zambia.

Island: Barbados, Maldives, Malta, Nauru, Papua New Guinea, St. Christopher-Nevis (St. Kitts-Nevis), Singapore, Trinidad and Tobago.

Cities (other than U.S.): Bridgetown, Barbados; Belmopan, Belize; Gaborone, Botswana; Sofia, Bulgaria; Santiago, Chile; Bury, Cheltenham, Maidstone, Norwich and Todmorden, England; Toulouse, France; Bathurst, Gambia; Heidelberg and Strasbourg, Germany; Corinth and Crete, Greece; Bisau, Guinea-Bissau; Brindisi and Padova (Padua), Italy; Pyongyang, North Korea; Kuala Lumpur, Malaysia; Male, Maldives; Bamako, Mali; Valleta, Malta; Mexico City, Mexico; Yaren, Nauru; Port Moresby, Papua New Guinea; Doha, Qatar; Basse-Terre, (St. Kitts-Nevis), St. Christopher-Nevis; Riyadh, Saudi Arabia; Singapore, Singapore; Mbabane, Swaziland; Bern, Switzerland; Port-of-Spain, Trinidad and Tobago; Montevideo, Uruguay; Thohyandou, Venda; Aden, Yemen; San'a', Yemen Arab Republic; Lusaka, Zambia.

IN A VIRGO VIBRATION

It is easy to be a workaholic. In this town, you are extremely practical and materialistic. This locale brings out your desire for perfection. If you are too picky and critical, it may be difficult to make and keep friends. This is a studious environment. A great deal of your time is spent reading books and learning from everyday experiences; this knowledge is stored and used when needed. You are constantly analyzing people and situations which does not afford you too much time to talk. You may volunteer your services to the city or state; diet and health programs (weight centers, "fat" farms, health resorts or medicine), to "keep the city or state clean" campaigns.

VIRGO TRAITS

You seek and disseminate knowledge. You are industrious and excel in placing everything in its proper order. You are practical in all undertakings. You like to deal with the facts. You are meticulous, discriminating, skeptical and overly critical. Details are a must. You are well read and experienced. To be of service is your motto. You enjoy doing things for others, and thus often overlook your own needs. By nature, you are fussy and particular with associates, business deals, labor performed, and personal activities. You are picky and won't date just anyone. You can carry hygiene consciousness to such a degree that a potential mate could be turned off. Your best trait is the ability to analyze everything. Your downfall is criticism.

VIRGO COMPATIBILITY

With Virgo: Because you are both neat, efficient and learned, you are compatible with each other. You'll constantly analyze and mull over each other's every word and action. Lovemaking is calm but gratifying. With Capricorn: Both of you are industrious and understand one another's drive to keep busy. Conservative views may reign; however, you are more open to change than Capricorn. You both cover up your feelings. Sexually, you are both inhibited, but highly sensual once you let go. With Taurus: You appreciate this person's steadfastness. You have a lot in common; both are industrious, money hungry, calm, cool and collected and want a sure thing. Both of your bodies' erogenous zones are satisfied when you two are in the bedroom.

With Scorpio: Both pay attention to detail and strive to be perfect. Sarcasm can come from either one of you; however, it doesn't seem to bother this relationship. You are awakened sexually by Scorpio and may be surprised when you discover things about yourself which you never knew. With Cancer: This person's cooking and accommodating nature please you. You are able to help Cancer because you can analyze and discuss the "why" of Cancer's mood swings. You are moved by warm feelings and heartfelt love when the two of you become ever so intimate. With Leo: You admire Leo's intellect; thus, intellectual conversations enhance your relationship. You don't mind taking a back seat to Leo and waiting on this person hand and foot. Fleshly appetites are stimulated and appeased after exhilarating indulgence by the two of you.

With Libra: This one enjoys listening to you talk. You're able to relax those nerves with Libra. Romantic candlelight suppers, soft music and tender embraces lead to carnal pleasure. With Aquarius: This individual moves too fast and yaks too much for you. It seems that you can't get a word in edgewise — and you know how you like to talk. The "I-know-it-all" Aquarian may not want to listen to the facts and information you enjoy imparting. However, in the bedroom you don't mind experimenting with way-out things — unless you're still in a puritanical stage. With Gemini: This person's lack of continuity in speech drives your orderly mind berserk. Your nagging and criticism go over Gemini's head. This individual's lack of concentration in the sex act and constant yakking interfere in lovemaking.

With Sagittarius: Your practicality and Sagittarian's impracticality don't blend. You are too quiet, conservative and inhibited for wild, fun-loving and uninhibited Sagittarius. You are appalled by this person's lack of seriousness in the sex act and desire to dissipate in crazy antics. With Pisces: This person's childish and spend-thrift ways may not be to your liking. Pisces may be too sensitive and emotional for you — especially when you are picky and critical. You may not be ready for the Piscean's wantonness, but if you let yourself go you will enjoy it. With Aries: This individual's temper could bring your sarcastic tendencies to the fore; a battle might result. Aries rushes too fast and takes too many risks, which can be a threat to the relationship. You are overwhelmed by the Arien's strong sex drive — Aries is physical and you are mental; thus, problems could result.

VIRGO 2019 FORECAST

If you own a dwelling or land, the best time to sell and make a profit is from January 1st to March 6th. Also, this is a favorable time to add on an additional room on existing property. It is easy now to obtain a loan which involves real estate transactions. However, if you are marrieds, your spouse may not want to make any changes, thus be ready for disappointments. If your house or condo is up for sale, deals could fall through during this period. You cannot believe in the promises of others. Be careful of get-rich-quick schemes involving land, especially if someone tries to con you into investing in so-called resort areas or buying a lot. Things are not as they seem and you could fall for phony deals that sound too good to be true.

March 7th to December 31st, is a wonderful time to go on an overseas journey. Go with a loved one. You'll be on Cloud Nine as you explore and learn about other cultures. Take a cruise, if you do not want to fly. You will meet fascinating and interesting people on all long distance trips. If single, get married and honeymoon in exotic locales or a river cruise in a foreign destination. If you are single, you could meet someone an a trip abroad and elope. Don't be surprised if suddenly you hear wedding bells ringing. You may be in shock that you tied the nuptial knot so fast. But if that does not occur, you could receive a marriage proposal. Regardless of what transpires, you will feel safe, secure, make excellent plans, be cooperative and feel that you have found the person who could make your life blissful and that it may be a lasting relationship. This is also a favorable time with getting along with children whether they are yours or belong to someone else. Ambition and persistence prevail with creative endeavors. Follow your psychic impressions now with romance, taking care of your responsibilities and teamwork with loved ones. Promote all projects involving entertainment, fun, and pleasure with a serious attitude by planning everything in detail. Do not give up; now is the time to start to achieve your dreams.

Best Period For Romance... January 1-19 and December 22-31

Best Dates For Sex

Jan: 1, 10, 11, 15, 19, 28; Feb: 6, 7, 11, 12, 16, 24; Mar: 11, 15, 23, 24; Apr: 2, 7, 11, 12, 20, 29, 30; May: 9, 17, 27, 31; Jun: 1, 5, 14, 20, 25, 26, 28; Jul: 11, 20. 21, 30; Aug: 7. 16, 17, 21, 22, 26; Sep: 3, 13, 18, 23; Oct: 1, 10, 11, 15. 20, 28; Nov: 6, 7, 11, 16, 24, 25; Dec: 4, 9, 13, 22, 31.

CHAPTER SEVEN
LIBRA: THE SCALES... SEPTEMBER 23 — OCTOBER 22

To understand this chapter, read the Preface and Foreword. If you, know your rising sign, read the advice given for that sign as well as for your Sun sign. The combination of these two will give you more information than could be gained by simply reading only the Sun sign. Refer to pages 16 and 17 if you do not know what your rising sign is.

The following descriptions are typical for those born under the sign Libra. However, your own horoscope may contradict some of this, depending upon your rising sign and the signs occupied by the planets in your horoscope.

Libra is an air sign and is masculine and semi-fruitful. Venus is the planetary ruler. Each of the signs and/or planets has rulership over certain phases of life. The following are ruled by Libra or Venus:

COLORS
You may want to enhance your living quarters or wardrobe in these shades:
Venus: Bright yellow; such shades as butter, ripe lemons, the Sun or the yolk of an egg.
Libra: Light (pale) yellow; such shades as cream, straw, flaxen, canary, pineapple, champagne.

TALISMANIC GEMS
Amber, coral, diamond, yellow opal. You may want to magnetize the diamond or yellow opal for good luck and/or to protect you from harm. Refer to Part Two under Magnetizing Objects for auspicious dates to magnetize a talismanic gem.

STONES
White quartz, white marble. Therefore, you may accent your abode with these stones as accessories or wear them as jewelry. You may find that you have good luck when wearing or owning one of these stones.

METALLIC ELEMENT
Venus: Copper.

NUMBER
Number 3: You may want to bet this number, or perhaps favorable events will occur on this date. If you want to plan ahead for certain activities, you could use this date for something important, especially if it coincides with a date for that event in the Best Days section in Part Two.

DAY
Friday: You may want to plan important activities for Friday. Your energy is at its height on Fridays.

SENSES: PHYSICAL OR NON-PHYSICAL
Physical Sense: Touch
Physical Organ: Skin
Psychic Sense: Psychometry

MUSIC

Ballads, low-down jazz, instrumental, such as funky blues, romantic piano, violin and the yarning strains of the flute and harp; sexy saxophone sounds to make love by. Words and music with love themes.

PERFUMES

These fragrances bring out your charm, elegance, sophistication and add mystery to your aura. The tone is vampy, exciting, seductive, enchanting, bewitching, sexy and sensuous. Rhapsodic moments of love can be felt; your sweetheart will be swept up by your fascinating personality and held spellbound.

For the Female: Ajee by Revlon, Ambush by Dana, Aromatics Elixir by Clinque, Aviance, Bal a Versailles by Jean Desprez, Beautiful by Esteé Lauder, Bob Mackie, Diamonds and Emeralds by Elizabeth Taylor, Eau de Guerlain, First de Van Cleef & Arpels, Gucci No. 3, Intimate by Revlon, Jardanel, Khara, Magie Noire by Lancôme, Miss Dior, Navy by Cover Girl, Nuance, Nuit de Noel by Caron, Ombre Bleue by Jean-Charles Brosseau, Organza by Givenchy, Replique, Secret of Venus by Weil, Soft Youth Dew by Esteé Lauder, Tea Rose, Teatro alla Scalla, Tendre Poison by Christian Dior, Tribu by Bennetton, Ultima by Ultima II, Venezia by Laura Biagiotti.

For the Male: Aspen for Men, British Sterling, Cardin's Men's Cologne, Giorgio, Ho Hang, Mennen Skin Bracer, Roman Brio, Stetson.

FLOWERS

Flowers and flowering plants that are light (pale) and bright yellow, such as: Aaron's beard, carnation, chrysanthus, coreopsis, crosswort, Crown Imperiale, Dusty Miller, fawn Lily, globeflower, honeysuckle, hydrangea, iris, Love-in idleness (wild pansy), lutea (gentian), melilot, Primrose (including Evening Primrose), redroot, rose, (tea, pale yellow), St. John's wort, tulip (including lily-flowered), winter aconite, witch hazel and yellow pimpernel.

BOOKS

Art, ballet, dance, opera, music, beauty, fashion, etiquette, positive thinking and Hor d'oeuvres recipe books. Also romantic novels with love stories a la Romeo and Juliet.

FASHION

You are a clothes horse. Expensive clothes and luxurious accessories are a must for you. You would rather have a few costly outfits rather than many cheap ones. Your taste in fashion is excellent; elegance is desired and attained. It is important to you that your face and figure are shown to their best advantage. Your wearing apparel must allow your skin to breathe. Your coordinates must be properly matched; you are indecisive and therefore take your time choosing the right colors and outfits to go together.

If you are a Libra woman, you enjoy soft-feeling fabrics — silks, chiffons, velvets, jerseys, furs, and suede. Your wardrobe also consists of faille, velour, velveteen, satin finish polyester, acetate nylon crepe-back satin, crepe de chine, matte or nylon jersey, polyester-challis or lambs wool. Pleated skirts, blouses, silk shantung dresses, slinky or chiffon full evening gowns and sexy lingerie are hung in your closets and worn when the occasion arises. All shades of yellow — lemon, canary — appeal to you. When you don clothes or accessories in these colors, you will feel beautiful. You will be ready to go to, or give, a party.

If you are a Libra man, you are attracted to suede and fur parkas, velour vests, wool velour topcoats, wool flannel trousers, lambs wool V-neck sweaters and cotton-polyester slacks. You feel rich when you wear a black suit, white shirt and silk necktie. All shades of brown — cinnamon, beige, chocolate appeal to you. You may choose a yellow or pink accessory. When you don clothes or accessories in these colors, you feel handsome. You will be in the mood to entertain the opposite sex.

GIFTS

See preceding sections for type of books, flowers, music or perfume that may appeal to a Libran. Both male and female Librans adore elegance (they dislike anything gaudy), love to get dolled up, entertain and go to the best places. He/she is beauty conscious and enjoys being surrounded by pretty objects (sculptured statues, expensive paintings with gilded frames, valuable art objects, a figurine, decorative ashtray or switch plates, oriental flower vase or anything that is colorful or ornate). Librans love luxuries (furs, genuine jewelry — especially diamonds — yachts or expensive cars).

Libra enjoys the social scene. He/she charms everyone with his/her pleasant personality and fine manners. Buy Libra gifts for entertaining: silverware, silver tableware (or service), wine cradle, a set of guest towels, crystal decanter, bottle of fine wine or champagne. An hors d'oeuvres recipe book may appeal to a Libran. Treat Libra to tickets to the ballet, opera concert, theatre, gala or charity ball. Or make arrangements for Libra to be a member of a museum. Or perhaps the gift of a facial, massage, manicure, or spa treatment will make Libra glow. Libran's love to dress in the latest fashion; thus, give him/her designer clothes or a subscription to a fashion magazine.

Libra is ever so romantic; therefore, buy a book of poems, or give beautiful re-corded music, a love-greeting card, a vase with a single rose or an engraved watch, pendant, bracelet, or locket. For the Libran guy buy cologne, after shave lotion, cuff links, a tie clip, a silk tie, underwear, or an ascot. Libra knows how to relax and enjoys taking life easy, so give Libra a deck lounge, hammock, pool float, rocking chair, waterbed, chaise lounge, sleek designed sofa, or other furniture.

Buy the Libra gal something soft, lovely and expensive and you'll be "in" with her. She'll adore lace and silk underwear, sexy lingerie (silk chemise), silk scarf, satin sheets, perfume, soap basket set with perfumed soaps, perfume atomizer, cosmetics (make up, brush set, beauty kit), wig, hair dryer, lotions. Buy her a belt, fur (hat, jacket or coat), alligator purse, disco or evening bag. She has a sweet tooth; thus a box of chocolates, jams, jellies, or preserves will make her happy. A bed tray for a lazy morning breakfast would suit her fine.

For the Young: Paper dolls, dolls (like Barbie with beautiful clothes), coloring books or gorgeous illustrated books, rhinestone stud kit, mini-cosmetic case or beauty salon, dress-up trunk (gowns, clothes, hats, hi-heels), jewelry box, rings, charm bracelet, locket, and chain. Musical instruments (stringed) or tapes, CD's or records. Appeal to Libra's love of art: give crayons, easel, chalk board, finger paints, paint-by-number set, kits for arts and crafts — ceramics, bead making, stringing or a t-shirt decorating kit. Games that call for intellectual activity, such as board or card games (Libra craves companionship so games must be for one or more of his/her pals to play with). You can never go wrong with candy.

CELL SALTS
Natrum phosphoricum or phosphate of soda.

ZONES OF THE BODY
The fallopian tubes, internal generative (reproductive) organs, kidneys, lumbar area, ovaries, suprarenals, veins. Thus you could be subject to female problems such as PMS, kidney ailments such as kidney stones, ovarian difficulties, varicose veins.

HERBS
Effective herbs and plants for the Libra afflicted body zones are: Aloes, balm, beech, bethroot, birch, bitterroot, bittersweet, black or blue cohosh, bloodroot, broom, buckbean, camomile, carrot root/seed, catnip, cayenne, celandine (wild), chicory (endive), cleavers, comfrey, corn silk, dandelion root, elder, fringe tree, gentian root, golden seal, heartsease, holy thistle, hydrangea, hyssop, Indian hemp, juniper berries, lemon-thyme, mandrake, nettle, pansy, parsley, peach leaves/twigs, peppermint, Peruvian bark, plantain, pleurisy root, poke root, poplar, prickly ash, primrose, Queen of the meadow, ragwort, red sage, rosemary, rue, sage, sanicle, sassafras, saw palmetto berries, sea wrack, slippery elm, Solomon's Seal, sorrel, spearmint, spikenard, squaw vine, St. John's wort, strawberry, sweet balm, tansy, thyme, uva ursi, vervain, violet, watercress, water pepper, white oak bark, white pine, white pond lily, white rose, wild alum root, wild Oregon grape, wild yam, wood sage, and yarrow.

CLIMATE
Temperate, not liable to excessive heat or cold; thus, you may want to live or vacation in a temperate climate.

PART OF LAND AND COUNTRY
An arid, dry, parched with heat place far above the ground, or some other base level; pertaining to highland or inland regions rather than those near sea levels. Land that is not wanting in settlers, but that which is populated by towns, villages and cities, and is subdivided into numerous plots.

U.S. Cities: Cathedral City, Desert Hot Springs, Los Angeles, Riverside and San Bernardino, CA; Rock Island, IL; New Orleans, LA; Casnovia and Fruitland, MI; Edgewater, NJ; Roswell, NM; Charleston, NC; Eugene, OR; Rapid City, SD; Franklin and Nashville, TN; Waco, TX; Alexandria, VA.

U.S. State: (None).

U.S. Territory: Midway Islands.

Countries: Belize, Botswana, Bulgaria, China, France, Germany, Guinea, Guinea-Bissau, Lesotho, Libya, Mali, Nicaragua, Nigeria, Portugal, Saudi Arabia, South Africa, Syria, Transkei, Turkey, Uganda, and the Yemen Arab Republic.

Islands: Antigua and Barbuda, Fiji, Tuvalu

Cities (other than U.S.): St. John's, Antigua and Barbuda; Antwerp, Belgium; Belmopan, Belize; Gaborone, Botswana; Sofia, Bulgaria; Peking, China; Barkington, Leeds and Middleton, England; Suva, Fiji; Paris, France; Bonn and Frankfurt, Germany; Conakry, Guinea; Bissau, Guinea-Bissau; Gaeta, Italy; Maseru, Lesotho; Tripoli, Libya; Bamako, Mali; Managua, Nicaragua; Lagos, Nigeria; Lisbon, Portugal; Riyadh, Saudi Arabia; Fribourg, Switzerland; Damascus, Syria; Ankara, Turkey; Funafuti, Tuvalu; Kampala, Uganda, San'a', Yemen Arab Republic.

IN A LIBRA VIBRATION

You are inclined to make friends, have fun, fall in love, marry, and enjoy a leisure life. Your romantic nature is brought out here. Social events are the mainstream of the community. Fashion and beautifying is the rage. In this environment, you may be lazy and strive for peace and harmony. The ballet, opera or concerts and museums may keep you busy. You may become involved in a movement to further the arts and cultural activities in this locality. Perhaps you campaign to erect a bronze or marble statue of a town hero. Or you may wish to bring color to the city by suggesting that the artists paint and exhibit their works on designated streets.

LIBRA TRAITS

Art, fashion, beauty, music and the ballet, opera or theatre are areas that appeal to your aesthetic senses. You enjoy socializing. You're a great host/hostess. Your graciousness is noted by others. You dislike bad manners. It's hard for you to say "no" to people because you don't like to hurt their feelings. Thus, you tend to give in to the easy way out and say "yes." You are very easy going and strive for balance and a life without stress. You don't like to argue, but will fight when an injustice is done. Fairness is extremely important to you in all matters. You weigh the pros and cons of all issues and are able to see both sides of a coin. Your best trait is your charm. Your downfall is your indecisiveness.

LIBRA COMPATIBILITY

With Leo: You are a great match: both are interested in all phases of the arts and enjoy the finest — clothes, jewelry, home accessories, furniture. Wining and dining; romantic places with views and gazing lovingly into each other's eyes —is delightful. You are both rabid with passion while making love. With Gemini: This person's multiple personalities fascinate you. Gemini's wit and intellect is admired and mesmerizing. The two of you can talk for hours. Sex is a delight because you will never know what to expect. With Aquarius: This person's constant surprises have you smitten. Both are free spirits and give each other independence. Spur-of-the-moment activities are enchanting. Sexually, Aquarius has a spellbinding effect on you.

With Libra: The peace and harmony you strive for is found with someone born under your same sign. Both are in love with the idea of love — wining, dining, soft lights, music and gourmet food. Both of your wanton appetites flare up and explode over and over again with more than gratifying results. With Virgo: This person appeals to your desire for order, neatness and cleanliness. You like Virgo's analytical talents because they coincide with your weighing the pros and cons of all situations. You are content with Virgo's affectionate responses to your bodily and emotional needs while engaged in carnal activity. With Taurus: This person's love of beauty attracts you. You can relax with Taurus and are glad that this individual doesn't rush. You are enamored by the Taurean's clinches and libidinous nature.

With Sagittarius: You two have a good social life. However, the Sagittarian's restlessness and constant desire to be on the go can wear you out. Laughter reigns. Carnal joys are experienced. With Scorpio: Secretive Scorpio arouses your curiosity. You admire this person's strength to be in control of everything and everyone. You like Scorpio's romantic side. Sensual experiences in the bedroom have you aching for more, and with Scorpio it's never ending! With Pisces: You drift, dream, relax and let go — it's a quiet and peaceful relationship. Both are romantic, like poetry and to listen to slow and beautiful music for lovers only. Lovemaking is lewd, wild and unforgettable.

With Capricorn: Problems are likely to develop because this person is prone to curbing your spending habits; in fact, Capricorn could bring it to a complete stop. This person may be too selfish and ambitious for you. This individual's refraining from complete abandonment with sex could be a real turn-off. With Cancer: This person is too moody for you. You're a social butterfly and Cancer's a homebody and may not want to party when invited out. However, the pleasures of the flesh are extremely enthralling. With Aries: Your tranquility is disrupted by the Arien's desire for action and excitement. You're not the type to camp our and forego the comforts and luxuries of home; however, adventure in the bedroom excites you. Erotically, you could be overpowered by Aries.

LIBRA 2019 FORECAST

From January 1st to March 6th, is a fantastic time bringing good luck with communication and transportation areas. If you are an author, the public is fascinated by anything different, especially if it involves a new approach or anything educational, inventive, the latest in social media, technology, humor or a fad. You are intuitive with fresh ideas that pop into your conscious mind so fast that it appears like you are writing automatically. Mental activities keep you busy regardless of whether it is clerical work, creative writing or just talking on a phone. This is a period of many spontaneous and spur of the moment short distance trips. From March 7th to December 31st, the spotlight is on your living quarters. it is a beneficial time to purchase real estate at a bargain. Negotiations are planned using strategy on your approach. Sticking with your bid by abiding your time and patiently waiting for your terms to be agreed upon. Success comes from being calm, diplomatic and using foresight. Loans, mortgages and closings are favored with amazing results, Co-ops, condos, shopping centers (malls, plazas), apartment buildings and duplex homes are good investments and easy to acquire now. Locations near water (river, lake, ocean) in a resort area are ideal property areas. Use your ESP (extra sensory perception) and tune in to your dream deal. Persistence pays off. You are extremely ambitious to own land or structures. Renting to tenants is beneficial and can bring in extra income. The more you get, the more you will want. Taking on added responsibility may bring some sacrifice but in the long run it is in your favor and not that difficult during this time. Work done from the home may be your perfect office. You will feel relaxed and still be a workaholic. You can wheel and deal in all business transactions. Use your promotional skills by being an over-achiever and going that extra mile---the end result is security. And that is what it is all about, isn't it? If you have members of your household living with you, there is teamwork--everyone pitches in to help. If you live alone, you may want companionship; however, your workload could keep you so busy that you won't miss having people around you.

Best Period For Romance...January 20 — February 18

Best Dates For Sex

Jan: 1, 2, 3, 8, 17, 21, 28, 29, 30; Feb: 4, 14, 18, 24, 25, 26, 27; Mar: 3, 4, 13, 17, 23, 24, 25, 26, 30, 31; Apr: 9, 14, 20, 21, 22, 27; May: 6, 7, 11, 17, 18, 19, 24, 25; Jun: 7, 11, 12, 14, 15, 16, 20, 21, 30; Jul: 4, 5, 11, 12, 13, 18, 28; Aug: 1, 7, 8, 9, 10, 14, 24, 28; Sep: 3, 4, 5, 6, 10, 11, 20, 21, 25; Oct: 1`, 2, 3, 7, 8, 17, 18, 22, 28, 29, 30; Nov: 4, 14, 18, 24, 25, 26, 27; Dec: 1, 2, 11, 15, 16, 22, 23, 24, 29.

CHAPTER EIGHT
SCORPIO: THE SCORPION... OCTOBER 23 — NOVEMBER 22

To understand this chapter, read the Preface and Foreword. If you, know your rising sign, read the advice given for that sign as well as for your Sun sign. The combination of these two will give you more information than could be gained by simply reading only the Sun sign. Refer to pages 16 and 17 if you do not know what your rising sign is.

The following descriptions are typical for those born under the sign Scorpio. However, your own horoscope may contradict some of this, depending upon your rising sign and the signs occupied by the planets in your horoscope.

Scorpio is a water sign and is feminine and fruitful. The planetary rulers are Mars and Pluto. Each of the signs and/or planets has rulership over certain phases of life. The following are ruled by Scorpio, Mars or Pluto:

COLORS
You may want to enhance your living quarters or wardrobe in these shades:

Pluto: Shades of black, such as panther, tar, soot, blackberry or black currants. Shades of clay, such as umber. The brown hues such as chestnut, chocolate, mud and dark brown. Infra-red, which is a red-blue and below and beyond red. Ultraviolet, which is a purplish blue-black-red and beyond violet.

Mars: Bright red, such as blood red and ruby red.

Scorpio: Dark red, such as carmine, crimson, scarlet, hematite, claret, maroon, deep wine, dark strawberry, burgundy, and red with black.

TALISMANIC GEMS
Pluto: Black diamond (red and black hermatite).

Scorpio: Topaz.

You may thus want to magnetize these gems for good luck and/or to protect you from harm. Refer to Part Two under Magnetizing Objects for auspicious dates to magnetize a talismanic gem.

STONE
Pluto: Uncut black diamond.

Scorpio: Bloodstone, lodestone, vermillion, hermatite.

Mars: Iron stone (any rock or mineral which contains iron).

Therefore, you may accent your abode with these stones as accessories or wear them as jewelry. You may find that you have good luck when wearing or owning one of these stones.

METALLIC ELEMENT
Pluto: Plutonium.

Mars: Iron.

NUMBER
Number 4: You may want to bet with this number, or perhaps favorable events will occur on this date. If you want to plan ahead for certain activities you could

use this date for something important, especially if it coincides with a date for that event in the Best Days section in Part Two.

DAY

Tuesday: You may want to plan important activities for Tuesday. Your energy is at its height on Tuesdays.

SENSES: PHYSICAL OR NON-PHYSICAL

Physical Sense: The nerves of sensation; bodily contact
Physical Organs: Sexual parts of the body
Psychic Sense: Absorption of electromagnetic essences

MUSIC

That of Spain — the bullfight, Flamenco, Spanish guitar. Or Portugal's Fado music and Argentine's Tango. Oriental and Latin dance sounds — this brings your passionate nature out into the open. Also the troubadours singing of romance; torch songs, jazz, Cajun, African, Salsa, hip-hop, rag, songs that have a message, such as personal, political or environmental.

PERFUMES

These scents are rich, heady, strong, sexy and arouse romance to states of delirious seduction. It will be easy for you to weave a magic spell so your love is bound to you, because these fragrances bring out your magnetism. Wear them as an aphrodisiac to entice and snare your paramour into a web of eroticism.

For the Female: Albert Nippon, Animale by Suzanne de Lyon, Bulgari Eau Parfume, Casmir by Chopard, Danger, Enigma, Escada by Margaretha Ley, Fire and Ice by Revlon, Incognito by Cover Girl, Intoxication by D'Orsay, Joop! Safari by Ralph Lauren, Joy by Jean Patou, Maroc by Ultima II, Musk Oil by Jóvan, My Sin, Mystere de Rochas, Nahema by Guerlain, Night Musk, Nuits Indiennes by Jean-Louis Scherrer, Obsession by Calvin Klein, Opium by Yves Saint Laurent, Pheromome by Marilyn Miglin, Poison by Christian Dior, Royal Secret, Samsara by Guerlain, Sex Appeal by Jóvan, Shalimar by Guerlain, Tabu by Dana, True Love by Elizabeth Arden, Tuvara, Van Cleef by Van Cleef & Arpels, Volupte by Oscar de la Renta, White Musk, Wild Musk Patchouli by Coty.

For the Male: Actif Blue, Egoiste Platinum for Men by Chanel, Jade East, J.H.L. by Aramis, Macho by Fabergé, Monsieur Houbigant's Must, Obsession for Men by Calvin Klein, Old Spice, Sex Appeal by Jóvan.

FLOWERS

Pluto: Flowers and flowering plants that are black, such as: the black calla lily, poppy and ebony iris.

Scorpio: Flowers and flowering plants that are bright red (blood, carmine, crimson, scarlet and royal), and dark red (burgundy, maroon, deep wine), such as: Amaranth, azalea, bee-balm (bergamot), bleeding heart, Buddleia, Centranthus, roses, clematis, corn cockle, cosmos astrosanguinlus, "fairie" chrysanthemums, fuchsia, geranium, gladiolus (sword lily), heather, hibiscus, honeysuckle, hydrangea, Judas tree, larkspur, lily (amaryllis-Jacobean, guernsey, oriental), lycoris, peony (crimson), phlox paniculata, pitcher plant, poinciana (royal), potentilla, ranunculus, red clover, rose-campion, scarlet pimpernel, tulip (including lily-flowered), sweet William, Venus flytrap and zinnia.

BOOKS

Those that involve history, crime, murder, adventure, sex, UFO's, poetry, medicine, geology, geometry, radio, television, cable, the sea, the occult, the supernatural or research findings. Historical novels that are bloody, gory, cliffhangers, thrillers, shockers. Also computer, dream journals, detective stories, and books with mazes and games that challenge the mind.

FASHION

The clothes you buy are usually purchased on impulse. If you see something appealing, you are obsessed with it until it is yours; it is bought regardless of the price, quality or workmanship and it is worn until it falls apart. You are partial to raiments that make you appear mysterious, exotic and dramatic; thus, you are fond of Oriental fashion. Your wardrobe consists of hats which you love wearing because they hide part of your face. By nature, you are secretive and find using subtleness to allure, magnetize and snare others in your web; thus, you dress in an outfit that captivates the desired one.

If you are a Scorpio woman, you are the femme fatale of the Zodiac. You prefer slinky dresses, gowns and lingerie. Also, you adore tunics, skirts with side slits, blouses or dresses that are see-through or show cleavage, satin dresses or evening gowns, pantsuits with tunics, black leather, acrylic-knit suits, fur-lined parkas, trench coats, black broadtail coats, leather dresses and coats. Your favorite fabrics are satin, brocade, damask, crepe de chine, viols, foulard silks, leather, faille, wool jersey, French wool and acetate-nylon crepe-black satin. If you are a Scorpio man you are the macho lady-killer of the Zodiac. You prefer leather coats or jackets, trench coats, black trousers, suits and fur-lined parkas, wools, gaberdines, cotton-polyester, poplin, rayon and silk.

All shades of red — blood red, scarlet, dark red and deep wine appeal to you. When you don clothes or accessories in these colors, your gutsy side is revealed and you are ready to conquer the person desired. By the way, Scorpios love to combine black with shades of red.

GIFTS

See preceding sections for type of books, flowers, music or perfume that may appeal to a Scorpion. Do not buy Scorpio soaps, towels, bed linens or underwear — or anything too personal (unless Scorpio is your mate or relative). Your intentions could be misunderstood or Scorpio could feel insulted (especially with a gift of soap). Give presents that can be shown to others.

Scorpio has an investigative mind and enjoys solving problems, thus give a mystery book or purchase tickets for a mystery-drama game (usually played in special hotels or on special train trips) in which Scorpio participates with a cast of other players. The supernatural appeals to many Scorpion's, thus, arrange for a seance with your Scorpio guy/gal. Or how about tickets to a romantic locale where privacy with a loved one is shared?

This sign enjoys a challenge, thus give Scorpio a chess game. Other suggestions for both the male and female: shells, stamps, coins, lithograph prints, wine rack, bottle of booze, steak knives, afghan, microwave oven, stereo set, tape recorder, cassette tapes, CD's, CD player, CD Rom's, TV set, phonograph records (collectors), VCR, blank film or digital movie for VCR, radio (earplugs, transistor or table model). The Scorpio gal might enjoy a gift that enhances her sexy image: slinky lingerie (if you're intimately involved with her), lacy or see-through blouses, figure-flattering sweaters, designer jeans. Scorpio is secretive and loves to hide her treasures, thus, a jewelry box will keep her happy. Or perhaps a diary. She's a great record-keeper and is quite psychic in her dreams, therefore, give her a journal so she can keep track of her dreams and later decipher them. Other items that may appeal to her: a scarf, fur stole, jacket or coat; plastic decorations; jewelry (costume or genuine, especially topaz).

The Scorpio guy's obsessed with machinery he can take apart, fool around with, solve its riddle and put back together again. Give him a Do-It-Yourself kit and working tools or a hi-fi set he can destruct or construct. A Scorpio loves to snoop and is careful that no one gets into his business; therefore, he'd appreciate a telescope, binoculars, burglar alarm system for his car, home or office, paper shredder, photo developing kit and lab, or a camera. Most Scorpio's are attracted to water, so if you can afford it give him a boat, canoe, watercraft (jet skis), surfing gear, goggles, snorkel, boogie board, or diving equipment. He might be content with a computer, laser printer, electronic equipment, digital sound system, electric laminator to seal documents inside. Or, give him a leather wallet, tie pin, necktie, cuff links, smoking jacket or brief underwear (if the two of you are an intimate twosome).

For the Young: Vinyl snakes or insects, play tunnel, mini-sand digger, shovel and pail (for beach-dirt or sand), electronic doll, design mosaic kit, make-your-own musical instrument kit, Pound-a-ball kit with mallet, puzzle (cube, crossword), games (maze, Labyrinth, tumbling tower, detective), spy kit, toy guns, weapons; knives; sheriff or police officer badge and outfit or plastic police-cycle-driving dash. Chemistry set, science discovery set, medical kit, magnifying glass, mechanical toys, robot transformers, play copying machine, radio control jeep, electronic gadgets (hand-held games), building games, blocks, model ship building, ship in a bottle or stamp collecting kit.

CELL SALTS
Calcarea sulphurica or sulphate of lime.

ZONES OF THE BODY
The bladder, excretory organs, external generative (reproductive) glands (penis, testicle, vagina), groin, inguinal region, nose and nasal bones, pelvis, perineum, prostrate gland, rectum, sigmoid flexure, spermatic cord, sphincter, ureter, uterus, urogenital orifice. Thus you could be subject to problems involving the bladder (gall bladder, gall stones, incontinence), hemorrhoids, prostate, the uterus or external generative glands.

HERBS
Effective herbs and plants for the Scorpio afflicted body zones are: Aloes, apple

tree bark, balm, bean, beech, bethroot, bittersweet, black or blue cohosh, blackthorn, bloodroot, bramble, broom, buchu, burdock, burnet (pimpernel), camomile, carrot root/seed, cascara sagrada, celandine (wild), charlock, cleavers, comfrey, corn silk, cubeb berries, dandelion, fennel, fenugreek, fire-weed, fit root, fleabane, golden seal, heather, hemlock, hydrangea, hyssop, juniper berries, marjoram, milkweed root, mugwort, myrrh, nettle, parsley, peach leaves, pilewort, plantain, psylla, Queen of the meadow, red root, rue, sassafras, saw palmetto berries, shepherds'-purse, slippery elm, smartweed, Solomon's Seal, sorrel, spearmint, squaw vine, sumach berries, sweet balm, uva ursi, vervain, water pepper, white oak bark, white pond lily, wild alum root, wintergreen, witch hazel bark/leaves, wood sage, and yarrow.

CLIMATE

Humid, moist, damp, very hot, close and heavy with sweltering heat; thus, you may want to live in the Caribbean, southeastern portion of the United States or a place where the climate is of the preceding nature.

PART OF LAND AND COUNTRY

The country is below the general level, away from the sea, in a valley bounded by hills or mountains. Land that is wet and spongy, with soil composed mainly of decayed vegetable matter; a quagmire, marsh, swamp or a place where stagnant matter, muddy ground or a hot spring is located.

U.S. Cities: Fairbanks, AK; Little Rock, AR; Cathedral City, CA; Denver, CO; West Palm Beach, FL; Salina, KS; Rockville, MD; Fruitland, MI; St. Paul, MN; Jefferson City and St. Louis, MO; Allendale, Newark, Ridgewood, Trenton and Upper Saddle River, NJ; Charlotte, NC; Providence, RI; Aberdeen, SD; Chattanooga, Franklin and Knoxville, TN; Barre and Rutland, VT; Rock Springs, WY.

U.S. States: Montana, Nevada, North Carolina, North Dakota, Oklahoma, South Dakota, Washington.

Countries: Belgium, Brazil, Equatorial Guinea, Honduras, Hungary, Lebanon, Russia, South Africa, Transkei, Yemen, Zambia.

Islands: Antigua and Barbuda, Dominica, Dominican Republic, Fiji, Saint Vincent and the Grenadines, Tuvula.

Province: Angola.

Cities (other than U.S.): Luanda, Angola; St. John's, Antigua and Barbuda; Brussels, Belgium; Rio de Janeiro, Brazil; Winnipeg, Canada; Roseau, Dominica; Santo Domingo, Dominican Republic; Dover, East Grinstead, Glossop, Hull, Liverpool, Stockport and Worthing, England; Suva, Fiji; Tegucigalpia, Honduras; Budapest, Hungary; Newcastle, Ireland; Messina, Sicily, Italy; Beirut, Lebanon; Acapulco, Mexico; Fez (Fes), Morocco; St. John's, Newfoundland; Kingstown, Saint Vincent and the Grenadines; Cape Town, South Africa; Khartoum, Sudan; Umtata, Transkei; Ankara, Turkey; Funafuti, Tuvalu; Aden, Yemen; Lusaka, Zambia.

Areas: Bavaria, Germany.

IN A SCORPIO VIBRATION

You are capable of exerting immense pressure upon your surroundings. The force you exert is so tremendous it leaves others shaking in their pants. With your determination, persistence and untiring energy, you are able to accomplish goals. In this environment, you are demanding, resourceful and enterprising. You may feel compelled to start a drive to clean up crime. Perhaps you are a member of a secret society that does good deeds for the local citizens. Issues involving radioactive materials, missiles, drainage and sewerage systems may be your favorite causes. In this town, you may be a compulsive spender. Or perhaps you are jealous, possessive, oversexed and obsessed with a loved one, or take to criminal activities.

SCORPIO TRAITS

You are secretive in your personal activities and business affairs. Your desires are never-ending; there is always something more you want. And what's more — you usually get it! You don't do things halfway; your energies are concentrated on one goal with such intensity that others might call you obsessed. Your emotions are as strong as your demands. You must be in control — whether it's in commerce or in a relationship. You never forget a hurt and must be careful of being revengeful. Your sign is knows as "the bitch" — no one dares walk over you. The Scorpio sting hurts and is shown when someone crosses you. As a friend, you are extremely loyal and expect the same loyalty in return. You are jealous when in love. Your best trait is resourcefulness. Your downfall is possessiveness.

SCORPIO COMPATIBILITY

With Pisces: A fantastic match! Your Pisces lover will obey you. You cherish this person because the Piscean wants to hang on to you for dear life. Pisces will enjoy being a slave to your every desire. Frantic states of erotic pleasure have the two of you delirious — you may never want to come up for air! With Cancer: You are in awe of Cancer's caring, nurturing and protective nature. It's heavenly when Cancer constantly touches you. Lovemaking between the two of you is an emotional and lustful experience. With Libra: This one's charm appeals to you. You are able to help Libra overcome indecisiveness, especially when you call the shots! Sex starts romantically and winds up passionately and unending.

With Virgo: You are able to communicate on an intellectual and scientific basis with this person. Virgo gives you a safe and secure feeling. Both have similar goals. Carnally, Virgo's a challenge; you are deeply moved when you can get the Virgoan to respond with ecstasy to your brand of lovemaking.

With Capricorn: The business and financial interests of both of you blend well together. You two are great planners and can persist with your goals for success. Sex starts quietly and slowly but builds to tempestuous sensuality. With Sagittarius: Date this person if you want to brighten your life with laughter. You respect the Sagittarian's open, candid and honest nature. But you have problems with this individual's desire to be on the go. Carnality is fun and excessively enjoyed when you two get together.

With Scorpio: Both admire each other's persistence to accomplish tasks. You two are a jealous and possessive couple who can do great things together. You'll wear out each other sexually. With Aries: The two of you are a deadly combination with your constant challenges. This is a stormy and dangerous relationship. Both possess red-hot tempers and are oversexed; an explosion will inevitably occur in and out of bed. With Taurus: A stubborn twosome who are possessive and control-ling. Who will be the boss? Both have voluptuous appetites which can be appeased when your bodies meet. It is a fantastic match sexually.

With Gemini: In the beginning, Gemini's vacillating ways intrigue you, but later, you find it impossible to live in an unstable climate. The Geminian's mul-tiple personalities and restlessness drive you berserk. This person's love of variety in matters of the flesh fascinates you, but Gemini's lack of concentration during the sex act bugs you. With Aquarius: This person's too freedom loving for you. The moment you try to own Aquarius, you may find yourself alone. Sexually, the Aquarian is difficult to resist. In the bedroom, you'll flip out over all the carnal experimentation that Aquarius wants to try. With Leo: Leo wants to be the boss and you must be in control; therefore, expect challenges, arguments and stormy scenes. But a passionate embrace and kiss kindle a burning fire raging within, and it is inevitable that the two of you will meet — body and soul — and quench all existing flames.

SCORPIO 2019 FORECAST

From January 1st to March 6th, money comes pouring in so fast that your head will reel. You may be in a state of shock when the financial upswing comes from unexpected resources, new jobs, projects, inventions or innovative areas using the latest technology or in food, medical or health care industries. You'll be inspired to go for the gold by taking spontaneous action. Sales are stupendous. You'll go on spur of the moment spending sprees. You need to, but won't, curb extravagance. To you it is "easy come, easy go."

This is not the year to gamble or take any kind of risk with the stock market now, because you do not see through schemes, fraud and phony deals or people--your mind is spaced out and it is as if you are blinded by what is real and what is not. Loved ones, fun and pleasure could cost you plenty this entire year, but you do not care, your mood is to live it up and have a ball regardless of the cost. Entertainment, amusement centers, theme parks, movies, shows, night clubs, arenas, stadiums, games (board or video) are areas where your energy and money splurges abound--and it is always with loved ones that you want to make happy and show them a great time. Sexual fantasies can make you believe that you have found utopia.

From March 7th to December 31st, you will tend to business deals over the phone or by commuting back and forth on trips to nearby places (cities, states or in the vicinity where you live). Plan your strategy and then follow through by using diplomacy and your intuition in all negotiations. You are ambitious, calm, thorough, well-organized and know how to get what you want. Clients and partnerships are favored; however, you are in the driver's seat at all meetings, conference calls and business arrangements. Mergers are favored with you calling the shots. It is in your nature to always be the person in the controlling position. You will not allow anyone to tell you what to do, personally or professionally.

Best Period For Romance... February 18 — March 20
Best Dates For Sex

Jan: 1, 10, 11, 12, 13, 14, 15, 19, 28; Feb: 6, 7, 8, 9, 10, 11, 12, 16, 24; Mar: 8, 9, 10, 11, 15, 23, 24; Apr: 2, 4, 5, 6, 7, 11, 12, 20, 29, 30; May: 2, 9, 17, 27, 28, 29, 30, 31; Jun: 1, 5, 14, 20, 22, 25, 26, 27, 28; Jul: 11, 20, 21, 22, 23, 24, 25, 26, 30; Aug: 7, 16, 17, 19, 20, 21, 22, 26; Sep: 3, 13, 14, 15, 16, 17, 18, 23; Oct: 1, 10, 11, 12, 13, 14, 15, 20, 28; Nov: 6, 7, 8, 9, 10, 11, 16, 24, 25; Dec: 4, 5, 6, 7, 8, 9, 13, 22, 31.

CHAPTER NINE
SAGITTARIUS: THE CENTAUR... NOVEMBER 22 — DECEMBER 21

To understand this chapter, read the Preface and Foreword. If you, know your rising sign, read the advice given for that sign as well as for your Sun sign. The combination of these two will give you more information than could be gained by simply reading only the Sun sign. Refer to pages 16 and 17 if you do not know what your rising sign is.

The following descriptions are typical for those born under the sign Sagittarius. However, your own horoscope may contradict some of this, depending upon your rising sign and the signs occupied by the planets in your horoscope.

Sagittarius is a fire sign and is masculine and barren. The planetary ruler is Jupiter. Each of the signs and/or planets has rulership over certain phases of life. The following are ruled by Sagittarius or Jupiter:

COLORS
You may want to enhance your living quarters or wardrobe in these shades:

Jupiter: Indigo; such shades as deep-violet-blue; hues from dark bluish-purple to grayish-bluish purple. Bright purple, such as the brilliant purple hue known as "royal" purple.

Sagittarius: Light (pale) purple, such shades as orchid, lavender, lilac or light bluish-purple such as mauve.

TALISMANIC GEMS
Jade, red garnet. You may thus want to magnetize the jade or garnet for good luck and/or to protect you from harm. Refer to Part Two under Magnetizing Objects for auspicious dates to magnetize a talismanic gem.

STONES
Those with red and green mixed, such as turquoise and heliotrope (deep green chalcedony flocked with red jasper). Therefore, you may accent your abode with these stones as accessories or wear them as jewelry. You may find that you have good luck when wearing or owning one of these stones.

METALLIC ELEMENT
Juniper: Tin.

NUMBER
Number 7: You may want to bet with this number, or perhaps favorable events will occur on this date. If you want to plan ahead for certain activities, you could use this date for something important, especially if it coincides with a date for that event in the Best Days section in Part Two.

DAY
Thursday: You may want to plan important activities for Thursday. Your energy is at its height on Thursdays.

SENSES: PHYSICAL OR NON-PHYSICAL

Physical Sense:	Smell
Physical Organ:	Nose
Psychic Sense:	Aroma detection

MUSIC

Lively, bouncy sounds. Comedy, folk, polka, tarantella, country, religious (gospel, hymns, devotional), rock and roll, rhythm and blues; piano and violin — depending upon your mood.

PERFUMES

These scents satisfy your love of the outdoors — scenery, camping, traveling. You'll be in the mood to indulge in sports or other fun-filled moments, such as your desire to live it up and have a ball. Wear these fragrances when you want to have fun, and yet be close to the one dearest to your heart.

For the Female: Blue Jeans, Clinique Wrappings, Empriente, Equipage, Escape by Calvin Klein, Galore, Grass Oil, J'ai Ose by Guy Laroche, La Prairie, Lauren by Ralph Lauren, Le Sport, Liz Claiborne Fragrance, Octeé Perfumed Note 2, Seringa by Floris, Sport by Jóvan.

For the Male: Antaeus Pour Homme by Chanel, Canoe, Equipage, Escape by Calvin Klein, Grey Flannel by Jeoffrey Beene, Sport by Jóvan, Kouros by Yves Saint Laurent, Le de Givenchy, Versailles Pour Homme.

FLOWERS

Jupiter: Flowers and flowering plants that are indigo, such as the iris.

Sagittarius: Flowers and flowering plants that are light (pale) purple (lavender, lilac, mauve, orchid), such as Anemone patens, blanket flower, chrysanthus, crocus, dahlia, hardheads, honesty, hyacinth (grape), hydrangea, Japanese toad lily, lavender, lilac, magnolia, orchid (including the rosey-purple), passionflower, purple oxalis, snapdragon, sweet pea and verbena.

BOOKS

Those that are about travel, geography, horses, sports, the rugged outdoors, law, languages (learning), religion, theosophy, metaphysics, philosophy. Also comic books, humorous stories and joke books.

FASHION

You are an impulsive shopper and go on extravagant spending sprees. Quantity and quality in clothes is desired; nothing but the best for you. Your wearing apparel must be easy to jump in and out of and not require much care. You can not stand garments with buttons, snaps, hooks or zippers because if they are missing, torn or broken, you will not take the time to repair them.

You are a careless dresser, although you like the latest styles. You will dress for the occasion if it demands it. Your clothes are poorly coordinated and many do not match. You delight in wearing fun and/or sport ensembles. If you are a Sagittarius woman, you feel comfortable in blue jeans, denim jumpers, sweat shirts, pantsuits, knits, skirts, sweaters, blouses, slacks and dresses that are jumper, or slip-on. Your favorite fabrics are machine washable and drip dry because they are easy to care for. You are drawn to leather, suede, jersey, wrinkle-free polyester, lambs wool, acrylic and mohair sweaters. If you are a Sagittarius man, you enjoy jeans, casual slacks, Hawaiian shirts, jumpsuits, fur parkas, jackets of napa shearling or quilted action or western garb. Leather, rayon, denim and polyester-cotton fabrics are popular with you.

All shades of purple — light, orchid, mauve, magenta, lilac and lavender appeal to you. When you don clothes or accessories in these colors, you feel like laughing your way through life.

GIFTS

See preceding sections for type of books, flowers, music or perfume that may appeal to a Sagittarian. Sagittarian's relish the outdoors: a walk through the woods, to drive to scenic places and gaze at the scenery or to play out in the open air. Give Sagittarian a present that will appeal to his/her love of the outdoors; sleeping bag, camping gear (tent, cookware, portable, stove), compass, hiking boots or bag, lantern, fishing equipment (lure, rod, net), wool socks, sneakers, leg warmers, saddle for a horse or a trailer (if you can afford it). Surprise Sagittarius with a horse or riding lessons. Hunting equipment may be just what Sagittarius wants; thus, an archery set (with bow and arrows) could please this sign represented by The Archer. Informational video tapes that deal with camping, hunting or fishing could make Sagittarian beam.

Most Sagittarian's are interested in sports, either as a player or a spectator. Give tickets to his/her favorite sporting event. Or how about sporting equipment? — sled, skis, toboggan, snowmobile, bowling ball, baseball and bat (or cards), football, basketball, tennis racket and balls or outfit, Ping Pong, table and/or balls and paddle, roller skates, skateboard, ice skates, and exercise pad or warmup suit. This sign loves games: croquet, darts, horseshoe, monopoly. Or give a Sagittarian a bicycle, motor scooter or motorcycle. Sagittarius is restless and constantly on the go and likes to keep moving; therefore, these vehicles will satisfy his/her need to be busy and active.

Sagittarius is the sign of wanderlust; overseas travel keeps Sag's smiling. Give Sag an airline ticket to a foreign country or a curio that comes from an exotic locale. Treat Sagittarius to a weekend trip in the country, a journey to a national park (in the summer) or a skiing holiday (in the winter). Other great gifts: travel clothes, luggage, personalized luggage tags, travel scenic posters, a camera (especially panoramic to capture those wide-angle scenery shots Sags loves), a video camcorder to record every memorable moment this jet-loving sign thrives on, VCR travel videos, language tapes or a travel iron or alarm clock. Also, Sag would be delighted with a leather passport holder.

This fun loving sign enjoys a good laugh, regardless of his/her age. A crazy hat, joke book or harmless prank tricks could keep Sag rolling in the aisles. A religious Sagittarian would enjoy a bible, religious jewelry or other adornment. Other suggestions: leather goods, cheese tray, dip tray and bowl or jewelry (red garnet, turquoise or Native American ring, bracelet, pendant, necklace, especially a Squash Blossom necklace).

For the Young: Sag could be elated, if you can afford a real pony or a horse and have shelter for it. However, a rocking or wood hobby horse would be appreciated. Riding, dancing or figure-skating lessons can satisfy Sagittarian's spirited nature. Or a ski class may fit the bill. Give Sag a tricycle, pocket skit (for skishoeing), toy archery set, a swing or tree house. A puppy or kitten could bring joy into a Sagittarian's life. Or how about a cowboy/cowgirl outfit complete with hat, boots, holster and pistols? To satisfy his/her athletic nature, give a ball (baseball, basketball, football, volleyball), baseball holder, mitt, cap, clothes, and bat. Sag is into games (see adult list above for sports) as well as Parcheesi and Chinese Checkers. Other ideas: comic books, plastic acrobat clown, clown outfits (including make-up), kits (airport, travel, leathercraft or other creative do-it-yourself kits).

CELL SALTS

Silica or oxide of silicon.

ZONES OF THE BODY

The buttocks, fumur, gluteus, hips (locomotor muscles of the hips and thighs), ischium, legs (above the knees), liver, pancreas, sciatic nerve, sartorius, thighs. Thus you could be subject to diabetes, hepatitis, or problems with the hips, liver, pancreas or sciatica, or injuries to the hips, legs or thighs.

HERBS

Effective herbs and plants for the Sagittarius afflicted body zones are: Agrimony, aloes, angelica, balm, balmony, beech, bitterroot, bittersweet, black or blue cohosh, bloodroot, blueberry leaves, blue flag (iris, lily), borage (bugloss), broom, buchu, buckbean, burdock, butternut bark, camomile, carrot root/seed, cascara sagrada, cayenne, celandine (wild), celery root/seed, chicory (endive), cleavers, dandelion root, elder, featherfew, fennel, fringe tree, gentian root, golden seal, henna, hemp, holy thistle, hops, horehound, hyssop, Indian hemlock, leek, lobelia, lungwort, magnolia, mallow, mandrake, marjoram, milkweed, motherwort, parsley, peach (bark/kernels/leaves/twigs), pennyroyal, plantain, pleurisy root, poke root, poplar, prickly ash, Queen of the meadow, raspberry leaves, red root, red sage, rhubarb, rue, sage, saw palmetto berries, self-heal, sorrel, St. John's wort, sumach berries, tansy, uva ursi, wahoo, white oak bark, white pine, wild alum root, wild Oregon grape, wild yam, wintergreen, woad, wood betony, wormwood, yarrow and yellow dock.

CLIMATE

Very warm, hot and dry (and free from moisture): thus, you may want to live in such a climate.

PART OF LAND AND COUNTRY

A mountainous country that is not too lofty or elevated, but moderately situated above the ground or some other base level. This land is covered with trees or a wooded area; timber is plentiful.

U.S. Cities: Birmingham, Montgomery and Tuscaloosa, AL; Anchorage and Juneau, AK; Tucson, AZ; Coronado, Laguna Beach, Long Beach, Manhattan Beach, and Palm Desert, CA; Wilmington, DE; Pensacola, Tallahassee and Tampa, FL; Columbus and Macon, GA; Idaho Falls and Lewiston, ID; Muncie, IN; Baton Rouge, LA; Annapolis and Cumberland, MD; St. Louis, MO; Grand Island, NE; Roswell, NM; New York City (Manhattan), Tarrytown and Rochester, NY; Cincinnati and Youngstown, OH; Allentown and Lancaster, PA; Greenville, Hilton Head and Spartanburg, SC; Memphis, TN; Beaumont, Gastrop and San Antonio, TX; Barre, VT; Seattle and Spokane, WA; Cheyenne, WY.

U.S. States: Alabama, Delaware, Illinois, Indiana, Mississippi, New Jersey, Pennsylvania.

U.S. Territory: America Samoa.

Countries: Argentina. Bangladesh, Bophuthatswana, Bosnia-Herzegovina, Cameroon, Ciskei, El Savador, Kenya, Laos, Mauritania, Mongolia, Paraguay, Russia, Surinam, Transkei, United Arab Emirates, Venezuela.

Island: Australia, Barbados, Dominica, St. Christopher and Nevis (St. Kitts-Nevis), Taiwan (China).

Cities (other than U.S.): St. John's, Antigua and Barbuda; Melbourne, Victoria, Australia; Dacca, Bangladesh; Bridgetown, Barbados; Mmabatho, Bophuthatswana; Yaoude, Cameroon; Bisho, Ciskei; Roseau, Dominica; San Salvador, El Salvador; Bradford, Nottingham, Sheffield, Sunderland and West Bromrich, England; Helsinki, Finland; Avignon and Narbonne, France; Cologne, Rothenburg (Hessen) and Stuttgart, Germany; Taranto, Italy; Vientiane, Laos; Nouakchott, Mauritania; Ulan Bator, Mongolia; Asuncion, Paraguay; Basse-Terre, St. Kitts, St. Christopher-Nevis; Paramaribo, Surinam; Umtata, Transkei; Abu Dhabi, United Arab, Emirates; Caracas, Venezuela; Aden, Yemen.

IN A SAGITTARIUS VIBRATION

You want to live it up — fun and laughter reign. In this environment, you are easygoing, outspoken, footloose and fancy free. You may go on splurges and escapades that could cost you plenty, but you do not care. In this town, you may be a churchgoer, take up horse breeding, or suddenly journey to far away lands or nearby countries. Your confidence and enthusiasm show whether you are working or playing. Outdoor sports may keep you occupied a lot. Community issues involving the government, judicial systems, interstate commerce, colleges or religion may be your bag. You may take an active interest in tourism, overseas projects and people in general. Lectures may attract you, especially those on philosophy.

SAGITTARIUS TRAITS

You are optimistic and look at life through rose-colored glasses. You believe that everything happens for the best. People see your confidence. Others are inspired by your encouraging words. Decisions are promptly made. You leap into the fire and often get burnt but you don't care. Everything is done to excess. Your favorite role is playing Santa Claus — your generosity brings happiness to others. You are a good sport, fun loving, friendly, easy-going and happy-go-lucky. Your lack of diplomacy gets you into hot water when you aim your arrow with hurting and candid remarks. Often being too honest offends those you only want to help (because you want the best for everyone), though you don't realize it when you put your foot into your mouth. You trust people too much, which could be costly. You take loved ones for granted. Your thoughts are centered on the future; you don't look back to the past. By nature, you are impulsive and undisciplined. Your best trait is loyalty. Your downfall is outspokenness.

SAGITTARIUS COMPATIBILITY

With Gemini: You get along great because you are both outgoing and enjoy a good time and need to be on the go. No one can chain, enslave or hold either of you back. However, in time the Gemini flightiness and changeableness may disturb you. Sex will always consist of new thrills. With Aries: You admire one another. Both are fiery, adventuresome and speak out — no-holds barred conversations are challenging. The two of you lead each other into raptures of the most erotic nature — anything goes! With Sagittarius: Both enjoy the outdoors, whether it's looking at the scenery or engaging in sports. Pranks are played on each other as well as on others. It's a relationship of fun, excitement, lots of laughs and travel to exotic locales. In matters of the flesh, overindulgence is the norm for you two!

With Leo: You respect one another. The Leonine's large-scale operations and grandiose ideas appeal to you. Both enjoy spending money and living in the lap of luxury. The two of you are intoxicated by sensuality — carnal scenes are extremely erotic and naughty. With Libra: Social life with you two swings and is rewarding. Both are easygoing and enjoy the finer things in life. Lovemaking is tender and touches your heartstrings. With Aquarius: You are mesmerized by one another and complete freedom reigns in the relationship. You are delighted with the Aquarian's sudden and spur-of-the-moment fun-filled antics. You are both spellbound when engaging in electrifying and way-out carnal acts.

With Capricorn: You can learn diplomacy from this one. You are a giver and Capricorn tends to be a taker; thus, watch out that you are not used! This person may be too serious and conservative for you. However, you will relish every moment when you startle Capricorn with unusual forms of eroticism. With Scorpio: Everything goes well with you two until a rope is around your neck, then, you will dash off to greener pastures. Scorpio is too secretive for you. However, sex is an indescribable experience; it blows your mind when you are transported to realms you never knew existed. With Taurus: This person can stabilize you and make you feel comfortable. However, Taurus is too quiet, boring and stubborn for you who craves excitement and changes. However, with the Taurean you will know what sensual pleasure is.

With Cancer: This person is too sensitive for you; you dislike having to watch every word spoken. You go berserk when Cancer isn't in the mood to do planned activities. But lovemaking can be beautiful if you have the patience to endure the indecisiveness and slowness of the Cancerian. With Virgo: It is easy for you two to tangle in verbal battles, especially once the nagging starts. Egos are attacked quickly. Virgo is more mental than you, who lean toward the physical. If Virgo is the cold and prudish type sexually, you'll be turned off. However, if you attract a Virgoan who is hot-to-trot and desirous of experiencing new forms of sexual behavior, then have fun! With Pisces: This person is too emotional for you and, besides, Pisces will try to hold you back from being footloose and fancy-free. You, move fast; Pisces moves slow; thus, your nerves are frayed by the Piscean who refuses to quicken his/her pace. However, the two of you can be extremely lustful and yield to every inclination or impulse imaginable as if there were no tomorrow.

SAGITTARIUS 2019 FORECAST

January 1st to March 6th, celebrate! A time to live it up and have a ball with fun-loving, spontaneous antics by frolicking and laughing your way through life. A new person may suddenly enter your life and bring radical changes, surprises---it could be a magnetizing and spellbound relationship that has you flipped out . Or it is a love-them-and leave- them attitude with one night stands. Or you may win a jackpot, if you gamble. You are in a risk-taking, happy-go-lucky frame of mind. Or it is possible that a pregnancy occurs or a baby is born. Go to amusement centers, sporting events, arenas, stadiums, theme parks, shows or any form of entertainment when, and if, and the mood strikes. Let your hair down--reinvent yourself.
From March 7th to December 31st, your money increases; perhaps it is a sudden raise, a new job or transfer from one department to another, You can be conservative, make excellent financial plans, go on a budget or save money; security is uppermost on the agenda. Go into new ventures as a sideline or take on added work, responsibility --moonlighting is favored. You are ambitious and preoccupied to have a future devoid of financial woes. Persistence and sacrifice will pay off. If you own a company, merge with large corporations. Go to meetings; use diplomacy. Don't rush into any business deal. You can win and influence people to go along with you and be on your team.
Buying real estate is favorable; bargains are attracted. Negotiations are done slowly and in a wheel and deal fashion. Promoting property, land or dwellings, especially condos, duplexes or shopping malls can put money in your bank account. Resort areas near the water are beneficial for investment purposes. Income property and renting to tenants is a big boost to your income. The more you own, the more you will want. The best time to sell, especially if a profit is desirable, is after December 3rd. Follow your psychic impressions when dealing with any real estate transaction. Avoid day-dreaming, getting lazy or procrastinating.

Best Period For Romance... March 20 — April 19
Best Dates For Sex
Jan: 1, 8, 13, 21, 28; Feb: 4, 9, 18, 24; Mar: 3, 4, 8, 9, 17, 23, 24, 30, 31; Apr: 4, 14, 20, 27; May: 2, 11, 17, 24, 25, 29, 30; Jun 7, 14, 20, 21, 25, 26; Jul: 4, 5, 11, 18, 23; Aug: 1, 7, 14, 19, 20, 28; Sep: 3, 10, 11, 15, 16, 25; Oct: 1, 7, 8, 12, 22, 28; Nov: 4, 9, 18, 24, 25; Dec: 1, 2, 6, 7, 15, 16, 22, 29.

CHAPTER TEN
CAPRICORN: THE GOAT... DECEMBER 22 — JANUARY 20

To understand this chapter, read the Preface and Foreword. If you, know your rising sign, read the advice given for that sign as well as for your Sun sign. The combination of these two will give you more information than could be gained by simply reading only the Sun sign. Refer to pages 16 and 17 if you do not know what your rising sign is.

The following descriptions are typical for those born under the sign Capricorn. However, your own horoscope may contradict some of this, depending upon your rising sign and the signs occupied by the planets in your horoscope.

Capricorn is an earth sign and is feminine and semi-fruitful. The planetary ruler is Saturn. Each of the signs and/or planets has rulership over certain phases of life. The following are ruled by Capricorn or Saturn:

COLORS

You may want to enhance your living quarters or wardrobe in these shades:

Saturn: Bright or deep, pure blue, such as peacock, royal and some shades of cobalt blue. Gray; shades of gray (mixture of black and white), such as ash, lead, charcoal, smoky. Grayish-blue shades, such as cerulean, steel blue, steel gray, slate, pearl gray, pearl blue.

Capricorn: Dark blue; such shades as ultramarine, navy, sapphire, lapis luzuli, Dresden.

TALISMANIC GEMS

Onyx, sardonyx, jet, black opal, black tourmaline, smoky quartz (cairngorm). You may want to magnetize one of these gems for good luck and/or to protect you from harm. Refer to Part Two under Magnetizing Objects for auspicious dates to magnetize a talismanic gem.

STONES

Ash-colored or black minerals, such as coal. Therefore, you may accent your abode with these stones as accessories or wear them as jewelry. You may find that you have good luck when owning an ash-colored or black mineral stone such as coal.

METALLIC ELEMENT

Saturn: Lead.

NUMBER

Number 8: You may want to bet with this number, or perhaps favorable events will occur on this date. If you want to plan ahead for certain activities, you could use this date for something important, especially if it coincides with a date for that event in the Best Days section in Part Two.

DAY

Saturday: You may want to plan important activities for Saturday. Your energy is at its height on Saturdays.

SENSES: PHYSICAL OR NON-PHYSICAL

Physical Sense: Hearing
Physical Organs: Ears
Psychic Sense: Clairvoyant

MUSIC

Serious, heavy, solemn, sacred; Chamber, the minuet, Baroque, classical, choral, violin and piano symphonies. Although you may find the blues and loud rock music with a disco beat are a diversion from so much gravity.

PERFUMES

Go to the top with these essences. Under your cool and together venue is an earthy and seriously sensual person. Uncover your most hidden desires and make a definite statement with these scents. Wear them to bring out your quiet, unaffected, tantalizing and smoldering passions.

For the Female: Angel by Thierry Mugler, Bill Blass for Women, Comme des Garcons, Eau de Givenchy, Eau de Parfum, Essence Rare, Esteé Lauder, Germaine, Halston for Her, Hermés, Isadora, Tuscany Per Donna, V by Vanderbilt, Votre, Wildflower by Oscar de la Renta, Y by Yves Saint Laurent.

For the Male: Bijan Fragrance for Men, Black Tie, Giorgio Beverly Hills V.I.P. Special Reserve, Habit Rouge by Guerlain, Pino Silvestre, Santa Fe for Men, Tuscany by Aramis.

FLOWERS

Flowers and flowering plants, such as carnations, nightshade, saltice (the salt-marsh plant sea lavender), as well as those that are dark blue, such as: Alkanet, bluebell, fringed marsh, gentian (wildflower), globe thistle, harebell, hyacinth, larkspur, plumbago, scilla verna, vervain, Vipers' bugloss.

BOOKS

Those that are about history, business, economics, money, power, geology, geometry, archaeology; useful books that can help Capricorn get ahead, such as motivational (how-to-succeed) books. Documentaries and biographies of wealthy, powerful and successful people. Stories that are realistic and present the hard bare facts of life.

FASHION

You want good quality and durability in fabrics at cheap prices; thus, you hunt for bargains. Your eye for detail makes you notice all seams, linings, etc.; you dislike inferior workmanship. The clothes purchased are worn for years. New fads or styles are dismissed by you; it is the casual, elegant, conservative and old fashioned that you stick to. You cannot stand flashy colors or designs in wearing apparel. Simplicity is your key to dressing. Your wardrobe is in excellent taste and is well-kept. If you are a Capricorn woman, you feel best in tailored and straight garments. The shirtwaist, piped pocket, sweater and coat dress appeal to you. Knit or tailored pantsuits, skirts, blouses and sweaters equally attract you. You lean toward liking cabled knits, wools, polyesters, linen, cotton, gaberdine, crepe, satin, and short-haired furs. If you are a Capricorn man, flannel trousers, oxford button-down shirts, suits with vests and casual tailored slacks and/or shirts, suits with vests and casual tailored slacks and/or shirts will give comfort. Flannel, wool and cotton-polyester may be part of your wardrobe.

GIFTS

See preceding sections for type of books, flowers, music or perfume that may appeal to a Capricornian. Do not give Capricorn a present that is silly, frilly, gaudy, wasteful, tasteless or impractical. Give this sign a quality gift that appeals to his/her ambitious and professional-business-like side: Attaché or briefcase, appointment book, business cards, desk set, pen and pencil set, calendar, address book, personalized stationary, letter opener, fax or answering machine.

Capricorn has a strong desire to be organized; thus, presents along these lines are appreciated: organizers, storage bins or boxes, file cabinets, belt and tie rack, drawer divider, space-saving things for the closet, jewelry chest with drawers, crystal keepsake box or shoe racks. Workaholic Capricorn is delighted with a present that makes him/her feel safe, secure, or rich; a lock, safety chain, money, bonds (savings or corporate), gift certificate, stocks in a company or a CD from the bank. Or, if you can afford it — land, property, a condo or piece of real estate.

Hardworking Capricorn would enjoy a present that is useful and practical: work clothes, trousers, pantsuits, do-it-yourself items, tools, flashlight, calculator, adding machine, clock, toaster, doormat or How-to-be-successful books. When buying clothes for Capricorn, keep in mind that he/she is attracted to conservative, but fashionable, styles and prefers solid colors. Give Capricorn a scarf, ascot, tote bag, leather purse, handkerchief (personalized), necktie, stockings, pantyhose, belt (leather with simple designs) or hat. Durables that can be stored are great gifts for this sign: home-bottled jams, preserves or food products.

Capricorn is attracted to something old, solid, rare, historical or weather beaten: expensive or inexpensive items that have some sort of value — maybe from a collector's viewpoint. (This sign is the ratpack sign of the Zodiac; he/she seems to collect just about everything and can find a use for just about anything). Also cater to his/her hobby. Gifts that will delight Capricorn are signed historical letters and documents, woodcuts, silk screen prints, lithographs, engravings, authentic oil paintings, rare coins or books, jade objects d'art, malachite figurines, tapestries, oriental rugs, pottery, stone tablets or objects, antiquities (onyx statue), curio chests, or tables, antiques (furniture accessories), jewelry — cameos, lockets, stickpins, watches.

The over achieving and persevering Capricorn may be delighted with genuine jewelry or watches which contain onyx, sardonyx or black sapphire settings/stones. Other suggested items are throw rugs, live flowers or plants, framed photographs of memorable occasions, a shawl or goose-down comforter. Or what about tickets to a museum, ballet, opera, concert or musical show? Or the soundtrack (CD, cassette tape, video) of movies and Broadway hit shows.

For the Young: rocks (pet, magic, gem-rock or in its natural state), gems, stones, dolls (talking, walking), mechanical toys, caps, cap rack, wool pull-on hood, umbrella, learning watch, lunch box, school storage box for art work, photos, mementos; kits (ceramic, pottery wheel, cast plaques) carpenter work bench and tools, architectural blocks, construction sets/blocks (plastic, vinyl vehicles and workers), caterpillar pull toy, train with tracks, or games to bring out Capricorn's love of finances, industry and wheeling and dealing, such as monopoly.

CELL SALTS
Calcarea phosphoric or phosphate of lime.

ZONES OF THE BODY
The bones, bony-skeleton-framework of the body, cartilages, joints, knees, kneecaps, teeth (bone and bone-like structure part of the teeth). Thus you could be subject to arthiritis, bone disease, knee problems, rheumatism.

HERBS
Effective herbs and plants for the Capricorn afflicted body zones are: Balm of Gilead, birch, bitter root, bittersweet, black or blue cohosh, black poppy, blue flag, buckbean, buckthorn bark, burdock, cayenne, celery seed, colombo, elder, henbane, hydrangea, Indian hemp, leadwort, lobelia, mugwort, nettle, night shade, origanum, peppermint, pleurisy root, poke root, poplar, prickly ash, quassia, Queen of the meadow, sarsaparilla, skullcap, skunk cabbage, twinleaf, white pine, wild Oregon grape, wild yam, willow, wintergreen, wormwood, and yellow dock.

CLIMATE
Frigid, chilly and cold with a fairly large or very great snowfall; thus, you may want to live in this type of area.

PART OF LAND AND COUNTRY
Country that is high up in rocky, roughly broken, and rugged mountains with plenty of dense growth of bushes, shrubs or underwood; partly wooded, but not too many, large trees. Land where the soil is so poor that it is difficult to grow crops, but weeds, thorns and prickles are overflowing. An area which is suited for mining ores.

U.S. Cities: Huntsville and Mobile, AL; Anchorage, AK; Prescott, AZ; Fort Smith and Pine Bluff, AR; Hermosa Beach, CA; New Haven and New London, Ct; Key West, Jacksonville, St. Augustine and Tallahassee, FL; Albany, Atlanta and Savannah, GA; Honolulu, HI; Idaho Falls and Lewiston, ID; Rockford, IL; Cedar Rapids, Dubuque and Sioux City, IA; Paducah, KY; Cumberland, MD; Boston, MA; Detroit and Moorland, MI; Grand Island and North Platte, NE; Camden and Jersey City, NJ; New York City (Manhattan), NY; Asheville and Chapel Hill, NC; Bismarck and Fargo, ND; Cincinnati, OH; Enid, OK; Salem, OR; Lancaster, PA; Pierre, SD; Memphis, TN; Abilene, Austin, Gastrop and San Angelo, TX; Provo and Salt Lake City, UT; Chesapeake, Newport News and Virginia Beach, VA; Wenatchee, WA; Wheeling, WV.

U.S. States: Alaska, Connecticut, Georgia, Iowa, New Mexico, Texas, Utah. Panamian Canal Zone.

Countries: Albania, Bosnia-Herzegovinia, Burma, Cameroon, Croatia, Czechoslovakia, Ecuador, El Salvador, Eritrea, Finland, Germany, Hungary, Kenya, Libya, Mauritania, Poland, Romania, Slovenia, Sudan, Uruguay.

Islands: Australia, Cuba, Indonesia, Samoa (Western), United Kingdom (England).

Cities (other than U.S.): Tirana, Albania; Melbourne, Victoria, Australia; Rangoon, Burma; Yaoude, Cameroon; Havana, Cuba; Quito, Ecuador; San Salvador, El Salvador; Keighly and Oxford, England; Fayence, France; Bonn, Brandenburg and Konstanz, Germany; Budapest, Hungary; Jakarta, Java, Indonesia; Tortona, Italy; Nairobi, Kenya; Tripoli, Libya; Nouakchott, Mauritania; Warsaw, Poland; Bucharest, Romania; Apia, Samoa; Khartoum, Sudan; London, England (U.K.); Montevideo, Uruguay.

IN A CAPRICORN VIBRATION

Life may seem hard and difficult, especially if you have taken on added work, responsibility or live on a budget. In this environment, you are ambitious, materialistic, practical, or a miser. Either you will adapt to every requirement to gain your ends or you will gripe and complain about your lot in life. You may feel lonely here because you are afraid to meet and trust people, or you use others to climb to the top. Your organization ability is enhanced. You may believe it is your civic duty to get involved in town or state issues — pollution control, country improvement of toll roads, highways or lights; renovation of old buildings and homes; care for the aged or poor.

CAPRICORN TRAITS

You use, keep (rat-pack) and save. You hate waste and tend to conserve in your personal life as well as in the environment. You'll patiently wait for your plans to mature and will make sacrifices along the way. Your self-control is marvelous. Your own advantage is always kept in mind. You are selfish, greedy and money-hungry. You strive to be on top and may have obstacles along the way, but your persistence and hard work will bring success. You are ambitious and cautious in all ventures — business and personal. You are practical and conservative. By nature, you are serious and don't laugh too often. Stubbornness prevails; it's difficult for you to change your habits — you just don't give in. Thus, you can be your own worst enemy. You carry the troubles of others, especially family and loved ones; often, you feel responsible toward them. People can depend upon you; you'll be there "come rain or come shine." You are reserved and undemonstrative; however, you do feel things to the depths of your soul. Your best trait is diplomacy. Your downfall is negativity.

CAPRICORN COMPATIBILITY

With Taurus: You will get along fine because both of you are money and business oriented. The two of you are efficient, self-reliant, practical, stubborn and quiet.

However, Taurus will wake up passions in you that you never knew existed; sexual pleasures are heavenly. With Virgo: You appreciate this person's conservativeness. Both are workaholics; Virgo doesn't compete with you. The Virgoan encourages your industrious nature. Moderation in sex is observed; happy states of satisfaction are achieved. With Scorpio: This individual's seriousness appeals to you. Both are persistent and thrive for success. You may clash when one tries to control the other. You are amazed at how Scorpio brings out and gratifies your hidden erotic desires.

With Aquarius: You are fascinated by this person's interest in new things. However, Aquarius is too unpredictable and erratic for you. You prefer more stability and enjoy making plans, whereas the Aquarian enjoys doing things on the spur-of-the-moment. However, you will not be able to resist for too long the Aquarian's magnetic pull; sensual delights could hypnotize as well as shock you. With Sagittarius: This person cheers you up so life does not seem to be so rough. You are in awe of this individual's spendthrift ways and confidence that money will continue to flow. Lovemaking is stimulating; however, your moderation may make the Sagittarian look for greener pastures unless you use your famous manipulative powers to keep Sagittarius near you. With Pisces: You adore the Piscean's desire to serve you like a slave. Pisces is so warm and kind that you feel spoiled and pampered. Sexually, the two of you believe you have found Shangri-La.

With Cancer: This one's need for constant variety does not blend with your set habits. You are too cold for this warm, sensitive and loving individual. You'll be turned off by Cancer's bucketful of tears. However, sex is a moving and an elating experience with the Cancerian. With Gemini: You are much too stable for this person; Gemini will drive you bats with his/her constant changes. You'll be secretive because you'll be fearful that talkative Gemini will gossip about you. Carnality is dissatisfying because Gemini rushes you, or stops to chatter in midstream, or wants to try too many kinky things. With Aries: This person's impatience and impulsiveness clash with your patience and cautiousness. You want a sure thing — something familiar. Aries is a pioneer and likes to start new things. Both are selfish. You'll balk when Aries orders you to hurry. Sexually, this person's too licentious for conservative you.

With Libra: Spending money is the problem with you two; Libra is extravagant and you are thrifty; thus, problems develop easily. You won't want to stop working just to relax and be a companion to Libra, whom you think is lazy. You may not want to waste your time socializing (unless it benefits you) or constantly fulfilling Libra's sexual needs. With Leo: You are both leaders; thus, who is going to be the ruler? You will adore Leo's generosity, but you may not take the time to give Leo the attention he/she craves. Carnal delights are thrilling and bring to the surface all those wild and naughty things you'd always wanted to try. With Capricorn: This is a bad match because the two of you are shrewd and suspicious. Who will use whom? However, both are ambitious and work hard; thus, there may not be much time for each other. In the bedroom, you tend to have an icy air; thus you take too long to warm up to each other, but once aroused sex is deeply enthralling.

CAPRICORN 2019 FORECAST

From March 7th to December 31, is a time to make serious plans in your personal life. You feel secure with a fascinating loved one who you believe you can trust and have a lasting relationship. It is a time to make changes in the way you have been living. Take your time pursuing the object of your affections. You are not the type to lead a tops-turvy existence. Therefore, be patient, diplomatic and observant to the other person's speech and actions. Make sure that you do not make any mistakes in any approach used. This loved one could be a secret and personal obsession. You may be on Cloud Nine when talking on the phone, however, you are a master at disguising your feelings and intentions. Plan and take short distance romantic trips. Go on a cruise. Or take a train or drive to recreational areas near water such as a lake, river or ocean.

This is a great year to promote business deals online, through direct mail or traveling and meeting with important people--c.e.o's, owners of a corporation--- mergers, teamwork and cooperative effort by one and all can be expected. Go to conventions, wheel and deal, use tact, diplomacy, state your terms and negotiate by following your instincts. Your judgment is good--you know what you want and are great at manipulation. You tend to get your way now so go for the brass ring! Take a trip nearby or visit relatives. This is a great time to express your dramatic talents by writing a play, movie or book; it could pour from your brain in an automatic fashion--so let your ESP (extra sensory perception) out. Educational pursuits could be mind-boggling. Set a deadline date for mental activities. Be persistent and you can finish it on time.

From January 1st to March 6th, sell real estate, move or just be happy hibernating in your home. But do not be surprised at people dropping by unexpectedly. Do not gripe or complain if others bring disruptions and changes of plans which affect your living quarters. Go with the flow and make the best of all situations. Do not allow anyone to use you.

Best Period For Romance... April 20 — May 20
Best Dates For Sex
Jan: 1. 10, 11, 15, 21, 28; Feb: 6, 7, 11, 12, 18, 24; Mar: 6, 11, 17, 23, 24; Apr: 2, 7, 14, 20, 29, 30; May: 11, 17, 27, 31; Jun: 1, 7, 14, 23, 28; Jul: 4, 5, 11, 20, 21, 25, 26; Aug: 1, 7, 16, 17, 21, 22, 28; Sep: 3, 13, 18, 25; Oct: 1, 10, 11, 15, 22, 28; Nov: 6, 7, 11, 18, 24, 25; Dec: 4, 9, 15, 16, 22, 31.

CHAPTER 11
AQUARIUS: THE WATER BEARER... JANUARY 20 — FEBRUARY 18

To understand this chapter, read the Preface and Foreword. If you, know your rising sign, read the advice given for that sign as well as for your Sun sign. The combination of these two will give you more information than could be gained by simply reading only the Sun sign. Refer to pages 16 and 17 if you do not know what your rising sign is.

The following descriptions are typical for those born under the sign Aquarius. However, your own horoscope may contradict some of this, depending upon your rising sign and the signs occupied by the planets in your horoscope.

Aquarius is an air sign and is masculine and barren. The planetary rulers are Uranus and Saturn. Each of the signs and/or planets has rulership over certain phases of life. The following are ruled by Aquarius, Uranus or Saturn:

COLORS
You may want to enhance your living quarters in these shades:

Uranus: Dazzling white, like a bed of new-fallen snow in the sunshine. Such shades that are luminous, incandescent and are reminiscent of white heat (shining with intense brilliance).

Aquarius: Light (pale) blue, such as the clear blue sky, azure, baby, powder, sea-blue, electric, (metallic, luminous and emanating light) blue. Intense blue, such as royal, peacock, sapphire and Wedgewood.

Saturn: Bright or deep, pure blue, such as peacock, royal and some shades of cobalt blue. Gray; shades of gray (mixed with black and white), such as ash, lead, charcoal, smoky. Grayish-blue shades, such as cerulean, steel blue, steel gray, slate, pearl gray, pearl blue.

TALISMANIC GEMS
Blue sapphire, asteria, jacinth, sky-blue sapphire, blue opal, blue tourmaline, lapis lazuli, blue spinel, sapphirine. You may want to magnetize one of these gems for good luck and/or to protect you from harm. Refer to Part Two under Magnetizing Objects for auspicious dates to magnetize a talismanic gem.

STONES
Black pearl, chalcedony and obsidian. Therefore, you may accent your abode with these stones as accessories or wear them as jewelry. You may find that you have good luck when wearing or owning one of these stones.

METALLIC ELEMENT
Uranus: Uranium.

NUMBER
Number 9; You may want to bet with this number, or perhaps favorable events will occur on this date. If you want to plan ahead for certain activities, you could use this date for something important, especially if it coincides with a date for that event in the Best Days section in Part Two.

DAYS

Wednesday and Saturday: You may want to plan important activities for Wednesday or Saturday. Your energy is at its height on these days.

SENSES: PHYSICAL OR NON-PHYSICAL

Physical Sense: The mind without using analysis or reasoning
Physical Organ: Body electricity
Psychic Sense: Intuition

MUSIC

It depends upon your momentary whim as to whether you'll listen to any of the following: Offbeat, improvisational — classical and jazz. The latest craze, Merengue, cumbia, punk rock, hip-hop, etc. Operettas, Baroque, classical, electronic sounds. Reggae (a blend of African percussion, contemporary electronics, and lyrics that give melodic voice to religious, political and social commentary), disco rock beat, fox trot, swing, ragtime, boogie-woogie, rock and roll, musical comedy, blue grass, folk songs or chants.

PERFUMES

Be an individualist and make your own statements. Feel free to indulge in new adventures. These fragrances make you sparkle brilliantly. Sprinkle them on to express your complex whims. These scents tell the world you're ready for anything and everything. Wear them when you want to have a hypnotic effect on someone.

For the Female: Cachet, Courege, Eau d'Aliage, Eau de Guerlain, Ex'cla-ma'tion, Far Away by Avon, Jaipur de Boucheron, Longing by Coty, Mary McFadden, New West Skinscent for Her by Aramis, No Regrets by Alexandra de Markoff, Ô de Lancôme, Privilege, Sun, Moon, Stars by Karl Lagerfeld, Tocade by Rochas, White Linen.

For the Male: C. Halston, Courreges Homme, K L Homme by Parfums Lagerfeld, Rive Gauche by Yves Saint Laurent, Ted Lapidus, YSL Pour Homme.

FLOWERS

Uranus: Flowering and flowering plants that are dazzling white, such as Anemone, clematis, crocus, hibiscus, hyacinth, Madonna Lily, monarda (scarlet) narcissus, Oriental lily, oxalis, petunia, pheasants eye, phlox, paniculata, snowdrops.

Aquarius: Flowers and flowering plants that are light (pale) and intense blue, such as Anemone, aster, bachelor buttons, balloonflower, blue-eyed Mary, blue squill, bluets (innocents, quaker ladies), bugloss (wildflower), chrysanthus, clover, columbine, crocus, flax, forget-me-not, freesia, geranium, Glory-of-the-snow, hyacinth (wood), hydrangea, iris, leadwort, orris, plumbago, speedwell, Virginia bluebell (cowslip).

BOOKS

Those that are unusual, way out, allegorical, or deal with new theories, research, science, UFO's, outer space, science fiction, space travel, the esoteric, New Age (astrology, parapsychology, ghosts, mediums, psychics, prophecies, witchcraft, ceremonial magic), antiques, antiquities, electricity, electronics, computers, robots, new gadgets, inventions, or those that explore the mind — psychology, hypnosis, motivation, etc.

FASHION

You buy clothes suddenly on a whim. The garments chosen are cheap or expensive; however, good quality and workmanship are overlooked if you like something. It is possible that you will buy the mode of the day and not wear it. You are unpredictable and dress mainly to please yourself.

You create new fashion and are ahead of the times in the garb you wear. Because you are an individualist, you alter an outfit by giving it your personal touch with, perhaps, by adding a pocket or new buttons. You never wear an ensemble you have seen someone else in.

Your wardrobe could change from Bohemian, beatnik, hippie or Gypsy to conservative and old-fashioned. You are not always conscious of clothes, and could be seen in a flower-child raiment or the latest haute couture. Your closet probably contains raiments or accessories in stripes, checks, polka dots, plaids or tweeds.

If you are an Aquarian woman, you might be partial to dresses that are long and flowing, Levis, denim jeans, jumpers or hand screened print dresses or plaid skirts. The fabrics you might easily take to are seersucker, acrylic, washable cotton, corduroy, polyester, silk, leather or knit. If you are an Aquarian man, you probably prefer denim jeans, Levis, corduroy slacks, wool or turtleneck sweaters and leather jackets. Your favorite fabrics are cotton, polyester, denim, acrylic with plaid design or tweed.

All shades of blue — light, sky, electric, royal, baby, powder, sapphire and sea appeal to you. When you don clothes or accessories in these colors, you feel like exploring new areas of your personality. You could go on some mind boggling trips.

GIFTS

See preceding sections for type of books, flowers, music or perfume that appeal to an Aquarian. Those born under the sign of Aquarius, have a wide range of tastes from modern, avante garde, futuristic, ultra-progressive to different, unusual, kooky, novel, way-out, inventive or to old and conservative. Contemporary items appeal to Aquarius. Gift suggestions: an antique, antiquity (Tiki, wooden mask), abstract painting, African wall hanging or astrological items (book, magazine subscription, personal horoscope by an astrologer, Zodiac design or napkins, tablecloth, drinking glasses, and towels. Or appeal to his/her weird side: witchcraft oil, talismanic gem (or object), divining pendulum or mini-pyramid. Aquarians are fascinated by metal or mobile sculpture. He/she is delighted with a gift that is original; one-of-a-kind or personally designed with him/her in mind.

The intellectual Aquarian loves working with his/her mind. Aquarius likes to be "in" with the times and latest trends. The perfect present is the newest gadget on the market, especially if it is operated electrically or electronically. You can't go wrong with appliances (blender, vegetable steamer or electric can opener), machines (juice, popcorn, Cappuccino coffee maker, fax, answering, food processor), or high-tech gifts — home computer, talking or hand-held calculator, robot (one that gives service), telephone (cordless, self-dialing), video or TV game or sound responding alarm or light.

Aquarius may be pleased with any of these items; duffel bag, sweatshirt, car accessory, automobile (if you can afford it), jewelry (blue sapphire), subscription to a science magazine, outer-space map and chart, musical instrument (harp, guitar, zither, marimba, accordion, harmonica, xylophone), anklets, socks, stockings, chimes. Or give Aquarius tickets (opera, ballet, concert, movie, theatre, modern dance, New Age, or to a lecture). Or, perhaps, you can enroll Aquarius in a class such as astrology, high-tech, science or special short term course (preferable to a long term, due to the Aquarian's short attention span and desire to learn fast).

For the Young: Outer space toys (space kit/outfit, battery-operated miniature jet or spaceship, space shuttle cockpit, mini-space capsule or ship, home planetarium, telescope) or games mesmerize Aquarian kids. Aquarius is inquisitive and scientific-minded; thus, give a science kit, toy, book, video, magazine or mini-lab for scientific research products. An Aquarian kid is into high-technology just as much as an adult under this sign. Therefore, he/she would enjoy a robot designer kit or a battery operated-walking robot. Or a portable or play computer, blocks (magnet, electronic or magnetic learning), electronic doll (for a gal), sky plane transformer, remote controlled planes or boats, model airplane, building kit, computer game, calculator or any toy that is operated electrically or electronically. Other suggestions: a kite, mini-automobile or kits (coin collecting, jewelry-crafts, monster-creator or ghost makeup).

CELL SALTS
Natrum muriaticum, or chloride of soda.

ZONES OF THE BODY
The Achilles tendon, ankles, calves, circulation, legs (below the knees), shins. Thus you could be subject to problems with the ankles (swollen, sprained, twisted), arthritis, circulatory problems, leg spasms, paralysis.

HERBS
Effective herbs and plants for the Aquarius afflicted body zones are: Black or blue cohosh, catnip, cayenne, cedron, celery root/seed, elder, fennel, fit root, frankincense, gentian root, ginger, ginkgo biloba, golden seal, holy thistle, hydrangea, hyssop, Lady's slipper, lily of the valley, masterwort, mistletoe, myrrh, origanum (wild marjoram), pennyroyal, Peruvian bark, red clover, red root, rue, sanicle, sassafras, self-heal, skullcap, skunk cabbage, spearmint, spikenard, twinleaf, valerian, vervain, wild yam, witch hazel bark, wood betony and wood sage.

CLIMATE
Not excessively hot or cold, and weather that is changeable.

PART OF LAND AND COUNTRY
The country is neither lying below nor situated far above the general ground base level; it is thickly populated with cities and crowded conditions. The land is not roughly broken, rocky or hilly, but easy to walk on; yet it has a view that is satisfying to the aesthetic senses. The land is used chiefly for residences and other structures (business, etc.).

U.S. Cities: Tucson, AZ; Anaheim, Bakersfield, Beverly Hills, Capitola, Coronado and Huntington Beach, CA; Fort Collins, CO; Jacksonville, FL; Atlanta and Augusta, GA; East St. Louis, IL; Evansville, Indianapolis and Terre Haute, IN; Council Bluffs and Davenport, IA; Manhattan and Topeka, KS; Bowling Green and Louisville, KY; New Orleans, LA; Augusta, ME; Hagerstown, MD; New Bedford and Oak Bluffs, MA; Flint, Laketon and Lansing, MI; Biloxi, Jackson and Meridian, MS; Missoula, MT; Omaha, NE; Carson City, NV; Camden and Orange, NJ; Chapel Hill and Raleigh, NC; Canton, Cleveland, Columbus and Dayton, OH; Corpus Christi, Dallas, Fort Worth, Galveston and Gastrop, TX; Brigham City and Provo, UT; Olympia, WA; Fairmont, WV; Madison, WI.

U.S. States: Arizona, Kansas, Massachusetts, Michigan, Oregon.

U.S. Territory: Virgin Islands.

Countries: Costa Rica, Czechoslovakia, Gambia, Greece, Iran, Iraq, Nepal, Slovakia.

Panamian Canal Zone.

Principality: Liechtenstein

Independent State: Vatican City

Islands: Grenada, Haiti, Nauru, Sri Lanka.

Cities (other than US.): Salzburg, Austria; Toronto, Canada; Taipei, Taiwan, China; San Jose, Costa Rica; Brighton and Salisbury, England; Bathurst, Gambia; Bremen, Hamburg, Ingolstadt and Trent, Germany; Athens, Greece; St. Georges, Grenada; Port-au-Prince, Haiti; Teheran, Iran; Vaduz, Liechtenstein; Yaren, Nauru; Katmandu, Nepal; Colombo, Sri Lanka, Vatican City State.

IN AN AQUARIAN VIBRATION

You enjoy the society of others and the interchange of ideas. People are fascinated by your pleasant and magnetic personality; friends are made quickly. Your involvement in astrology and the esoteric might make you very popular. In this environment, you are unpredictable — anything goes. A topsy-turvy life with constant excitement suits you fine. You do not want to be tied down, must be independent and do your "thing". Your views are ultra-progressive.

You search for change which can benefit the masses; possibly, you will campaign for new laws, reform or invent something that can aid the metropolis or state. You may be abrupt and opinionated, and be known as the town know-it-all.

AQUARIAN TRAITS

You never know what your are going to do from one moment to another. Often, your life is turned upside down. You're an individualist and a free spirit and can't stand being chained by anyone in business or your personal life. You're erratic and can swing from a security-conscious attitude to being a person who couldn't care less about monetary concerns. You are quite a talker; others have trouble getting a word in edgewise. Your ideas are usually ahead of the times. You are intuitive and inventive and lean toward originality and being different. Your greatest virtue is that you understand human nature. You want verification of all theories. Science appeals to you. You can be contrary, especially when debating. You are the rebel and reformer who isn't afraid of breaking laws or setting precedents. Your magnetic personality is irresistible. Romantically, you want someone who is difficult to conquer. Your best trait is humanitarianism. Your downfall is abruptness.

AQUARIUS COMPATIBILITY

With Gemini: Because you both like to do new and different things on the spur of the moment, you are a good match. You two can stay up all night yakking about everything from soup to nuts. Sexually, constant and intriguing surprises are in store for you — anything goes! With Sagittarius: You will never cease to be amazed by this person's good sense of humor, optimistic outlook and ability to make life fun. Neither of you will be a prisoner in this relationship — you're both independent and freedom-loving. The unusual carnal experiments the two of you indulge in are ingenious and have you completely bewitched. With Libra: You are smitten by Libra's charm and gentle, kind ways and intellectual skills. Both enjoy flitting about like social butterflies. Eroticism intoxicates the two of you to the point of believing that you are surely in the Garden of Eden.

With Aries: You are attracted to this person because there is constant excitement without dependence upon one another. Both are impulsive and enjoy the adventure of new things. Risk-taking-sex, in public places, or way-out-carnal activity makes you both ecstatic and takes you to frenzied states. With Pisces: This person's warmth and quietness sooth your nerves. You may not like the Piscean clinging to you, but you'll try to unravel his/her mysterious ways. Both of you are sensually gratified when your bodies and souls unite. With Aquarius: An interesting match, but you both are too opinionated. Who can tell the other one anything when you both feel you know it all? Sex is indescribably marvelous; you are overwhelmed by each other's diversity in bed.

With Capricorn: This person's old-fashioned thoughts and actions clash with your modern ones. You enjoy shaking up Capricorn with startling shocks, surprises and your unpredictableness. You relish arousing Capricorn to great heights of passion and gratifying his/her fleshly appetites. With Cancer: You have to mind your p's and q's with this person because your abruptness hurts his/her feelings. Also, this individual frowns upon your straying from home too much. Sex with Cancer is captivating and lustful, but you may not want to spend so much time in bed — especially when new horizons beckon. With Virgo: This person tends to be too analytical and slow for your fast-racing mind. You dislike criticism and being nagged; therefore, the moment Virgo starts you're ready to bolt. If Virgo is prudish, you'll be turned off. However, if you've become involved with a Virgoan who wants to experience new sensations, then you won't hesitate to take quick action along these lines.

With Taurus: It is in your best interest to avoid this person because you will not like being possessed. Both of you are fixed in your ideas and ways; stalemate conditions are met. However, there is an irresistible attraction; lovemaking is won-drously ardent, but you may not care to continue the wanton pace you are caught up in. With Scorpio: You refuse to be tied down with this person. You'll disappear the moment Scorpio tries to control you. You may have difficulty conversing with Scorpio because he/she is just too quiet and secretive for you. You could be shaken by the depth of sensuality felt when you two are together. However, in spite of erotic bliss you will break the chains that bind you too tightly. With Leo: This individual's ego is too much for you to put up with. You refuse to be bossed by Leo; after all, you're a free spirit. But opposites attract and both may find it a fascinating relationship. Sex is extremely passionate and lewd, but you may tire of excessive pleasure in the bedroom.

AQUARIUS 2019 FORECAST

From January 1st to March 6th, a sudden increase of phone calls keeps you busy talking to friends and relatives, You encourage each other. Faith and belief in each other's personal and professional endeavors is inspirational. Jokes may be told. Conversations are humorous, uplifting and philosophical. New Age topics may be discussed. You'll be fascinated by all the unusual, way out or technical things learned. The latest fad in technology is mind-boggling. Spur of the moment short distance visits with pals is fun with lots of laughs. Your outings and get-togethers with buddies is expensive, but you don't care how costly it is. If you spend too much time living it up with lunches, dinners and trips, it will be difficult to work; thus, your bank account could dwindle.

From March 7th to December 31st, the emphasis is on your home; you may enjoy solitude. Moments spent alone may give you the time you need to make serious plans for the future. You could contemplate moving or getting involved in real estate transactions. A part of you may not want to be tied down to having the responsibility of owing land or a structure. However, that can be changed because the desire to always have a roof over your head is very strong this year. Your foresight is excellent. You could look at a piece of property and know that is can be valuable, if not now, later. This is a beneficial time to attract a bargain. Be secretive and make a low price bid based upon a methodical and systematic strategy. You are clever, observant and have done your homework on the house you want. Therefore, follow your instincts when it is time to negotiate and stick with your organized plan. The end result may astound you, especially when you now own your dream home. The money spent on decorating is put to good, practical use. Comfort is important to you. Finances can increase through promoting real estate that belongs to you or others. You can be psychic, so wheel and deal. Perhaps, you want to decorate or upgrade your living quarters. If so, this is the time to do it. If you move, give a housewarming party. Your friends will surprise you with gifts for your new home. Do some landscaping, plant a flower garden and spruce up your residence.

Best Period For Romance... May 21 — June 20
Best Dates For Sex

Jan: 1, 2, 3, 10, 11, 12, 13, 17, 28, 29, 30; Feb: 6, 7, 8, 9, 14, 18, 24, 25, 26, 27; Mar: 6, 7, 8, 9, 12,17, 23, 24, 25, 26; Apr: 2, 3, 4, 9, 14, 19, 20, 21, 22, 29, 30; May: 1, 2, 6, 7, 11, 17, 18, 19, 20, 27, 28, 29, 30; Jun: 7, 14, 15, 16, 23, 24, 25, 26, 30; Jul: 4, 5, 10, 11, 12, 13, 20, 21, 22, 23, 28; Aug: 1, 7, 8, 9, 10, 16, 17, 18, 19, 21, 24, 30; Sep: 3, 4, 5, 6, 13, 14, 15, 16, 20, 21, 25; Oct: 1, 2, 3, 10, 11, 12, 17, 18, 22, 28, 29, 30; Nov: 6, 7, 8, 9, 14, 18, 24, 25, 26, 27; Dec: 4, 5, 6, 9, 11, 15, 16, 22, 23, 24, 31.

CHAPTER TWELVE
PISCES: THE FISHES... FEBRUARY 19 — MARCH 20

To understand this chapter, read the Preface and Foreword. If you, know your rising sign, read the advice given for that sign as well as for your Sun sign. The combination of these two will give you more information than could be gained by simply reading only the Sun sign. Refer to pages 16 and 17 if you do not know what your rising sign is.

The following descriptions are typical for those born under the sign Pisces. However, your own horoscope may contradict some of this, depending upon your rising sign and the signs occupied by the planets in your horoscope.

Pisces is a water sign and is feminine and fruitful. The planetary rulers are Neptune and Jupiter. Each of the signs and/or planets has rulership over certain phases of life. The following are ruled by Pisces, Neptune or Jupiter:

COLORS

You may want to enhance your living quarter or wardrobe in these shades:

Neptune: Changing iridescence pearl and mother-of-pearl.

Jupiter: Indigo, such shades as deep violet-blue; hues from dark bluish-purple to grayish-bluish purple. Bright purple, such as the brilliant purple hue known as "royal" purple.

Pisces: Dark purple hues, such as dark plum, magenta, royal, grape and purplish-reddish-violet shades such as mauve. Shades of greenish-blue, such as aquamarine, sea-green, turquoise blue, and some shades of peacock and cobalt blue.

TALISMANIC GEMS

Peridot (olivine) pearl and pearly white opal. You may want to magnetize one of these gems for good luck and/or to protect you from harm. Refer to Part Two under Magnetizing Objects for auspicious dates to magnetize a talismanic gem.

STONES

Coral, gravel, pumice and sand. Therefore, you may accent your abode with these stones as accessories or wear coral as jewelry. You may find that you have good luck when wearing coral or owning one of these stones.

METALLIC ELEMENT

Neptune: Neptunian.

NUMBER

Number 12: You may want to bet with this number, or perhaps favorable events will occur on this date. If you want to plan ahead for certain activities, you could use this date for something important, especially if it coincides with a date for that event in the Best Days section in Part Two.

DAYS

Thursday and Friday: You may want to plan important activities for Thursday or Friday. Your energy is at its height on these days.

SENSES: PHYSICAL OR NON-PHYSICAL

Physical Sense: ....Meditation
Physical Organ: .... Pineal gland (the 3ʳᵈ eye)
Psychic Sense: Aroma detection, visions, illuminations and ESP
                    dreams

MUSIC

Haunting, sensual, dreamy, romantic and sentimental sounds. A nocturne, rhapsody, concerto, sonata, serenade; poetry or love song being recited with soft, melodious background music. The harp, violin and zither makes you believe you are hearing the music of the spheres. Devotional organ hymns, a requiem, lullaby or spiritual music makes you feel as if you're one with the universe. A waltz, rock and roll and dance music puts you in the mood to trip the light fantastic.

PERFUMES

These intoxicating fragrances may evoke images that may satisfy your desire to be mysterious, alluring, intriguing, sensuous and playfully provocative. These scents bring out the soul of a poet and make you feel heavenly. Wear these essences when you want a strong emotional response or to be seductive; you'll appear tempting enough to captivate your paramour.

For the Female: Belle de Jovan, Calvin Klein, Cardin de Pierre Cardin, Chantilly by Houbigant, Cinnebar, Coco by Chanel, Coriandre by Jean Couturier, Courant, Decadence by Prince Matchabelli, Deneuve, Most Precious by Evyan, Farouche, Femina by Alberta Ferretti, Fendi, Heartland by Bath and Body Works, Imari by Avon, L'Aire de Temps by Nina Ricci, L'Heure Bleu by Guerlain, Oscar by Oscar de la Renta, Quadrille, Spellbound by Esteé Lauder, Sublime by Jean Patou, Tiffany by Tiffany, Vivid by Liz Claiborne.

For the Male: CK One by Calvin Klein, Drakkar Noir, E. Pierre Cardin, K L Homme by Parfums Lagerfeld, Monsieur De Givenchy, One Man Show, Pour Homme by Maxim, Tabac.

FLOWERS

Neptune: Flowers and flowering plants that are iridescent, such as Buddleia and Guernsey lily (mother-of-pearl).

Jupiter: Flowers and flowering plants that are indigo, such as iris.

Pisces: Flowers and flowering plants that are dark purple (grape, plum, royal), such as: Althea, aster, bittersweet, chrysanthus, clematis, closed (bottle) gentian, colchicum, cornflower, crocus, cuckoopint, daylily, delphinium, eyebright, figwort, fuchsia, iris, monarda (beebalm, bergamot), nightshade, persicaria, petunia, phlox paniculata, pimpernel, rhododendron, rose root, snapdragon, sweet pea, sweet William, tulip, vervain and woody nightshade.

BOOKS

Those that touch one's imagination so one lives vicariously and escapes to the world of make believe. Fantasy, nursery rhymes, fairy and folk tales, fables or love stories. Books that delve with dreams, psychic phenomenon, mystical, spiritual and esoteric areas. Or those that deal with animals, physics, photography, painting, acting, poetry or tragedy, the theatre, ballet, circus, carnival or the sea. Also books about the Piscean's favorite star (actor/actress, singer or musician).

FASHION

Money is spent foolishly and quickly on clothes. Your impracticality is seen when you buy one ensemble that you expect to wear only once, or one that is above your means in price. The quality or workmanship means nothing to you; the look and feel are your determining factors.

All styles of clothing appeal to your imagination; thus, when wearing them you play the part of whomever you wish to be — and you do long to be so many different people. Your flair for drama shows in your wearing apparel and/or behavior.

If you are a Pisces woman, you dress in something that makes you appear mysterious, alluring, seductive. The raiments you don bring out your romantic and poetic side. You prefer an aesthetic, Oriental, or old-fashioned look to a casual one; you are able to achieve your heart's desire. You are partial to dresses or gowns that are loose, flowing and billowy; thus, you feel free to flow gracefully through life as if you live in the clouds. However, you can switch from dreamy to everyday clothes in a flash; it all depends upon your emotional needs of the moment. You are attracted to caftans, shifts, smocks or tent dresses and muu-muu gowns because they camouflage your weight. Your favorite fabrics are chiffon, silk, nylon, petitpoint lace, faille, moire, taffeta and jersey.

If you are a Pisces man, you delight in many changes of wardrobe; you dress for the occasion. When you are in a lazy mood, you do not care what you wear as long as it is loose, comfortable and allows you to be sloppy. You are partial to soft fabrics and lightweight clothes, but will wear wool slacks and be heavily bundled up in a wool or cashmere sweater and heavy coat when the weather is cold. Other materials you wear with ease and enjoy are cotton, corduroy, polyester and silk (shirts and neckties).

All shades of purple — light, dark, lilac, mauve, lavender and orchid appeal to you, as well as aquamarine, sea-green, iridescent and mother-of-pearl. When you don clothes or accessories in these colors, you can be unusually psychic or feel visionary and may want to meditate, dance or make rapturous love.

GIFTS

See preceding sections for types of books, flowers, music or perfume that may appeal to a Piscean. Appeal to his/her poetic, romantic or sentimental nature: book (love poems), music box, dreamy music (CD, cassette tape). If the gift is personalized (write your own song, poem or greeting card), Pisces will treasure it forever. Or give Pisces a collectible: vase (especially small, for one flower), art object (crystal figurine, small sculpture, beautiful print, oil or water color painting), or plate (commemorative or special edition).

Pisces is artistic, creative, loves beauty, colors and working with his/her hands; thus for a Piscean of all ages, give a ceramic, (especially a theatrical mask set), tote bag for cosmetics or art supplies, canvas, easel, paints, brushes, artist's smock. Or a kit for making jewelry, soap, ceramics or for flower pressing, bead stringing, loom weaving or make-up. Cater to the Piscean dramatic flair by giving acting or dancing lessons, wigs, costumes, beautiful feathers to decorate a room or video's (drama, romance, fantasy, dance, ballet).

Let Pisces live out his daydreams in his/her unrealistic world of wonderland; thus, give him/her tickets to the circus, ice-figure-skating show or extravaganza in a cabaret or to see his/her favorite star perform. Or give him/her seasonal theatre tickets to plays, musicals or the ballet. Present Pisces with music lessons or a musical instrument (piano, string — especially the harp). Pisceans are great photographers; thus, give him/her a camera (digital), photo album, film developing equipment, slide machine holder, view or movie film complete with a projector and screen. Or gift Pisces with photography lessons.

Water-sign Pisces will be thrilled with tickets for a cruise or a weekend spent by a lake, river, ocean, bay or babbling brook, especially if the setting is romantic and picturesque. Or consider perfumed bath soap, bubble bath set, hot tub, water fountain, underwater camera, fishing or scuba lessons, an aquarium filled with fish or rent or buy (if you can afford it) a raft, canoe, boat, yacht, sailboat.

For the Piscean feet (ruled by Pisces): a pumice stone, callus remover, pedicure set, foot soak basin and solution, shoehorn, shoe rack, shoe bag/tote, panty hose, tapestry, foot stool or shoes, boots, slippers or stockings. Animal loving Piscean's adore pets. Other suggested items: semi-precious gems/stones, pearls (faux or genuine), ties, scarves, pajamas, plastic gadgets, artificial items, herb plants, cocktail glasses, coasters or a bottle of liquor, parachute, humidifier, heating pad or air conditioner.

For the Young: (Note: many of the preceding items are also for kids). Pisces loves glamour; thus, he/she would have fun with feather-bedecked hats, boas, fantasy dress-up, costumes for playing make-believe or a mini theatre (puppets, or, fairytale), play set (pirate, power-geared carnival). Other suggestions: a doll (especially rag), cuddly stuffed animal (teddy bear), balloon, bubble-making machine, muppet video, animal slippers, birdhouse, butterfly or window bird feeder, animals (live, vinyl, plastic, rubber), wind-up bathtub toys (duck, fish, seal, turtle) zoo book (press-and-listen), slate (to doodle, design), paints (washable, non-toxic) with brush set, books (coloring, fairytale, ocean and fish stories), story stickers (creative picture stories) or a trinket that may become a keepsake (locket, jewelry).

CELL SALTS
Ferrum phosphoricum or phosphate of iron.

ZONES OF THE BODY
The feet, metatarsus, phalanges, plantaris, tarsus, toes. Thus you could be subject to bunions, callouses, corns, fallen arches, flat feet, hammer toes and other foot problems such as fungus of the toes.

HERBS
Effective herbs and plants for the Pisces afflicted body zones are: Ferns, henbane, mosses which grow in water (algae, kelp, seaweed).

CLIMATE
Moderately cold, where there are rainstorms, rainfall or showers and fog.

PARTS OF LAND AND COUNTRY

Country that is not too extremely low, is greatly uneven and irregular, enclosed on all sides by hills, and is cut up by long hollows or gores worn by a flowing stream. Land where there are fish ponds, or through which rivers or small, inactive and slow creeks flow. Or near large bodies of water, such as lakes wholly surrounded by land, or where there are moderately cold springs of water coming from the surface of the earth.

U.S. Cities: Phoenix and Yuma, AZ; Newport Beach and Sacramento, CA; Newark, DE; Miami Beach and St. Petersburg, FL; Champaign and Urbana, IL; Evansville, IN; Cedar Rapids, Council Bluffs, Davenport and Sioux City, IA; Bowling Green and Frankfort, KY; Lake Charles and Shreveport, LA; Augusta, Bangor and Lewiston, ME; Fall River, Lowell and New Bedford, MA; Ann Arbor, Battle Creek, Cedar Creek, Flint, Fruitport and Ravenna, MI; Mankato, Minneapolis, St. Cloud and St. Paul, MN; Hattiesburg, MS; Springfield, MO; Billings, Butte, Helena and Missoula, MT; Lincoln and Omaha, NE; Las Vegas, Reno and Sparks, NV; Atlantic City and Paterson, NJ; Ithaca, Schenectady and Yonkers, NY; Greensboro, NC; Grand Forks, ND; Cleveland, OH; Medford, OR; Allentown, PA; Pawtucket, RI; Sioux Falls, SD; Amarillo, Dallas, Grand Prairie, TX; Ogden and Price, UT; Burlington, VT; Portsmouth, VA; Huntington, WV; Eau Claire and Madison, WI; Laramie, WY.

U.S. States: Florida, Maine, Nebraska, Ohio, Vermont.

Principality: Monaco

Countries: Andorra, Ghana, Morocco, Nepal, Netherlands (Holland), Switzerland.

Islands: Maurutius, Saint Lucia, Taiwan (China).

Cities (other than U.S.): Cowes, Victoria, Australia; Toronto, Canada; Taipei, Taiwan, China; Bornemouth, Christchurch, Farnham, Grimsby, King's Lynn, Lancaster, Preston and Southpost, England; Regensburg and Worms, Germany; Accra, Ghana; Port Louis, Mauritius; Compostela, Mexico; Monaco-Ville and Monte Carlo, Monaco; Rabat, Morocco; Katmandu, Nepal; The Hague, Netherlands (Holland); Castries, Saint Lucia; Bern, Switzerland.

IN A PISCES VIBRATION

Your imagination is extremely lively; mystery and intrigue mesmerize you. In this environment, you are sensitive, emotional, demonstrative and loving. Romance may be a dream or reality, depending upon whether you mix and mingle with others or stay home alone. This is a great town for practicing transcendental meditation and to develop yourself spiritually and psychically. Visions of a Utopia may be satisfied when your idealistic views are put to use in prisons or hospitals, or getting involved in charity or social work. Or perhaps you will be part of a movement to build amusement centers, theatres or aquariums for the enjoyment of the citizens to attract tourism.

PISCEAN TRAITS

You believe in people, life and ideas, and are easily misled, swayed and stepped on. You're vulnerable to schemes of overnight riches that in reality helps you to quickly part with your dough. You are impractical and spend money foolishly. You are too kind, sympathetic and unselfish. You worry about everything — small and large. By nature, you are idealistic and want peace for mankind. You slip away from reality as you drift and dream about a world where everything is akin to Shangri-La. You are psychic, dramatic and can emote like a natural actor/actress. You dislike discipline and tend to procrastinate. You are prone to all kinds of excesses. You tend to be subservient and enjoy serving others almost slave-like. Your best trait is devotion. Your downfall is your emotions.

PISCES COMPATIBILITY

With Cancer: Because you are both demonstrative and loving, this is a relationship that could be said to have been made in Heaven. Both are sensitive, emotional and caring. In the bed, every moment is breathtakingly beautiful as each of you pour your heart and soul into the sex act, or even just an embrace. With Scorpio: You adore Scorpio. You want to cling and be possessed by this person. Scorpio is your dream come true. Erotically, the Scorpion makes you feel so enchanted that you truly believe you have found the Utopia you have been searching for. With Pisces: Both are intriguing and romantic; thus, the two of you share many pleasurable moments together. You're a couple who can be lazy, procrastinate and drift and dream. How will any work get done? You are deeply touched and deeply moved by each other's endearing words, hugs, kisses and sensuality.

With Taurus: You feel secure with this person. You enjoy the fact that Taurus wants to own you. Like a clinging vine, you won't let go. The two of you are lustful; every physical craving is vehemently gratified. With Capricorn: You revere this individual's ambition. Buy you may not like it when Capricorn tightens the purse strings or gives more attention to a career than to you. It is a game for you to entice Capricorn; once this person is in your clutches, highly erotic states leading to sublime bliss is felt by both of you. With Aries: You are bedazzled by the Arien's aggressiveness and nerve. You worry about the risks Aries takes. This person has so much energy, it's easy for you to get exhausted in his/her company. Fleshly appetites are appeased when the two of you indulge in fervid and sensational carnal acts.

With Aquarius: It is as if a spell was cast and you are powerless to break it. You enjoy listening to Aquarius do all the talking. But you get bugged when the Aquarian makes hasty departures and keeps you in suspense. Lovemaking is overwhelming; you are so enraptured that you envision that you have escaped earthly pleasures because you have found heavenly ones. With Leo: You respect, admire and adulate this person. You like Leo to be the boss. You enjoy staying in the background while Leo is on center stage. Your sensual yearnings are satisfied by a hot blooded gal/guy. With Libra: You are elated by this person's quiet, peaceful and beautiful nature. Both can be lazy and enjoy relaxing too much. It's difficult to get moving, especially toward a career. The two of you feel as if you are floating on a cloud while listening to soul-stirring music and impassionately touching one's innermost being in the act of making love.

With Virgo: This one's neatness and your sloppiness do not mix. Your feelings will constantly be hurt when Virgo nit-picks. Virgo is too busy working to give you the attention you need. You are turned off by the Virgoan's sexual inhibitions; but once they are lifted, carnal pleasure is experienced. With Gemini: This individual's too fickle for you. Gemini makes you worry and cry because you never know whether this Dr. Jekyll and Mr. Hyde truly loves you. The Geminian runs as soon as you cling. But you do find Gemini intriguing, especially when you are both carried away with new forms of eroticism. With Sagittarius: When you become frustrated, Sagittarius makes your tears flow by being too frank. Both of you look through rose-colored glasses and get carried away with your dreams. But the Sagittarian takes you for granted and isn't always there when you need him/ her. However, everything sensual is tried, rabidly, and to the point of exhaustion.

PISCES 2019 FORECAST

This year obstacles exist between your personal and professional life. You cannot be in two places at one time. It is either work or play. It could be health issues that interfere with your career. If you tend to business, your bank account could increase between January 1st and March 6th. It could be a raise in your wages or a title promotion. You could go on a big spending splurge at this time. You are happy to part with huge sums of money. You need to watch laziness and procrastination. People may think you are high on a drug or booze because you seem to be spaced out and/or not all there. However, it could be that you are day dreaming and imagine that you are living in paradise--utopia. Perhaps, you believe you have found shangri-la. If you find that it is difficult (a hardship) to live in the mundane real world then you will want to escape from reality to the unreal world where everything is peachy-keen. Talk to your pals--they can help stabilize you with words of wisdom. Listen to their advice because they care for you and are 100% in your corner. One-on-one conversations are useful as well as getting together with a group of friends, especially if you are a member of a club. However, from January 1st to March 6th, do not listen to their ideas involving your money and how you should invest it. Financial mistakes could be made through leaping in too fast or waiting too long to decide what it is you want to do.

From March 7th to December 31st, go on a vacation at a nearby location. Enjoy picturesque scenery. Visit relatives, meet new people and see your buddies. Talk on the phone, send e-mails and keep in touch with others---the result can keep you grounded. Friends make you feel safe, secure and can hold you spellbound with fascinating stories, especially with the latest in technology. Do keep occupied with Twitter, be on Facebook, and send Instagrams. Take photos with your cell phone and send them to your pals. Reinvent yourself--glamorize or be comfortable with a new look. You can charm others with a charismatic personality.

Best Period For Romance... June 21 — July 22
Best Dates For Sex
Jan: 1, 10, 11, 12, 13, 14, 15, 19, 28; Feb: 6, 7, 8, 9, 10, 11, 12, 16, 24; Mar: 8, 9, 10, 11, 15, 23, 24; Apr: 2, 4, 5, 6, 7, 11, 12, 20, 29, 30; May: 2, 9, 17, 27, 28, 29. 30, 31; Jun: 1, 5, 14, 20, 22, 25, 26, 27, 28; Jul: 11, 20, 21, 22, 23, 24, 25, 26, 30; Aug: 7, 16,17, 19, 20, 21, 22, 26; Sep: 3, 13, 14, 15, 16, 17, 18, 23; Oct: 1, 10, 11, 12, 13, 14, 15, 20, 28; Nov: 6, 7, 8, 9, 10, 11, 16, 24, 25; Dec: 4, 5, 6, 7, 8, 9, 13, 22, 31.

PART TWO

BEST DAYS GUIDE FOR DAILY ACTIVITIES

INTRODUCTION

Use Part Two for the best day to go to the movies, propose, make love, attend a party, etc. This section of the Astrological Almanac is a little different from Sun sign astrology, although it is based upon the daily (transit) planets. To understand Part Two, read the Forward, page 12. In Part Two there are approximately 500 categories to guide you in your daily activities.

My telephone constantly rings with questions from clients and strangers. The inquiries range through every possible subject:

"Is this a good time to sign a contract?"

"When is the best time to look for an apartment?"

"Can you tell me what would be a good day to advertise?"

"Is an operation on the stomach favorable on _____ day?"

"When should I start a business?"

"Can you tell me if tomorrow is a good day to begin looking for a job?"

"When is a good time to go to the dentist?"

"I want to have a baby. Are there any dates when I am more prone to getting pregnant?"

" Is next month a good time to go fishing?"

"I loaned money to a friend. When would the best time be to ask for it back?"

"Am I compatible with someone born under the sign of _____?"

"I have trouble buying shoes. Could you give me a favorable date to purchase them?"

Many valuable hours have been spent answering these individual requests or help. With the growth of interest in astrology, the telephone calls have increased. If I continue along these lines, it will be difficult for me to accomplish anything else! However, I realize that there are many people who cannot afford their own astrologer. Others do not have the correct time of birth; thus, they cannot have an accurate horoscope cast without having it rectified by a reliable astrologer. By precalculating and publishing in book form the answers to everyday questions, many people have benefited.

Since 1957, I've researched and experimented with these daily "activity" forecasts. I have found them to be invaluable. They really work even though an individual horoscope or Sun sign is not involved. Part Two applies to everyone, regardless of your Sun Sign. Every possible venture has been included in Part Two of the Astrological Almanac. All of the dates given were calculated according to the aspects of the transiting planets and the events which they govern. The Moon has been taken into consideration, as it aspects all of the planets approximately every two and a half days.

There are eight planets and two luminaries (Sun and Moon). For the sake of convenience, I will call the Sun and Moon planets. Each of these planets rules a particular kind of behavior or thought, as well as specific activities and events. The distances these planets are from one to another are called "aspects." Some aspects are harmonious and bring auspicious events while others are inharmonious and bring inauspicious events.

In many cases, the sign the Moon is in will cause an event to happen regardless of the aspects. For instance, it is a well known fact — that the Moon influences the tides and that during a Full Moon there are more flare-ups involving crime than at any other time. Furthermore, a woman's menstrual period is every 27 1/2 days, which also corresponds to the Moon's cycle through the 12 signs of the Zodiac.

It is therefore logical to assume that if the Moon can influence the preceding events, it can also cause other activities to occur. However, it is not only the Moon but all the other planets that, together, bring various events into our lives. The planets, including the Sun and the Moon, are composed of electromagnetic energies that radiate different kinds of vibrations (dependent upon the astrological meaning of the planet) to us here on the Earth.

In astrological terms, the planets which influence everyday events and activities are called transits; everyone is affected by them. A baby is born and these planets are a child's natal (birth) horoscope. For a person already living, these transiting planets trigger both everyday occurrences and major events. These planets can affect great masses of people at one time; for instance, they may bring airplane crashes, bombings, highjackings, earthquakes, fires, hurricanes and other calamities; or favorable events, such as rain when the farmer needs it, or any of the auspicious activates that are categorized.

Your individual horoscope always comes before anything else. The days listed will usually coincide with an individualized horoscope and will help, rather than hinder, you. The activities mentioned will apply only to the extent that other things not stated are equal. For example: You had a haircut on a date other than the one listed. It came out beautifully. Perhaps in your own horoscope you had a favorable Venus (hair) aspect. However, if you had gone to the hair salon on a day listed you would have had a better haircut.

There are favorable dates for making good and lasting impressions. For example: You go for an audition on a day listed but you are not hired. What went wrong? Either your own horoscope was afflicted or you were not the type the producer was seeking for the part. Do not be discouraged if this happens. Perhaps, you auditioned on a date when you could make a good and lasting impression. The producer will probably call you at a later time when he has the perfect role for you.

In this Astrological Almanac, there are favorable time periods to sign contracts and dates to avoid signing papers. Before you sign a document, cross-check these categories in Part Two. If there is a day you want to sign a contract and it is not listed as favorable, turn to the Avoid page and see if it is given there. If it is not and you feel you must sign, then do so on a date that is not listed on the Avoid page.

Each sign of the Zodiac governs a different zone of the physical body; thus, if an operation is performed on a zone corresponding to a sign in which the Moon is located on the day of surgery, it could be fatal or more painful than it should be or it may have to be repeated at a later time. For years, statistics have demonstrated that more hemorrhaging occurs during the Full Moon than at any other time.

Have you ever had an operation that was repeated at a later date? If so, the Moon was in the wrong sign of the Zodiac at the time of surgery. Possibly the Moon was making an inharmonious aspect to Mars, which rules cutting. If you took a long time to heal, it was because the Moon was on the decrease or making discordant aspects to the Sun or perhaps your individual horoscope was afflicted when you had surgery.

Numerous clients of mine looked up dates for their friends to have surgery and reported that the operations were successful and quick recoveries were made. In fact, in one case the doctor was stunned because his patient, who was in his seventies, healed more quickly than the doctor had anticipated.

Part Two contains dates when to have and when to avoid surgery. Concerning operations the following must be clearly understood: If surgery cannot be avoided because of a life or death situation, then it is advisable to have the operation even though the dates are not favorable for performing surgery on that zone of the body. Perhaps, in your own individualized horoscope, you have auspicious aspects for an operation (with Mars, the planet of surgery) even though the transiting Moon or Mars does not favor it. Thus, from your own horoscope's aspect, you will pull through the operation successfully even though the recovery may be painful or slow.

Or it is possible that your own horoscope is afflicted for an operation during a certain time period, but surgery is necessary; then select a favorable time listed under the Surgery category. By so doing, you will enhance your chances for a quick recovery.

On the positive side, many events too numerous to mention have transpired with people who used the Astrological Almanac — here are just a few that occurred: A friend of mine went fishing according to the dates listed for fishing, and each time he caught more fish than he ever had in the past and prior to using the Astrological Almanac dates. Many students at Manhattan College in New York City improved their grades by studying on the dates listed under the category Exams, Tests, Studies.

The following will explain, as simply as possible to the layman, how it all works. Have you ever been in pain when you had your teeth cleaned by the dentist? If so, the transiting Moon was in Aries or Taurus. Have you ever attended a party that was boring? If so, Venus was making an unfavorable aspect to Saturn or another planet. Have you ever mailed a letter or an important document that took, seemingly, forever to be received or answered, or that was lost? If so, either Mercury was retrograde (appearing to us here on Earth to be moving backwards) or poorly aspected to the other planets, and at the same time the Moon was on the decrease.

Have you ever wondered why a Broadway show opened and closed in a few weeks, yet was enjoyed by those who saw it? It is because the show opened on the waning of the Moon (decreasing from Full Moon to New Moon) and/or there were unfavorable Neptune aspects in the sky at the same time.

On April 28, 1983, Elizabeth Taylor and Richard Burton opened in their first preview of Noel Coward's play Private Lives at the Lunt-Fontanne Theater in New York City for a limited engagement. The official opening date was May 8, 1983. Both the preview (which is the one that counts astrologically under the category Shows in Part Two) and the opening night were not listed under Shows (to open) in my Astrological Almanac for 1983. Not even the Taylor-Burton famous and appealing name draw could bring the public in the way the producers anticipated. When the play first opened, it was announced that the engagement would be extended for one month beyond the closing date. However, by the end of June it was announced that business was not as had been expected; therefore, Private Lives would not be extended for another month. This could have been avoided if the producers had opened the show while the Moon was increasing in light instead of decreasing in light.

In the 1983 edition of my Astrological Almanac, there were other incidents which took place under various categories. Avoid: Dental Work (April 12, two dentists' hands slipped while cleaning their patients' teeth; both were injured and suffered pain for several weeks.). Two strikes were called under the category Avoid: Strikes (March 1, New Jersey transit strike, it lasted one month; March 8, New York City Metro transit strike, lasted about six weeks).

Under the Avoid: Falls category, on January 21, in the New York City area, a little boy who climbed on the roof, fell to his death. Under the Avoid: Fires category, February 21 (huge fire, New Jersey); March 15 (oil truck on expressway, Brooklyn); also huge fires in other sections of the New York City area; March 21 (hotel fire, New York City). Under the Avoid: Accidents category, January 21 (car and bus collided, New York City area), April 3 (oil barge collision in St. Louis; truck with oil accident, New Jersey; railroad car tanker explosion of nitric acid fumes, Denver, Colorado; train derailed, West Virginia; Amtrak train derailed, Rockford Gap, Virginia); April 4 (freight train derailed, east coast); April 28 (Amtrak train derailed, New Haven, Connecticut, people seriously injured); May 10 (New York City, subway train derailed; May 31, Brooklyn, subway train derailed; June 6, (New York City) building wall collapsed, people injured; also New York City, subway train derailed; June 7 (Long Island, New York), deck collapsed at cocktail party at a country club); March 15, 2000, Amtrak train derailed in Kansas (on the way to Los Angeles, California) 35 people suffered minor injuries.

In the 1998 edition of my Astrological Almanac, under the category Avoid: Danger, major catastrophies occured such as: major earthquakes ranging from 7.0 to 7.4 magnitude; as well as tornadoes; there was an earthquake on March 29 in the Fiji Islands; also on March 29 there were several tornadoes in southwestern and south-central Minnesota and also near Maxville, Wisconsin; April 1 there was an earthquake off the coast of Southern Chile; May 3, earthquake southwest Taiwan. The 2003 edition of my Astrological Almanac, under the category Avoid: Danger, from May 4th to May 8th, over 280 tornedos caused disaster, destruction of property, towns demolished and people killed in the U.S. States: Arkansas, Kansas, Nebraska, Oklahoma and Tennessee, as well as Toronto, Canada.

In the 2001 edition of my Astrological Almanac, under the category Avoid: Danger, January 17, New York City had a 2.4 magnitude earthquake; January 26, worst earthquake in 50 years, 7.9 magnitude, near Hyderabad, India, more than 50 high rise buildings reduced to rubble, many injured, over 100,000 people killed. It affected people as far away as Bombay. Altogether over 500,000 people are homeless in the regions it affected. February 8, India, another earthquake; February 17, earthquake in El Salvador. In the 2005 edition of my Astrological Almanac, under the category Avoid: Danger, July 7, 2005, London, England bombs and explosions on busses, trains. Under the same category, on August 25, Hurricane Katrina hit Florida (6 people killed) and continued on its path of destruction, on August 29, it laid waste to parts of Mississippi, Alabama and Louisiana — New Orleans was destroyed. In the 2006 edition of my Astrological Almanac, under the category Avoid: Danger, earthquakes occurred October 15 (Hawaiian Islands), and October 20, in Peru and Turkey.

In the 2001 edition of my Astrological Almanac, under the category Avoid: Accidents, January 26, Interstate highway near Joliet, Illinois, a Salvation Army van and tractor trailer collided, 10 people killed; February 1, Los Angeles, California,

2 passenger cable cars collided. February 5, 2001, Syracuse, New York, an Amtrak train and a freight train crashed into each other. February 15, 2001 there was a 30 car pile up on icy roads in Oklahoma; and on March 17, an Amtrak Train derailment in Iowa, one person died, over 40 injured; April 27, school bus crash in Canada, 5 children killed; October 3, Manchester, Tennessee, Greyhound Bus crashed when passenger slit driver's throat with a razor, 7 killed, 32 injured. (Note: the April 27 and October 3 dates were also listed under the category Avoid: Travel By Land.) In the 1993 edition of my Astrological Almanac, under the category Avoid: Terrorist Attacks, February 26, the bombing of the New York City World Trade Center. In the 2000 edition of my Astrological Almanac, under the category Avoid: Terrorist Attacks, January 18, Yemen; February 11, Spain; February 13, Yugoslavia; February 29, Yugoslavia; March 2, Yemen; March 3, India; March 21, India; May 19, 20, India; May 27, Indonesia; June 1, Georgia; June 2, Namibia; June 2, India; June 8, Sierra Leone; June 8, Greece; July 20, Angola; July 24, India; July 27, Colombia; August 2, India; September 7, Guinea; September 13, 15, Colombia; September 17, Guinea; September 30, India; October 1, Tajikistan; October 2, Uganda; October 12, Ecuador; October 12, Bosnia; October 14, South Africa; October 19, Sri Lanka; November 19, Nambia, Jordan; December 31, Thailand.

Under the category Avoid: Terrorist Attacks, October 12, 2000, the U.S. Naval Destroyer "Cole" was docked for refueling in the Gulf of Aden in Yemen. Two terrorists, on a suicide mission, were in a small boat loaded with ammunition. Their boat pulled alongside the U.S. Naval Destroyer "Cole," and exploded. As a result, 39 Americans were wounded and 17 killed, and many were missing. The following day (October 13) in Yemen, there was an explosion at the British Embassy — a bomb had been thrown over the wall, but did not hit the Embassy building nor injure anyone.

In the 2001 edition of my Astrological Almanac, under the category Avoid: Terrorist Attacks, September 11, New York City World Trade Center, thousands killed, many injured, many still missing; September 23, Jakarta, Indonesia; September 26, three Israeli soldiers injured by booby trap bomb when it exploded near Gaza-Israeli border; October 3, Algeria; October 3, Philippines; October 13, Madrid, Spain, car bomb explosion, many injured; December 1, Jerusalem, car bombs and other bombs in Mall, 10 dead, 180 injured.

Under the category Avoid: Terrorist Attacks, March 11, 2004, terrorists bombed three different commuter trains in Madrid, Spain — 190 people died, over 1,400 were injured. This date was also listed under Avoid: Danger and Avoid: Travel by Land. July 30, 2004, three suicide bombings occurred in Tashkent, Uzbekistan, including one outside the U.S. Embassy. September 9, 2004 in Jakarta, Indonesia, near the Australian Embassy, explosives killed many people and buildings eight blocks away were severely damaged.

In the 2000 edition of my Astrological Almanac, these incidents took place under various categories. Under the category Avoid: Travel By Water, September 26, a ferry boat ran aground and crashed into a reef off the island of Paros in Greece. Some people were missing; 53 were confirmed dead. The Captain and crew were arrested because they had been watching TV when the accident occurred. April 5, 2007, a Greek cruise ship in Santorini, Greece crashed into reefs. The ship sank, but the 1,600 on board survived, except for two people who are (were) missing.

In my Astrological Almanac for 2000, under the category Mercury Retrograde, the dates listed were from October 18 to November 8. The United States Presidential Election was on November 7. When Mercury is Retrograde confusion occurs with communications, filling out forms, signing papers and other mental activities. Thus, it's better to avoid these things when Mercury is Retrograde. The United States Presidential Election is perfect proof of what can go wrong — some people did not understand (confusion) the ballot, the recall occurred and the country was uncertain as to who would be the next President. This is a good example of what occurs when Mercury is Retrograde.

INCIDENTS UNDER AVOID: TRAVEL BY AIR

Some of the dates of airplane crashes and incidents that occurred in various years and that were listed under my Avoid: Travel by Air dates are listed below. When I list these dates in my Astrological Almanac, it does not mean there will be a crash; it implies that these are the most likely dates for a crash to occur.

1982 — January 13 (Washington D.C.), February 4 (Africa), February 9 (Japan), September 11 (helicopter, West Germany), September 13 (Spain).

1983 — January 11 (cargo jet, Detroit); January 16 (Turkey, jet crashes) and flight scheduled to depart from Los Angeles to New York City canceled due to plane difficulties (people evacuated; no injuries); January 28 (small plane crash, Arizona); airplane forced to land in Reno, everyone was safe; on the East coast of the USA, a jet's wing fell off, no one was hurt; March 11 (jet crash, Venezuela); April 3 (small airplane with two people in it disappeared after leaving Long Island, New York); April 30 (three airplane crashes — student pilot in New York City area. U.S. Navy plane in Florida, small plane in South Carolina); May 5 (jet forced to land in Florida due to maintenance error); May 22 (in Frankfort, Germany, Canadians performing in air show landed on highway, plane hit cars on road, people killed, pilot jumped to safety, not injured); June 22 (Air Canada DC-9 emergency landing in Cincinnati, fire broke out on board, 30 people were burned and died); September 1, Korean jet left U.S., shot down by Russians.

1985 — September 15, Beirut plane hijacked, hostages held; November 23, Egyptian jet hijacked, hostages held; December 12, U.S. military plane crashed in Gander, Newfoundland, 250 people killed.

1987 — May 1, people killed when two planes collided in Orlando, Florida; May 9, worst Polish aircraft disaster, everyone killed; July 30, helicopter crash, and a cargo airplane crashed into a restaurant near Mexico City (35 people killed); August 16. Detroit air crash (153 killed); September 4, a B-1 bomber crashed in Colorado; October 20, Indianapolis, many people killed in air crash; November 8, plane crashed in Tijuana, Mexico.

1988 — January 10, plane crashed in water in Japan; February 17, air crash in Australia during air show; February 25, Texas helicopter crash; people killed; April 28, Hawaii, worst plane crash, jet torn apart; September 21, Albany, New York plane crash; October 18, in India two bad crashes, people killed; December 8, missile attack on jet; December 11, TWA plane hijacked from Puerto Rico; Russian military plane crashed on way to earthquake disaster; December 12, another military plane crash in Russia on way to earthquake disaster; December 21, Pan Am 747 exploded in flames and crashed in Scotland.

1989 — September 20, La Guardia, New York airplane crash.

1990 — January 18, two planes collided, Atlanta, Georgia — a large and a small plane; July 28/29, in New York State, small plane crashes.

1991 — March 3, Illinois plane crash; March 16, Otay, California crash, country singers; March 21, San Diego, California crash, and a crash in Saudi Arabia; April 5, Lexington, Kentucky crash; May 27, an explosion and crash minutes after take-off from Thailand with Austria as the destination point; June 30, California crash; October 16, Newark, New Jersey, two planes clipped each other's wings; December 10, airplane crash in Grand Canyon; December 11, a small plane crash in Georgia.

1992 — April 16, Kenya air crash, people killed; La Guardia, New York, plane crash due to fire; no one killed.

1993 — January 13, Grand Canyon airplane crash; July 23, Scotland crash; North Korea crash.

1994 — April 10, Farmingdale, New York, small plane crash.

1995 — February 13, plane crashed in Grand Canyon; 8 killed, 2 lived.

1996 — July 17, TWA jet mid-air explosion off Long Island coast, New York (everyone killed). August 26, terrorists hijacked Cypress Jet. October 19, New York City plane hit an approach light, skidded, 4 slightly injured. October 20, New Brunswick, Canada, plane crash, 8 killed. October 22, Florida, small plane crash, plane landed on top of grocery store. October 31, San Paolo, Brazil, plane crash, people killed. November 21, Arizona, small plane crash, people killed. November 30, California, small plane crash.

1997 — March 2, Utah, near airfield, small plane crash, 1 killed, 3 injured. March 14, plane crash. March 15, Wisconsin, 2 small planes collided, people killed. March 15, Los Angeles, California, small plane crash, hit shed by a house. March 18, Russia, plane crash, people killed. March 18, Florida, 2 Army planes collided in air show, people killed. April 2, Air Force jet disappeared after leaving Arizona, found in Colorado Mountains at a later date. April 6, Harbor, Maine, single-engine plane crashed on the front lawn of residence, pilot and 2 people injured; August 10, Taiwan, small passenger plane collided into mountain.

1998 — January 13, Pakistan plane crash, people killed; April 20, Bogota, Columbia airplane crash.

1999 — July 2, Swiss Airline crash over the coast of Nova Scotia, everyone killed; September 26, plane crashed into volcano in Hawaii; October 31, Egyptian air liner crashed near Nantucket Island, Massachusetts, 217 people killed.

2000 — January 31, Alaska airline crash off Point Mugu, California, 88 people killed; February 16, cargo airplane crash over Rancho Cordova, California; March 16, Texas helicopter crash, everyone killed; April 18, Philippines air crash, 131 killed, no survivors; July 17, an American Airlines jet with 133 people on board took off from Grapevine, Texas and circled the air for 45 minutes and then landed, due to smoke filling the cockpit. No one was injured; the cause of the smoke was undetermined. August 9, there was a double plane collision when two airplanes crashed; one plane went into a house; the other into a field — everyone was killed. On August 23, just off the coast of Manama, Bahrain, a plane crashed into the Persian Gulf as it was approaching Bahrain en route from Cairo, 123 people were killed. No cause for the crash was determined. Also on August 23, an American Airlines plane made an emergency landing, due to turbulence, in Houston, Texas. People were injured and taken to the hospital.

On August 24, 2000, at Newark Airport in New Jersey, a Continental Airlines jet spun around and blew out four tires after its brakes locked upon landing. The 27 people on board the plane were not injured. On August 25, an American Airlines jet enroute from London to New York city was forced to make an emergency landing in Goose Bay, Newfoundland, Canada. The reason for the emergency landing was "smoke in the cockpit." No cause for the smoke was determined and the 172 people on board were not injured. On October 25, 2000, 25 people died in a plane crash in the country of Georgia.

In the 2001 edition of my Astrological Almanac, under the category Avoid: Travel By Air, February 15, Long Beach, California, 2 small planes collided; February 15, in Oklahoma, an American Airlines jet flight aborted, jet on take off was on the runway and slid in the mud; March 28, Los Angeles, 10 injured by emergency landing of jet. In the 2002 edition of my Astrological Almanac, under the category Avoid: Travel By Air, January 5, Tampa, Florida, 15 year old boy committed suicide by flying an airplane into a high rise building by the Bank of America offices; January 5, two small plane crashes; January 28, Ecuador jet liner crashed into Andes mountains near Colombian border, 94 people killed; October 24, 2002, Senator Wellstone, wife, daughter and staff members killed in plane crash near Eveleth, Minnesota. In my Astrological Almanac For 2003, on February 1: Columbia Space Shuttle broke up, all 7 Astronauts died; May 25, China Air crash, everyone killed. In my Astrological Almanac For 2004, on January 3, 148 people killed on an Egyptian Air flight, crash occurred in the Red Sea. In the 2004 edition of my Astrological Almanac, under the category Avoid: Travel By Air, on August 24, two Russian airplanes crashed in Russia within minutes of each other, 94 people killed. In the 2005 edition of my Astrological Almanac, under the category Avoid: Travel By Air, Peru airplane crashed, 48 people killed.

IF YOU ARE ONE DAY AHEAD OF ENGLAND OR THE USA

All of the activities were calculated so you could use them for the entire day given, regardless of what time zone you are in on the western hemisphere (England, North or South America, Hawaii, Alaska, etc.). The same applies if you are in a time zone in the eastern hemisphere and are on the same day as England; however, if you are one day ahead of England or the U.S., etc., use the day after all dates listed in this Almanac (this also applies to Part One, the Sun Sign section of this book).

For example, if you live in Tokyo, you are one day ahead of the U.S. and most of the time nine hours ahead of England (depending upon daylight and summer times, etc.), which means that when it's 4:00 p.m. in England it is 1:00 a.m. of the next day in Tokyo.

Thus, when you are a day ahead of Greenwich, England, and want to select a favorable day on which to start advertising in January 2019, turn to the Advertising section page. You will note that January 6 is given, but, because you are a day ahead in time, you are simultaneously a day after what is listed in the Almanac; therefore, adjust the date given in the Almanac to January 7. In other words, use the day after the dates listed and stop the day after the last date given, as illustrated.

NOTE: Dates that could have been listed for some localities would not have been in aspect at the same time they were for other places. For example: England is eight hours ahead of California (when standard time is used by both places). Dates are given in this Almanac are for both England and California. A day before or after the dates listed would not have been favorable for both England and California simultaneously; therefore, those dates are not given.

CATEGORIES

ACQUISITIONS

These are favorable dates to acquire something, especially as an addition to an established category, group — such as a corporation taking over (acquiring) a company. If quick results are desired, start discussions and/or acquisitions on the underlined dates. See Mergers, page 172.

Jan.: 6-10, 15, 16, 24, 28-31; Feb.: 3, 5-8, 11, 13-15, 17, 18, 20, 21, 23-25, 27, 28; Mar.: 3-5, 31; Apr.: 2, 3; May: 23-25, 27, 28, 31; Jun.: 1, 2, 4, 7-9, 21-24, 27-30; Jul.: 1, 4, 5; Aug.: 2-4, 6, 8-10, 13, 14, 16-18, 21, 22, 24, 25, 28, 29, 31; Sep.: 3, 4, 6, 7, 9-13, 18; Oct.: 1, 3, 16-19, 30; Nov.: 20, 21, 25, 27, 28, 30; Dec.: 1-3, 8-11, 13, 15-17.

ACUPUNCTURE

For optimum physical performance and health, these dates are best to see an Acupuncturist. However, do not have needles administered on the dates listed below IF THEY ALSO APPEAR under Avoid: Surgery (pages 114-117) — for the part of the body needles are to be administered.

Jan.: 2, 13-16, 24, 27, 28; Feb.: 5-7, 24-28; Mar.: 1, 10, 12-17, 19, 21, 22; Apr.: 2-4, 6, 11, 13, 18; May: 9-13, 15-17, 19, 20, 22-24, 26, 30, 31; Jun.: 1-10, 24, 29; Jul.: 3, 22-24, 28, 30; Aug.: 5, 10, 21, 25-29; Sep.: 1, 6, 7, 17-20, 23, 30; Oct.: 1-3, 10, 11, 14, 17, 28, 30; Nov.: 9-11, 13-15, 19, 27-30; Dec.: 2-6, 10, 11, 13-15, 17-21, 23-25, 27.

ADVERTISING

An ad should appear on any one of these dates. Place it beforehand. Advertising includes brochures, concerts, direct mail, film (movies) fliers, magazines, newspapers, nightclubs, radio, tabloids, television, theatre and all types of products, shows and exhibits. See Printing, 181.

Jan.: 6-13, 15-20; Feb.: 5-11, 13-18; Mar.: None; Apr.: 6-11, 13-18; May: 5-10, 12-17; Jun.: 4-9, 11-16; Jul.: 3-6; Aug.: 1-6, 8-14, 31; Sep.: 1-4, 6-13, 29, 30; Oct.: 1-4, 6-12, 28-30; Nov.: 27-30; Dec.: 1-3, 5-11, 27-31.

AFFECTIONAL INTERESTS

Pep up your life! Affectional interests will prosper more quickly if undertaken on these dates. See Dating, page 142; see Romance, page 190.

Jan.: 1, 6, 15, 25-28, 30, 31; Feb.: 1-3, 11, 12, 14, 15, 17-21, 23-25; Mar.: 8, 12-14, 25-28; Apr.: 1-4, 7, 8, 10-15, 17-22, 26, 29; May: 2, 4, 10-15, 17-21, 27-31; Jun.: 1-4, 6, 12-14, 20, 26, 29; Jul.: 1, 3, 4, 6, 7, 9, 10, 19, 21, 26; Aug.: 5, 6, 9, 16, 20, 21, 31; Sep.: 1, 2, 7, 9-13, 15, 18, 20, 25, 27-30; Oct.: 1-4, 9, 10, 18-21, 23-27, 29; Nov.: 3, 8, 9, 11, 19, 22-30; Dec.: 1-5, 7-12, 18, 24, 28-31.

AGENTS (LITERARY, SCREEN, TELEVISION, THEATRICAL)

See an agent on one of these dates. If you want quick results contact an agent, by mail or telephone on the underlined dates.

Jan.: 2-4, 10, 15, 25, 30; Feb.: 1-10, 15-18, 21-26; Mar.: 1-4, 31; Apr.: 5-9, 11, 12, 18, 21, 27, 29; May: 5, 8, 13, 15-17, 20-24; Jun.: 1, 6-9, 14, 24; Jul.: None; Aug.: 3, 8, 19-21, 24; Sep.: 9-13, 15, 24, 25, 30; Oct.: 1-4, 10, 12, 14, 16-21, 29, 30; Nov.: 20, 22, 26-30; Dec.: 1, 3, 4, 9, 15, 22-25, 29-31.

ALCOHOL

Do you want to stop drinking? If so, try one of the following dates to initiate the desired resolution. You will find that on these dates it is easy to stick to your plans. This includes ale, beer, champagne, liquor, wine and hard liquor such as gin, scotch, vodka and whiskey.

Jan.: 1, 28; Feb.: 24; Mar.: 3, 4, 23, 24, 30, 31; Apr.: 20, 27; May: 24, 25, 31; Jun.: 1, 20, 21, 28; Jul.: 18, 25, 26; Aug.: 21, 22, 28; Sep.: 18, 25; Oct.: 15, 22; Nov.: 18, 24, 25; Dec.: 15, 16, 22.

AMUSEMENTS

Escape into another world by going to an arcade, amusement center, circus, fair or exposition (artistic or industrial development, etc.), or take a whirl at either Disneyland or Sea World on any of the dates which follow:

Jan.: 7-10, 27-30; Feb.: 5-7, 17, 18, 23-27; Mar.: 3-7, 13, 14, 17, 23, 25, 26, 31; Apr.: 1, 2, 4, 13, 14; May: 24-28; Jun.: 3, 4, 7, 20-25, 30; Jul.: 1, 4, 5, 18-21, 29; Aug.: 6, 7, 9, 10, 16, 17, 24, 25; Sep.: 2-6, 30; Oct.: 1-3, 11, 17-19, 21, 30; Nov.: 4-8, 14, 15, 17, 18, 27; Dec.: 1-5, 11-13.

ANIMALS: BIRTH

Animals, (horses, pets, cattle) born on the following dates make good breeding stock, mature quickly and are, in general, healthy, thus, mate them so their young will be born on the days that are not underlined. If beauty and grace are required, such as for racing and showing, plan for the young to be born on the underlined dates. See Avoid: Animals Spay or Neuter, page 109.

Jan.: 10, 11, 15, 19; Feb.: 6, 7, 11, 12, 16; Mar.: 11, 15; Apr.: 7, 11, 12, 18; May: 9, 15, 17; Jun.: 5, 11, 12, 14; Jul.: 9, 11; Aug.: 5, 7; Sep.: 1, 3, 13, 29; Oct.: 1, 10, 11, 28; Nov.: 4, 11; Dec.: 1, 2, 9, 11, 31.

ANIMALS: TRAINING

Jan.: 10, 15, 24, 27; Feb.: 6, 7, 17, 18, 20, 24; Mar.: 6, 7, 10, 11, 17-19, 23, 24; Apr.:2, 3, 13, 14, 16; May: 31; Jun.: 1, 7-10, 23-25, 27, 28; Jul.: 4, 5, 20-22, 24-26, 31; Aug.: 1-4, 6, 7, 16-18, 21, 22, 28-30, 31; Sep.: 7, 18, 25, 27; Oct.: 1, 14, 15, 21; Nov.: 10, 11, 12, 18-21, 30; Dec.: 8, 9, 15-18.

APOLOGIZING

Do you want to apologize to someone? If so, these dates are favorable because the other person is inclined to accept the apology.

Jan.: 25-27; Feb.: 6, 7, 15-18, 20-25; Mar.: None; Apr.: 17, 18, 20-22; May: 7-10, 15, 19, 20, 31; Jun.: 1-4, 11, 12; Jul.: None; Aug.: 5-14, 20, 21; Sep.: 24, 29, 30; Oct.: 3, 19-24, 30; Nov.: 20, 21, 27; Dec.: 2-4, 10, 11, 24, 26, 27, 29, 30.

APPLICATIONS: (ID. CARD, PASSPORT, PERMIT, VISA)

Apply for an ID card, passport, permit or visa on these dates. The underlined dates are for quick results. See Job: Apply for Work, page 163. For License Applications, see page 168; for photo for ID card or passport, see Photography, page 178.
Jan.: 2-4, 10, 15, 25, 30; Feb.: 1-10, 15-18, 21-26; Mar.: 1-4, 31; Apr.: 5-9, 11, 12, 18, 21, 27, 29; May: 5, 8, 13, 15-17, 20-24; Jun.: 1, 6-9, 14, 24; Jul.: None; Aug.: 3, 8, 19-21, 24; Sep.: 9-13, 15, 24, 25, 30; Oct.: 1-4, 10, 12, 14, 16-21, 29, 30; Nov.: 20, 22, 26-30; Dec.: 1, 3, 4, 9, 15, 22-25, 29-31.

APPRAISALS, ASSESSMENTS: HIGH

High appraisals or assessments are easily obtained on any of the following dates:
Jan.: 2, 3, 8, 13, 18, 25, 26, 28, 30; Feb.: 6-9, 18, 23-25, 27; Mar.: 3, 4; Apr.: 1-4, 9-11, 13, 14, 18, 20-22, 27-30; May: 1, 2, 6-8, 15, 19, 20, 24, 25, 27, 28, 30; Jun.: 7, 12-16, 20-24, 26, 30; Jul.: 4; Aug.: 1, 5, 6, 8-10, 14, 16-20, 24, 25; Sep.: 4, 6, 15, 16, 23-25, 29, 30; Oct.: 1, 3, 7-11, 18, 19, 22, 26; Nov.: 22-25, 27; Dec.: 2, 21, 23, 24, 28, 30.

APPRAISALS, ASSESSMENTS: LOW

Low appraisals or assessments are easily obtained on any of the following dates:
Jan.: 1, 6, 7, 15-17, 19, 20, 22-24; Feb.: 1-3, 10, 11, 13-17, 20-22; Mar.: 1, 2; Apr.: 6-8, 16; May: 5, 9, 10, 13, 16, 17, 22, 23, 29, 31; Jun.: 1, 2, 4-6, 8, 9, 11, 18, 19, 27-29; Jul.: 1, 3, 5, 6; Aug.: 2-4, 11-13, 21, 22, 26-29, 31; Sep.: 1-3,8-11, 18, 27; Oct.: 12, 14-17, 20, 23-25, 28; Nov.: 20, 21, 29, 30; Dec.: 9-11, 14-17, 19, 20, 22, 27, 29.

ARCHITECTURAL PLANS — DRAW SUBMIT

Draw up plans on any of these dates. Submit the plans on the underlined dates.
Jan.: 9, 10, 15, 27; Feb.: 5-7, 17, 18, 20, 21, 23-25; Mar.: 3-5, 31; Apr.: 2, 3; May: 24-27, 31; Jun.: 1-3, 4, 25, 27-30; Jul.: 1; Aug.: 4, 6-10, 13, 14, 18, 21-25, 28-30, 31; Sep.: 18, 27; Oct.: 3, 16-19, 21, 30; Nov.: 20, 21, 27, 28, 30; Dec.: 10, 11, 15-17.

ARCHITECTURAL PLANS — FOR APPROVAL

Get your plans approved on these dates.
Jan.: 4, 7, 8, 10, 15, 28, 30; Feb.: 3, 4, 6-8, 10, 18, 25; Mar.: 2, 4, 31; Apr.: None; May: 24, 25, 31; Jun.: 1, 21, 24; Jul.: 4, 5; Aug.: 1, 5, 7-9, 14, 21, 24; Sep.: None; Oct.: 1, 3, 4, 18, 19, 21; Nov.: 20, 22, 27, 28, 30; Dec.: 4, 11, 15, 16.

ART

Artistic endeavors such as drawing, painting, graphics, sketching, arranging flowers, and painting pottery are favored on the following dates. See Exhibits, page 148; see Sculpting, page 191.
Jan.: 1, 6, 15, 17-28, 30, 31; Feb.: 1-3, 11, 12, 14-28; Mar.: 2, 8, 11-14, 16-22, 25-28; Apr.: 1-4, 7-15, 17-22, 26, 29; May: 2, 4-21, 27-31; Jun.: 1-4, 6, 12-14, 20, 26, 29; Jul.: 1, 3, 4, 6-10, 16-19, 21, 26, 29; Aug.: 5, 6, 9, 16, 20-26, 31; Sep.: 1-7, 9-15, 18, 20, 25, 27-30; Oct.: 1-4, 9-14, 18-27, 29; Nov.: 3, 8, 9, 11, 13-15, 19, 21-30; Dec.: 1-12, 18, 23, 24, 28-31.

AUCTIONS: BUY

Attend auctions and bid for a low price on these dates. These are dates when buying is favored — this includes auctions over the Internet.
Jan.: 6, 7, 14-17, 22-24; Feb.: 1-4, 10-15, 20, 21; Mar.: 2, 31; Apr.: 6-8, 16; May: 3, 5, 11-13, 16, 17, 22-25, 29-31; Jun.: 1-10, 28, 29; Jul.: 1-5; Aug.: 2-4,

12, 13, 21-31; Sep.: 1-3, 8-11, 18, 19, 26, 27; Oct.: 14-20, 23-25, 27, 28; Nov.: 20, 21, 29, 30; Dec.: 8-11, 14-20, 22, 27, 29.

AUCTIONS: SELL

Auction goods (including books, clothes, jewelry, furniture, art, antiques, etc.) or animals on these dates. These dates favor high prices; the customer will have the money to spend plenty on the desired object. The preceding includes auctions over the Internet.

Jan.: 1-3, 8, 10, 11, 13, 18-20, 25-28, 30; Feb.: 4, 6-9, 16-18, 22-27; Mar.: 3, 4; Apr.: 1-5, 9-14, 18, 20-22, 27-30; May: 1, 2, 6-10, 15, 19, 20, 26; Jun.: 11-16, 20-23, 25-27, 30; Jul.: 31; Aug.: 1, 5-10, 14, 16-20; Sep.: 4-6, 15, 16, 23-25, 29, 30; Oct.: 1, 3, 7-12, 21, 22, 26; Nov.: 22-27; Dec.: 2, 4, 21, 23, 24, 30, 31.

AUDITIONS: ACTORS AND ACTRESSES

Acting is best expressed (performed) on any of the following dates:

Jan.: 5-10, 15, 16, 25-31; Feb.: 1-28; Mar.: 1-4, 28, 31; Apr.: 2, 20; May: 4-9, 15-17, 22-27, 31; Jun.: 1-5, 11-14, 18-20, 25-30; Jul.: 1, 2; Aug.: 5-14, 22, 26; Sep.: 18; Oct.: 1, 16-30; Nov.: 25-29; Dec.: 4, 13, 22, 29, 31.

AUDITIONS: COMEDY

Comedy (stand-up, film, T.V., and clowns) is best expressed (performed) on any of the following dates.

Jan.: 8, 18, 21, 22, 24, 27, 28, 30; Feb.: 3, 4, 6-8, 17-19, 21, 23-28; Mar.: 2-4; Apr.: 1-4, 13-15, 17; May: 24-28; Jun.: 1-4, 7-10, 13, 20-25, 27, 29, 30; Jul.: 1, 4, 5; Aug.: 1, 2, 4, 6-10, 13-18, 23-25, 28-31; Sep.: 1-7, 9-11, 24, 25, 28, 30; Oct.: 1, 3, 11, 14, 16-19, 21-23, 25, 27; Nov.: 21, 22, 24-27; Dec.: 2, 8, 10, 17.

AUDITIONS: DANCERS

Dancing is best expressed (performed) on any of the following days:

Jan.: 1, 6, 10, 11, 24-27; Feb.: 6, 7, 16-25; Mar.: 8, 11-14, 25-28; Apr.: 1-4, 7-15, 17-22; May: 2, 4, 12-21, 27-31; Jun.: 1-4, 6, 7, 26, 29; Jul.: 1, 3-6, 26, 29; Aug.: 5, 6, 9, 16, 17, 20, 23-26, 28, 31; Sep.: 1, 6, 7, 20, 27, 28; Oct.: 3, 4, 9, 10, 17-21; Nov.: 9, 19, 21, 27-30; Dec.: 1-12, 15, 18, 24, 28-31.

AUDITIONS: MUSICIANS

Musical ability is best expressed (performed) on any of the following dates:

Jan.: 6-10, 15, 16, 24, 27-31; Feb.: 3-8, 10-15, 17, 18; Mar.: 2-7, 10-14, 17-19, 24, 26, 31; Apr.: 2, 3, 13, 14, 16; May: 27, 31; Jun.: 1-4, 7-10, 20-25, 27-30; Jul.: 1, 4, 5, 13, 18-22, 24-29, 31; Aug.: 1-4, 6-10, 13-18, 21-25, 28-31; Sep.: 2-7, 9-11, 13, 18, 27; Oct.: 1, 3, 11, 14-19, 21, 30, 31; Nov.: 3-8, 10-15, 17-21, 25, 27, 28, 30; Dec.: 4, 9-13,15-18.

AUDITIONS: SINGERS

Singing is best expressed (performed) on any of the following dates:

Jan.: 2-4, 10, 15, 25, 30; Feb.: 1-10, 15-18, 21-26; Mar.: 1-4, 31; Apr.: 4-9, 11, 12, 18, 21, 27, 29; May: 3, 5, 8, 13, 15-17, 20-24; Jun.: 1, 6-9, 14, 24; Jul.: None; Aug.: 3, 8, 19-21, 24; Sep.: 9-13, 15, 30; Oct.: 1-4, 10, 12, 14, 16-21, 25, 29, 30; Nov.: 20, 22, 26-30; Dec.: 1, 3, 4, 9, 15, 22-25, 29-31.

AUTHORITIES

Deal with someone in an authoritative position on any of the following dates. The underlined days bring quick results.

Jan.: 1-5, 8, 11, 16, 25; Feb.: 1-4, 6-10, 16-18, 23-28; Mar.: 3; Apr.: 6, 7, 10, 13-15, 17, 18, 20-22, 29; May: 7-9, 12-14, 23-26, 29-31; Jun.: 1, 5, 7, 12, 22, 25-27; Jul.: 5; Aug.: 1, 5-14, 16, 20, 28-30; Sep.: 1, 3-6, 8, 11-13, 19, 24, 25, 30; Oct.: 8, 11, 12, 14, 18, 22, 23; Nov.: 20, 21, 25-30; Dec.: 1-11, 13-16, 21, 23, 24, 26-28, 31.

AVOID: ACCIDENTS

Accidents such as burns, cuts, fires, bumping into objects or mishaps while riding on a horse or land vehicles (bus, train, trailer, RV, truck, van, motorcycle, or a cable, passenger or street car) are easily attracted on any of the following dates. Thus, extreme caution and a slow pace should be maintained. Also, train and subway accidents such as derailments are likely to occur on these days. See Avoid: Danger, page 110; see Avoid: Falls, page 112.

Jan.: 4, 6-8, 12, 17-23, 25, 26, 28-31; Feb.: 1-4, 8-15, 17, 23; Mar.: 3, 11, 16-24; Apr.: 1, 9, 15, 16, 22-30; May: 1-3, 7, 14, 21, 29; Jun.: 4, 11-21, 26, 27; Jul.: 4, 6-14, 17, 18, 25, 26; Aug.: 1, 8, 15, 23, 26-31; Sep.: 1-16, 21, 27; Oct.: 4, 12, 20, 22-29; Nov.: 1-8, 10, 17, 22-26; Dec.: 1, 9, 16, 22, 30.

AVOID: ANGER

Anger on any of the following dates could have dire results. Thus, avoid problems by directing the same anger energy to creative outlets, such as sexual activities or games that are not too hazardous.

Jan.: 4, 6-8, 12, 17-23, 25, 26, 28-31; Feb.: 1-4, 8-15, 17, 23; Mar.: 3, 11, 16-24; Apr.: 1, 9, 15, 16, 22-30; May: 1-3, 7, 14, 21, 29; Jun.: 4, 11-21, 26, 27; Jul.: 4, 6-14, 17, 18, 25, 26; Aug.: 1, 8, 15, 23, 26-31; Sep.: 1-16, 21, 27; Oct.: 4, 12, 20, 22-29; Nov.: 1-8, 10, 17, 22-26; Dec.: 1, 9, 16, 22, 30.

AVOID: ANIMALS SPAY OR NEUTER

Never spay or neuter an animal on any of the following dates.

Jan.: 1, 2, 22-29; Feb.: 19-25; Mar.: 18-25; Apr.: 15-21; May: 12-18; Jun.: 8-15; Jul.: 6-12; Aug.: 2-8, 29-31; Sep.: 1-4, 26-30; Oct.: 1, 2, 23-29; Nov.: 19-26; Dec.: 17-23.

AVOID: BLIND DATES

You may be romantically inclined on these dates, but it is best to avoid a blind date. The person could be a disappointment or you will not enjoy yourself. See Dating, page 142.

Jan.: 3, 9, 17-24, 30; Feb.: 8, 14, 16, 20, 22, 26-28; Mar.: 1, 2, 10, 11, 13, 16-24, 26; Apr.: 9, 10, 16, 22-24; May: 5-11, 13, 16, 19, 20, 24; Jun.: 3, 8, 10, 15, 16, 21-24, 30; Jul.: 1, 6-8, 13-21, 28, 31; Aug.: 1-3, 7, 9, 10, 14, 15, 23, 24, 30; Sep.: 2-6, 14, 20-27, 29, 30; Oct.: 1-3, 6, 11-15, 17, 18, 22, 24, 25, 30; Nov.: 6, 12-15, 20, 21, 27; Dec.: 6, 11, 14, 18, 19-24.

AVOID: BUYING OR WEARING CLOTHING
(FOR THE FIRST TIME)

Clothing should not be purchased or first worn on any of the following dates. See Buying: Clothes, page 123.

Jan.: 1, 2, 20-22, 27-29; Feb.: 17-19, 23-25; Mar.: 16-18, 22-25; Apr.: 13-15, 19-21; May: 10-12, 16-18; Jun.: 6-8, 13-15; Jul.: 3-6, 10-12, 31; Aug.: 1, 2, 6-8, 27-29; Sep.: 2-4, 24-26, 30; Oct.: 1, 2, 21-23, 27-29; Nov.: 17-19, 24-26; Dec.: 14-17, 21-23.

AVOID: BUYING OR WEARING SHOES, BOOTS,
SNEAKERS OR SLIPPERS (FOR THE FIRST TIME)

Do not buy or wear shoes, boots, sneakers or slippers (for the first time) on any of the following dates because problems are likely to develop with your feet or toes. For the best dates to break in new shoes, boots, sneakers or slippers see Shoes, Boots, Sneakers, Slippers: Wear For The First Time, page 193.

Jan.: 5, 6, 12, 13, 19, 20, 25, 26; Feb.: 1, 2, 9, 16, 22; Mar.: 1, 8, 9, 15, 16, 21, 22, 28, 29; Apr.: 5, 12, 18, 24, 25; May: 2, 3, 9, 15, 16, 22, 29, 30; Jun.: 5, 6, 11, 12, 18, 19, 26; Jul.: 2, 3, 9, 15, 16, 23, 30; Aug.: 5, 11, 12, 19, 20, 26, 27; Sep.: 1, 8, 15, 16, 22, 23, 29; Oct.: 5, 12, 13, 20, 26; Nov.: 1, 2, 9, 16, 23, 29; Dec.: 6, 7, 14, 20, 26, 27.

AVOID CONTRACTS (DRAWING OR SIGNING)

Do not draw up or sign a contract, agreement, document, paper or lease on any of the following dates because a problem could later occur with it. See Contracts: Draw/Sign, page 141.

Jan.: 1-4, 6-8, 11-14, 20-24, 27-31; Feb.: 1-3, 13, 19-23, 27, 28; Mar.: 1-27, 29-31; Apr.: 1-4, 9-13, 17, 19, 24, 27-30; May: 1-4, 10, 18, 26-31; Jun.: 1, 2, 11, 15-20, 26-30; Jul.: 1, 3-31; Aug.: 1, 6, 13, 15-17, 22, 24-29; Sep.: 2-8, 14, 20-28; Oct.: 5-8, 13, 15, 22-26, 31; Nov.: 1-25; Dec.: 2, 10, 12, 17-25.

AVOID: CUTTING CLOTH

Cloth should not be cut on any of the following dates. See Cloth Cutting, page 138.

Jan.: 21, 22; Feb.: 17-19; Mar.: 16-18; Apr.: 13-15; May: 10-12; Jun.: 6-8; Jul.: 3-5, 31; Aug.: 1, 2, 27-29; Sep.: 24-26; Oct.: 21-23; Nov.: 17-19; Dec.: 14-17.

AVOID: CUTTING TIMBER

Timber should not be cut on any of the following dates. See Timber: Cutting, page 204.

Jan.: 1, 10, 11, 19, 28; Feb.: 6, 7, 16, 24; Mar.: 15, 23, 24; Apr.: 2, 11, 12, 20, 29, 30; May: 9, 17, 27; Jun.: 5, 14, 20; Jul.: 11, 20, 21, 30; Aug.: 7, 16, 17, 26; Sep.: 3, 13, 23; Oct.: 1, 10, 11, 20, 28; Nov.: 6, 7, 16, 24, 25; Dec.: 4, 13, 22, 31.

AVOID: DANGER
BOMBS, EATHRQUAKES, EXPLOSIVES, HURRICANES

Guard against assaults and all types of hazards (especially occupational) on the following dates. Dangerous sports and taking mad chances could attract catastrophes during these times. Earthquakes, volcanic eruptions, tornadoes and hurricanes could cause major disasters. Avoid behaving in a temperamental manner, lest this leads to fights or quarrels. Also be careful of overhanging objects that could fall, as well as bombs and explosives. Corrosive and mechanical dangers can be attracted on any of these dates. Watch out for insect attacks such as wasp and locusts. See Avoid: Accidents, page 109; see Avoid: Fires, page 112.

Jan.: 4, 6-8, 12, 17-23, 25, 26, 28-31; Feb.: 1-4, 8-15, 17, 23; Mar.: 3, 11, 16-24; Apr.: 1, 9, 15, 16, 22-30; May: 1-3, 7, 14, 21, 29; Jun.: 4, 11-21, 26, 27; Jul.: 4, 6-14, 17, 18, 25, 26; Aug.: 1, 8, 15, 23, 26-31; Sep.: 1-16, 21, 27; Oct.: 4, 12, 20, 22-29; Nov.: 1-8, 10, 17, 22-26; Dec.: 1, 9, 16, 22, 30.

AVOID: DEBTS

Do not borrow money or charge bills on any of the following dates because it will be difficult to pay it back. The worst days are underlined. To charge bills, see Credit: Applications, Purchases, page 142; see Money: Borrow or Lending, page 173

Jan.: 1-4, 21, 22, 24, 25-27, 29, 31; Feb.: 3, 21-23, 25, 26, 27, 28; Mar.: 1-5, 20-23, 25, 27-31; Apr.: 1, 4, 19, 21, 22, 23-28, 29; May: 1-3, 18, 19, 21-26, 28; Jun.: 2, 17-20, 22, 24-26, 27, 29, 30; Jul.: 1, 16, 17, 19, 22, 23, 24, 27-30; Aug.: 15, 16, 18, 19, 20, 21, 23-27, 28, 29; Sep.: 14-17, 19-26; Oct.: 16, 17, 22, 23, 25, 26; Nov.: 12, 16, 17, 18, 19, 22-24; Dec.: 12-14, 15, 16, 17, 19-21, 24, 25.

AVOID: DENTAL CLEANING

Do not have your teeth cleaned on these dates. See Dental Cleaning, page 143.

Jan.: 12-14, 21; Feb.: 8-10, 19; Mar.: 7-10, 20; Apr.: 3-6, 19; May: 1-3, 18, 28-31; Jun.: 17, 24-27; Jul.: 16, 22-24; Aug.: 15, 18-21; Sep.: 14-17; Oct.: 12-14; Nov.: 8-10, 12; Dec.: 5-8, 12.

AVOID: DENTAL WORK
BONDINGS, BRACES, BRIDGES, CAPS, EXTRACTIONS,
FILLINGS, PLATE IMPRESSIONS, RECONSTRUCTION
OR ROOT CANAL, SURGERY AND X-RAYS

Do not have dental work such as bondings, braces, bridges, caps, extractions, fillings, plate impressions, or reconstruction, root canal, surgery or X-rays on any of the following days. Problems such as hemorrhaging, acute pain, caps or false teeth that do not fit or slow healing could result if performed on these dates. See Avoid: Dental Cleaning (preceding category); see Avoid Surgery (gums), page 114; see Dental Cleaning, Extraction, Work, page 143; see Surgery (gums), page 198.

Jan.: 5, 11-15, 20-22; Feb.: 4, 7-11, 18-20; Mar.: 6-11, 19-21; Apr.: 3-6, 18-20; May: 1-5, 17-19, 28-31; Jun.: 3, 16-18, 24-28; Jul.: 2, 15-17, 21-25, 31; Aug.: 14-22, 30; Sep.: 13-17, 28; Oct.: 12-15, 27; Nov.: 7-13, 26; Dec.: 4-9, 11-13, 26.

AVOID: EAR PIERCING

Avoid having your ears pierced on any of these dates; also see Avoid: Surgery (Ears), page 114. For the best day to have your ears pierced, see Ear Piercing, page 145.

Jan.: 5, 13-16, 20-22; Feb.: 4, 9-13, 18-20; Mar.: 6, 9-13, 19-21; Apr.: 5-9, 18, 19; May: 2-6, 17-19, 30, 31; Jun.: 1-3, 16-18, 26-29; Jul.: 2, 15-17, 23-27, 31;

Aug.: 14-16, 20-24, 30; Sep.: 13-20, 28; Oct.: 12-17, 27; Nov.: 9-13, 26; Dec.: 7-13, 26.

AVOID: EATING SUGAR AND STARCHES

These are the dates you should avoid eating sweets and starches.

Jan.: 15, 17-22, 25, 26; Feb.: 11, 12, 22, 26-28; Mar.: 1, 2, 11, 21; Apr.: 7, 13-18; May: 7-11, 15, 31; Jun.: 1, 11, 12, 21-24, 28; Jul.: 9, 18-21, 25, 26, 31; Aug.: 1-3, 5, 11, 21, 22; Sep.: 1-5, 18, 29, 30; Oct.: 1, 2, 11-15, 26; Nov.: 11-15, 22, 23; Dec.: 9, 19-23.

AVOID: FALLS

Falls can be attracted easily on any of the following dates; thus, use caution. See Avoid: Accidents, page 109.

Jan.: 6, 12, 13, 17-23, 25, 26, 28-31; Feb.: 1-4, 8-15, 26; Mar.: 1, 9, 24, 26, 28; Apr.: 9, 22-29; May: 1-3, 19, 22, 29, 30; Jun.: 11-21, 25, 26, 30; Jul.: 6-14, 28; Aug.: 7, 9, 12, 24; Sep.: 5, 6, 8-16, 20, 21; Oct.: 5, 12, 18, 20, 22-30; Nov.: 1-9, 14, 22-26; Dec.: 6, 7, 11, 24.

AVOID: FIRES

Use extra safety precautions on these dates, thus avoiding the chance of fire. See Avoid: Accidents, page 109.

Jan.: 4, 6-8, 12, 17-23, 25, 26, 28-31; Feb.: 1-4, 8-15, 17, 23; Mar.: 3, 11, 16-24; Apr.: 1, 9, 15, 16, 22-30; May: 1-3, 7, 14, 21, 29; Jun.: 4, 11-21, 26, 27; Jul.: 4, 6-14, 17, 18, 25, 26; Aug.: 1, 8, 15, 23, 26-31; Sep.: 1-16, 21, 27; Oct.: 4, 12, 20, 22-29; Nov.: 1-8, 10, 17, 22-26; Dec.: 1, 9, 16, 22, 30.

AVOID: GOSSIP

If you gossip on these days it will spread quickly, be misinterpreted and hurt another person; thus, avoid gossiping.

Jan.: 12, 13, 17-20; Feb.: 9, 13-16; Mar.: 8, 9, 13-16; Apr.: 9-13, 17; May: 6-10; Jun.: 5, 16; Jul.: 3, 13; Aug.: 9, 10; Sep.: 2, 5-7; Oct.: 3, 12, 30; Nov.: 5, 27; Dec.: 7, 10, 11.

AVOID: HAIR TRANSPLANTS

Avoid having hair transplants on these dates.

Jan.: 5, 12-14, 21; Feb.: 4, 8-10, 19; Mar.: 6-10, 20; Apr.: 3-6, 19; May: 1-4, 18, 28-31; Jun.: 3, 17, 24-27; Jul.: 2, 16, 22-24, 31; Aug.: 15, 18-21, 30; Sep.: 14-17, 28; Oct.: 12-14, 27; Nov.: 8-10, 12, 26; Dec.: 5-8, 12, 26.

AVOID: HARVESTING

If root crops are dug on any of these dates they will "sweat", become soggy and show rot. See Harvesting, page 157.

Jan.: 1, 10, 11, 19, 28; Feb.: 6, 7, 16, 24; Mar.: 15, 23, 24; Apr.: 2, 11, 12, 20, 29, 30; May: 9, 17, 27; Jun.: 5, 14, 20; Jul.: 11, 20, 21, 30; Aug.: 7, 16, 17, 26; Sep.: 3, 13, 23; Oct.: 1, 10, 11, 20, 28; Nov.: 6, 7, 16, 24, 25; Dec.: 4, 13, 22, 31.

AVOID: HIRING EMPLOYEES

Do not hire anyone on the following dates because either a problem will occur or the person will not remain on the job for any length of time. See Job: Hiring Employees, pages 163 and 164.

Jan.: 1, 2, 5, 14, 21, 27-29; Feb.: 4, 12, 19, 23-26; Mar.: 5-28; Apr.: 5, 12, 19-21, 26; May: 4, 11, 16-18, 26; Jun.: 3, 10, 13-15, 17, 25; Jul.: 2, 7-31; Aug.: 6-8, 15, 23, 30; Sep.: 2-5, 14, 21, 28, 30; Oct.: 1, 2, 5, 13, 21, 27-29, 31; Nov.: 1-19, 24-26; Dec.: 4, 12, 18, 21-23, 26.

AVOID: MAKING IMPORTANT DECISIONS

There is too much confusion and communication with others appears to be chaotic; thus, misunderstandings and misinterpretations are likely to occur. You may be indecisive because everything seems to be up in the air or subject to change; therefore, avoid making important decisions on any of these dates.

Jan.: 6-8, 11-14, 20-24, 27; Feb.: 13, 20-23, 27, 28; Mar.: 5-27; Apr.: 9-13, 17, 24, 30; May: 1-4, 10, 18, 26-30; Jun.: 11, 15-20, 27; Jul.: 3-31; Aug.: 1, 6, 13, 15-17, 22; Sep.: 2-8, 14, 20-23, 25-28; Oct.: 5-8, 15, 23, 31; Nov.: 1-19; Dec.: 2, 10, 17-21.

AVOID: MANICURES

Do not cut ingrown fingernails on the following dates. The worst dates are underlined. See Manicures, page 170.

Jan.: 1-3, 4, 21-24, 25, 26, 27-31; Feb.: 1, 2, 3, 19-21, 22, 23, 24-28; Mar.: 1, 2, 3, 4, 5, 20, 21, 22, 23, 24, 25-27, 28, 29, 30, 31; Apr.: 1, 2-4, 19-21, 22, 23, 24, 25, 26-29, 30; May: 1, 2, 3, 18-20, 21, 22, 23-28, 29, 30, 31; Jun.: 1, 2, 17, 18, 19, 20-25, 26, 27, 28, 29, 30; Jul.: 1, 16-18, 19-22, 23, 24, 25-30; Aug.: 15, 16-18, 19, 20, 21, 22, 23-27, 28, 29; Sep.: 14, 15, 16, 17, 18, 19-23, 24-26, 27; Oct.: 13, 14, 15, 16-20, 21-25, 26; Nov.: 12, 13-17, 18-22, 23, 24, 25; Dec.: 12, 13, 14, 15, 16, 17-19, 20, 21, 22, 23-25.

AVOID: MOVING

Do not move on any of the following dates because confusion results, objects or personal property is lost, stolen or damaged, or other difficulties are encountered. See Moving, page 174.

Jan.: 1, 2, 27-29; Feb.: 23-25; Mar.: 22-25; Apr.: 19-21; May: 16-18; Jun.: 13-15; Jul.: 10-12; Aug.: 6-8; Sep.: 2-4, 30; Oct.: 1, 2, 27-29; Nov.: 24-26; Dec.: 21-23.

AVOID: NUCLEAR POWER AREAS

The following dates are the most likely days when nuclear power plants could have leakage of chemicals or radioactive materials.

Jan.: 13, 20, 26, 28-31; Feb.: 1-4, 10, 16, 22; Mar.: 1, 2, 9, 16, 22; Apr.: 5, 10-16, 18-30; May: 1-23, 30; Jun.: 5, 6, 12-20, 26; Jul.: 3, 9, 12-16, 18-21, 23, 24, 30, 31; Aug.: 1, 5, 20, 27; Sep.: 2, 16, 23, 25-30; Oct.: 1, 2, 10-15, 20, 26, 27; Nov.: 1-10, 16, 17, 23; Dec.: 7, 14, 19-31.

AVOID: PEDICURES

Do not cut ingrown toenails on the following dates. The worst dates are under-lined. See Manicures and Pedicures, page 170.

Jan.: 1-3, <u>4</u>, 21-24, <u>25</u>, <u>26</u>, 27-31; Feb.: <u>1</u>, <u>2</u>, 3, 19-21, <u>22</u>, <u>23</u>, 24-28; Mar.: <u>1</u>, 2, <u>3</u>, 4, <u>5</u>, 20, <u>21</u>, <u>22</u>, 23, <u>24</u>, 25-27, <u>28</u>, <u>29</u>, 30, 31; Apr.: <u>1-3</u>, 4 19-21, <u>22</u>, 23, 24, <u>25</u>, 26, 27, <u>28-30</u>; May: <u>1-3</u>, 18-20, <u>21</u>, <u>22</u>, 23-25, <u>26-30</u>, 31; Jun.: 1, 2, 17, <u>18</u>, <u>19</u>, 20, 21, <u>22-24</u>, 25, <u>26</u>, <u>27</u>, 28-30; Jul.: 1, <u>16-23</u>, 24, <u>25</u>, <u>26</u>, 27-29, <u>30</u>; Aug.: <u>15-20</u>, 21, 22, <u>23</u>, 24, 25, <u>26</u>, <u>27</u>, 28, 29; Sep.: <u>14-16</u>, 17-20, <u>21-23</u>, 24-26, <u>27</u>; Oct.: <u>13</u>, 14-19, <u>20</u>, 21-25, <u>26</u>; Nov.: 12-15, <u>16</u>, <u>17</u>, 18-22, <u>23</u>, <u>24</u>, 25; Dec.: 12, 13, <u>14</u>, 15, <u>16</u>, 17-19, <u>20</u>, 21, <u>22</u>, 23-25.

AVOID: SCHEMES

On the following dates be on guard for con artists, phonies and get-rich-quick schemes. See Computer: Fraud, page 140.

Jan.: 1-20, 24, 30. Feb.: 14, 20, 26, 27; Mar.: 13, 19, 20, 26; Apr.: 9, 10, 16, 22-29; May: 7, 13, 19, 20, 28-31; Jun.: 1-25, 30; Jul.: 1, 6, 7, 13, 14, 28; Aug.: 3, 9, 10, 24, 30, 31; Sep.: 1-28; Oct.: 3, 17, 18, 24, 25, 30; Nov.: 12-15, 20, 21, 27; Dec.: 5-9, 11, 18, 19-21, 24.

AVOID: STRIKES

If you strike on any of the following dates it will last a long time. The <u>underlined</u> dates are when both sides will be stubborn, and thus, reach a stalemate. See Strikes, page 198.

Jan.: <u>1</u>, 2-4, <u>8</u>, <u>15</u>, 21-27, <u>28</u>, 29-31; Feb.: 1-3, <u>11</u>, <u>12</u>, <u>18</u>, 19-23, <u>24</u>, 25-28; Mar.: 1, 2, <u>3</u>, <u>4</u>, 5-10, <u>11</u>, 12-16, <u>17</u>, 18-22, <u>23</u>, <u>24</u>, 25-29, <u>30</u>, <u>31</u>; Apr.: 1-4, <u>7</u>, <u>14</u>, 19, <u>20</u>, 21-26, <u>27</u>, 28-30; May: 1-3, <u>11</u>, <u>17</u>, 18-23, <u>24</u>, <u>25</u>, 26-30, <u>31</u>; Jun.: <u>1</u>, 2, 17-19, <u>20</u>, <u>21</u>, 22-27, <u>28</u>, 29, 30; Jul.: 1, <u>4</u>, <u>5</u>, 7-10, <u>11</u>, 12-17, <u>18</u>, 19-24, <u>25</u>, <u>26</u>, 27-30; Aug.: <u>1</u>, <u>7</u>, <u>14</u>, 15-20, <u>21</u>, <u>22</u>, 23-27, <u>28</u>, 29; Sep.: <u>3</u>, <u>10</u>, <u>11</u>, 14-17, <u>18</u>, 19-24, <u>25</u>, 26, 27; Oct.: <u>1</u>, <u>7</u>, <u>8</u>, 13, 14, <u>15</u>, 16-21, <u>22</u>, 23-26, <u>28</u>, 31; Nov.: 1-3, <u>4</u>, 5-10, <u>11</u>, 12-17, <u>18</u>, 19-23, <u>24</u>, <u>25</u>; Dec.: <u>1</u>, <u>2</u>, <u>9</u>, 12-14, <u>15</u>, <u>16</u>, 17-21, <u>22</u>, 23-25, <u>29</u>.

AVOID: SURGERY

Do not have an operation on any of the following dates if the surgery is to be per-formed on any of the following regions of the body: The brain (upper hemisphere); brow, cerebrum, cheeks, eyelids, eyes, face, forehead, gums, head, jaw (upper), lips, mouth, nose, teeth (upper). The worst dates for operations are <u>underlined</u>. For the best days for surgery in these are as, see page 198.

Jan.: <u>5</u>, 9, 10, <u>11-14</u>, 15, 16, <u>21</u>; Feb.: <u>4</u>, 5-7, <u>8-10</u>, 11-13, <u>19</u>; Mar.: 5, <u>6-10</u>, 11, 12, <u>20</u>; Apr.: 1, 2, <u>3-6</u>, 7, 8, <u>19</u>, 28-30; May: <u>1-4</u>, 5, <u>18</u>, 26, 27, <u>28-31</u>; Jun.: 1, 2, <u>3</u>, <u>17</u>, 22, 23, <u>24-27</u>, 28, 29; Jul.: <u>2</u>, <u>16</u>, 19-21, <u>22-24</u>, 25-27, <u>31</u>; Aug.: <u>15</u>, 16, 17, <u>18-21</u>, 22, 23, <u>30</u>; Sep.: 12, 13, <u>14-17</u>, 18, 19, <u>28</u>; Oct.: 9-11, <u>12-14</u>, 15, 16, <u>27</u>; Nov.: <u>5-10</u>, 11, <u>12</u>, 13, <u>26</u>; Dec.: 3-10, <u>12</u>, <u>26</u>.

AVOID: SURGERY

Do not have an operation on any of the following dates if the surgery is to be performed on any of the following regions of the body: The blood vessels (of the carotid arteries), brain (base, lower lobes), carotid arteries, cerebellum, ears, jaw (lower), larynx, neck (and its bony structure), occipital region (bone), palate, pharynx, teeth (lower), throat, thyroid gland, tonsils, vein (jugular), vocal cords. The worst dates for operations are underlined. For the best dates for surgery in these areas, see page 198.

Jan.: 5, 11, 12, 13, 14-16, 17, 18, 21; Feb.: 4, 8, 9, 10-13, 14, 15, 19; Mar.: 6, 7-9, 10, 11, 12-14, 20; Apr.: 3, 4, 5-8, 9, 10, 19; May: 1, 2, 3-5, 6-8, 18, 28-30, 31; Jun.: 1-3, 4, 17, 24-30; Jul.: 1, 2, 16, 22, 23, 24-29, 31; Aug.: 15, 18-20, 21-23, 24, 25, 30; Sep.: 14, 15, 16, 17-19, 20-22, 28; Oct.: 12, 13-16, 17-19, 27; Nov.: 8, 9, 10-13, 14, 15, 26; Dec.: 5-7, 8-10, 11, 12, 26.

AVOID: SURGERY

Do not have an operation on any of the following dates if the surgery is to be performed on any of the following regions of the body: The arms, bronchi (bronchial tubes), clavicle (collarbone), fingers, hands, lungs (upper lobes), nervous system (central), respiratory system (upper), ribs, shoulders and shoulder blades, windpipe, wrists. The worst dates for operations are underlined. For the best days for surgery in these areas, see page 199.

Jan.: 5, 14, 15, 16-18, 19, 20, 21; Feb.: 4, 10-12, 13-15, 16, 17, 19; Mar.: 6, 10, 11, 12-14, 15, 16, 20; Apr.: 5, 6, 7, 8-10, 11-13, 19; May: 3, 4-8, 9, 10, 18, 31; Jun.: 1, 2-4, 5, 6, 17, 27, 28, 29, 30; Jul.: 1, 2, 3, 16, 24-26, 27-29, 30, 31; Aug.: 15, 21, 22, 23-25, 26, 27, 30; Sep.: 14, 17, 18, 19-22, 23, 24, 28; Oct.: 13, 14, 15, 16-19, 20, 21, 27; Nov.: 10, 11, 12-15, 16, 17, 26; Dec.: 8, 9, 10-12, 13, 14, 26.

AVOID: SURGERY

Do not have an operation on any of the following dates if the surgery is to be performed on any of the following regions of the body: The breasts, diaphragm, digestive organs, lacteals (lymph carrying vessels), lungs (lower lobes), respiratory system (lower), stomach, womb (belly). The worst dates are underlined. For the best days for surgery in these areas, see page 199.

Jan.: 5, 16, 17, 18-21, 22; Feb.: 4, 13, 14, 15-17, 18, 19; Mar.: 6, 12, 13, 14-16, 17, 18, 20; Apr.: 5, 8, 9, 10-13, 14, 15, 19; May: 4, 5-7, 8-10, 11, 12, 18; Jun.: 2, 3-6, 7, 8, 17, 29, 30; Jul.: 1-3, 4-6, 16, 27, 28, 29-31; Aug.: 1, 2, 15, 23, 24, 25-27, 28, 29, 30; Sep.: 14, 19-21, 22-24, 25, 26, 28; Oct.: 13, 16-18, 19-21, 22, 23, 27; Nov.: 12, 13, 14, 15-17, 18, 19, 26; Dec.: 10, 11, 12-14, 15-17, 26.

AVOID: SURGERY

Do not have an operation on any of the following dates if the surgery is to be performed on any of the following regions of the body: The aorta, back, heart, spine (and the marrow and nerves of the spine), spleen. The worst dates for operations are underlined. For the best dates for surgery in these areas, see page 199.

Jan.: 5, 18, 19, 20-22, 23, 24; Feb.: 4, 15, 16, 17-19, 20, 21; Mar.: 6, 14, 15, 16-18, 19, 20; Apr.: 5, 10-12, 13-15, 16, 17; May: 4, 8, 9, 10-12, 13, 14, 18; Jun.: 3, 4, 5, 6-8, 9, 10, 17; Jul.: 1, 2-6, 7, 8, 16, 29, 30, 31; Aug.: 1, 2, 3, 4, 15, 25, 26,

27-30; Sep.: 14, 22, 23, 24-26, 27, 28; Oct.: 13, 19, 20, 21-23, 24, 25, 27; Nov.: 12, 15, 16, 17-19, 20, 21, 26; Dec.: 12, 13, 14-17, 18, 19, 26.

AVOID: SURGERY

Do not have an operation on any of the following dates if the surgery is to be performed on any of the following regions of the body: The abdominal region, appendix, bowels, ,chylification, colon, duodenum, gastro-intestinal system, intestinal canal tract, mesenteric glands, navel, peristaltic action of the bowels, pyloris glands, small intestines, umbilical cord. The worst dates for operations are underlined. For the best days for surgery in these areas, see page 200.

Jan.: 5, 20, 21-24, 25-27; Feb.: 4, 17, 18, 19-21, 22, 23; Mar.: 6, 16, 17, 18-20, 21, 22; Apr.: 5, 13, 14, 15-17, 18, 19; May: 4, 10, 11, 12-14, 15, 16, 18; Jun.: 3, 6, 7, 8-10, 11-13, 17; Jul.: 2, 3-5, 6-8, 9, 10, 16, 31; Aug.: 1, 2-4, 5, 6, 15; 27, 28, 29-31; Sep.: 1, 2, 14, 24, 25, 26-28, 29, 30; Oct.: 13, 21, 22, 23-25, 26, 27; Nov.: 12, 17, 18, 19-21, 22-24, 26; Dec.: 12, 14-16, 17-19, 20, 21, 26.

AVOID: SURGERY

Do not have an operation on any of the following dates if the surgery is to be performed on any of the following regions of the body: The fallopian tubes, internal generative (reproductive) organs, kidneys, lumbar area, ovaries, suprarenals, veins. The worst dates for operations are underlined. For the best days for surgery in these areas, see page 200.

Jan.: 1, 2, 5, 21, 22-29; Feb.: 4, 19, 20-25; Mar.: 6, 18, 19, 20, 21-25; Apr.: 5, 15-18, 19, 20, 21; May: 4, 12-17, 18; Jun.: 3, 8-15, 17; Jul.: 2, 6-12, 16, 31; Aug.: 2-8, 15, 29, 30, 31; Sep.: 1-4, 14, 26, 27, 28, 29, 30; Oct.: 1, 2, 13, 23-26, 27, 28, 29; Nov.: 12, 19-25, 26; Dec.: 12, 17-23, 26.

AVOID: SURGERY

Do not have an operation on any of the following dates if the surgery is to be performed on any of the following regions of the body: The bladder and gall bladder, excretory organs, external generative (reproductive) glands (penis, testicle, vagina), groin, inguinal region, kidneys (sinus or pelvic areas), nose and nasal bones, pelvis, perineum, prostrate gland, rectum, sigmoid flexure, spermatic cord, sphincter, ureter, uterus, urogenital orifice. The worst dates for operations are underlined. For the best days for surgery in these areas, see page 201.

Jan.: 1, 2-4, 5, 21, 24-26, 27-29, 30, 31; Feb.: 4, 19, 21, 22, 23-25, 26-28; Mar.: 6, 20, 21, 22-25, 26, 27; Apr.: 5, 17, 18, 19-21, 22, 23; May: 4, 14, 15, 16, 17, 18, 19-21; Jun.: 3, 10-12, 13-15, 16, 17; Jul.: 2, 8, 9, 10-12, 13, 14, 16, 31; Aug.: 4, 5, 6-8, 9-11, 15, 30, 31; Sep.: 1, 2-4, 5-7, 14, 28, 29, 30; Oct.: 1, 2-4, 13, 25, 26, 27-29, 30, 31; Nov.: 12, 21-23, 24-26, 27, 28; Dec.: 12, 19, 20, 21-23, 24, 25, 26.

AVOID: SURGERY

Do not have an operation on any of the following dates if the surgery is to be performed on the following regions of the body: The buttocks, femur, gluteus, hips (locomotor muscles of the hips and thighs), ischium, legs (above the knees), liver, pancreas, sciatic nerve, sartorius, thighs, lumbar. The worst dates for operations are underlined. For the best days for surgery on these areas, see page 201.

Jan.: 1, 2-5, 6, 7, 21, 27, 28, 29-31; Feb.: 1-3, 4, 19, 23, 24, 25-28; Mar.: 1, 2, 6, 20, 22-24, 25-27, 28, 29; Apr.: 5, 19-23, 24-26; May: 4, 16, 17, 18-21, 22, 23; Jun.: 3, 13, 14, 15-17, 18, 19; Jul.: 2, 10, 11, 12-14, 15, 16, 17, 31; Aug.: 6, 7, 8-11, 12, 13, 15, 30; Sep.: 2, 3, 4-7, 8, 9, 14, 28, 30; Oct.: 1, 2-4, 5, 6, 13, 27, 28, 29-31; Nov.: 1-3, 12, 24, 25, 26-28, 29, 30; Dec.: 12, 13, 21-23, 24, 25, 26, 27, 28.

AVOID: SURGERY

Do not have an operation on any of the following dates if the surgery is to be performed on the bones, bony-skeleton-framework of the body, cartilages, joints, kneecaps, knees, teeth (bone and bone-like structure part of the teeth). The worst dates for operations are underlined. For the best days for surgery on these areas, see page 201.

Jan.: 2, 3, 4-7, 8, 9, 21, 29, 30, 31; Feb.: 1-4, 19, 25-27, 28; Mar.: 1, 2, 3-5, 6, 20, 25, 26, 27-29, 30, 31; Apr.: 1, 5, 19, 21, 22, 23-26, 27, 28; May: 4, 18, 19, 20, 21-23, 24-26; Jun.: 3, 15, 16, 17-19, 20-22; Jul.: 2, 12, 13, 14-17, 18, 19, 31; Aug.: 8-10, 11-13, 14, 15, 30; Sep.: 4-6, 7-9, 10-12, 14, 28; Oct.: 2, 3, 4-6, 7-9, 13, 27, 29, 30, 31; Nov.: 1-3, 4, 5, 12, 26, 27, 28-30; Dec.: 1-3, 12, 23, 24, 25-28, 29, 30.

AVOID: SURGERY

Do not have an operation on any of the following dates if the surgery is to be performed on the Achilles tendon, ankles, calves, circulation, legs (below the knees), shins. The worst dates for operations are underlined. For the best days for surgery on these areas, see page 202.

Jan.: 4, 5, 6, 7-9, 10-12, 21, 31; Feb.: 1, 2, 3-5, 6-8, 19, 28; Mar.: 1, 2-6, 7, 20, 27, 28, 29-31; Apr.: 1, 2, 3, 5, 19, 24, 25, 26-28, 29, 30; May: 1, 4, 18, 21, 22, 23-26, 27, 28; Jun.: 3, 17, 18, 19-22, 23, 24; Jul.: 2, 14, 15, 16-19, 20-22, 31; Aug.: 11, 12, 13-15, 16-18, 30; Sep.: 7, 8, 9-12, 13, 14, 28; Oct.: 4, 5, 6-9, 10-12, 14, 27, 31; Nov.: 1, 2, 3-5, 6-8, 12, 26, 28, 29, 30; Dec.: 1-3, 4, 5, 12, 25, 26, 27, 28-30, 31.

AVOID: SURGERY

Do not have an operation on any of the following dates if the surgery is to be performed on the feet, metatarsus, phalanges, plantaris, tarsus, toes. The worst date for operations are underlined. For the best days for surgery on these areas, see page 202.

Jan.: <u>5</u>, 7, 8, <u>9-12</u>, 13, 14, <u>21</u>; Feb.: 3, <u>4-8</u>, 9, 10, <u>19</u>; Mar.: 2-4, <u>5-7</u>, 8-10, <u>20</u>, 29-31; Apr.: <u>1-3</u>, 4, <u>5</u>, 6, <u>19</u>, 27, <u>28-30</u>; May: <u>1</u>, 2, 3, <u>4</u>, <u>18</u>, 23-25, <u>26-28</u>, 29-31; Jun.: <u>3</u>, <u>17</u>, 19-21, <u>22-24</u>, 25-27; Jul.: <u>2</u>, <u>16</u>, 17, 18, <u>19-22</u>, 23, 24, <u>31</u>; Aug.: 13, 14, <u>15-18</u>, 19-21, <u>30</u>; Sep.: 9-11, <u>12-14</u>, 15-17, <u>28</u>; Oct.: 6-8, <u>9-13</u>, 14, <u>27</u>; Nov.: 3, 4, <u>5-8</u>, 9, 10, <u>12</u>, <u>26</u>, 30; Dec.: 1, 2, <u>3-5</u>, 6-8, <u>12</u>, <u>26</u>, 28, 29, <u>30</u>, <u>31</u>.

AVOID: TERRORIST ATTACKS

These are the dates when terrorist attacks are most likely to occur:
Jan.: 13, 20, 26, 28-31; Feb.: 1-4, 10, 16, 22; Mar.: 1, 2, 9, 16, 22; Apr.: 5, 10-16, 18-30; May: 1-23, 30; Jun.: 5, 6, 12-20, 26; Jul.: 3, 9, 12-16, 18-21, 23, 24, 30, 31; Aug.: 1, 5, 20, 27; Sep.: 2, 16, 23, 25-30; Oct.: 1, 2, 10-15, 20, 26, 27; Nov.: 1-10, 16, 17, 23; Dec.: 7, 14, 19-31.

AVOID: THEFT

Use extra caution on these dates to protect yourself against muggings, robberies or theft, including car-jacking and car theft.
Jan.: 13, 20, 26, 28-31; Feb.: 1-4, 10, 16, 22; Mar.: 1, 2, 9, 16, 22; Apr.: 5, 10-16, 18-30; May: 1-23, 30; Jun.: 5, 6, 12-20, 26; Jul.: 3, 9, 12-16, 18-21, 23, 24, 30, 31; Aug.: 1, 5, 20, 27; Sep.: 2, 16, 23, 25-30; Oct.: 1, 2, 10-15, 20, 26, 27; Nov.: 1-10, 16, 17, 23; Dec.: 7, 14, 19-31.

AVOID: TRAVEL BY AIR

Travel by air should be avoided on these dates. This includes hot air balloons, gliders, helicopters or parachutes.
Jan.: 1-26; Feb.: 1, 2, 6, 14-18; Mar.: 7-12, 14, 15; Apr.: 4, 5, 7-11, 13, 14, 22-30; May: 2-6, 12, 15, 16, 27-31; Jun.: 1-25; Jul.: 8, 16-19, 28; Aug.: 5, 6, 14, 15, 30, 31; Sep.: 1-28; Oct.: 12, 14-17, 19-22, 30, 31; Nov.: 10, 12-15, 19, 20, 26-29; Dec.: 5-15, 18-21.

AVOID: TRAVEL BY LAND

Travel by bus, cable car, car, motorcycle, street car, train, trailer, tram, RV (recreation vehicle), truck or van should be avoided on these dates. See Travel: By Land, page 204.
Jan.: 4, 6-8, 12, 17-23, 25, 26, 28-31; Feb.: 1-4, 8-15, 17, 23; Mar.: 3, 11, 16-24; Apr.: 1, 9, 15, 16, 22-30; May: 1-3, 7, 14, 21, 29; Jun.: 4, 11-21, 26, 27; Jul.: 4, 6-14, 17, 18, 25, 26; Aug.: 1, 8, 15, 23, 26-31; Sep.: 1-16, 21, 27; Oct.: 4, 12, 20, 22-29; Nov.: 1-10, 17, 22-26; Dec.: 1, 9, 16, 22, 30.

AVOID: TRAVEL BY WATER

Travel on a boat, sailboat, ship, yacht, etc. should be avoided on the following dates. See Travel: By Water, page 205.
Jan.: 3-22, 24, 28-31; Feb.: 1-4, 8-15, 20, 26, 27; Mar.: 1, 3, 13, 19, 20, 26; Apr.: 9, 10, 16, 22-29; May: 7, 13, 19, 20, 28-31; Jun.: 1-25, 30; Jul.: 1, 6-14, 28; Aug.: 3, 9, 10, 24, 30, 31; Sep.: 1-27; Oct.: 3, 17, 18, 24, 25, 30; Nov.: 1-8, 12-15, 20-27; Dec.: 5-9, 11, 18-21, 24.

BAKING

Baking progresses best if done on any of the following dates. However, food baked on the <u>underlined</u> days will rise better than food which is prepared on the other dates. The preceding includes baking in kilns, microwaves and ovens.

Jan.: 6, 13, 19, <u>25</u>, <u>26</u>; Feb.: <u>1</u>, <u>2</u>, 9, 16, <u>22</u>; Mar.: <u>1</u>, 8, 9, 15, <u>21</u>, <u>28</u>; Apr.: <u>4</u>, 11, 12, 18, <u>24</u>, <u>25</u>; May: <u>2</u>, 9, 15, <u>22</u>, <u>29</u>, <u>30</u>; Jun.: 5, 11, 12, <u>18</u>, <u>25</u>, <u>26</u>; Jul.: 9, 15, <u>23</u>, <u>30</u>; Aug.: 5, 12, <u>19</u>, <u>20</u>, <u>26</u>; Sep.: 1, 8, <u>15</u>, <u>16</u>, <u>23</u>, 29; Oct.: 5, 12, <u>20</u>, <u>26</u>; Nov.: 1, 2, 9, <u>16</u>, <u>22</u>, <u>23</u>, 29; Dec.: 6, 7, <u>13</u>, <u>20</u>, 27.

BALLOONS: HOT-AIR RIDE

Have you been yearning to take a ride in a hot-air balloon? Have fun sailing through the air on these dates. See Avoid: Travel by Air, page 118.

Jan.: 27-29, 31; Feb.: 3-5, 7, 19, 21, 22, 24, 25, 28; Mar.: 1, 2, 4-6, 23, 28, 31; Apr.: 12, 20; May: 8, 9, 17, 22-25; Jun.: None; Jul.: 2, 23, 26, 30; Aug.: 7, 12, 22, 26; Sep.: 30; Oct.: 1, 2, 23, 27-29; Nov.: 1-9, 11, 16-18; Dec.: 13, 22, 29.

BANKERS

These dates are great for dealing with bankers during business hours or while socializing. The <u>underlined</u> days are when quick results are obtained.

Jan.: <u>8</u>, <u>15</u>, 30; Feb.: 3, <u>6-8</u>, <u>17</u>, <u>18</u>, 21; Mar.: 3, 4; Apr.: 1-4, <u>17</u>, 22, 27-29; May: <u>14</u>, 19, 20, 23-25, 27, 31; Jun.: 1, 2, <u>4</u>, 27-30; Jul.: 1; Aug.: <u>4</u>, <u>10</u>, <u>13</u>, <u>14</u>, 18, 21, 22, 24, 25, 28, 29; Sep.: None; Oct.: <u>3</u>, 16-19; Nov.: 22, <u>27</u>, <u>30</u>; Dec.: <u>2</u>, <u>3</u>, <u>10</u>, <u>11</u>, 13, 24, <u>28</u>, <u>30</u>.

BARBECUES, CLAMBAKES, LUAU'S

Are you in the mood for fun and good food? If so, go to a <u>luau</u> and feast on roasted pig and other victuals. Or go to a <u>clambake</u>, if you're near the seashore and picnic on clams, corn, and other foods baked in layers on buried hot stones. Or go to a <u>barbecue</u> and eat grilled corn, meat or chicken roasted over <u>live</u> coals. Enjoy yourself on these dates.

Jan.: 2, 3, 15, 16, 27; Feb.: 5-7, 18, 21, 24-27; Mar.: 10, 12-14, 17, 26; Apr.: 2-4, 6, 7, 11; May: 5, 8, 10, 11-13, 17-20, 23, 24, 26, 31; Jun.: 1-3, 7, 24, 28, 29; Jul.: 5, 22, 24, 28, 31; Aug.: 6, 7, 9, 10, 21, 22, 25, 28, 29; Sep.: 6, 17-19, 24, 25, 28, 30; Oct.: 1-3, 10, 11, 14, 15, 17, 21, 30; Nov.: 11-15, 18, 19, 27; Dec.: 2-5, 10-13, 15, 19, 21, 23, 24.

BEAUTY APPOINTMENTS

Beautify yourself on these dates; you will like the results and so will everyone else. See Hair, pages 155-157; See Manicures and Pedicures, page 170; for cosmetic surgery, the operation should be performed on any of the best days listed for that part of the body on which surgery is to be performed, e.g., the Face, page 198. The Zones of the Body are found in Part One, under each of the 12 Zodiac signs, or see Surgery, pages 198-202.

Jan.: 1, 6, 15, 25-28, 30, 31; Feb.: 1-3, 11, 12, 14, 15, 17-21, 23-25; Mar.: 8, 12-14, 25-28; Apr.: 1-4, 7, 8, 10-15, 17-22, 26, 29; May: 2, 4, 10-15, 17-21, 27-31; Jun.: 1-4, 6, 12-14, 20, 26, 29; Jul.: 1, 3, 4, 6, 7, 9, 10, 19, 21, 26; Aug.: 5, 6, 9, 16, 20, 21, 31; Sep.: 1, 2, 7, 9-13, 15, 18, 20, 25, 27-30; Oct.: 1-4, 9, 10, 18-21, 23-27, 29; Nov.: 3, 8, 9, 11, 19, 22-30; Dec.: 1-5, 7-12, 18, 24, 28-31.

BEER BREWING
Try these date to brew your own beer.

Jan.: 2, 7, 10, 15, 17, 23, 28, 30, 31; Feb.: 4, 5, 7, 11, 12, 15, 20, 24, 28; Mar.: 1, 10-15, 17, 23, 24, 26, 29, 31; Apr.: 2, 3, 6-8, 11, 13, 16, 18, 20, 27, 30; May: 2, 5, 12, 13, 20, 26, 27, 31; Jun.: 1, 7, 9, 10, 14, 21, 23, 24, 28, 29; Jul.: 6-8, 12, 18, 20, 21, 24-26, 28, 30; Aug.: 3, 5, 7, 9, 10, 14, 16, 17, 21, 22, 26, 30; Sep.: 1, 3-10, 13, 18, 23, 27; Oct.: 1, 5, 10, 15, 17, 22, 24, 28, 30; Nov.: 4, 6, 7, 11, 14, 16, 19-21, 25, 27, 28; Dec.: 3, 4, 9, 13-20, 22, 27, 29, 31.

BODY PIERCING
Do you want toe rings? Or, perhaps, you are into ear, navel, nose, mouth or tongue piercing. For favorable dates to indulge in body piercing, see the area to be pierced listed under Surgery, pages 198-202. For unfavorable dates, see the area to be pierced under Avoid: Surgery, pages 114-117. See Ears: Pierced, page 145.

BOSSES: GOODWILL
Seek the goodwill of the boss on one of these dates. If quick results are desired, take action on the underlined days.

Jan.: 1-5, 8, 11, 16, 25; Feb.: 1-4, 6-10, 16-18, 23-28; Mar.: 3; Apr.: 6, 7, 10, 13-15, 17, 18, 20-22, 29; May: 7-9, 12-14, 23-26, 29-31; Jun.: 1, 5, 7, 12, 22, 25-27; Jul.: 5; Aug.: 1, 5-14, 16, 20, 28-30; Sep.: 1, 3-6, 8, 11-13, 19, 24, 25, 30; Oct.: 8, 11, 12, 14, 18, 22, 23; Nov.: 20, 21, 25-30; Dec.: 1-11, 13-16, 21, 23, 24, 26-28, 31.

BUDGET
Start to economize on any of the following dates. It is easy to stick to the budget if it is commenced on one of the underlined days.

Jan.: 6, 7, 8, 9-14, 15, 16-20; Feb.: 5-10, 11, 12, 13-17, 18; Mar.: None; Apr.: 5, 6, 7, 8-13, 14, 16; May: 5, 9, 10, 11, 13, 16, 17; Jun.: 4-6, 7, 8-13, 14, 15, 16; Jul.: 3, 4, 5, 6; Aug.: 1, 2-6, 7, 8-13, 14, 31; Sep.: 1, 2, 3, 4-9, 10, 11, 13; Oct.: 1, 3, 5, 10, 12, 28, 29-31; Nov.: 27-30; Dec.: 9, 10, 11, 27, 29, 30, 31.

BUILDING: CONSTRUCTION
To build a structure so it will better resist destruction, turn the first dirt or lay the cornerstone on any of the following days. If the building is begun on one of the underlined dates, the project will be finished quickly. This includes: apartment, casino, condo, hospital, house, inn, lodge, marina, medical, motel, office, restaurant, shopping mall, skyscraper, store. See Architectural Plans, page 107; see Buying: Headgear, Helmets, page 127; see Cement Poured, page 135; see Designing, page 143; see Roof, page 190.

Jan.: 8, 15; Feb.: 11, 18; Mar.: 3, 4, 30, 31; Apr.: 7, 14, 27; May: 24, 25, 31; Jun.: 1, 7, 20, 21, 28; Jul.: 4, 5; Aug.: 1, 14, 21, 22, 28; Sep: 10, 11, 18, 25; Oct.: 7, 8, 15, 22; Nov.: None; Dec.: 1, 2, 9, 15, 16, 29.

BUILDING: DEMOLITION, IMPLOSION
Wreck or destroy a building through using electrical or mechanical equipment on these dates. However, if explosives are used, especially with an implosion (building falling inwardly), the underlined dates are best.

Jan.: 22-28, 30; Feb.: 23-28; Mar.: 1, 21, 22; Apr.: 1-4, 27, 29, 30; May: 1, 2, 19-23, 24, 26, 30, 31; Jun.: 1, 2, 24, 29; Jul.: 22-26, 28, 30; Aug.: 21, 25-29; Sep.: 15-20, 23; Oct.: 14, 17, 22; Nov.: 13-15, 19, 25; Dec.: 13-17, 18-24, 25.

BUNION REMOVAL

Get relief and have that painful bunion removed on one of these dates. The preferred dates are underlined. However, if surgery is performed see Avoid: Surgery, page 117; also see Surgery, page 202.

Jan.: 23, 30; Feb.: 20, 26, 27; Mar.: 3, 4, 26, 30, 31; Apr.: 4, 22, 27; May: 2, 19, 20, 24, 25, 29, 30; Jun.: 20, 21, 25, 26, 30; Jul.: 18, 23, 28; Aug.: 19, 20, 24, 28; Sep.: 15, 16, 20, 21, 25-27; Oct.: 17, 18, 22-24; Nov.: 4, 18, 19, 20; Dec.: 15-18, 24.

BUSINESS: COMMENCE

Open your business on one of these dates to insure greater success. On these dates, the public will flock to your establishment and continue to patronize you. The best dates are underlined. The preceding involves all types of business such as: Accounting, Advertising, Body Building, Collection Agency, Employment Agency, Gym, Model Agency, Public Relations, Real Estate, Restaurant, School (acting, dancing, martial arts training, public, private, specialized, tutoring), Service Business, Tanning Salon, Theatrical Agency, Stores, (Department, Flower, Furniture, Deli, Grocery, Jewelry, Book, Dry Cleaning, Liquor, Music, Photography, Shoe). See Shows: Open, page 194.

Jan.: 6, 7, 8, 9, 10, 15-18; Feb.: 5, 6-8, 10, 11, 13-15, 17, 18; Mar.: None; Apr.: 6-11, 13-17; May: None; Jun.: 4, 7-9, 13, 14; Jul.: 4, 5; Aug.: 1-4, 6, 8-10, 13, 14, 31; Sep.: 2-4, 30; Oct.: 1, 2, 3, 4, 11, 28-30; Nov.: 27, 28, 30; Dec.: 1, 2, 3, 5, 8-10, 11.

BUSINESS: DEALS

Because communication is good, these dates are favorable to talk deals with others in business. The best dates are underlined. See Favors, page 149; see Projects and Propositions, pages 181, 182.

Jan.: 27, 28, 30; Feb.: 3, 4, 5, 6-8, 10, 15, 17, 18, 20, 21, 23-28; Mar.: 1-4; Apr.: 1-4, 17; May: 24-27, 31; Jun.: 1-4; Jul.: None; Aug.: 2-4, 6-10, 13, 14, 18, 21-25, 28-31; Sep.: 12, 13, 24, 30; Oct.: 1-3, 16-19, 21; Nov.: 20, 21, 22, 24-27, 28, 30; Dec.: 1-3, 10, 17.

BUSINESS: EXPAND

For large quarters, big profits and quick results, start to expand a business on one of these dates.

Jan.: 8, 10; Feb.: 6-8, 17, 18; Mar.: None; Apr.: 13-17; May: None; Jun.: 4, 7-9; Jul.: 4, 5; Aug.: 1-4, 6, 8-10, 13, 14, 31; Sep.: 2-4, 6, 7, 9-11, 13, 30; Oct.: 1, 3, 11; Nov.: 20-22, 24, 25, 27; Dec.: 2, 8-10.

BUST DEVELOPMENT

Start exercises to enlarge your bust on any of these dates. For the breasts to remain firm, commence bust development exercises on the underlined days, you'll find it easy to stick with the exercise program on these same dates.

Jan.: 8, 10, 11, 13, 14, 18-20; Feb.: 6-9, 16, 18; Mar.: 9, 15, 18, 19; Apr.: 11-13, 14, 15; May: 7-10, 11, 12, 16, 27; Jun.: 5, 7, 12, 14, 16; Jul.: 4, 5, 9, 11, 13; Aug.: 1, 5, 6, 7, 8-10, 14; Sep.: 1, 5, 6, 8, 10, 13, 29, 30; Oct.: 1, 3, 8, 10-12, 30, 31; Nov.: 2, 5-10, 11, 27; Dec.: 2, 4, 8, 9, 10, 27, 28, 30, 31.

BUYING ANTIQUES

Go shopping for antiques on these dates. If you are going to charge an antique, do so on the days below if it also appears on page 142 under

Credit Purchases.
  Jan.: 1-4, 7-10, 15, 16, 18, 27-31; Feb.: 3-7, 18-20; Mar.: 3-7, 10-14, 18-20,25-27, 31; Apr.: 1-4, 6-11, 14-16, 20-22, 24, 27, 29; May: 12, 13, 18-21, 24-26, 31; Jun.: 1-4, 7-10, 25, 27-30; Jul.: 1, 6, 18-22, 24-29; Aug.: 4, 7-10, 14, 18, 21-25, 29-31; Sep.: 9, 11-13, 18, 27; Oct.: 1, 3, 4, 9, 10, 15-19, 21, 30, 31; Nov.: 4-8,10, 11, 17, 19-21, 27, 28, 30; Dec.: 3, 9-12, 16, 17, 24, 29-31.

BUYING: AUTOMOBILES, MOTORCYCLES, TRUCKS, TRAILERS, VANS

  Purchase a vehicle on these dates; thus, enhancing your chances for satisfactory mechanical and electrical service. If you are going to charge these vehicles do so on the days below if they also appear on page 142 under Credit Purchases. See Avoid: Theft, page 118; see Insurance, page 162; see Repairs, Automobiles, page 187; see Sports Activities, page 196.
Jan.: 2-4, 8, 9, 30, 31; Feb.: 1, 3, 5-7, 16, 18, 20; Mar.: 3, 4, 31; Apr.: 1-4, 15, 18, 21, 22, 24, 27, 29; May: 1, 8, 12, 16, 19-22, 24-26; Jun.: 5, 7, 8, 12, 14, 21, 22, 25-27; Jul.: None; Aug.: 11, 23-27, 29; Sep.: 1, 7, 11, 12, 15, 22, 26; Oct.: 4, 9, 17, 19; Nov.: 20, 27-29; Dec.: 3, 10, 17, 24, 29-31.

BUYING: BALLOONS, AIR CONDITIONERS

  Buy balloons as a gift or for a party (etc.) or if you need to cool off, purchase an air conditioner also on any of these dates. If you are going to charge your purchase, do so if it also appears on page 142 under Credit Purchases.
Jan.: 4-16, 23, 25-29, 31; Feb.: 1-13, 15-19, 21-25, 28; Mar.: 1-12, 14, 15, 23, 28, 31; Apr.: 6-8, 11, 12, 20, 30; May: 2, 4-6, 8, 9, 15-17, 22-27, 31; Jun.: 1, 2, 4, 5, 11-15, 17, 18; Jul.: 2-5, 8-12, 16-19, 23, 26, 30; Aug.: 7, 12, 22, 26; Sep.: 18, 23; Oct.: 1, 5, 8, 14-16, 19-23, 26-29, 31; Nov.: 1-11, 25, 26, 28, 29; Dec.: 13, 22, 29.

BUYING: BARGAINS

  Go shopping on any of the following dates because bargains, good buys or sales are attracted. However, if you are going to charge anything, do so on the dates below if they also appear on page 142 under Credit Purchases.
Jan.: 27-31; Feb.: 3-6, 8, 10-13, 15, 17, 18, 24-28; Mar.: 2-5, 31; Apr.: 2, 3, 6-8, 20; May: 5, 10, 11, 17, 20, 21, 23-26; Jun.: 27-29; Jul.: 4, 5, 31; Aug.: 1, 2, 4, 6-10, 13, 14, 18, 21-23, 25, 28, 29; Sep.: None; Oct.: 1, 3, 14-17, 19, 21-24, 27-30; Nov.: 20, 25, 27, 28, 30; Dec.: 9-11, 15-18, 22, 23, 29, 31.

BUYING: CAMERAS

  Do you have the photography bug? Then buy a camera on one of these dates and click away! Buy a digital camera on the underlined dates. If you are going to charge it, do so on the dates below if it also appears on page 142 under Credit Purchases.
  Jan.: 4-16, 19-23, 25-29, 31; Feb.: 1-4, 5, 6, 7-9, 10-13, 15-19, 21, 23, 24, 25, 28; Mar.: 1-10, 11-15, 17-21, 23, 28, 31; Apr.: 2, 6-8, 9, 10, 11, 12, 20, 30; May: 2, 4-6, 8, 9, 15-17,22-27, 31; Jun.: 1, 2, 4-8, 11-15, 17-29; Jul.: 2-5, 8-12, 16-19, 23, 26, 30; Aug.: 7, 12, 16, 17, 22, 26; Sep.: 3, 4, 7, 9, 11-15, 17, 18, 19-22, 23; Oct.: 1, 5, 8, 10, 11, 14-16, 18, 19, 21, 22, 23, 26-29, 31; Nov.: 1-11, 12-14, 15-19, 25, 26, 28, 29, 30; Dec.: 1-3, 4-9, 12, 13, 18, 22, 29, 31.

BUYING: CD ROM, SOFTWARE, LASER PRINTER

Use for the first time CD Rom and software on these dates. The underlined dates are best for buying a Laser Printer. If you are going to charge any of these items do so on dates below if they also appear on page 142 under Credit Purchases.

Jan.: 1-4, 8, 9, 11, 16, 18, 28, 31; Feb.: 5, 6, 7, 9, 20, 21, 23, 24, 25, 27; Mar.: 1, 3, 4, 7, 11, 12-15, 17-19, 21, 27; Apr.: 1-4, 8, 9, 15, 16, 18, 20, 24, 29, 30; May: 1, 2, 5, 8, 19-22, 24-27; Jun.: 1, 5, 7-10, 14, 21, 22, 24, 25, 29; Jul.: 2, 6, 11, 15, 20, 21, 26, 27, 29; Aug.: 2, 3, 7, 10, 11, 22, 25-27, 29-31; Sep.: 1, 4, 6, 7, 8, 9, 11, 12, 13, 15, 17, 18, 19, 20, 22, 26; Oct.: 1-4, 9, 12, 17, 18, 19, 21, 27; Nov.: 1, 6-8, 13, 14, 15, 20, 21, 28, 30; Dec.: 1, 2, 3, 4, 9, 10, 13, 17, 18, 22, 24, 25, 29-31.

BUYING: CLOCKS, WATCHES

Buy clocks on the following dates. The best dates to purchase a watch are on the underlined dates. If you are going to charge your purchase, do so if it also appears on page 142 under Credit Purchases.

Jan.: 9, 10, 15, 16, 24, 27-31; Feb.: 3-8, 10-15, 17, 18, 19, 20, 21, 23-28; Mar.: 2-5, 31; Apr.: 2, 3, 13, 14, 16, 20; May: 5, 10, 11, 13, 17, 20, 21, 23-28, 31; Jun.: 1-4, 7-10, 20-25, 27-30; Jul.: 1, 4, 5, 31; Aug.: 1-4, 6-10, 13-18, 21-25, 28-30, 31; Sep.: 5-7, 9, 10, 11, 13, 18, 27; Oct.: 1, 3, 14, 15, 16, 17, 18, 19, 21, 30; Nov.: 20, 21, 25, 27, 28, 30; Dec.: 9-12, 15-19, 22, 23, 29, 31.

BUYING: CLOTHES (CASUAL, SPORTSWEAR)

For casual clothing or sportswear (baseball, basketball, camping, climbing, exercise, football, jogging, skiing, swimwear, tennis, etc.) these dates are favorable to treat yourself to a new outfit. If you are going to charge your purchases, do so on the dates below if they also appear on page 142 under Credit Purchases. See Avoid: Buying Or Wearing Clothing, page 110.

Jan.: 13, 17-19, 23, 30, 31; Feb.: 1-3, 20; Mar.: 8, 13, 14, 19, 26; Apr.: 4, 12, 22; May: 2, 9, 13; Jun.: 20, 26; Jul.: 1, 7, 18, 29; Aug.: 9, 20, 24-26; Sep.: 5-7, 10, 11, 20, 27; Oct.: 3, 13, 20, 24; Nov.: 9, 14, 15, 30; Dec.: 1, 2, 6, 18, 24, 28, 29.

BUYING: CLOTHES (GLAMOROUS, LINGERIE, SEXY)

Do you want something glamorous to wear for a night out on the town? Go dancing or to clubs, galas, banquets or parties by buying fantastic clothing on these dates. Lingerie shopping is favored, also, on these dates. Night Wear (Peignoir, teddie, sexy nightgown or sleep wear) also is favored to buy on these days. If you are going to charge your purchases, do so on the date below if they also appear on page 142 under Credit Purchases. See Avoid: Buying Or Wearing Clothing, page 110; see Buy: Tuxedo, page 133.

Jan.: 10, 11, 15; Feb.: 6, 7, 11, 12; Mar.: 11; Apr.: 2, 7, 29; May: 4, 15, 27; Jun.: 1, 28; Jul.: 20, 21, 26; Aug.: 5, 16, 17, 22; Sep.: 1, 18, 29; Oct.: 10, 11, 26; Nov.: 22, 23; Dec.: 4, 9, 31.

BUYING: COMPUTER SCANNERS

These are the dates to buy a scanner for a computer; thus, you can scan books, manuscripts, etc. If you are going to charge it, do so on the days below if it also appears on page 142 under Credit Purchases.

Jan.: 2, 4, 5, 6, 8-15, 25, 28, 29, 31; Feb.: 1, 3-7, 16, 18, 19, 21, 22, 24, 25; Mar.: 3, 4, 31; Apr.: 1-4, 6-8, 11, 12, 15, 18, 20, 21, 30; May: 5, 6, 8, 9, 12, 15, 16, 18, 21, 22, 24-27, 31; Jun.: 1, 2, 4, 5, 11, 12, 14, 15, 25-29; Jul.: 2; Aug.: 7, 11, 12, 22, 23, 25-27, 29; Sep.: 1, 7, 18, 22, 23; Oct.: 1, 4, 9, 15, 16, 19-21, 23, 29, 31; Nov.: 28, 29; Dec.: 3, 10, 13, 17, 29-31.

BUYING: COSMETICS, JEWELRY

Buy cosmetics or jewelry (including cuff links, tie pins, etc.) on these fantastic dates. If you are going to charge your purchases, do so on the dates below if they also appear on page 142 under Credit Purchases.

Jan.: 15, 17-19, 23-26, 30, 31; Feb.: 1-3, 11, 12, 14-16, 20-22, 26-28; Mar.: 2, 8, 11-14, 19-22, 26-28; Apr.: 1-4, 7-12, 17, 18, 22, 26, 29; May: 2, 4, 9, 13-15, 19-21, 27-31; Jun.: 1-4, 12, 20, 26, 29; Jul.: 1, 6-9, 18, 19, 21, 26, 29; Aug.: 5, 9, 16, 20-26, 31; Sep.: 1, 5-7, 9-15, 18, 20, 27-29; Oct.: 3, 4, 9-14, 18-20, 24-26; Nov.: 3, 8, 9, 11, 13-15, 21-23, 27-30; Dec.: 1-12, 18, 24, 28-31.

BUYING: CURIOS, DOLLS, HATS, LINENS, (TOWELS, BEDDING), ORNAMENTS, SCARVES

Purchase hats and scarves on these dates. Buy curios, dolls, linens and ornaments. If you are going to charge your purchases, do so on the dates below if they also appear on page 142 under Credit Purchases.

Jan.: 1, 6, 15, 25-28, 30, 31; Feb.: 1-3, 11, 12, 14, 15, 17-21, 23-25; Mar.: 8, 12-14, 25-28; Apr.: 1-4, 7, 8, 10-15, 17-22, 26, 29; May: 2, 4, 12-15, 17-21, 27-31; Jun.: 1-4, 6, 12-14, 20, 26, 29; Jul.: 1, 3, 4, 6, 7, 9, 10, 23, 26, 29; Aug.: 5, 6, 9, 16, 19-22, 24-26, 31; Sep.: 1, 7, 9-13, 15, 18, 20, 27, 28; Oct.: 3, 4, 9, 10, 18-21, 23-27, 29; Nov.: 3, 8, 9, 11, 19, 22-30; Dec.: 1-5, 7-12, 18, 24, 28-31.

BUYING: ELECTRICAL APPLIANCES OR EQUIPMENT

Purchase appliances and other products which use electricity on these dates. Such items as an adding or answering machines or an electrical typewriter or a calculator, dishwasher, hair dryer, heater, iron, lamp, refrigerator, stove, vacuum cleaner or washer/dryer machine. If you are going to charge them, do so on any of the dates below if they also appear on page 142 under Credit Purchases. For Microwaves, see Buying, page 128.

Jan.: 1-4, 8, 9, 11; Feb.: 5, 7, 18, 20, 24, 25; Mar.: 3, 4; Apr.: 1-4, 8, 9, 20-22, 24, 27, 29, 30; May: 5, 8, 12-14, 19-22, 24, 25, 27, 31; Jun.: 1, 2, 4, 7, 8, 22, 24, 27, 29; Jul.: 6; Aug.: 10, 11, 14, 22, 24-26, 29, 31; Sep.: 1, 4, 6-9, 11-13, 15, 18, 22; Oct.: 1, 3, 4, 9, 16-19, 23, 24, 29; Nov.: 20, 21, 27-30; Dec.: 2, 3, 6, 8-10, 13, 17, 24, 29-31.

BUYING: ELECTRONIC EQUIPMENT (BEEPER, COMPUTER, FAX, I-POD, PAGER, TABLET)

Purchase electronic equipment on these dates, such as a beeper, computer, fax, pager, printer, tablet or word processor. If you are going to charge it, do so on the days below if they also appear on page 142 under Credit Purchases. For Buying: CDROM's, see page 123; to Buy: Modems, see page 128; to Buy: Software for Computers, see page 123; to Buy: TV Sets, see page 130; to Install FAX Machines, see page 160.

Jan.: 2-4, 7-9, 30, 31; Feb.: 1, 3, 5, 15, 16, 18, 20; Mar.: 3, 4, 31; Apr.: 1-4, 6, 11, 15, 18, 21, 22, 24, 27, 29; May: 1, 2, 5, 8, 12, 16, 19-22, 24, 25, 31; Jun.: 5, 7-9, 12, 14, 21, 22, 24, 26, 27, 29; Jul.: 6; Aug.: 5, 10, 11, 14, 21, 24-27, 29; Sep.: 1, 7, 8, 11, 12, 15, 18, 22, 23, 26; Oct.: 4, 9, 17, 19, 22, 30; Nov.: 20, 27-29; Dec.: 2, 3, 10, 13, 17, 24, 27, 29-31.

BUYING: EXERCISE EQUIPMENT

For mechanical and other exercise equipment, to serve you best, buy on these dates. If you are going to charge your purchases, do so on the dates below if they also appear on page 142 under Credit Purchases. For Exercising: Physical, see page 148.

Jan.: 2, 13-16, 24, 27; Feb.: 5-7, 24-28; Mar.: 1, 10, 12-17, 19-22; Apr.: 2-4, 6, 11, 13, 18; May: 9-13, 15-20, 22-24, 26, 30, 31; Jun.: 1-3, 5-10, 24, 29; Jul.: 3, 22-24, 28, 30; Aug.: 5, 10, 21, 25-29; Sep.: 1, 6, 7, 17-20, 23, 30; Oct.: 1-3, 10, 11, 13, 14, 17, 28, 30; Nov.: 9, 11-15, 19, 27-30; Dec.: 2-6, 10-15, 17-21, 23-25, 27.

BUYING: FLOORING (CARPET, LINOLEUM, VINYL TILE)

Buy carpets or linoleum, or vinyl tile flooring on these favorable dates. See Buying: Bargains, page 122; see Buying: Flooring (stone, wood), the following category; see Installation: Flooring (carpet, linoleum, vinyl, tile), page 161. If you are going to charge the flooring, do so on the days below if they also appear on page 142 under Credit Purchases.

Jan.: 1-4, 6-10, 15, 16, 24, 27-31; Feb.: 3-8, 10-15, 17, 18; Mar.: 2-7, 10, 11-14, 17-19, 24, 26, 31; Apr.: 2, 3, 6-11, 13, 14, 16; May: 17; Jun.: 1-4, 7-10, 20-25, 27-30; Jul.: 1, 4-8, 10-14, 17-22, 24-29, 31; Aug.: 1-4, 6-10, 13-18, 21-25, 28-31; Sep.: 2-7, 9-11, 13, 18, 27; Oct.: 1, 3, 10, 14-19, 21, 30, 31; Nov.: 3-8, 10-15, 17-21, 25, 27, 28, 30; Dec.: 9-12, 15-18.

BUYING: FLOORING (STONE, TILE, WOOD)

Buy stone, (granite, flagstone, etc.), tile (brick, ceramic), or wood (cherry, parquet) flooring on these dates. See Installations: Flooring (stone, tile, wood), page 161. If you are going to charge the flooring do so on the days below if it also appears on page 142 under Credit Purchases.

Jan.: 1, 2, 4, 6-10, 15, 16, 27-31; Feb.: 3-8, 10-13, 15, 17-19, 21, 23-25, 28; Mar.: 2-7, 10-12, 14, 17, 18, 23, 24, 31; Apr.: 2, 3, 6-8, 11, 13, 14, 20; May: 4-6, 8, 10, 11, 17, 23-27, 31; Jun.: 1, 2, 4, 7, 8, 20-25, 27-29; Jul.: 1, 8, 10-12, 17-22, 24-27, 29, 31; Aug.: 1, 2, 4, 6-8, 13, 14, 18, 21-23, 25, 28, 29, 31; Sep.: 2-4, 18; Oct.: 1, 10, 14-16, 19, 21, 31; Nov.: 3-8, 10-13, 15, 17-19, 25, 26, 28, 30; Dec.: 5, 8-10, 12, 13, 15-17, 22, 23, 29, 31.

BUYING: FLOWERS

These are good days to buy and give flowers. For the type of flower, if the flowers are a gift, see Part One, under the person's Zodiac sign — Flowers ruled by that sign. If you are going to charge your purchase, do so if it also appears on page 142 under Credit Purchases.

Jan.: 1, 6, 15, 17-28, 30, 31; Feb.: 1-3, 11, 12, 14-28; Mar.: 2, 8, 11-14, 16-22, 25-28; Apr.: 1-4, 7-15, 17-22, 26, 29; May: 2, 4, 9-21, 27-31; Jun.: 1-4, 6, 12-14, 20, 26, 28, 29; Jul.: 1, 3, 4, 6-10, 18, 19, 21, 26, 29; Aug.: 5, 6, 9, 16, 20-26, 31; Sep.: 1-7, 9-15, 18, 20, 27-30; Oct.: 1-4, 9-14, 18-27, 29; Nov.: 3, 8, 9, 11, 13-15, 19, 21-30; Dec.: 1-12, 18, 23, 24, 28-31.

BUYING: FRANCHISE

Buy a franchise on any of the following dates because the price will be right. If you are going to borrow money to buy a franchise, do so on any of the dates below if it also appears on page 142 under Credit Purchases.

Jan.: 1-4, 10, 15-19, 25; Feb.: 5-9, 11, 13-15, 17, 18, 20, 21, 23-25, 27, 28; Mar.: 3, 4, 31; Apr.: 2, 3, 6-9; May: 24, 25, 27, 31; Jun.: 1, 2, 4, 7-9, 11, 22-24, 27-30; Jul.: None; Aug.: 2-4, 6, 8-14, 18, 19, 21, 22, 24-26, 28, 29, 31; Sep.: 1, 6-13, 18; Oct.: 3, 16-19, 22-25, 28-30; Nov.: 20, 21, 25, 27-30; Dec.: 1-3, 6, 8-11, 13, 15-17.

BUYING: FURNITURE — HOME FURNISHINGS/ACCESSORIES

Buy furniture for its beauty on any of the following dates. Also buy accessories on these dates. If you are going to charge them, do so on any of the dates below if they also appear on page 142 under Credit Purchases. See Furniture: Good Service, page 152.

Jan.: 1, 6, 15, 17-28, 30, 31; Feb.: 1-3, 11, 12, 14-28; Mar.: 2, 8, 11-14, 16-22, 25-28; Apr.: 1-4, 7-15, 17-22, 26, 29; May: 2, 4, 9-21, 27-31; Jun.: 1-4, 6, 12-14, 20, 26, 28, 29; Jul.: 1, 3, 4, 6-10, 18, 19, 21, 26, 29; Aug.: 5, 6, 9, 16, 20-26, 31; Sep.: 1-7, 9-15, 18, 20, 27-30; Oct.: 1-4, 9-14,18-27, 29; Nov.: 3, 8, 9, 11, 13-15, 19, 21-30; Dec.: 1-12, 18, 23, 24, 28-31.

BUYING: GAMES, TOYS

Buy games or toys on these days, if they are mechanical. The underlined dates are best for buying, when the game or toy is wireless or battery operated. If you are going to charge your purchases, do so if they also appear on page 142 under Credit Purchases.

Jan.: _1_, 2, _3_, 4, _5_, _8_, _11_, _16_, _22_, 24, 27; Feb.: 5, 6, _7_, 8, 9, _12_, 15, _20_, _24_, 25, 26, _27_, 28; Mar.: 1, _4_, _7_, 10, 12, 13, _14_, 15, _20_, _24_; Apr.: 2, _3_, 4, 6, _8-10_, 11, _13-16_, 18, 30; May: 1, 2, 5, 8-13, 15, 16, _17_, 18-20, 22-24, _25_, 26, _27_, 30, _31_; Jun.: _1_, 2, 3, 5-9, _10_, _24_, 29; Jul.: 3, _7_, _11_, 22-24, _26_, 28, 30; Aug.: _3_, 5, _7_, 10, _17_, 21, _22_, 25-29, _31_; Sep.: 1, _4_, 6, 7, _9_, _11_, _12_, 17, _18_, 19, 20, 30; Oct.: 2, 3, _8_, 10, _11_, 13, 14, _16_, 17, _18_, _19_, _21_, 22, _23-25_, 28, _29_, 30; Nov.: 9, 11,_12_, 13-15, 19, _21_, _25_, 28, _30_; Dec.: _1_, 2-6, _8_, 10, 11, _12_, 13-15, 17, _18_, 19-25, 27.

BUYING: GLASS, MIRRORS, OPTICAL EQUIPMENT

For mirrors and glass items (artistic objects, binoculars, drinking vessels, eye glasses, microscopes, telescopes or any item which involves a lens, lenses, an aid to vision or that is reflective, transparent and translucent) buy on these dates. If you are going to charge your purchase do so if it also appears on page 142 under Credit Purchases.

Jan.: 4-16, 23, 25-29, 31; Feb.: 1-13, 15-19, 21-25, 28; Mar.: 1-12, 14, 15, 23, 28, 31; Apr.: 6-8, 11, 12, 20, 30; May: 2, 4-6, 8, 9, 15-17, 22-27, 31; Jun.: 1, 2, 4, 5, 11-15, 17, 18; Jul.: 2-5, 8-12, 16-19, 23, 26, 30; Aug.: 7, 12, 22, 26; Sep.: 18, 23; Oct.: 1, 5, 8, 14-16, 19-23, 26-29, 31; Nov.: 1-11, 25, 26, 28, 29; Dec.: 13, 22, 29.

BUYING: HEADGEAR, HELMETS

These are favorable dates to buy headgear such as is used in construction work, fencing, riding a motorcycle, baseball (as a catcher) snorkeling, deep sea diving or the harness part over a horses head. The best dates are underlined. If you are going to charge your purchase, do so if it also appears on page 142 under Credit Purchases.

Jan.: 1-3, 6-11, 14-16, 24, 27; Feb.: 5-7, 18, 24-28; Mar.: 2, 4-7, 10, 12-14, 17, 19, 20, 26, 31; Apr.: 2, 3, 6-8, 10, 11, 13, 14, 20; May: 1, 5, 8, 10-13, 17-20, 23, 24, 26, 31; Jun.: 1-3, 7-10, 22-24, 27-30; Jul.: 1, 5, 6, 19-22, 24, 27-29, 31; Aug.: 2-4, 6, 7, 9, 10, 13, 14, 16-18, 19, 21, 22, 24, 25, 28, 29, 31; Sep.: 2-4, 6, 7, 17-20, 30; Oct.: 1-3, 10, 11, 14-19, 21, 30, 31; Nov.: 11-15, 18-21, 27, 28, 30; Dec.: 2-5, 11-13, 15, 17-19, 21, 23-25, 29, 31.

BUYING: HORSE

Buy a horse for personal or professional use on any of these dates. If you are going to charge, or borrow money to buy the horse, do so if it also appears on page 142 under Credit Purchases.

Jan.: 7, 10, 15-18, 24, 27, 28, 30, 31; Feb.: 3-8, 11, 12, 15, 19, 20, 24, 27, 28; Mar.: 10-14, 17, 24, 26, 31; Apr.: 2, 3, 6-8, 11, 13, 16; May: 24-27, 31; Jun.: 1-4, 7-10, 20-25, 27-30; Jul.: 1, 4, 5, 13, 14, 17-22, 24-28, 31; Aug.: 1-4, 6-10, 13-18, 21-25, 28-31; Sep.: 2-4, 18, 27, 30; Oct.: 1-3, 14, 15, 17, 30; Nov.: 4, 6-8, 10-15, 19-22, 24-28, 30; Dec.: 2-5, 8-13, 15-17.

BUYING: LUGGAGE, ATTACHÉ CASE, BRIEFCASE, PORTFOLIO CASE

Buy luggage or other small cases on these dates. If you are going to charge your purchase, do so if it also appears on page 142 under Credit Purchases.

Jan.: 2-4, 10, 15, 25, 30; Feb.: 1-10, 15-19, 21-26; Mar.: 1-4, 31; Apr.: 5-9, 11, 12, 18, 19, 21, 27, 29; May: 5, 8, 13, 15-17, 20-24; Jun.: 1, 6-9, 14, 24; Jul.: None; Aug.: 3, 8, 19-21, 24; Sep.: 9-13, 15, 24, 30; Oct.: 1-4, 10, 12-14, 16-21, 25, 29, 30; Nov.: 20, 22, 26-30; Dec.: 1, 3, 4, 9, 15, 22-25, 29-31.

BUYING: MACHINERY, TOOLS, IMPLEMENTS

Do you need any new machinery? Or what about tools or implements? You will be happy with them if you buy them on these dates. If you are going to charge them, do so on any of the dates below if they also appear on page 142 under Credit Purchases.

Jan.: 2, 13-16, 27; Feb.: 5-7, 24-28; Mar.: 1, 10, 12-17, 19-22; Apr.: 2-4, 6, 11, 13, 18; May: 9-13, 15-20, 22-24, 26, 30, 31; Jun.: 1-3, 5-10, 24, 29; Jul.: 3, 22-24, 28, 30; Aug.: 5, 10, 21, 25-29; Sep.: 1, 6, 7, 17-20, 23, 30; Oct.: 1-3, 10, 11, 13, 14, 17, 28, 30; Nov.: 9, 11-15, 19, 27-30; Dec.: 2-6, 10-15, 17-21, 23-25, 27.

BUYING: MEDICAL INSTRUMENTS, SCISSORS, KNIVES, TWEEZERS, CUTLERY

Buy sharp instruments on the dates below. If you are going to charge your purchase, do so on any of the dates below if it also appears on page 142 under Credit Purchases.

Jan.: 2, 13-16, 24, 27; Feb.: 5-7, 24-28; Mar.: 1, 10, 12-17, 19-22; Apr.: 2-4, 6, 11, 13, 18; May: 9-13, 15-20, 22-24, 26, 30, 31; Jun.: 1-3, 5-10, 24, 29; Jul.: 22-24, 28, 30; Aug.: 5, 10, 21, 25-29; Sep.: 1, 6, 7, 17-20, 23, 30; Oct.: 1-3, 10, 11, 13, 14, 17, 28, 30; Nov.: 9, 11-15, 19, 27-30; Dec.: 2-6, 10-15, 17-21, 23-25, 27.

BUYING: MICROWAVE OVENS

Buy a microwave oven on any of these dates. If you are going to charge it, do so if it also appears on page 142 under Credit Purchases.

Jan.: 1, 3, 16, 24, 25, 27; Feb.: 7, 20, 24, 25, 27; Mar.: 4-7, 10-14, 19, 20, 24; Apr.: 1-4, 8, 9; May: 25, 27, 31; Jun.: 1-4, 10, 24, 29; Jul.: 21, 26; Aug.: 3, 7, 10, 17, 22, 25, 26, 28-31; Sep.: 5-7, 18; Oct.: 1, 3, 8, 16, 18, 19, 21; Nov.: 12-14, 21, 30; Dec.: 1-4, 6, 8, 9, 12, 13, 15-18.

BUYING: MODEM FOR COMPUTER OR WORD PROCESSOR

Exchange files and messages with others (friends, business associates, etc.) and obtain access to commercial data bases and electronic mail services. If you are going to charge the modem, do so on the days below if it also appears on page 142 under Credit Purchases.

Jan.: 1-5, 9, 18, 25; Feb.: 5, 7, 18-20, 24, 25, 27; Mar.: 3, 4; Apr.: 1-4, 8-11, 14-16; May: 18, 24-27, 31; Jun.: 1-4, 7, 8, 10, 22, 24, 25, 27, 29; Jul.: None; Aug.: 2, 4, 7-9, 11, 12, 14, 18, 23-26, 29, 30; Sep.: 1, 9, 11-13, 15, 18; Oct.: 1, 3, 4, 9, 16-19, 21-25, 29; Nov.: 20, 21, 27-30; Dec.: 2-4, 6, 8-10, 12, 13, 17.

BUYING: MUSICAL INSTRUMENTS

Buy musical instruments on these dates. If you are going to charge your purchase, do so if it also appears on page 142 under Credit Purchases. See Lessons: Musical Instruments, page 167.

Jan.: 2-4, 10, 15, 16, 28, 30, 31; Feb.: 3-8, 10-12, 14, 15, 17-21, 23-28; Mar.: 2-4, 11, 14, 17-19, 24-27, 31; Apr.: 2, 3, 6-11, 13, 14, 16, 19-22; May: 4-6, 10-14, 17-20, 23, 24, 27, 31; Jun.: 1, 7-10, 21, 23, 28; Jul.: 6-8, 17-21, 25, 26; Aug.: 3, 7, 9, 14, 22-25, 30, 31; Sep.: 2-4, 18, 27, 30; Oct.: 1-3, 10, 11, 14-19, 21; Nov.: 4, 6, 7, 11, 13-15, 20, 21, 25-28, 30; Dec.: 1-5, 8, 9, 22-25, 29-31.

BUYING: PERFUME

Buy perfume on these dates. If the perfume is to be a gift, see Part One under the persons Zodiac sign — Perfume. If you are going to charge the perfume, do so if it also appears on page 142 under Credit Purchases.

Jan.: 1, 6, 15, 17-28, 30, 31; Feb.: 1-3, 11, 12, 14-28; Mar.: 2, 8, 11-14, 16-22, 25-28; Apr.: 1-4, 7-15, 17-22, 26, 29; May: 2, 4, 9-21, 27-31; Jun.: 1-4, 6, 12-14, 20, 26, 28, 29; Jul.: 1, 3, 4, 6-10, 18, 19, 21, 26, 29; Aug.: 5, 6, 9, 16, 20-26, 31; Sep.: 1-7, 9-15, 18, 20, 27-30; Oct.: 1-4, 9-14, 18-27, 29; Nov.: 3, 8, 9, 11, 13-15, 19, 21-30; Dec.: 1-12, 18, 23, 24, 28-31.

BUYING: PETS

Buy a pet on one of these dates; the best days are underlined. If you are going to charge or borrow money to purchase a pet, do so on any of the dates below if it also appears on page 142 under Credit Purchases.

Jan.: 6-10, 15, 16, 24, 27-31; Feb.: 3-8, 10-15, 17, 18; Mar.: 2-7, 10-14, 17-19, 24, 26, 31; Apr.: 2, 3, 13, 14, 16; May: 27; Jun.: 1-4, 7-10, 20-25, 27-30; Jul.: 1, 4, 5, 13, 18-22, 24-29, 31; Aug.: 1-4, 6-10, 13, 14, 16-18, 21-25, 28-31; Sep.: 2-4, 11, 13, 17, 18, 24, 25, 27; Oct.: 1, 3, 11, 12, 14-21, 30, 31; Nov.: 3-8, 10, 11, 13-15, 17-21, 25, 27, 28, 30; Dec.: 4, 9-11, 15-18.

BUYING: PEWTER

Buy objects made with pewter on these dates. If you are going to charge your purchases do so if it also appears on page 142 under Credit Purchases.

Jan.: 1-5, 8, 24-28, 30; Feb.: 2-4, 6-9, 16-28; Mar.: 1-22, 24, 29; Apr.: 1-29; May: 3, 4, 9-31; Jun.: 1-10, 18-30; Jul.: 1-13, 18-31; Aug.: 1-31; Sep.: 1-11, 15, 16, 27-30; Oct.: 1, 3, 6-21, 31; Nov.: 2, 5-15, 17-27; Dec.: 2, 8-10, 17, 19, 21, 23, 24, 26-28, 30.

BUYING: PHOTOCOPIER

Buy a photocopier machine on these dates. If you are going to charge it, do so if it also appears on page 142 under Credit Purchases.

Jan.: 4, 5, 9, 10, 15, 16, 19, 20, 25-27; Feb.: 5-7, 16-19, 21-25, 28; Mar.: 1-4, 28, 31; Apr.: 1-4, 6-8, 11-13, 18-20; May: 5, 6, 8, 9, 15-18, 21-27, 31; Jun.: 1, 2, 4-8, 11, 12, 22-29; Jul.: 2; Aug.: 7, 12, 22, 25-29; Sep.: 1, 15-19; Oct.: 1, 14-16, 19-23, 26-29; Nov.: 28-30; Dec.: 1-3, 5-9, 13, 22, 23, 29-31.

BUYING: PLASTICS, SYNTHETIC FABRICS/MATERIALS

Buy any item made of plastic or synthetics, on one of these dates. If you are going to charge your purchase, do so if it also appears on page 142 under Credit Purchases.

Jan.: 4-16, 23, 25-29, 31; Feb.: 1-13, 15-19, 21-25, 28; Mar.: 1-12, 14, 15, 23, 28, 31; Apr.: 6-8, 11, 12, 20, 30; May: 2, 4-6, 8, 9, 15-17, 22-27, 31; Jun.: 1, 2, 4, 5, 11-15, 17, 18; Jul.: 2-5, 8-12, 16-19, 23, 26, 30; Aug.: 7, 12, 22, 26; Sep.: 18, 23; Oct.: 1, 5, 8, 14-16, 19-23, 26-29, 31; Nov.: 1-11, 25, 26, 28, 29; Dec.: 13, 22, 29.

BUYING: POTTERY

Buy pottery on these dates. The best dates are underlined. If you are going to charge it, do so if it also appears on page 142 under Credit Purchases.

Jan.: 1-5, 9, 10, 15, 16, 24, 25-31; Feb.: 1-3, 4-13, 14-18; Mar.: 1-15, 26, 31; Apr.: 2, 3, 5, 6, 7-14, 16, 20; May: 9-11, 13, 16, 17, 20, 30; Jun.: 1-4, 5-10, 20-30; Jul.: 1-5, 11-13, 18, 19, 20-31; Aug.: 1-7, 8-16, 17-22, 23-26, 27-30, 31; Sep.: 1, 5-9, 10, 11, 13, 18, 27; Oct.: 1, 3, 10, 12-17, 18-21, 30, 31; Nov.: 1-21, 25, 27-29, 30; Dec.: 9-12, 14, 15, 16-20, 22, 23, 29, 31.

BUYING: RADAR DETECTOR

Do you want to detect objects and determine their position, or velocity, by analysis of very high frequency radio waves reflected from their surfaces? If so, buy a radar detector on any of these dates. If you are going to charge your purchase, do so if it also appears on page 142 under Credit Purchases.

Jan.: 1, 3, 5, 8, 16, 21-25, 27; Feb.: 7-9, 12, 20, 24, 25, 27; Mar.: 4-7, 11-14, 19, 20, 24; Apr.: 3, 8, 9; May: 17, 18, 25, 27, 31; Jun.: 1-4, 10, 24, 29; Jul.: 7, 11, 21, 26; Aug.: 3, 7, 10, 17, 22, 31; Sep.: 4-9, 11-13, 18; Oct.: 1, 3, 8, 16, 18, 19, 21-25, 29; Nov.: 12-14, 21, 25, 30; Dec.: 1-4, 6, 8, 9, 12, 13, 18.

BUYING: RADIOS, RECORDERS/MIXERS, TELEVISION SETS, VCR'S, PHONOGRAPH MACHINES/RECORDS, HI-FI SETS, STEREO SYSTEMS, COMPACT PLAYERS/DISCS, TAPE DECKS, DVD's, VIDEO DISC/GAMES, KINDLES AND CASSETTE TAPES

You'll avoid getting a lemon by purchasing these products on these dates. If you are going to charge any of these products, then do so on the dates below, if they also appear on page 142 under Credit Purchases.

Jan.: 1, 3, 5, 8, 16, 21-25, 27; Feb.: 7-9, 12, 20, 24, 25, 27; Mar.: 4-7, 11-14, 19, 20, 24; Apr.: 3, 8, 9; May: 17, 18, 25, 27, 31; Jun.: 1-4, 10, 24, 29; Jul.: 7, 11, 21, 26; Aug.: 3, 7, 10, 17, 22, 31; Sep.: 4-9, 11-13, 18; Oct.: 1, 3, 8, 16, 18, 19, 21-25, 29; Nov.: 12-14, 21, 25, 30; Dec.: 1-4, 6, 8, 9, 12, 13, 18.

BUYING: REAL ESTATE

You will hold onto real estate (land) longer if it is purchased on any of these dates. For the transaction to transpire quickly (including land purchase) and to also pay off the mortgage faster, buy property on the underlined days. To purchase real estate at a cheap price, and to get a good deal, see Buying: Bargains, page 122; see Land: Develop, page 164.

Jan.: 6-10, 15, 16, 24, 30, 31; Feb.: 3, 5-8, 10, 11, 13-15, 17, 18, 20, 21, 27, 28; Mar.: 2-5, 31; Apr.: 2, 3, 13, 14, 16; May: 24, 25, 27, 28, 31; Jun.: 1, 2, 4, 7-9, 20-24, 27-30; Jul.: 1, 4, 5; Aug.: 1-4, 9, 10, 13, 14, 16-18, 21, 22, 24, 25, 28, 29, 31; Sep.: 6, 7, 9-11, 13, 18, 27; Oct.: 3, 14-19, 30; Nov.: 20, 21, 27, 28, 30; Dec.: 9-11, 15-17.

BUYING: RELIGIOUS ITEMS

These are favorable dates to buy religious items such as a bible, statue, altar, candle, or rosary beads. If you are going to charge your purchase, do so if it also appears on page 142 under Credit Purchases.

Jan.: 1-5, 8, 24-28, 30; Feb.: 2-4, 6-9, 16-28; Mar.: 1-22, 24, 29; Apr.: 1-29; May: 3, 4, 9-31; Jun.: 1-10, 18-30; Jul.: 1-13, 18-31; Aug.: 1-31; Sep.: 1-11, 15, 16, 27-30; Oct.: 1, 3, 6-21, 31; Nov.: 2, 5-15, 17-27; Dec.: 2, 8-10, 17, 19, 21, 23, 24, 26-28, 30.

BUYING: ROBOTS

How would you like to own a robot to give you service by performing human tasks? Or a robot machine or device that works automatically or by remote control may be appealing. Buy robots on any of these dates. If you are going to charge or borrow money for your purchase, do so on any of the dates below if it also appears on page 142 under Credit Purchases.

Jan.: 1-5, 8, 9, 11, 18, 25, 27; Feb.: 5, 7, 17-20, 24, 25, 27; Mar.: 3-7, 11-14, 19-21, 25-28, 31; Apr.: 1-4, 8, 9, 18; May: 24-27, 31; Jun.: 1-4, 7, 8, 10, 22, 24, 25, 27, 29; Jul.: 2, 6, 18, 20, 21; Aug.: 2, 3, 7, 10, 11, 14, 22-26, 29-31; Sep.: 1, 4-9, 11-13, 15, 18, 22; Oct.: 1, 3, 4, 9, 16-19, 21, 23, 24, 29; Nov.: 12-15, 20, 21, 27-30; Dec.: 2-4, 6, 8-10, 12, 13, 17, 18.

BUYING: SATELLITE DISH

Buy a satellite dish on any of these dates. If you are going to charge your purchase, do so if it also appears on page 142 under Credit Purchases.

Jan.: 1-5, 8, 9, 16, 18, 25, 27; Feb.: 5, 7, 19, 20, 24, 25, 27; Mar.: 3, 4; Apr.: 1-4, 8-11, 13-16, 19, 24, 26, 29; May: 5, 8, 10, 12-14, 17-23, 25-27, 31; Jun.: 1-4, 7-10, 22, 24, 25, 29; Jul.: 2, 6; Aug.: 2, 3, 7, 10, 11, 22, 25, 26, 28-31; Sep.: 1, 4-9, 11-13, 15, 18; Oct.: 1, 3, 4, 9, 11, 12, 16-19, 21-25, 29; Nov.: 20, 21, 28, 30; Dec.: 1-4, 6, 8-10, 12, 13, 17, 18, 22, 29-31.

BUYING: SHOES, BOOTS, SNEAKERS, SLIPPERS

Have you ever purchased shoes or boots that later felt uncomfortable or that caused foot problems? If so, you probably purchased them at the wrong time astrologically (see Avoid: Buying or Wearing Shoes or Boots, page 110). Thus, buy footwear on any of the following dates and you will escape being miserable. If you are going to charge them, do so on any of the dates below if they also appear on page 142 under Credit Purchases. See Shoes or Boots, page 193; see Shoes: Custom Made, page 193; see Shoes: Dying, page 193.

Jan.: 3, 4, 7-11, 14-18, 21-24, 27-31; Feb.: 3-8, 10-15, 17-21, 23-28; Mar.: 2-7, 10-14, 23, 31; Apr.: 2, 6-11, 20, 27, 29, 30; May: 4-8, 17, 23-28, 31; Jun.: 1-4, 7-10, 13-17, 20-25, 27-30; Jul.: 1, 4-8, 10-12, 17-21, 26; Aug.: 7, 16, 17, 22; Sep.: 3, 4, 18; Oct.: 1, 8, 10, 11, 14-19, 21-25, 27-31; Nov.: 3-8, 10-15, 17-19, 25-28; Dec.: 4, 5, 8, 9, 13, 22, 29, 31.

BUYING: SIGNS

Buy signs (billboard, display, door, office, poster, street, etc.) on these dates. For neon signs the underlined dates are best. If you are going to charge it, do so on the dates below if it also appears on page 142 of Credit Purchases. See Designing, page 143; see Installation: Elevators, page 161; see Printing, page 181.

Jan.: 4-7, <u>8</u>, 9-12, <u>13</u>, 14, <u>15</u>, 16, <u>19</u>, 23, 25-27, <u>28</u>, 29, 31; Feb.: 1-10, <u>11</u>, 12, 13, 15, <u>16</u>, 17-19, 21-23, <u>24</u>, 25, 28; Mar.: <u>1</u>, 2-10, <u>11</u>, 12, 14, <u>15</u>, <u>23</u>, <u>28</u>, <u>31</u>; Apr.: 5-8, 11, <u>12</u>, <u>20</u>, <u>25</u>, <u>27</u>, 30; May: 1, 2, 4-6, 8-11, 15-18, <u>22</u>, 23-27, 31; Jun.: <u>1</u>, 2, 4, <u>5</u>, 11-13, <u>14</u>, 15, <u>17</u>, <u>18</u>, 19, 20, 21, 25, <u>26</u>, 27-29; Jul.: 2, <u>3</u>, 4, 5, 8-10, <u>11</u>, 12, 16, 17, <u>18</u>, 19, <u>23</u>, <u>26</u>, <u>30</u>; Aug.: 5, 6, <u>7</u>, 8, 11, <u>12</u>, 13-16, 20, 21, <u>22</u>, <u>26</u>; Sep.: <u>3</u>, <u>16</u>, <u>18</u>, <u>23</u>, 30; Oct.: 1, 2, <u>5</u>, <u>8</u>, 12-16, 19, <u>20</u>, 21-23, 26, 27, <u>28</u>, 29, 31; Nov.: <u>1</u>, 2, 3, <u>4</u>, 5-11, <u>16</u>, 17-19, <u>25</u>, 26, 28-30; Dec.: 1-3, 10, 12, <u>13</u>, 14, 15, 22, 23, 25, <u>29</u>.

BUYING: SILVER

Buy silver items (silver buillon, silverware, tea sets and frames for photos, jewelry, etc.) on these dates. If you are going to charge your purchase, do so if it also appears on page 142 under Credit Purchases.

Jan.: 1-4, 8-10, 15, 16, 18, 22, 24, 28, 30, 31; Feb.: 4-7, 11, 12, 15, 18, 20, 24, 25, 27, 28; Mar.: 4, 7, 11, 13, 23, 25, 27, 30, 31; Apr.: 2, 4, 6-8, 11, 13-16, 21, 27-29; May: 5, 8, 12, 13, 17, 20, 21, 25-27, 31; Jun.: 7, 9, 10, 14, 21, 22, 24, 28, 29; Jul.: 1, 5, 7, 8, 11-13, 18, 20-22, 26, 27, 29; Aug.: 2, 9-11, 14, 16, 17, 21, 22, 28, 30, 31; Sep.: 3, 4, 7, 9, 11, 12, 18, 19, 25, 26, 30; Oct.: 1, 3, 8-11, 16, 17, 19, 22-25, 28, 29, 31; Nov.: 4, 6, 8, 11, 13, 15, 20, 22, 25, 27, 28; Dec.: 3, 4, 8, 9, 13, 15, 17, 18, 22, 23, 29.

BUYING: SPORTS EQUIPMENT

These are the favorable dates to buy sports equipment such as tables (pool, Ping Pong), racquets (tennis, racquetball), balls (baseball, basketball, bowling, football, golf, Ping Pong, tennis), darts, golf clubs, paddles, racquets (racquet ball, tennis), rollerblades, ice skates, roller skates, scooter skate boards, skate boards, sleds, skis, snowshoes, snowmobile, etc. The underlined dates are best; they'll last longer if bought on these dates. If you are going to charge your purchases do so if they also appear on page 142 under Credit Purchases.

Jan.: 2, 13, 14, 15, 16, 24, 27; Feb.: 5-7, 24, 25-28; Mar.: 1, 10, 12-16, 17, 19-22; Apr.: 2-4, 6, 11, 18; May: 1, 2, 5, 8-10, 11, 12, 13, 15, 16, 17, 18, 19, 20, 22-24, 26, 30, 31; Jun.: 1-3, 5, 6-10, 24, 29; Jul.: 3, 22-24, 28, 30; Aug.: 5, 10, 21, 25-27, 28, 29; Sep.: 1, 6, 7, 17, 18, 19, 20, 23, 30; Oct.: 1, 2, 3, 10, 11, 13, 14, 17, 30; Nov.: 9, 11, 12-15, 19, 28, 30; Dec.: 2, 3-6, 10-14, 15, 17-21, 23-25, 27.

BUYING: SURVEILLANCE SYSTEMS

Buy surveillance equipment and/or systems (burglar alarms, locks, vaults, and hi-tech security equipment) on these dates. If you are going to charge your purchases, do so on the dates below if they also appear on page 142 under Credit Purchases. See Hire: Consultant, page 159; see Install: Surveillance Systems, page 161.

Jan.: 9, 10, 15; Feb.: 5-7, 18-21, 24-28; Mar.: 3-7, 10-15, 18-20, 24, 26, 31; Apr.: 1-4; May: 24-27, 31; Jun.: 1-3, 7-9, 22-25, 27-30; Jul.: 1, 18-22, 25; Aug.: 2-4, 7-10, 14, 18, 21-25, 29-31; Sep.: 9, 18; Oct.: 1, 3, 4, 16-19, 21, 30, 31; Nov.: 11-15, 19-21, 27, 28, 30; Dec.: 2-4, 8-13, 16-18.

BUYING: TELEPHONES — WIRELESS

Buy a wireless (cellular, cordless, mobile) phone on these dates. If you are going to charge it, do so on any of the dates below if it also appears on page 142 under Credit Purchases.

Jan.: 1, 3, 5, 16, 27; Feb.: 7, 20, 24, 25, 27; Mar.: 4; Apr.: 3, 8-11, 13-16; May: 25, 27, 31; Jun.: 1-4, 10, 24, 29; Jul.: None; Aug.: 3, 7, 10, 22, 31; Sep.: 18; Oct.: 1, 3, 11, 16, 18, 19, 21-25, 29; Nov.: 21, 30; Dec.: 1-4, 6, 8, 9, 12, 13.

BUYING: TELEPHONES — WIRE TRANSMITTED

Buy a telephone transmitted by wire (land phone) on any of these dates. If you are going to charge it, do so on any of the dates below if it also appears on page 142 under Credit Purchases.

Jan.: 2-4, 10, 15, 25, 30; Feb.: 1-10, 15-18, 21-26; Mar.: 1-4, 31; Apr.: 5-9, 11, 12, 18, 21, 27, 29; May: 5, 8, 13, 15-17, 20-24; Jun.: 1, 6-9, 14, 24; Jul.: None; Aug.: 3, 8, 19-21, 24; Sep.: 9-13, 15, 24, 30; Oct.: 1-4, 10, 12, 14, 16-21, 25, 29, 30; Nov.: 20, 22, 26-30; Dec.: 1, 3, 4, 9, 15, 22-25, 29-31.

BUYING: THRIFT SHOP ITEMS

Get a good price, and help a charity, by purchasing thrift shop items on these dates. See Charity: Donations, page 135.

Jan.: 1, 2, 6-8, 14-16, 21, 22, 27, 28; Feb.: 3, 4, 10-13, 15, 17, 18; Mar.: 2-4, 10-13, 17-19, 24, 31; Apr.: 6-9, 11, 13, 14, 20; May: 10, 11, 17, 31; Jun.: 1, 2, 4, 7, 8, 13, 14, 25, 27, 29; Jul.: 4, 5, 8, 10, 11, 18, 25-29, 31; Aug.: 1-4, 6, 7, 14, 22-25, 28-31; Sep.: 2, 3, 27; Oct.: 14-19, 21-24, 27, 28; Nov.: 3, 4, 10-13, 15, 17-20, 25, 30; Dec.: 9-12, 15-18, 22, 29, 31.

BUYING: TIRES, WATER FILTERS
(TO PURIFY SWIMMING POOLS)

Do you need new tires or a water filter? If so, buy them on these dates. However, if you are going to purchase retread tires, the underlined dates are best. If you are going to charge your purchase, do so on the dates below if it also appears on page 142 under Credit Purchases.

Jan.: 6-9, 10, 15, 16, 27, 28, 29, 31; Feb.: 3, 4, 5, 6, 7, 8, 10, 11, 12, 13, 15, 17, 18, 19, 21, 23, 24, 25, 28; Mar.: 2-7, 10-12, 14, 23, 31; Apr.: 20; May: 4, 17, 23-26, 27, 31; Jun.: 1, 2, 4, 20, 25, 27, 28, 29; Jul.: 4, 5, 18, 19, 26; Aug.: 7, 22; Sep.: 18; Oct.: 1, 14, 15, 16, 19, 21, 31; Nov.: 3, 4, 5, 6, 7, 8-10, 11, 17-19, 25, 26, 28; Dec.: 13, 22, 29.

BUYING: TUXEDO

Buy a tuxedo on these dates. If you are going to charge it, do so on the dates below if it also appears on page 142 under Credit Purchases. See Renting: Tuxedo, page 187.

Jan.: 1-4, 6-8, 10, 15, 16, 27-31; Feb.: 3-7, 10-15, 17-21, 23-25; Mar.: 3-7, 12-14, 25-27, 31; Apr.: 1-4, 6-8, 10, 11, 13-15, 17-22, 26, 29; May: 4, 12-14, 17-21, 27, 28, 31; Jun.: 1-4, 7, 9, 10, 13, 14, 20, 25, 27-30; Jul.: 1, 4-7, 10-13, 22, 25-29; Aug.: 4, 6, 8-10, 13, 16-18, 21, 24, 25, 28-31; Sep.: 7, 9-13, 18, 27, 28; Oct.: 3, 4, 9, 10, 16-19, 21, 23-25, 27-31; Nov.: 3-5, 7, 8, 10, 11, 17-20, 22, 24-28, 30; Dec.: 1-5, 8-12, 15-18, 24, 28-31.

BUYING: UNIFORMS

Do you need to purchase a uniform? If so, buy it on any of these dates. If you are going to charge the uniform, do so on the dates below if it also appears on page 142 under Credit Purchases.

Jan.: 1, 3, 5, 8, 16, 21-25, 27; Feb.: 7-9, 12, 20, 24, 25; Mar.: 4-7, 11-14, 19, 20, 24; Apr.: 3, 8, 9; May: 17, 18, 25, 27, 31; Jun.: 1-4, 10, 24, 29; Jul.: 7, 11, 26; Aug.: 7, 10, 17, 22, 31; Sep.: 4-9, 11-13, 18; Oct.: 3, 8, 16, 18, 19, 21-25, 29; Nov.: 12-14, 21, 25, 30; Dec.: 1-4, 6, 8, 9, 12, 13, 18.

BUYING: WATERCRAFT
(BOATS, YACHTS, JET SKIS, RAFTS, WAVE RUNNERS,
WATER SCOOTERS, PWC'S-PERSONAL WATER CRAFT),
SURFBOARDS, SNORKELING
OR UNDERSEA DIVING EQUIPMENT

Buy these exciting items for fun in the water. If you are going to charge or borrow money to purchase them, do so on any of these dates below, if they also appear on page 142 under Credit Purchases.

Jan.: 4-16, 23, 25-29, 31; Feb.: 1-13, 15-19, 21-25, 28; Mar.: 1-12, 14, 15, 23, 28, 31; Apr.: 2, 6-8, 11, 12, 20, 30; May: 2, 4-6, 8, 9, 15-18, 21-27, 31; Jun.: 1, 2, 4, 5, 11-15, 17-20, 25-29; Jul.: 2-5, 8-12, 16-21, 23, 26, 30; Aug.: 7, 12, 16, 17, 22, 26; Sep.: 18, 23; Oct.: 1, 5, 8, 10, 11, 14-16, 19-23, 26-29, 31; Nov.: 1-11, 16-19, 25, 26, 28, 29; Dec.: 1-4, 10, 12-17, 22, 23, 25, 29, 31.

BUYING: WHEELCHAIRS

Buy manual wheelchairs on these dates. However, buy electric wheelchairs on the underlined dates. If you are going to charge your purchase, do so if it also appears on page 142 under Credit Purchases. See Renting: Wheelchairs, page 187.

Jan.: 2, 3, 4, 9, 13-15, 16, 18, 24, 27, 28, 30, 31; Feb.: 1, 3, 5-7, 16, 18-20, 24-26, 27, 28; Mar.: 1, 3, 4, 7, 10, 12-17, 19, 20, 21, 22, 25-28; Apr.: 2, 3, 4, 6, 11, 15, 18, 21, 22, 24, 27, 29; May: 1, 2, 5, 8, 9-11, 12, 13, 15, 16, 17-20, 21, 22-24, 25, 26, 30, 31; Jun.: 1-3, 5, 6, 7, 8, 9, 10, 12, 14, 22, 24, 25-27, 29; Jul.: 2, 3, 6, 15, 20, 22-24, 27, 28, 29, 30; Aug.: 2, 5, 10, 11, 21, 23, 24, 25, 26, 27, 28, 29, 30; Sep.: 1, 6, 7, 8-10, 12, 14, 15, 16-20, 22, 23, 26, 30; Oct.: 1-3, 4, 9, 10, 11, 12, 13, 14, 17, 19, 30; Nov.: 1, 4, 6, 7, 8, 9, 11, 12, 13, 14, 15, 19, 20, 27, 28, 29, 30; Dec.: 2, 3, 4-6, 10, 11-15, 17, 18-21, 23, 24, 25, 27, 29-31.

BUYING: WIGS, TOUPEES, HAIR PIECES

Beautify, improve your looks and change your appearance on these dates by buying a wig, toupee or other hair piece (falls, curls, braids, extensions, etc.). If you are going to charge your purchase, do so if it also appears on page 142 under Credit Purchases. See Hair Extensions, Weaving, page 156.

Jan.: 1, 6, 15, 25-28, 30, 31; Feb.: 1-3, 11, 12, 14, 15, 17-21, 23-25; Mar.: 8, 12-14, 25-28; Apr.: 1-4, 7, 8, 10-15, 17-22, 26, 29; May: 2, 4, 10-15, 17-21, 27-31; Jun.: 1-4, 6, 12-14, 20, 26, 29; Jul.: 1, 3, 4, 6, 7, 9, 10, 19, 21, 26; Aug.: 5, 6, 9, 16, 20, 21, 31; Sep.: 1, 2, 7, 9-13, 15, 18, 20, 25, 27-30; Oct.: 1-4, 9, 10, 18-21, 23-27, 29; Nov.: 3, 8, 9, 11, 19, 22-30; Dec.: 1-5, 7-12, 18, 24, 28-31.

BUYING: WOOD

Buy wood items (book cases, cabinets, desks, wall units), objects (carvings), and paneling on these dates. Also see Buying: Flooring, page 125; see Buying: Furniture, page 126; see Furniture: Good Service, page 152; see Furniture: Refinish, page 152; see Installation: Flooring, page 161. If you are going to charge your purchase, do so if it also appears on page 142 under Credit Purchases.

Jan.: 1-31; Feb.: 1-18; Mar.: 1-19, 24, 26, 31; Apr.: 2, 3, 5-14, 16, 20, 30; May: 5, 9-11, 13, 16, 17, 20, 30; Jun.: 1-30; Jul.: 1-31; Aug.: 1-31; Sep.: 1-11, 13, 18, 27; Oct.: 1, 3, 10, 12-31; Nov.: 1-21, 25, 27-30; Dec.: 9-12, 14-20, 22, 23, 29, 31.

CALLUSES: REMOVAL

These are the best days to remove those unwanted calluses from your feet. The preferred dates are underlined. However, if surgery is to be performed, see Avoid: Surgery, page 117; also, see Surgery, page 202.

Jan.: 23, 30; Feb.: 20, 26, 27; Mar.: 3, 4, 26, 30, 31; Apr.: 4, 22, 27; May: 2, 19, 20, 24, 25, 29, 30; Jun.: 20, 21, 25, 26, 30; Jul.: 18, 23, 28; Aug.: 19, 20, 24, 28; Sep.: 15, 16, 20, 21, 25-27; Oct.: 17, 18, 22-24; Nov.: 14, 18, 19, 20; Dec.: 15-18, 24.

CAMPAIGNS: COMMENCE

Start a campaign on one of these dates and see how easily impressed the public will be. The underlined dates are when it is easier to stick with the campaign.

Jan.: 7, 8, 9-11, 14, 15, 16-18; Feb.: 5-8, 10, 11, 12, 13-15, 18; Mar.: None; Apr.: 6, 7, 8-11, 14, 16; May: 11, 13; Jun.: 4, 7, 8-10, 16; Jul.: 5, 6; Aug.: 1, 2-4, 9, 10, 14, 31; Sep.: 2, 4-7, 9, 11, 13; Oct.: 3, 10, 30, 31; Nov.: 27, 28, 30; Dec.: 9, 10, 11, 29, 30, 31.

CANNING
Canning should be done on the following dates because the food will keep longer and taste better. For the best results, can preserves, jams and jellies on the underlined days.

Jan.: 1, 2-4, 22-27, 28, 29-31; Feb.: 1-3, 20-23, 24, 25-28; Mar.: 1-5, 21, 22, 23, 24, 25-31; Apr.: 1, 2, 3, 4, 20, 21-28, 29, 30; May: 1-3, 19-26, 27, 28-31; Jun.: 1, 2, 18, 19, 20, 21-30; Jul.: 1, 17-19, 20, 21, 22-29, 30; Aug.: 16, 17, 18-25, 26, 27-29; Sep.: 15-22, 23, 24-27; Oct.: 14-19, 20, 21-26; Nov.: 13-15, 16, 17-23, 24, 25; Dec.: 13, 14-21, 22, 23-25.

CANVASSING
Ask for opinions, votes or subscriptions on these dates and you will receive quick results.

Jan.: 10, 15; Feb.: 5-10, 15-18; Mar.: None; Apr.: 6-9, 11, 12, 18; May: 5, 8, 13, 15-17; Jun.: 6-9, 14; Jul.: None; Aug.: 3, 8; Sep.: 9-13, 30; Oct.: 1-4, 10, 12, 29, 30; Nov.: 27-30; Dec.: 1, 3, 4, 9, 29-31.

CARPET: SHAMPOOING
Shampoo your carpet on these favorable dates. The job will be done quickly on the underlined dates.

Jan.: 4, 5, 6-16, 23, 25-29, 31; Feb.: 1-4, 5-13, 15-18, 19, 21-25, 28; Mar.: 1-6, 7-12, 14-18, 23, 28, 31; Apr.: 5, 6-8, 11-14, 20, 30; May: 2, 4, 5, 6, 8, 9,15-17, 22-27, 31; Jun.: 1, 2, 4, 5, 11-15, 17-20, 25-29; Jul.: 2, 3-5, 8-12, 15, 16-19, 23, 26, 30; Aug.: 7, 12, 21, 22, 26, 31; Sep.: 1, 18, 23; Oct.: 1, 5, 8, 12, 13-16, 19-23, 26, 27, 28, 29, 31; Nov.: 1-11, 16-19, 25, 26, 28-30; Dec.: 13-17, 22, 23, 27, 29.

CEMENT POURED
Cement will last longer if poured on any of the following dates.

Jan.: 1, 28; Feb.: 24; Mar.: 3, 4, 23, 24, 30, 31; Apr.: 20, 27; May: 24, 25, 31; Jun.: 1, 20, 21, 28; Jul.: 18, 25, 26; Aug.: 21, 22, 28; Sep.: 18, 25; Oct.: 15, 22; Nov.: 18, 24, 25; Dec.: 15, 16, 22.

CHARITY: DONATE TO
These are favorable dates to donate money to charity, clothes to a thrift shop, or items that are auctioned and the proceeds go to charity.

Jan.: 8, 10, 24, 27-30; Feb.: 3, 4, 6-8, 14, 15, 17-19, 21, 23-28; Mar.: 2-7, 10, 12-14, 17, 18, 20, 24, 26; Apr.: 1-4, 13-15, 17; May: 24-28; Jun.: 2-4, 7, 8, 10, 13, 14, 20-25, 27, 29, 30; Jul.: 1, 4, 5, 13, 18-22, 24, 27-29, 31; Aug.: 1, 2, 4, 6-10, 13-18, 23-25, 28-31; Sep.: 2-7, 9-11, 13, 28, 30; Oct.: 1, 3, 11, 14, 16-19, 21-23, 25, 27, 30, 31; Nov.: 5-8, 10, 12-15, 17-19, 21, 22, 24-27; Dec.: 2, 4, 5, 8, 10, 17, 19, 21, 23, 24, 28, 30, 31.

CHARITY: SOLICIT DONATIONS, FUND RAISING
Do you want to raise funds for a cause or yourself (such as a business venture)? Solicit donations for charities and raise funds on these days which can be to your advantage. (People are more inclined to favor you, or a cause, when requests are made on these dates.) If quick results are desired, initiate all action on the underlined dates. See Shows, page 194; see Volunteer Work, page 206.

Jan.: 8, 10,15, 16, 27, 28, 30; Feb.: 3, 4, 6-8, 14, 15, 17, 18, 23-28; Mar.: 3, 4; Apr.: 1-4, 13, 14, 17; May: 24-28, 31; Jun.: 1-3, 4, 7, 8; Jul.: 1, 4, 5, 31; Aug.: 1-4, 6-10, 13, 14, 16-18, 21-25, 28, 29; Sep.: 4-6, 10, 13, 28, 30; Oct.: 1, 3, 11, 14-19, 21; Nov.: 22, 24-26, 27, 30; Dec.: 1-5, 8-11, 13.

CHECK GIMMICK: THE LAW OF ABUNDANCE

Many people through the years have reported winning money at bingo, in addition to winning on raffle tickets and small amounts on lotteries. One woman in New York City won the $50,000 Wingo newspaper contest. She told me she held her written Law of Abundance check in her hand and said, "Come on Law of Abundance check bring me that money; make me a winner." In June 1982 I appeared on the People Are Talking TV show, co-hosted by Oprah Winfrey in Baltimore, Maryland. The following month a man appeared on the same TV show and told how a neighbor who had seen me on the People Are Talking TV show, had explained to him how to do the check gimmick. He did it and immediately won the million dollar lottery! Therefore, do not hesitate to try the Check Gimmick. If you do not have a bank account, write it on a piece of paper in the form of a check, and, who knows, you may be the next million dollar lottery winner!

To attract more money, use these dates to do this check gimmick. Make the check payable to you and sign it, "The Law of Abundance"; on the line between your name and the signature write "Paid In Full". Do not void the check stub; just write on it that the check is for the Law of Abundance. If you do the check gimmick every month or more than once, do not throw the previous checks away unless you are writing the check because it is on a new bank account. Do not date the check or write in any amount; leave those lines blank. Fold the check, place it in your wallet or checkbook and forget about it. (This releases the energy so it will work for you to attract money.).

Jan.: 6-20; Feb.: 5-18; Mar.: None; Apr.: 6-18; May: 5-17; Jun.: 4-16; Jul.: 3-6; Aug.: 1-14, 31; Sep.: 1-13, 29, 30; Oct.: 1-12, 28-30; Nov.: 27-30; Dec.: 1-11, 27-31.

CHEMISTRY EXPERIMENTS

Experiment with chemicals and maybe you could make a discovery on one of the following dates. See Research, page 189.

Jan.: 1-4, 8, 9, 11, 25; Feb.: 5, 18, 20, 24, 25; Mar.: 3, 4; Apr.: 1-4, 8, 9, 20-22, 24, 27, 29, 30; May: 1, 5, 8, 12-14, 19-22, 24, 25, 27, 31; Jun.: 1, 2, 4, 7, 8, 22, 24, 27, 29; Jul.: 6; Aug.: 10, 11, 14, 22, 24-26, 29, 31; Sep.: 1, 4, 6-9, 11-13, 15, 18, 22; Oct.: 1, 3, 4, 9, 16-19, 23, 24, 29; Nov.: 20, 21, 27-30; Dec.: 1-3, 6, 8-10, 13, 17, 24, 29-31.

CHIROPRACTIC TREATMENTS

These are favorable dates for chiropractic treatments/adjustments.

Jan.: 1-3, 9, 13-16; Feb.: 5-7,16, 18-21, 22, 24-28; Mar.: 1, 4, 7, 10, 12-16, 19-22, 25-28, 30, 31; Apr.: 2-4, 6, 10, 11, 18, 21; May: 1, 2, 5, 8, 9, 11-13, 15, 16, 18-20, 22, 24-26, 30, 31; Jun.: 1-3, 5, 7-10, 22, 24, 25, 29; Jul.: 2, 15, 20, 22-24, 27-30; Aug.: 2, 5, 10, 21, 24, 25; Sep.: 6, 7, 17-20, 22, 23, 26; Oct.: 1-3, 9-11, 13-15, 17-19, 21, 30; Nov.: 9, 11-15, 19, 20, 27-30; Dec.: 2-6,10-14, 17-20, 23-25, 27, 29, 31.

CIGARETTES

Stop smoking cigarettes on any of these dates and it will be easy to stick to your resolution.

Jan.: 1, 28; Feb.: 24; Mar.: 3, 4, 23, 24, 30, 31; Apr.: 20, 27; May: 24, 25, 31; Jun.: 1, 20, 21, 28; Jul.: 18, 25, 26; Aug.: 21, 22, 28; Sep.: 18, 25; Oct.: 15, 22; Nov.: 18, 24, 25; Dec.: 15, 16, 22.

CLASSES: ASTROLOGY

These are favorable dates to attend astrology classes. For dates to study, see Exams, pages 147 and 148.

Jan.: 1-5, 8, 9, 11, 25, 27; Feb.: 5-7, 18, 20, 24, 25; Mar.: 3, 4, 30, 31; Apr.: 1-4, 8-11, 14-16, 20-22, 24, 27, 29, 30; May: 5, 8, 12-14, 19-22, 24-27, 31; Jun.: 1-4, 7, 8, 10, 22, 24, 25, 27, 29; Jul.: 2, 6; Aug.: 7, 10, 11, 14, 22-26, 29-31; Sep.: 1, 4, 9, 11-13, 15, 18, 22; Oct.: 1, 3, 4, 9, 16-19, 21, 23, 24, 29; Nov.: 20, 21, 27-30; Dec.: 2-4, 6, 8-10, 13, 17, 24, 29-31.

CLASSES: COOKING

Go to a cooking school and learn how to be a first class Chef on any of these dates.

Jan.: 2-4, 10, 13-15, 25, 30; Feb.: 1-10, 15-28; Mar.: 1-4, 15, 31; Apr.: 5-12, 18, 19, 21, 27, 29, 30; May: 1-3, 5, 8, 13, 15-24, 31; Jun.: 1-14, 24-27; Jul.: 11, 12, 16-19; Aug.: 3, 8, 19-21, 24; Sep.: 9-15, 20, 23-25, 30; Oct.: 1-4, 10, 12-21, 25, 29, 30; Nov.: 20, 22, 26-30; Dec.: 1-4, 9, 10, 13, 15, 22-25, 29-31.

CLASSES: MEDITATION

Join in with others and learn various types of meditation on these dates. See Illuminations, page 160. See Psychic Endeavors (For Psychic Development), page 182.

Jan.: 1, 5, 9-11, 15, 25, 27, 28; Feb.: 1, 3-7, 16, 18-22, 24, 28; Mar.: 1, 3, 4, 28, 31; Apr.: 2, 7, 11, 12, 20, 25, 27, 29, 30; May: 4, 9, 15, 16, 22, 24-27, 31; Jun.: 1, 5, 7-12, 14, 21-23, 28-30; Jul.: 2; Aug.: 7, 12, 22, 26; Sep.: 13, 18, 23; Oct.: 1, 5, 8, 10, 11, 15, 22, 23; Nov.: 29; Dec.: 4, 8, 9, 13, 22, 29, 31.

CLASSES: MODELING

Would you like to be a model? Try these dates to learn how to be a print, television or runway model.

Jan.: 1, 6, 15, 17-28, 30, 31; Feb.: 1-3, 11, 12, 14-28; Mar.: 2, 8, 11-14, 16-22, 25-28; Apr.: 1-4, 7-15, 17-22, 26, 29; May: 2, 4, 9-21, 27-31; Jun.: 1-4, 6, 12-14, 20, 26, 28, 29; Jul.: 1, 3, 4, 6-10, 18, 19, 21, 26, 29; Aug.: 5, 6, 9, 16, 20-26, 31; Sep.: 1-7, 9-15, 18, 20, 27-30; Oct.: 1-4, 9-14, 18-27, 29; Nov.: 3, 8, 9, 11, 13-15, 19, 21-30; Dec.: 1-12, 18, 23, 24, 28-31.

CLASSES, SEMINARS, WORKSHOPS

Teach a class, seminar or workshop on these dates and the attendance will be good. The best days are underlined. See Exams, Tests, Studies, pages 147 and 148.

Jan.: 6, 7, 8, 9, 10, 11, 12-15, 16, 17-20; Feb.: 5, 6, 7-9, 10, 11, 12, 13-18; Mar.: None; Apr.: 6, 7, 8-10, 11-14, 15-18; May: 5, 6-11, 12-14, 15, 16, 17; Jun.: 4, 5-9, 10, 11-13, 14, 15, 16; Jul.: 3-6; Aug.: 1, 2, 3, 4-6, 7, 8, 9, 10, 11-14, 31; Sep.: 1-3, 4-9, 10, 11-13, 29, 30; Oct.: 1, 2, 3, 4-7, 8, 9, 10, 11, 12, 28-30; Nov.: 27-29, 30; Dec.: 1-4, 5, 6-9, 10, 11, 27, 28, 29, 30, 31.

CLEANING

Your "spring cleaning" is done best on these days because you will do a thorough job and get into every nook and cranny. Or if you hire someone to do it for you, make sure these are the days the work is performed. This applies to a boat, room, office, house, apartment, chimney or dry cleaning.

Jan.: 1, 6, 15, 23, 28; Feb.: 1, 2, 11, 12, 20, 24; Mar.: 1, 11, 19, 23, 24, 28; Apr.: 7, 16, 20, 24, 25; May: 13, 17, 22, 31; Jun.: 1, 9, 14, 15, 18, 28; Jul.: 7, 11, 25, 26; Aug.: 3, 7, 12, 21, 22; Sep.: 3, 8, 18, 27; Oct.: 1, 5, 15, 24, 28; Nov.: 1, 2, 11, 20, 24, 25, 29; Dec.: 9, 18, 22, 27.

CLOTH: CUT

If you want to make a beautiful and neat cut, the cloth should be cut on any of the following dates. See Avoid: Cutting Cloth, page 110.

Jan.: 15, 25, 26; Feb.: 11, 12, 22; Mar.: 11, 21; Apr.: 7, 18; May: 15, 31; Jun.: 1, 11, 12, 28; Jul.: 9, 25, 26; Aug.: 5, 21, 22; Sep.: 1, 18, 29; Oct.: 15, 26; Nov.: 11, 22, 23; Dec.: 9, 20.

CLOTH: DYE

Dye cloth on the following dates and the color will tend to last longer.

Jan.: 1, 28; Feb.: 24; Mar.: 3, 4, 23, 24, 30, 31; Apr.: 20, 27; May: 24, 25, 31; Jun.: 1, 20, 21, 28; Jul.: 18, 25, 26; Aug.: 21, 22, 28; Sep.: 18, 25; Oct.: 15, 22; Nov.: 18, 24, 25; Dec.: 15, 16, 22.

CLUBS: JOIN

Become a member of a club (public, private, literary, music, dance, drama or a fraternity or sorority) by joining on these dates. Take, send or sign the application on these dates. If you're in a hurry, join on the underlined dates. See the following category Clubs: Join (Athletic, Gun, Sports); see Group Activities, page 155.

Jan.: 1-3, <u>16</u>, <u>17</u>; Feb.: <u>5-9</u>, <u>15</u>, 20, 24, 25, 27, 28; Mar.: 4; Apr.: 3, <u>6</u>, <u>8</u>; May: 24, 25, 27, 31; Jun.: 1, 2, <u>7</u>, <u>9</u>, 24, 29; Jul.: None; Aug.: <u>3</u>, <u>10</u>, 19, 21, 22, 24, 26, <u>31</u>; Sep.: <u>1</u>, <u>9</u>, <u>11</u>, <u>12</u>, 18; Oct.: <u>3</u>, <u>11</u>, 16-19, 22-25, <u>28-30</u>; Nov.: 21, 25, <u>28</u>, <u>30</u>; Dec.: <u>2</u>, <u>3</u>, <u>6</u>, <u>8</u>, 13.

CLUBS: JOIN (ATHLETIC, GUN, SPORTS)

Become a member of a gun, athletic or sports club on these dates. If you're in a hurry, join on the underlined dates. See Group Activities, page 155.

Jan.: 1, 3, <u>8</u>, <u>11</u>, <u>16</u>, 22-25; Feb.: <u>7-9</u>, 20, 24, 25, 27; Mar.: 4; Apr.: 3, <u>8</u>, <u>9</u>; May: 25, 27, 31; Jun.: 1, 2, <u>4</u>, 21, 24, 29; Jul.: None; Aug.: <u>3</u>, <u>10</u>, 17, 22, <u>31</u>; Sep.: <u>4</u>, <u>6-9</u>, <u>11-13</u>,18; Oct.: <u>3</u>, <u>8</u>, 16, 18, 19, 21-25, <u>29</u>; Nov.: 21, 25, <u>30</u>; Dec.: <u>1-3</u>, <u>6</u>, <u>8</u>, <u>9</u>, 13.

COLLECTION AGENCY: DEALING WITH

Do you get upset every time you talk to someone from a collection agency? Try dealing with personnel on any of the following dates.

Jan.: 8; Feb.: 5-7, 17, 18, 20, 21, 27, 28; Mar.: 3, 4; Apr.: 1, 2, 7-11, 13-17; May: 24, 25, 27, 31; Jun.: 1, 2, 4, 22-24, 27-30; Jul.: 1, 6; Aug.: 2-4, 9, 10, 14, 21, 22, 24, 25, 28, 29, 31; Sep.: 12, 13, 24; Oct.: 3, 16-19; Nov.: 20, 21, 27; Dec.: 1-3, 10, 11, 17.

COLONIC IRRIGATION

Detox by getting a colonic (colon therapy) on these dates and you'll feel great afterwards. The underlined dates are best for ridding the body of waste matter through a colonic irrigation.

Jan.: 1-4, 5-21, 22-31; Feb.: 1-3, 4-18; Mar.: 1-5, 6-19, 24, 26, 31; Apr.: 2, 3, 5-14, 16, 20, 30; May: 5, 9-11, 13, 16, 17, 20, 30; Jun.: 1, 2, 3-17, 18-30; Jul.: 1, 2-16, 17-30, 31; Aug.: 1-15, 16-29, 30, 31; Sep.: 1-11, 13, 18, 27; Oct.: 1, 3, 10, 12, 13, 14-26, 27-31; Nov.: 1-12, 13-21, 25, 27-30; Dec.: 9-12, 14-20, 22, 23, 29, 31.

COMIC: BOOKS, STRIPS

Draw, develop and write comic strips for magazines, newspapers or comic books on any of these dates. See Manuscripts, Outlines and Proposals, page 171; see Selling, page 191.

Jan.: 10, 15, 18, 27, 28, 30; Feb.: 3-8, 10, 17-21, 23-28; Mar.: 2-7, 10-14, 17-20, 24; Apr.: 1, 4, 5, 13, 14, 17, 18; May: 24, 25, 27, 31; Jun.: 1-4, 7-10, 20-25, 27-30; Jul.: 1, 13, 18-22, 24-29, 31; Aug.: 1-4, 6-10, 13, 14, 18, 21-25, 28-31; Sep.: 5-7, 9-11, 27, 28, 30; Oct.: 1-3,11, 14-19, 21, 31; Nov.: 5-8, 10-15, 17-22, 24-28, 30; Dec.: 1-4, 8-10, 17.

COMMERCIALS AND INFOMERCIALS: RADIO OR TELEVISION

These are good dates for commercials or infomercials to be broadcast for the first time. The products advertised will click instantly with the public on the underlined days. For Commercials to appear, see Advertising, page 105.

Jan.: 6, 7, 8, 9, 10, 11, 12-15, 16, 17-20; Feb.: 5, 6, 7-9, 10, 11, 12, 13-18; Mar.: None; Apr.: 6, 7, 8-10, 11-14, 15-18; May: 5, 6-11, 12-14, 15, 16, 17; Jun.: 4, 5-9, 10, 11-13, 14, 15, 16; Jul.: 3-6; Aug.: 1, 2, 3, 4-6, 7, 8, 9, 10, 11-14, 31; Sep.: 1-3, 4-9, 10, 11-13, 29, 30; Oct.: 1, 2, 3, 4-7, 8, 9, 10, 11, 12, 28-30; Nov.: 27-29, 30; Dec.: 1-4, 5, 6-9, 10, 11, 27, 28, 29, 30, 31.

COMMITTEES

Communication and cooperation at meetings are favored on the following dates.

Jan.: 1, 3, 8, 11, 16, 22-25; Feb.: 7-9, 20, 24, 25, 27; Mar.: 4; Apr.: 3, 8, 9; May: 25, 27, 31; Jun.: 1, 2, 4, 21, 24, 29; Jul.: None; Aug.: 3, 10, 17, 22, 31; Sep.: 4, 6-9, 11-13, 18; Oct.: 3, 8, 16, 18, 19, 22-25, 29; Nov.: 21, 25, 30; Dec.: 1-3, 6, 8, 9, 13.

COMPUTER: E-MAIL

Do you want an e-mail address so you can receive your mail electronically? These are favorable dates to apply and/or start your e-mail service.

Jan.: 2-4, 9, 10, 15, 16, 18, 25; Feb.: 5-7, 16, 18, 20-22, 24-28; Mar.: 1, 3, 4, 31; Apr.: 1-12, 15, 18, 21, 22, 24, 27, 29; May: 5, 8, 12, 13, 15, 16, 19-22, 24-26; Jun.: 1, 5, 7-9, 12, 22, 24-27; Jul.: 2; Aug.: 2, 3, 8, 11, 14, 19-21, 23-27, 29, 30; Sep.: 1, 9, 11, 12, 15-19; Oct.: 1-4, 9, 10, 12, 14-21, 25, 29, 30; Nov.: 20, 27-30; Dec.: 2-4, 9, 10, 17, 22-25, 29-31.

COMPUTER: FRAUD, SCAM

Be aware of shell games (bogus vacation, insurance and travel scams, etc.), because online rip offs could be attracted on these dates; their web sites can vanish in an instant when the screen is wiped clean. Their telephone lines can, also, be turned off in a second.

Jan.: 1-20, 24, 28-31; Feb.: 1-4, 14, 20, 26, 27; Mar.: 13, 19, 20, 26; Apr.: 9-16, 19-30; May: 1-23, 28-31; Jun.: 1-25, 30; Jul.: 1, 6, 7, 12-16, 28, 31; Aug.: 1, 3, 9, 10, 24, 30, 31; Sep.: 1-28; Oct.: 3, 10-15, 17, 18, 24, 25, 30; Nov.: 1-8, 12-15, 20, 21, 27; Dec.: 5-9, 11, 18-31.

COMPUTER: GAMES — CREATE

Create a computerized game on these dates; you'll have brilliant ideas. To finish it quickly, start creating it on the underlined dates. See Designing, page 143; see Selling, page 191.

Jan.: 4, 5, 9-15, 25, 27-29, 31; Feb.: 1, 3, 4, 5-7, 16, 18, 19, 21, 22, 24, 25; Mar.: 3-6, 7-12, 14, 15, 27, 28, 31; Apr.: 1, 2, 4, 5, 6-8, 11, 12, 14, 15, 20, 30; May: 1, 2, 4, 5, 6, 8, 9, 11, 12, 14-16, 21, 22, 24-27, 31; Jun.: 1, 2, 4, 5, 11, 12, 14, 25-29; Jul.: 2, 15, 16, 18-21, 23; Aug.: 7, 11, 12, 14, 19, 20, 22, 26; Sep.: 18, 23, 25; Oct.: 1, 4, 9-12, 13-16, 19-21, 23, 29, 31; Nov.: 1, 2, 4-11, 16, 17, 19, 28-30; Dec.: 2-4, 10, 13, 17, 29-31.

COMPUTER: GAMES — PLAY

Play online games in Cyberspace on these dates. You'll be alert, confident and have a great time.

Jan.: 2, 3, 7-10, 15, 16, 27; Feb.: 5-7, 18-21, 24, 25; Mar.: 4-7, 10, 12-14, 19, 20, 25-27, 31; Apr.: 2-4, 6-8, 10, 11, 14, 17, 20, 21; May: 4, 11-13, 18-20, 24-26, 31; Jun.: 1-3, 7-9, 22, 24, 25; Jul.: 6, 19, 20, 22, 24, 27, 29; Aug.: 7, 9, 14, 21, 24, 25, 29; Sep.: 3, 28; Oct.: 1-3, 9, 10, 15-19, 21, 31; Nov.: 11-15, 19-21, 27, 28, 30; Dec.: 2-5, 8, 10-13, 17, 24, 25, 29, 31.

COMPUTER: PROGRAM

Do you have a formula, system or anything else you want programmed on a computer? If so, program, or hire a programmer, on these favorable dates. Use the finished product (software) commercially or for your personal use. The underlined dates are best, if you want to finish quickly.

Jan.: 1-4, 9, 10, 15, 18, 25; Feb.: 5, 7, 20, 21, 24, 25, 27; Mar.: 3, 4, 31; Apr.: 1-4, 7-9; May: 24-27, 29; Jun.: 1, 4, 7-10, 14, 22, 24, 25, 29; Jul.: 2; Aug.: 2, 3, 7, 8, 11, 19, 22, 24-26, 29, 30, 31; Sep.: 1, 6-9, 11-13, 15, 17-19; Oct.: 1-4, 9, 16-19, 21, 24, 29; Nov.: 20, 21, 28-30; Dec.: 2-4, 9, 11, 17, 18.

COMPUTER: SECRET CODES

These are the best dates to put in a secret code on your computer. The best dates are underlined.

Jan.: 22-27; Feb.: 20-23, 24, 25; Mar.: 21, 22, 23, 24, 25, 28; Apr.: 20, 21, 24-26; May: 22-26; Jun.: 18-24; Jul.: 17-22; Aug.: 16-18, 21, 22, 23; Sep.: 17, 18, 19; Oct.: 14, 15, 16, 21; Nov.: 13, 17-19; Dec.: 15-18.

COMPUTER SERVICES: INTERNET, ONLINE

Subscribe to the internet, online services on the following dates and you'll find it educational and helpful. Test your I.Q., research family, medical, or other areas, puzzles or interact with audience members. Also, log on to auctions, travel, stock market, financial and investment fields,etc. Be online with celebrity interviews. The underlined dates are best. See Computer Fraud, page 140; see Computer: Games, page 140; see Voice Mail, page 206.

Jan.: 1-5, 10, 15, 16, 18, 25; Feb.: 5-7, 18, 21, 24-26; Mar.: 3, 4, 31; Apr.: 1-4, 6-9; May: 24, 25, 31; Jun.: 1-3, 4, 7-10, 21, 22, 24, 25, 29; Jul.: 2; Aug.: 2, 3, 7, 8, 10, 11, 19, 21, 23-26, 29, 30, 31; Sep.: 1, 18; Oct.: 3, 4, 9, 16-19, 21, 24, 25, 29, 30; Nov.: 20, 21, 27-30; Dec.: 3, 4, 6, 8, 9, 13.

COMPUTER: WEB SITE

Start your own home page on the following dates. Design it, or have it designed on the underlined dates. See Designing, page 143.

Jan.: 6. 8. 9, 10, 11, 12-15, 16, 18; Feb.: 5, 6, 7-9, 11, 12, 13, 15, 16, 18; Mar.: None; Apr.: 6, 7, 8, 9, 11, 12; May: 5, 9, 14, 15; Jun.: 4, 5, 6-8, 10, 11, 14, 15; Jul.: 3-5, 6; Aug.: 2, 3, 7, 10, 11, 12, 31; Sep.: 1, 4—9, 11-13; Oct.: 1, 3, 4, 5, 8, 9, 28, 29; Nov.: 27, 28, 29, 30; Dec.: 2-4, 6, 8-10, 29, 30, 31.

CONTRACTS: DRAWING OR SIGNING

For the greatest chance of success, draw or sign a contract, document, paper, lease or an agreement on any of the following dates. If quick results are desired, draw or sign the papers on the underlined dates. See Avoid: Contracts (Drawing or Signing), page 110; also see Legal Action, pages 165, 166.

Jan.: 10, 15, 25; Feb.: 4, 5-10, 15-18, 24-26; Mar.: None; Apr.: 5, 6-8, 18, 21; May: 5, 8, 13, 15-17, 20-24; Jun.: 6-9, 14, 24; Jul.: None; Aug.: 3, 8, 19-21; Sep.: 9-13, 15, 30; Oct.: 1-4, 10, 12, 14, 16-21, 29, 30; Nov.: 26, 27-30; Dec.: 1, 3, 4, 9, 15, 29-31.

CORNS: REMOVAL

These are favorable days to remove those ugly, old and painful corns on your toes. The preferred dates are underlined. However, if surgery is to be performed see the toe/foot areas listed under Avoid: Surgery, page 117; also, see Surgery, page 202.

Jan.: 23, 30; Feb.: 20, 26, 27; Mar.: 3, 4, 26, 30, 31; Apr.: 4, 22, 27; May: 2, 19, 20, 24, 25, 29, 30; Jun.: 20, 21, 25, 26, 30; Jul.: 18, 23, 28; Aug.: 19, 20, 24, 28; Sep.: 15, 16, 20, 21, 25-27; Oct.: 17, 18, 22-24; Nov.: 14, 18, 19, 20; Dec.: 15-18, 24.

COURAGE

Do you need courage to confront someone, drive a car for the first time, indulge in a dangerous sport, or to make love to someone? If so, you will feel more gutsy on the following dates:

Jan.: 15, 16, 27; Feb.: 18, 24-27; Mar.: 10, 12, 13, 17, 23; Apr.: 4, 14; May: 8-10, 13, 15-17, 22-24, 31; Jun.: 1-3, 7, 29; Jul.: 22, 24, 28; Aug.: 9, 10, 21, 25; Sep.: 17-19, 25, 30; Oct.: 1-3, 14, 17, 30; Nov.: 11-14, 19, 27, 30; Dec.: 2, 10-12, 15, 23-25.

CREDIT: APPLICATIONS, PURCHASES

Apply for credit (in person or by mail) on any of these dates (this includes credit cards, banks and credit unions). The best days to apply for credit are underlined. The credit purchase will be paid quickly if charged on these days. See Avoid: Debts, page 111; see Money: Borrow or Lending, page 173.

Jan.: 6-12, 13, 15-20; Feb.: 5, 6-8, 9-11, 13-15, 16-18; Mar.: None; Apr.: 6-11, 15, 16, 17, 18; May: 5-10,12-17; Jun.: 4-6, 7, 8, 9, 11-15, 16; Jul.: 3, 4, 5, 6; Aug.: 1-4, 5, 6, 8-13, 31; Sep.: 1-4, 6-13, 29, 30; Oct.: 1, 2, 3, 4, 6-10, 11, 12, 28-30; Nov.: 28-30; Dec.: 1, 2, 3, 5-11, 27, 28-31.

CRUSADES: COMMENCE

If you want quick action for universal causes and the masses to be cooperative, try the following dates to commence your crusade. The underlined days are when it will be easier to stick with the crusade. See Reforms: Commence, page 184.

Jan.: 8, 11, 16; Feb.: 7-9, 12; Mar.: None; Apr.: 8, 9; May: 5, 12-14, 17; Jun.: 4, 10; Jul.: None; Aug.: 3, 7, 10, 31; Sep.: 4-9, 11, 12, 13; Oct.: 3, 8, 29; Nov.: 30; Dec.: 1, 2, 3, 4, 6, 8, 9, 29, 31.

DATING

Date someone for the first time on these dates. See Avoid: Blind Dates, page 109. If it is someone you had been out with previously, see Romance, page 190.

Jan.: 1, 6, 12-16, 25-28, 31; Feb.: 1-3,11, 15, 17, 18, 21, 23-25; Mar.: None; Apr.: 1, 4, 7, 8, 11-15, 17, 18, 20, 21, 26, 29; May: 2, 12, 14, 15, 17, 19-21, 27-31; Jun.: 1, 2, 4, 6, 12-14, 20, 26, 29; Jul.: 3, 4, 26; Aug.: 5, 6, 16, 20-22, 25, 26, 31; Sep.: 1, 7, 9-13,15, 18, 28; Oct.: 4, 9, 10, 19-21, 23, 26, 27, 29; Nov.: 11, 22-26, 28-30; Dec.: 1-5, 7-10, 28-31.

DEBATE: CONTROVERSY

On the following dates, your ideas will be readily expressed and understood by others. Controversy and unusual views will flourish and be accepted quickly on the underlined dates.

Jan.: 2-4, 9, 30, 31; Feb.: 1, 3, 5-7, 16, 18; Mar.: 1, 3, 4, 31; Apr.: 1-4, 15, 18, 21, 22, 27, 29; May: 8, 12, 16, 19-22, 24, 25; Jun.: 5, 7, 8, 12, 14, 21, 22, 26; Jul.: None; Aug.: 2, 11, 14, 24-27, 29; Sep.: 1, 11, 12, 15; Oct.: 4, 9, 12, 17, 19; Nov.: 20, 27-29; Dec.: 3, 23, 24, 29-31.

DEBTS: COLLECT

If anyone owes you money, attempt to collect it on these dates; thus bill (or call) clients, customers or others who owe you. If quick results are desired, try the underlined dates.

Jan.: 30; Feb.: 3, 20, 21, 27; Mar.: None; Apr.: 23, 28; May: 9, 10, 12, 20; Jun.: None; Jul.: None; Aug.: 6, 8, 9; Sep.: 27, 30; Oct.: 3, 19; Nov.: 21, 22, 24, 27; Dec.: 9, 10, 17, 23, 24, 28, 30.

DECORATING

Be an interior decorator and try one of these dates if you want to be extra neat and blend the right colors, fabrics, accessories and furniture. The job page 143 (below).

Jan.: 1, 6, 12, 15, 23-28, 30, 31; Feb.: 1-3, 11, 12, 14-18, 20-25; Mar.: 8, 11-14, 26, 29; Apr.: 1-4, 7-15, 17, 18, 20-22, 26, 29; May: 2, 4, 12-17, 19-21, 27-31; Jun.: 1-3, 4, 6, 12-14, 20, 26, 29; Jul.: 1, 3, 4, 6-10, 26, 29; Aug.: 5, 6, 9, 16, 20-26, 30, 31; Sep.: 1, 6, 7, 9-13, 15, 18, 20, 27, 28; Oct.: 3, 4, 9, 10, 18-27, 29; Nov.: 3, 8, 9, 11, 19, 21-26, 27-30; Dec.: 1-11, 18, 24, 28-31.

DENTAL WORK: BONDING, BRACES, BRIDGES, CAPS, FILLINGS, PLATE IMPRESSIONS, RECONSTRUCTION, ROOT CANAL AND X-RAYS

Braces and fillings will remain intact, and plate impressions, reconstruction, root canal and x-rays work well and give good results on any of the following days. If the preceding work is done on a date not listed, it might be necessary to have the filling fixed again, or you could return many times before you get good plate impressions, or a problem may occur with the braces, bridges, false teeth or root canal work. See Avoid: Dental Work, page 111.

Jan.: 1, 2, 28; Feb.: 24; Mar.: 3, 4, 23, 24, 30, 31; Apr.: 27; May: 24, 25; Jun.: 20, 21; Jul.: 18; Aug.: 28; Sep.: 25; Oct.: 22; Nov.: 18, 25; Dec.: 15, 16, 22.

DENTAL WORK: CLEANING

For painless cleaning of the gums or teeth, it is best to go to the dentist or perio-dentist on any of the following days. See Avoid: Dental Cleaning, page 111.

Jan.: 1-11, 15-20, 22-31; Feb.: 1-7, 11-18, 20-28; Mar.: 1-6, 11-19, 21-31; Apr.: 1, 2, 7-18, 20-30; May: 4-17, 19-27; Jun.: 1-16, 18-23, 28-30; Jul.: 1-15, 17-21, 25-31; Aug.: 1-14, 16, 17, 22-31; Sep.: 1-13, 18-30; Oct.: 1-11, 15-31; Nov.: 1-7, 11, 13-30; Dec.: 1-4, 9-11, 13-31.

DENTAL WORK: EXTRACTIONS

Less pain and quick healing will take place if an extraction is performed on any of the following dates. See Avoid: Dental Work, page 111.

Jan.: 17; Feb.: 14; Mar.: 13; Apr.: 9, 16; May: 6, 7, 13; Jun.: 9; Jul.: 7, 13; Aug.: 3, 9, 10; Sep.: 5, 6; Oct.: 3, 30; Nov.: 27; Dec.: None.

DESIGNING

Design a house or work of art on one of these dates, because your imagination will soar as your artistic and creative talents are fully released. This includes interior and exterior designs on announcements, badges, banners, business cards, ceramics, certificates (awards/prizes, etc.), chimneys, clocks, clothes, decals, emblems, furniture, graphics, jewelry, kilns, landscaping, linens, logos, packaging, plates, sailboats, signs (including neon), uniforms, windows. Also, all structures — casinos, condos, hotels, inns, motels, lodges, shopping centers. See Architectural Plans, page 107.

Jan.: 4-16, 23, 25-29, 31; Feb.: 1-13, 15-19, 21-25; Mar.: 3-12, 14, 15, 25, 27, 28, 31; Apr.: 2, 6-8, 11-15, 17-21, 30; May: 2, 4, 12, 14-18, 22-27,31; Jun.: 1, 2, 4, 5, 11-15, 17-20, 25-29; Jul.: 2-5, 8-12, 23-26, 30; Aug.: 6-8, 11-17, 22, 26; Sep.: 18, 28; Oct.: 5, 8, 10, 15, 16, 19-23, 26-29, 31; Nov.: 1-11, 16-19, 25, 26, 28, 29; Dec.: 4, 13, 29-31.

DIET: GAIN WEIGHT

If gaining weight is your objective, increase the intake of food on the following days. The diet is easy to stick with if it is commenced on one of the underlined dates.

Jan.: 9-11, 13, 18-20; Feb.: 6-9, 16, 18; Mar.: 9, 10, 11, 15, 18; Apr.: 11-13, 14, 15, 17; May: 8-10, 11, 12, 16; Jun.: 5, 8, 12, 14, 15, 16; Jul.: 4, 5, 8, 11, 13; Aug.: 1, 5, 6, 7, 8-10, 31; Sep.: 1, 2, 3, 4-6, 13, 29, 30; Oct.: 3, 10, 11, 30, 31; Nov.: 2, 5-7, 11, 27; Dec.: 4, 6, 8, 30, 31.

DIET: LOSE WEIGHT

Get rid of weight fast by starting a new diet on any of the following dates. It will be easy to stick to your regime if you begin a diet on any of these dates.

Jan.: 1, 28; Feb.: 24; Mar.: 3, 4, 23, 24, 30, 31; Apr.: 20, 27; May: 24, 25, 31; Jun.: 1, 20, 21, 28; Jul.: 18, 25, 26; Aug.: 21, 22, 28; Sep.: 18, 25; Oct.: 15, 22; Nov.: 18, 24, 25; Dec.: 15, 16, 22.

DINING: GOURMET

Enjoy haute cuisine on the following dates:

Jan.: 3, 14-18, 21-24, 27, 30, 31; Feb.: 3, 18, 20, 21, 27; Mar.: 19, 20; Apr.: 14; May: 10, 11, 20; Jun.: 7, 16; Jul.: 4, 5, 13; Aug.: 1, 5-10, 13-16, 28; Sep.: 27, 28, 30; Oct.: 3, 22-25, 27, 30; Nov.: 21, 22, 24-27; Dec.: 23, 24.

DISTRIBUTION: BOOKS, MAGAZINES, PRODUCTS

Contact by fax, mail or phone a distributor on any of these dates. For quick results, make contact on the underlined dates.

Jan.: 2-4, 10, 15, 25, 30; Feb.: 1-3, 5-10, 15-18, 21-25; Mar.: 1-4, 31; Apr.: 6-9, 11, 18, 21, 27, 29; May: 5, 8, 13, 15-17, 20-24; Jun.: 1, 6-9, 24; Jul.: None; Aug.: 3, 8, 19-21, 24; Sep.: 9-13, 15, 30; Oct.: 1-4, 10, 12, 14, 16-20, 25, 29, 30; Nov.: 20, 22, 27-30; Dec.: 1, 3, 9, 15, 22-25, 29-31.

DRAMATIC EXPRESSION

Fantasy, creative imagination and the dramatic expression of emotions are best expressed on any of the following dates. This includes acting, dancing, singing, movies, plays, TV shows, radio/TV commercials or poetry readings.

Jan.: 5-10, 15, 16, 25-29, 31; Feb.: 1-13, 15-19, 21-25, 28; Mar.: 1-12, 14, 15, 21, 23, 28, 31; Apr.: 2, 13-15, 17-20; May: 4, 9, 15-17, 22-27, 31; Jun.: 1, 2, 4, 5, 11-14, 18-20, 25-29; Jul.: 2, 18-21, 23, 26, 30; Aug.: 5-8, 11-14, 20-22, 26, 28; Sep.: 18; Oct.: 1, 11, 14-16, 19-23, 26-29, 31; Nov.: 1-11, 16-19, 25, 26, 28, 29; Dec.: 4, 13, 15, 22, 29, 31.

DRUGS

These are the dates when you find it easiest to stop taking drugs and to stick to your resolution.

Jan.: 1, 28; Feb.: 24; Mar.: 3, 4, 23, 24, 30, 31; Apr.: 20, 27; May: 24, 25, 31; Jun.: 1, 20, 21, 28; Jul.: 18, 25, 26; Aug.: 21, 22, 28; Sep.: 18, 25; Oct.: 15, 22; Nov.: 18, 24, 25; Dec.: 15, 16, 22.

DUDE — RANCHING

Take a great vacation by dude-ranching on these dates. If you'd rather take over a ranch, invite your own guests and shape the environment to your liking, then become a dude-rancher on the underlined dates.

Jan.: 1-3, 13, 14, 15, 16, 27; Feb.: 5, 6, 7, 24-28; Mar.: 1, 8, 10, 12-22; Apr.: 2-4, 6, 11, 13, 14, 18; May: 1, 2, 3, 5, 8-10, 11-13, 15-18, 19, 20, 22, 23, 24, 26, 31; Jun.: 1-3, 5-10, 24, 29; Jul.: 22-24, 28, 30; Aug.: 5-7, 9, 10, 19, 20, 21, 25; Sep.: 17-20, 23-25, 30; Oct.: 1-3, 10, 11, 13, 14, 17, 19, 21, 30; Nov.: 9, 11-15, 19, 20, 27, 28, 30; Dec.: 2-6, 10, 11-15, 17, 23, 24, 25, 26, 27.

EAR PIERCING

Try getting your ears pierced on one of these days; you will probably be happy with the results. You will heal quickest on the underlined dates. See Avoid: Ears Pierced, page 111.

Jan.: 1-4, 6-12, 17-19, 23-31; Feb.: 1-3, 5-8, 14-17, 21-28; Mar.: 1-5, 7, 8, 14-18, 22-31; Apr.: 1-4, 10-17, 21-30; May: 1, 7-16, 20-29; Jun.: 4-15, 19-25, 30; Jul.: 1, 3-14, 18-22, 28-30; Aug.: 1-13, 17-19, 25-29, 31; Sep.: 1-12, 21-27, 29, 30; Oct.: 1-11, 18-26, 28-31; Nov.: 1-8, 14-25, 26-30; Dec.: 1-6, 14-25, 27-31.

EARS: PLATE IMPRESSIONS

The best days for plate impressions for the ears are the following dates:
Jan.: 1, 28; Feb.: 24; Mar.: 3, 4, 23, 24, 30, 31; Apr.: 20, 27; May: 24, 25; Jun.: 20, 21; Jul.: 18; Aug.: 28; Sep.: 25; Oct.: 22; Nov.: 18, 24, 25; Dec.: 15, 16, 22.

EGGS: TO HATCH

Set eggs to hatch on the following dates if you do not care about the chicks' size or whether they mature quickly. The best days are underlined.

Jan.: 10, 11, 19; Feb.: 6, 7, 16; Mar.: 15; Apr.: 11, 12; May: 9, 17; Jun.: 5, 14; Jul.: 11; Aug.: 7; Sep.: 3, 13; Oct.: 1, 10, 11, 28; Nov.: 4; Dec.: 1, 2, 11, 31.

EGGS: SET TO HATCH FOR QUICK MATURITY

Set eggs to hatch on the following dates if you want chicks to mature quickly; otherwise, refer to the preceding category.

Jan.: 15-20; Feb.: 13-18; Mar.: 15-19; Apr.: 13-18; May: 12-17; Jun.: 11-16; Jul.: 10-15; Aug.: 8-14; Sep.: 6-13; Oct.: 6-12; Nov.: 5-11; Dec.: 5-11.

EGGS: SET TO HATCH FOR SIZE

Set eggs to hatch on the following dates if you want the chicks to be large; otherwise, see the preceding categories.

Jan.: 6-13; Feb.: 5-11; Mar.: 7-13; Apr.: 6-11; May: 5-10; Jun.: 4-9; Jul.: 3-8; Aug.: 1-6; Sep.: 1-4, 29, 30; Oct.: 1-4, 28-31; Nov.: 1-3, 27-30; Dec.: 1-3, 27-31.

ELECTROLYSIS

Remove unwanted hair on these favorable dates; preferred days are underlined.

Jan.: 3, 23, 30; Feb.: 20, 26, 27; Mar.: 3, 4, 26, 30, 31; Apr.: 4, 22, 27; May; 2, 19, 20, 24, 25, 29, 30; Jun.: 20, 21, 25, 26, 30; Jul.: 18, 23, 28; Aug.: 19, 20, 24, 28; Sep.: 15, 16, 20, 21, 25, 26, 27; Oct.: 17, 18, 22-24, 30; Nov.: 14, 18, 19, 20; Dec.: 15, 16, 17, 18, 24.

EMPLOYMENT AGENCY

Sign up with an employment agency on these dates. For opening an employment agency, see Business: Commence, page 121; for Employment Application or Resume, see Job: Apply for Work, page 163; see Job: Interviews, page 163.

Jan.: 2-4, 10, 15, 25, 30; Feb.: 1-3, 5-10, 15-18, 21-25; Mar.: 1-4, 31; Apr.: 6-9, 11, 18, 21, 27, 29; May: 3, 5, 8, 13, 15-17, 20-24; Jun.: 1, 6-9, 14, 24; Jul.: None; Aug.: 3, 8, 19-21, 24; Sep.: 9-13, 15, 24, 25, 30; Oct.: 1-4, 10, 12, 14, 16-20, 25, 29, 30; Nov.: 20, 22, 27-30; Dec.: 1, 3, 9, 15, 22-25, 29-31.

ENCOURAGEMENT

Encourage someone on any of the following dates and watch how quickly the person responds. However, for encouragement to be lasting, the underlined days are best.

Jan.: 30; Feb.: 4, 6-8, 17, 18, 26, 27; Mar.: 3, 4, 5-7, 13, 14, 17; Apr.: 1-4, 13, 14; May: 27, 31; Jun.: 1, 7, 8-10, 24, 25, 27, 28, 29; Jul.: 20-22, 24, 25, 26; Aug.: 9, 18, 28; Sep.: 10, 11; Oct.: 3, 11, 17-19, 21; Nov.: 5-8, 14, 15, 17, 18, 19-22, 24-27; Dec.: 2.

ENGAGEMENTS

Become engaged on any of these date. The underlined days are best. See Marriage Proposals, page 171.

Jan.: 1, 6, 12, 13, 15, 16, 25, 26, 28, 30, 31; Feb.: 1-3, 11, 14, 15, 17, 18, 20, 21, 23, 24, 25; Mar.: None; Apr.: 1, 4, 7, 8, 10-13, 15, 17-19, 21, 22, 26, 29; May: 2, 12-15, 17, 19-21, 27-30, 31; Jun.: 1, 2, 4, 6, 12, 13, 14, 20, 26, 29; Jul.: 1, 3, 4, 6; Aug.: 5, 6, 9, 16, 20, 21, 22, 24-26, 31; Sep.: 1, 7, 9, 10, 11, 12, 13, 15, 18, 20, 25, 27; Oct.: 3, 4, 9, 10, 18-20, 23-26, 29; Nov.: 22, 23, 24, 25, 27-30; Dec.: 1, 2, 3, 5, 7, 8, 9, 10, 11, 24, 28, 29, 30, 31.

ENGRAVING

Engraving will be done beautifully on any of the following dates. For quick service, take the item or object in for engraving on any of the underlined dates.

Jan.: 1, 2, 13, 15, 16; Feb.: 5-7, 18, 20, 21, 24, 25; Mar.: None; Apr.: 2-4, 6-8, 10, 11, 13, 14, 17, 18, 20, 21; May: 1, 2, 12, 13, 15, 17, 19, 20, 22, 23, 27, 28, 30, 31; Jun.: 1, 2, 5-7, 9, 29; Jul.: 1, 3; Aug.: 5, 6, 9, 10, 16, 20, 21, 24-29, 31; Sep.: 1, 7, 17-20, 30; Oct.: 2, 3, 9, 10, 17-19, 30; Nov.: 27-30; Dec.: 2, 3, 5, 7, 8, 10, 11, 13, 15, 17, 24, 25, 27-29, 31.

ENTERTAINMENT

Every type of entertainment is enjoyed and well received on any of the following dates. Note: this includes poetry readings, movies, plays, music or dance in arenas, stadiums, concert halls, theatres or night clubs, as well as home entertainment. Also, see Shows, page 194.

Jan.: 7-10, 27-30; Feb.: 5-7, 17, 18, 23-27; Mar.: 3-7, 13, 14, 17, 23, 25, 26, 31; Apr.: 1, 2, 4, 13, 14; May: 24-28; Jun.: 3, 4, 7, 20-25, 30; Jul.: 1, 4, 5, 18-21, 29; Aug.: 6-10, 16, 17, 24, 25; Sep.: 2-6, 30; Oct.: 1-3, 11, 17-19, 21, 30; Nov.: 4-8, 14, 15, 17, 18, 27; Dec.: 1-5, 11-13.

ERRANDS

For good service, send a messenger on any of the following dates. For quick delivery use the underlined days.

Jan.: 2-4, 10, 15, 25, 30; Feb.: 1-10, 15-18, 21-26; Mar.: 1-4, 31; Apr.: 5-9, 11, 12, 18, 21, 27, 29; May: 5, 8, 13, 15-17, 20-24; Jun.: 1, 6-9, 14, 24; Jul.: None; Aug.: 3, 8, 19-21, 24; Sep.: 9-13, 15, 24, 25, 30; Oct.: 1-4, 10, 12, 14, 16-21, 29, 30; Nov.: 20, 22, 26-30; Dec.: 1, 3, 4, 9, 22-25, 29-31.

EXAMS, TESTS, STUDIES:
FOR CONCENTRATION AND PERSISTENCE

Study or take a test on any of the following dates because concentration and determination are favored:

Jan.: 1, 13-15, 28; Feb.: 1, 2, 4, 5, 11, 12, 18-20, 23, 24; Mar.: 31; Apr.: 3, 5-8, 14, 16, 20; May: 5, 13, 16-18, 31; Jun.: 1, 7, 9, 10, 14, 21, 28; Jul.: None; Aug.: 3, 7, 14, 20-22, 28, 30; Sep.: 9, 18, 25, 27; Oct.: 1, 12-16, 19-22, 24, 28, 29; Nov.: 20, 21, 25, 28-30; Dec.: 1-3, 9, 15, 18, 22, 23, 26-30.

EXAMS, TESTS, STUDIES: FOR LEARNING QUICKLY

Learning is quick on the following dates because your mind is extra alert and sharp:

Jan.: 2, 3, 16, 17, 30, 31; Feb.: 3-5, 8-10, 18, 27; Mar.: 2-4; Apr.: 4, 13, 14, 18, 19, 27; May: 5, 20, 23, 24; Jun.: 25, 29; Jul.: None; Aug.: 9, 10, 19, 20, 28; Sep.: 15, 25, 30; Oct.: 1-3, 12, 17, 22, 28, 30; Nov.: 27; Dec.: 10, 15, 22-24, 29.

EXAMS, TESTS, STUDIES: FOR PSYCHICALLY TUNING IN

Try these dates, because from out of the ether the answers seem to flow from the subconscious to the conscious mind. However, the underlined days are best for psychically tuning in.

Jan.: 1-4, 10, 11, 15, 20, 21, 28; Feb.: 6, 7, 10, 11, 15, 17-21, 23-28; Mar.: 2-4, 30, 31; Apr.: 2, 6-11, 19, 20, 27, 29; May: 17, 18, 23, 25, 27; Jun.: 1, 7, 8, 14, 21, 28; Jul.: None; Aug.: 7, 14, 15, 22; Sep.: 11, 13, 14, 18; Oct.: 1, 10-17, 28; Nov.: 25-28; Dec.: 4, 9, 11-13, 22, 29, 30, 31.

EXAMS, TESTS, STUDIES: FOR RETENTION

It is easy to retain studies on the following dates. Any exams that are taken could be a snap because mental activities are favored.

Jan.: 15, 28; Feb.: 3-5, 8, 11, 12, 19, 20, 24; Mar.: 31; Apr.: 3, 6-8, 20; May: 5, 13, 18; Jun.: 1, 7-10, 14, 23, 28; Jul.: None; Aug.: 3, 7, 14, 21, 22; Sep.: 18; Oct.: 1, 14-16, 19, 21, 24, 29; Nov.: 20, 21, 25, 26, 28, 30; Dec.: 2, 3, 23, 29.

EXCURSIONS

These dates are great for fun, adventure and pleasure, especially when on an outing, short journey or tour of limited duration. See Amusements, page 106; see Avoid: Accidents, page 109; see Avoid Travel By Air, Land, Water, page 118; see Travel By Land, Water, page 204, 205; see Travel: City, Country or Island Hop, page 205; see Travel Enjoyment, page 205; see Travel Plans, page 205.

Jan.: 7, 8, 15, 16, 27; Feb.: 5, 18, 21, 24, 25; Mar.: 4, 10, 12-14, 17; Apr.: 3, 4, 13, 14, 17, 19-21; May: 17-20, 23, 24, 31; Jun.: 1-3, 7, 29; Jul.: 22, 24, 28; Aug.: 6, 7, 9, 10, 21; Sep.: 17-19; Oct.: 3, 17-19, 21, 30; Nov.: 11, 19, 27; Dec.: 2, 8, 10-13, 15, 24, 25.

EXERCISING (PHYSICAL)

If you start exercising on any of the following dates, you will stick with it on a continuing basis. This includes, jogging, aerobics and calisthenics. Also, your endurance is greatest on these dates. See Buying: Exercise Equipment, page 125; see Sports Activities, page 196.

Jan.: 8, 15; Feb.: 11, 12, 18; Mar.: 11, 17; Apr.: 7, 14; May: 11, 17; Jun.: 7, 14; Jul.: 4, 5, 11; Aug.: 1, 7, 14; Sep.: 3, 10, 11; Oct.: 1, 7, 8, 28; Nov.: 4, 11; Dec.: 1, 2, 9, 29.

EXHIBITS

For good and quick results, exhibit art, flowers (flower shows), manufactured products (such as at trade shows), athletic feats, body building, etc. on any of these dates.

Jan.: 5-20; Feb.: 4-18; Mar.: None; Apr.: 5-18; May: 4-19; Jun.: 2-16; Jul.: 2-6; Aug.: 1-14, 30, 31; Sep.: 1-13, 28-30; Oct.: 1-12, 27-30; Nov.: 26-30; Dec.: 1-11, 26-31.

EXPLORATION: GEOGRAPHICAL, SEARCH

Explore a geographical region; you might make interesting discoveries on these dates. If the exploration deals with a search, try the underlined dates.

Jan.: 1, 2-4, 7-10, 11, 13-15, 16, 24, 25, 30, 31; Feb.: 1, 5, 6, 7, 12, 16, 18-20, 21, 23-26, 28; Mar.: 3, 4, 30, 31; Apr.: 1, 2, 3, 4, 7, 8, 9, 12, 15, 17, 18, 21, 24, 27, 29, 30; May: 1, 2, 5, 8, 12, 13, 15-22, 24, 25, 26, 27, 29; Jun.: 1, 5, 7-9, 10, 11, 12, 14-17, 21, 22, 24, 25-27, 29; Jul.: 2, 6; Aug.: 3, 7, 8, 10, 11, 14, 17, 19, 22, 24-27, 29, 30, 31; Sep.: 3, 4, 6-8, 9, 11, 12, 13, 14, 15, 17-19, 20, 22, 25, 26; Oct.: 1-4, 6-8, 9, 10, 15, 16, 17, 18, 19, 20, 21, 24, 28, 29; Nov.: 20, 21, 25, 27-29, 30; Dec.: 1, 2, 3, 4, 9, 10-14, 17, 18, 24, 25, 29-31.

EXPLORATION: MEDICAL

If a medical exam for diagnostic purposes is involved, try these dates. Exploratory analysis is highly favored on these days.

Jan.: 1, 3, 10, 15, 16, 28, 30; Feb.: 1, 2, 4, 7, 11, 12, 19-21, 24, 25, 27; Mar.: 4, 31; Apr.: 2, 3, 5-8, 16, 20; May: 5, 13-18, 20, 25, 27, 31; Jun.: 1, 9, 10, 14, 21, 23, 24, 28, 29; Jul.: None; Aug.: 3, 7, 9, 10, 14, 21, 22, 30, 31; Sep.: 9-19; Oct.: 1, 3, 10-21, 24, 28-30; Nov.: 20, 21, 25-30; Dec.: 1-4, 9, 14-17, 22-24, 27, 29, 31.

EYE TESTS

Test your eyes for glasses or contact lenses, or have a regular eye exam on any of these dates.

Jan.: 1, 2, 13, 15, 16, 24; Feb.: 5-7, 20, 24, 25, 27, 28; Mar.: 1; Apr.: 2-4, 11, 13, 18; May: 1, 2, 5, 8-10, 12, 13, 15-17, 19, 20, 22-24, 31; Jun.: 1, 2, 5-9, 24, 29; Jul.: 3; Aug.: 5, 10, 19-21, 25-29; Sep.: 1, 17-20, 23, 30; Oct.: 1-3, 10, 11, 14, 17, 30; Nov.: 20, 27-30; Dec.: 2, 3, 5, 6, 10, 11, 13-15, 17, 23-25, 27.

FABRICS: BLEACHING, DYEING, TINTING

Use bleach, dye or tint on any of the following dates if permanency and lasting results are desired. The best days are underlined. Also, see Shoes: Dye, page 193.

Jan.: 1, 4-7, 8, 10-14, 15, 16, 25-29, 31; Feb.: 1-7, 9, 10, 11, 12, 13, 15, 17, 18, 19, 21, 23-25, 28; Mar.: 1-9, 12, 14-16, 17, 21-23, 25, 27, 28, 31; Apr.: 1, 4, 6, 7, 8, 11-13, 14, 15, 17-21, 30; May: 2, 4-6, 8, 10, 11, 12, 14, 15, 17, 18, 21-23, 25-27, 31; Jun.: 1, 2, 4, 5, 11, 12, 17-20, 25-27, 29; Jul.: 2, 4, 5, 11, 12, 17-19, 21, 23, 26, 29, 30; Aug.: 5, 6, 12, 16, 20-22, 25, 26, 31; Sep.: 1, 18, 23, 25, 28-30; Oct.: 1, 2, 4, 5, 8, 9-14, 16, 19-21, 23, 26, 27, 29; Nov.: 1-5, 7-10, 11, 16-19, 22-26, 28-30; Dec.: 1, 2, 3, 4, 10, 12, 13, 22, 23, 28, 29, 30, 31.

FADS

Be different, daring and original. Start a fad on any one of the following dates. The fad will catch on quickly if the public is first made aware of it on the underlined days.

Jan.: 2-4, 8, 9, 30, 31; Feb.: 1, 3, 5-7, 16, 18, 20; Mar.: 3, 4, 31; Apr.: 1-4, 15, 18, 21, 22, 24, 27, 29; May: 1, 8, 12, 16, 19-22, 24, 25; Jun.: 5, 7, 8, 12, 14, 21, 22, 26, 27; Jul.: 6; Aug.: 11, 14, 24-27, 29; Sep.: 1, 7, 11, 12, 15, 22, 26; Oct.: 4, 9, 17, 19; Nov.: 20, 27-29; Dec.: 3, 10, 17, 24, 29-31.

FASTING

All of the following days are favored to commence a fast. However, if will power to stick with it is needed, it is best to start the fast on the underlined dates.

Jan.: 1, 2, 22-27, 28; Feb.: 1-3, 20-23, 24; Mar.: 1, 2, 3, 4, 24, 26, 31; Apr.: 2, 3, 20, 30; May: 1-3, 22, 23, 24, 28; Jun.: 1, 2, 18, 19, 20, 21, 22-27, 28, 29, 30; Jul.: 17, 18, 19-24, 25, 26, 27, 28; Aug.: 16-20, 21, 22, 23, 24, 28, 29; Sep.: 18, 27; Oct.: 14, 15, 16-18, 22, 23-26; Nov.: 13, 14, 18, 19, 20, 25; Dec.: 15, 16, 17-20, 22.

FAVORS

Others will be more inclined to help you on these days; thus, seek their good will. Request a salary raise. The underlined dates are best if you want quick results.

Jan.: 30; Feb.: 4, 6-8, 17, 18, 20, 21, 26, 27; Mar.: 3, 4; Apr.: 1-4, 13-17; May: 24-27, 31; Jun.: 1-3, 4, 7-10, 20-25, 27-30; Jul.: 1, 31; Aug.: 1-4, 9, 10, 14, 18, 21-25, 28-30, 31; Sep.: 11, 27, 28; Oct.: 3, 9-11, 14-19, 21; Nov.: 20-22, 27; Dec.: 2, 8-10, 17.

FERTILIZING

These dates are good to fertilize crops if you use a chemical fertilizer; however, if you use an organic fertilizer, the underlined days are auspicious.

Jan.: 1, 10, 11, 19, 25, 26; Feb.: 6, 7, 16, 24; Mar.: 15, 23, 24; Apr.: 2, 11, 12, 20, 29, 30; May: 9, 17, 27; Jun.: 5, 14, 20; Jul.: 11, 20, 21, 30; Aug.: 7, 16, 17, 26; Sep.: 3, 13, 23; Oct.: 1, 10, 11, 20, 28; Nov.: 4, 16, 24, 25; Dec.: 1, 2, 11, 13, 22, 31.

FILIBUSTERING

On the following dates, confusion and long-windedness are the order of the day. On the underlined dates, persistence and stubbornness reign.

Jan.: 7, 10, 15, 25, 27, 30; Feb.: 10, 13, 14, 16, 20, 25, 27, 28; Mar.: 2, 20, 26, 31; Apr.: 4, 17, 21, 24, 27, 29; May: 5, 7, 8, 13, 15, 18, 22, 23, 24, 26-30; Jun.: 1, 9, 19, 24, 27, 30; Jul.: 3, 17, 19, 24, 28; Aug.: 3, 6, 8, 13, 19, 20, 22, 24; Sep.: 2, 3, 11, 12-15, 25; Oct.: 4, 16-18, 20; Nov.: 5, 12, 14, 18, 20, 22, 26, 27; Dec.: 2, 4, 21, 24, 30.

FINGERNAILS: FALSE

Apply false fingernails (sculptured nails) on any of the following dates, because they will last longer than if applied on other days.

Jan.: 1, 8, 15, 28; Feb.: 11, 12, 18, 24; Mar.: 3, 4, 11, 17, 23, 24, 30, 31; Apr.: 7, 14, 20, 27; May: 11, 17, 24, 25, 31; Jun.: 1, 7, 14, 20, 21, 28; Jul.: 4, 5, 11, 18, 25, 26; Aug.: 1, 7, 14, 21, 22, 28; Sep.: 3, 10, 11, 18, 25; Oct.: 1, 7, 8, 15, 22, 28; Nov.: 4, 11, 18, 24, 25; Dec.: 1, 2, 9, 15, 16, 22, 29.

FIREWORKS: MAKE, SHOOT

Make fireworks and/or shoot them on these dates.

Jan.: 2, 13-16, 27; Feb.: 5-7, 24-28; Mar.: 1; Apr.: 2-4, 6, 11, 13, 18; May: 9-13, 15-20, 22-24, 26, 31; Jun.: 1-3, 5-10, 24, 29; Jul.: None; Aug.: 5, 10, 21, 25; Sep.: 17-20, 23, 30; Oct.: 1-3, 10, 11, 13, 14, 17, 30; Nov.: 27-30; Dec.: 2-6, 10-15, 17, 23-25, 27.

FISHING (OTHER THAN SHELLFISH)

Fishing is excellent on the following dates, but the fish bite best on the underlined dates.

Jan.: 1, 5, 10, 11, 18-20, 21, 22-24, 28; Feb.: 4, 6, 7, 16-18, 19, 20-22, 24; Mar.: 6, 15, 17-19, 20, 21-23, 24; Apr.: 2, 5, 11, 12, 16-18, 19, 20-22, 29, 30; May: 4, 9, 15-17, 18, 19-21, 27; Jun.: 3, 5, 14-16, 17, 18-20, 23; Jul.: 2, 11, 13-15, 16, 17-19, 20, 21, 30, 31; Aug.: 7, 12-14, 15, 16-18, 26, 30; Sep.: 3, 11-13, 14, 15-17, 23, 28; Oct.: 1, 10-12, 13, 14-16, 20, 27, 28; Nov.: 6, 7, 9-15, 16, 24-26; Dec.: 4, 9-11, 12, 13-15, 22, 26, 31.

FISHING: SHELLFISH

Because they are more plentiful, the following dates are the best for catching shellfish (clams, crabs, shrimp, lobsters, mussels, etc.):
Jan.: 21; Feb.: 19; Mar.: 20; Apr.: 19; May: 18; Jun.: 17; Jul.: 16; Aug.: 15; Sep.: 14; Oct.: 13; Nov.: 12; Dec.: 12.

FOODS: DEHYDRATED OR DRY

For good results, dehydrate or dry foods on any of these dates:
Jan.: 3, 30; Feb.: 26, 27; Mar.: 26; Apr.: 4, 22; May: 2, 19, 20, 29, 30; Jun.: 25, 26; Jul.: 23; Aug.: 19, 20, 28; Sep.: 15, 16, 25; Oct.: 22; Nov.: 18; Dec.: 15, 16, 24.

FOODS: FREEZING

Freezing should be done on the following dates. For best results, freeze foods on any of the underlined days.
Jan.: 1-4, 22, 23, 24-27, 28, 29, 30, 31; Feb.: 1-3, 20, 21-23, 24, 25-28; Mar.: 1-5, 21-23, 24, 25, 26, 27-30, 31; Apr.: 1, 2, 3, 4, 20, 21-29, 30; May: 1-3, 19, 20, 21-26, 27, 28-31; Jun.: 1, 2, 18-20, 21, 22, 23, 24-27, 28, 29, 30; Jul.: 1, 17, 18, 19, 20, 21, 22-24, 25, 26, 27-30; Aug.: 16, 17, 18-21, 22, 23-29; Sep.: 15-17, 18, 19-26, 27; Oct.: 14, 15, 16-23, 24, 25, 26; Nov.: 13-19, 20, 21, 22-24, 25; Dec.: 13-17, 18, 19-21, 22, 23-25.

FOOT TREATMENTS

Do you have a fungus under your toenails or any other annoying foot problem? These are the best dates to see a podiatrist. Do not have your feet or toenails treated on the underlined dates. For Bunions: Removal, see page 121 ; see Calluses, page 134; see Corns, page 141. If surgery is needed, see Avoid: Surgery, page 117 (for foot and toe area) and Surgery (foot and toe area), page 202.
Jan.: 1, 4, 5-8, 10-12, 13-16, 23, 25, 26, 27-29, 31; Feb.: 1, 2, 3, 4, 5-8, 9, 10, 11-13, 15, 16, 17, 18, 19, 21, 22, 23, 24, 25, 28; Mar.: 1, 2, 3, 4, 5-7, 8-10, 11, 12, 14-17, 18, 21-23, 27, 28, 31; Apr.: 1-3, 4-8, 11-14, 15, 17, 18, 19, 20, 30; May: 2, 4-6, 8, 9, 15-17, 18, 21, 22-25, 26, 27; Jun.: 1, 2, 4, 5, 11, 12, 13-15, 17, 18, 19, 20, 25, 26, 27, 28, 29; Jul.: 2, 3, 4, 5, 8, 9, 10, 11, 12, 16-22, 23, 24, 25, 26, 30; Aug.: 7, 12, 16, 17, 22, 25-29; Sep.: 17-19, 23; Oct.: 1, 5, 8, 10, 11, 14-16, 19, 20, 21-23, 26, 27-29, 31; Nov.: 1, 2, 3, 4, 5-8, 9, 10, 11, 16, 17, 18, 19, 25, 26, 28-30; Dec.: 4, 10, 12, 13-15, 16, 17, 22, 23, 29, 31.

FORECLOSURE

Foreclosure is readily attained if started on any of the following dates. Commence foreclosure proceedings on any of the underlined dates, if quick results are desired.
Jan.: 6-10, 15, 16, 28-31; Feb.: 3, 5-7, 17, 18, 20, 21, 23-25, 27, 28; Mar.: 2-5, 31; Apr.: 2, 3, 13, 14, 16; May: 24, 25, 27, 28, 31; Jun.: 1, 2, 4, 7-9, 20-24, 27-30; Jul.: 1; Aug.: 1-4, 6, 8-10, 13, 14, 21, 22, 24, 25, 28, 29, 31; Sep.: 2-4, 6, 7, 9-11, 13, 18, 27; Oct.: 1, 3, 14-19, 30; Nov.: 20, 21, 27, 28, 30; Dec.: 9-11, 15-17.

FRUIT

Fruit keeps best if picked on the following dates. Do not pick fruit on the underlined dates.

Jan.: 1, 2, 3, 4, 22-26, 27-29, 30, 31; Feb.: 1, 2, 20-22, 23-25, 26-28; Mar.: 1-4, 5, 21, 22-25, 26-31; Apr.: 1-3, 4, 19-21, 22-27, 28-30; May: 1, 2, 3, 18, 19-25, 26-28, 29-31; Jun.: 1, 2, 18-21, 22-24, 25-30; Jul.: 1, 17, 18, 19-22, 23-28, 29, 30; Aug.: 15-18, 19-24, 25-27, 28, 29; Sep.: 15-21, 22-24, 25-27; Oct.: 14-18, 19-21, 22-26; Nov.: 13, 14, 15-17, 18-23, 24, 25; Dec.: 12-14, 15-20, 21-23, 24, 25.

FURNITURE: BUILD

These are favorable days to build furniture. To finish the job quickly, start the work on the underlined dates. For Furniture: Good Service, see the following category; see Furniture: Refinish, below.

Jan.: 9, 10, 15, 16, 27; Feb.: 5-7, 18, 19-21, 24-28; Mar.: 2, 4-6, 7, 10, 12-14, 17, 19, 20, 26, 31; Apr.: 2-4, 13, 14; May: 18, 24-27, 31; Jun.: 1-3, 7-10, 22-25, 28-30; Jul.: 1, 19-22, 24, 27-29, 31; Aug.: 2-4, 6, 7, 9, 10, 13, 14, 18, 21, 22, 24, 25; Sep.: 17-19, 30; Oct.: 1-3, 11, 14-19, 21, 30, 31; Nov.: 11, 12-15, 18-21, 27, 28, 30; Dec.: 2-5, 10, 11-13, 15, 17.

FURNITURE: GOOD SERVICE

New furniture will give good service if it is used for the first time on any of the following dates. See Buying: Furniture, page 126.

Jan.: 15; Feb.: 11, 12; Mar.: 11, 31; Apr.: 7; May: None; Jun.: 21, 28; Jul.: 18, 25, 26; Aug.: 14, 22; Sep.: 18; Oct.: 15; Nov.: 4, 11; Dec.: 9, 29.

FURNITURE: REFINISH

The following dates are excellent to refinish furniture. For the job to be done quickly, try the underlined dates.

Jan.: 1, 2, 9, 10, 15, 16, 24, 27; Feb.: 5-8, 17, 18, 19-21, 23-25; Mar.: 3-6, 7, 10-14, 17-19, 20, 24-27, 31; Apr.: 1-4, 6-8, 10, 11, 13, 14, 16, 20-22; May: 5, 10-14, 17, 18-21, 23-27, 31; Jun.: 1-3, 4, 7-10, 25, 27-30; Jul.: 1, 18, 20, 21, 25, 26; Aug.: 7, 9, 14, 17, 21-25, 28-30, 31; Sep.: 18, 27; Oct.: 1, 3, 10, 15-19, 21, 30, 31; Nov.: 10, 11, 17-21, 27, 28, 30; Dec.: 1-5, 9-11, 12, 13, 15-17, 24, 29, 31 .

GAMBLING

Lady Luck may be smiling at you on these dates. The following are general trends for all types of gambling — raffle, lottery, table games, slot machines, contests and sweepstakes. Combine the gambling dates with the Sun sign dates for your best chances to win. The fifth house in an individual horoscope indicates how you will fare with gambling. If you wish to know if you have a lucky horoscope for winning, contact your personal astrologer or call the American Federation of Astrologers (in Tempe, Arizona) for a referral to an astrologer in your area.

Jan.: 8, 10, 27, 28, 30; Feb.: 4, 6-8, 17, 18, 23-27; Mar.: 3-7, 13, 14, 17, 24; Apr.: 1-4, 13, 14; May: 24-28; Jun.: 3, 4, 7, 13, 14, 20-25, 30; Jul.: 1, 4, 5, 13, 18-22, 28, 29, 31; Aug.: 1, 6-10, 14-18, 24, 25, 28; Sep.: 2-6, 10, 11, 30; Oct.: 1, 3, 11, 17-19, 21, 22, 27; Nov.: 5-8, 14, 15, 17, 18, 22, 24-27; Dec.: 2, 4.

GAMBLING: SUN SIGN DATES

Aries
Jan. 20 - Feb. 18; May 21 - June 20; Jul. 22 - Aug. 22; Nov. 22 - Dec. 21

Taurus
Jan. 1 - 19; Feb. 18 - Mar. 20; Jun. 21 - Jul. 22; Aug. 23 - Sep. 22; Dec. 22 - 31

Gemini
Jan. 20 - Feb. 18; Mar. 20 - Apr. 19; Jul. 22 - Aug. 22; Sep. 23 - Oct. 22

Cancer
Feb. 18 - Mar. 20; Apr. 20 - May 20; Aug. 23 - Sep. 22; Oct. 23 - Nov. 21

Leo
Mar. 20 - Apr. 19; May 21 - Jun. 20; Sep. 22 - Oct. 23; Nov. 22 - Dec. 21

Virgo
Jan. 1 - 19; Apr. 20 - May 20; Jun. 21 - Jul. 22; Oct. 23 - Nov. 21; Dec. 22 - 31

Libra
Jan. 20 - Feb. 18; May 21 - Jun. 20; Jul. 22 - Aug. 22; Nov. 22 - Dec. 21

Scorpio
Jan. 1 - 19; Feb. 18 - Mar. 20; Jun. 21 - Jul. 22; Aug. 23 - Sep. 22; Dec. 22 - 31

Sagittarius
Jan. 20 - Feb. 18; Mar. 20 - Apr. 19; Jul. 22 - Aug. 22; Sep. 23 - Oct. 22

Capricorn
Feb. 18 - Mar. 20; Apr. 20 - May 20; Aug. 23 - Sep. 22; Oct. 23 - Nov. 21

Aquarius
Mar. 20 - Apr. 19; May 21 - Jun. 20; Sep. 22 - Oct. 23; Nov. 22 - Dec. 21

Pisces
Jan. 1 - 19; Apr. 20 - May 20; Jun. 20 - Jul. 22; Oct. 23 - Nov. 21; Dec. 20 - 31

GAMES, TOYS: CREATE (BATTERY OPERATED)

These are favorable dates to create a board game that is battery operated (wireless). See Advertising, page 105; see Designing, page 143; see Inventions: Marketing, page 162; see Projects, pages 181, 182; see Selling, page 191.

Jan.: 1, 3, 5, 8, 16, 21-25, 27; Feb.: 7-9, 12, 20, 24, 25, 27; Mar.: 4-7, 11-14, 19, 20, 24; Apr.: 3, 8, 9; May: 17, 18, 25, 31; Jun.: 1-4, 10, 24, 29; Jul.: 7, 11, 21, 26; Aug.: 3, 7, 10, 17, 22, 31; Sep.: 4-9, 11-13, 18; Oct.: 1, 3, 8, 16, 18, 19, 21-25, 29; Nov.: 12-14, 21, 25, 30; Dec.: 1-4, 6, 8, 9, 12, 13, 18.

GAMES, TOYS: CREATE (MECHANICAL)

Be creative and create a board game on these dates. However, if mechanics are involved, the underlined dates are best for games that use electricity. See Advertising, page 105; see Designing, page 143; see Inventions: Marketing, page 162; see Projects, pages 181, 182.

Jan.: 2-4, 9, 13-15, 24, 27, 30, 31; Feb.: 1, 3, 5, 6, 7, 16, 18-20, 24-26, 28; Mar.: 3, 4, 10, 12-17, 19, 20, 21, 22, 25-28, 29; Apr.: 1-4, 6, 11, 13, 15, 18, 19, 21, 22, 24, 29; May: 1, 2, 5, 8, 9-11, 12, 13, 15, 16-18, 20-22, 23, 24, 25, 30, 31; Jun.: 1-3, 5, 7, 8, 9, 10, 12, 14, 22, 24, 25-27, 29; Jul.: 2, 3, 15, 20, 22-24, 28, 30; Aug.: 2, 5, 10, 11, 21, 23-25, 26, 27, 29, 30; Sep.: 1, 6, 7, 12, 15, 17-20, 22, 23, 26, 30; Oct.: 1-3, 4, 9, 10, 11, 13, 14, 17, 19, 30; Nov.: 1, 6, 8, 9, 11, 12, 13, 14, 15, 19, 20, 27-29, 30; Dec.: 2, 3, 4-6, 10, 11-15, 17, 18-21, 24, 25, 27, 29-31.

GAS STATION, PHOTO SHOP OR STUDIO: OPEN

These are favorable days to open these types of business:

Jan.: 6-13, 15, 16; Feb.: 5-11, 13, 15-18; Mar.: None; Apr.: 6-8, 11; May: 5-9, 15-17; Jun.: 4, 5, 11-15; Jul.: 3-5; Aug.: 12; Sep.: None; Oct.: 1, 8, 28, 29; Nov.: 28, 29; Dec.: 10, 29.

GIFTS

Make someone happy by giving a gift on one of these dates. Have you ever given a present that was thrown out later or given to someone else by your recipient? To avoid that possibility, give your gift on any of the underlined dates. See Gifts in Part One under the Sun Sign section of the person for whom you are going to purchase the gift.

Jan.: 1, 6, 12-14, 15, 16, 25-27, 28, 30, 31; Feb.: 1-3, 11, 12, 14, 15, 17, 18, 19-21, 23, 24, 25; Mar.: 28; Apr.: 1, 4, 7, 8, 10-13, 14, 15, 17-19, 20, 21, 22, 26, 29; May: 2, 4, 12-15, 17, 18-21, 27-30, 31; Jun.: 1, 2-4, 6, 12, 13, 14, 20, 26, 29; Jul.: 1, 3, 4, 6; Aug.: 5, 6, 9, 16, 20, 21, 22, 24-26, 31; Sep.: 1, 7, 9, 10, 11, 12, 13, 15, 18, 20, 27, 28; Oct.: 3, 4, 9, 10, 18-21, 23-27, 29; Nov.: 22, 23, 24, 25, 26-30; Dec.: 1, 2, 3-5, 7, 8, 9, 10-12, 18, 24, 28, 29, 30, 31.

GOVERNMENT

Government dealings are favored on the following dates. Take advantage of the underlined dates if quick action and results are desired.

Jan.: 1-5, 8, 11, 16, 25; Feb.: 1-4, 6-10, 16-18, 23-28; Mar.: 3; Apr.: 6, 7, 10, 13-15, 17, 18, 20-22, 29; May: 7-9, 12-14, 23-26, 29-31; Jun.: 1, 5, 7, 12, 22, 25-27; Jul.: 5; Aug.: 1, 5-14, 16, 20, 28-30; Sep.: 1, 3-6, 8, 11-13, 19, 24, 25, 30; Oct.: 8, 11, 12, 14, 18, 22, 23; Nov.: 20, 21, 25-30; Dec.: 1-11, 13-16, 21, 23, 24, 26-28, 31.

GRAFTING AND POLLINATING

Graft, bud, pollinate, transplant, make root separations or take cuttings to root on the following dates because they will grow extremely well:

Jan.: 10, 11, 19; Feb.: 6, 7, 16; Mar.: 15; Apr.: 11, 12; May: 9, 17; Jun.: 5, 14; Jul.: 11; Aug.: 7, Sep.: 3, 13; Oct.: 1, 10, 11, 28; Nov.: 4; Dec.: 1, 2, 11, 31.

GRAIN: HARVESTING

Grain will keep better for seed on these dates. See Avoid: Harvesting, page 112.
Jan.: None; Feb.: 22; Mar.: 21; Apr.: 22; May: 19, 20; Jun.: 20; Jul.: 18; Aug.: 19; Sep.: 15, 16; Oct.: 17, 18; Nov.: 14; Dec.: 15, 16.

GRAIN: PLANTING

Grain planted on any of the following dates will grow well and quickly.
Jan.: 19; Feb.: 16; Mar.: 15; Apr.: None; May: 17; Jun.: 14; Jul.: 11; Aug.: None; Sep.: 13; Oct.: 10, 11; Nov.: 6, 7; Dec.: None.

GRASS: CUTTING

Cut grass so it will grow fast and beautiful on any of the dates that are not underlined. However, if you want to decrease the growth, mow the grass on the underlined dates.
Jan.: 1-4, 5-20, 21-31; Feb.: 1-3, 4-18, 19-28; Mar.: 1-5, 6-19, 20-31; Apr.: 1-4, 5-18, 19-30; May: 1-3, 4-17, 18-31; Jun.: 1, 2, 3-16, 17-30; Jul.: 1, 2-15, 16-30, 31; Aug.: 1-14, 15-29, 30, 31; Sep.: 1-13, 14-27, 28-30; Oct.: 1-12, 13-26, 27-31; Nov.: 1-11, 12-25, 26-30; Dec.: 1-11, 12-25, 26-31.

GROUP ACTIVITIES

Be with crowds or with the gang on the following dates because group activities are favored.
Jan.: 1, 3, 8, 11, 16, 22-25, 27; Feb.: 7-9, 12, 20, 24, 25, 27; Mar.: 4; Apr.: 3, 8, 9; May: 25, 27, 31; Jun.: 1, 2, 4, 10, 24, 29; Jul.: None; Aug.: 3, 7, 10, 17, 22, 31; Sep.: 4-9, 11-13, 18; Oct.: 3, 8, 16, 18, 19, 21-25, 29; Nov.: 21, 25, 30; Dec.: 1-4, 6, 8, 9, 13, 18.

HAIR: COLORING

Bleach, dye, frost, tint or apply a color rinse to the hair (or beard) on any of the following dates. The underlined dates are favorable if you want it to last a long time.
Jan.: 4-7, 8, 9-14, 15, 16, 23, 25-29, 31; Feb.: 1-10, 11, 12, 13, 15-17, 18, 19, 21-25, 28; Mar.: 1-10, 11, 12, 14, 15, 23, 31; Apr.: 6, 7, 8, 11, 12, 20, 30; May: 2, 4-6, 8, 9, 15, 16, 17, 22-27, 31; Jun.: 1, 2, 4, 5, 11-13, 14, 15, 17-20, 25-29; Jul.: 2, 3, 4, 5, 8-10, 11, 12, 16-19, 23, 26, 30; Aug.: 7, 12, 22, 26; Sep.: 18, 23; Oct.: 1, 5, 8, 14-16, 19-23, 26, 27, 28, 29, 31; Nov.: 1-3, 4, 5-10, 11, 16-19, 25, 26, 28, 29; Dec.: 13, 22, 29.

HAIR: CUTTING OR TRIMMING FOR BEAUTY

Have your hair or beard cut on any of the following dates if you want a beautiful cut. The underlined dates are best.
Jan.: 6, 12-20; Feb.: 11, 12, 14-18; Mar.: 8, 11-14, 16-19; Apr.: 6-18; May: 5-17; Jun.: 4, 6, 11-14; Jul.: 3, 4, 6-10; Aug.: 5, 6, 9, 31; Sep.: 1-7, 9-13, 29, 30; Oct.: 1-4, 9-12, 29; Nov.: 3, 8, 9, 11, 27-30; Dec.: 1-11, 27-31.

HAIR: CUTTING OR TRIMMING FOR LUXURIANT GROWTH

Cut hair or a beard for luxuriant growth on any of the following dates:

Jan.: 10, 11, 19; Feb.: 6, 7, 16; Mar.: 15; Apr.: 11, 12; May: 9, 17; Jun.: 5, 14; Jul.: 11; Aug.: 7; Sep.: 3, 13; Oct.: 1, 10, 11, 28; Nov.: 4; Dec.: 1, 2, 11, 31.

HAIR: CUTTING OR TRIMMING FOR QUICK GROWTH

For hair or beards to grow fast, have the ends trimmed or the beard trimmed on any of these dates. The best dates are underlined.

Jan.: 6-12, 13-20; Feb.: 5, 6-9, 10-13, 14-18; Mar.: 7-9, 10, 11-14, 15, 16-19; Apr.: 6-15, 16, 17, 18; May: 5-17; Jun.: 4, 5-11,12-14, 15, 16; Jul.: 3, 4, 5, 6-12, 13-15; Aug.: 1-4, 5-14, 31; Sep.: 1-7, 8, 9, 10-13, 29, 30; Oct.: 1-9, 10-12, 28-30, 31; Nov.: 1-5, 6, 7, 8-11, 27-30; Dec.: 1-11, 27, 28, 29, 30, 31.

HAIR: CUTTING OR TRIMMING FOR SLOW GROWTH

Cut hair or beards on any of the following dates because regrowth will be slow, thus lessening visits to the beauty parlor or barber shop. The best days are underlined.

Jan.: 1, 2, 3, 4, 22, 23, 24, 25, 26, 27-29, 30, 31; Feb.: 1, 2, 3, 20, 21, 22, 23-25, 26, 27, 28; Mar.: 1, 2, 3, 4, 5, 21, 22, 23-25, 26, 27, 28-31; Apr.: 1-3, 4, 20, 21, 22, 23, 24, 25, 26, 27, 28-30; May: 1, 2, 3, 19, 20, 21, 22, 23, 24, 25, 26-28, 29, 30, 31; Jun.: 1, 2, 18-21, 22-24, 25, 26, 27-29, 30; Jul.: 1, 17, 18, 19-22, 23, 24-27, 28, 29, 30; Aug.: 16-18, 19-21, 22, 23, 24, 25, 26-28, 29; Sep.: 15, 16, 17-19, 20-23, 24, 25, 26, 27; Oct.: 14-16, 17, 18, 19, 20, 21, 22, 23, 24, 25, 26; Nov.: 13, 14, 15, 16, 17, 18, 19, 20, 21, 22, 23, 24, 25; Dec.: 13, 14-16, 17, 18, 19, 20, 21-23, 24, 25.

HAIR: CUTTING OR TRIMMING FOR THICKNESS

For hair or beards to grow thick, have them cut or trimmed on these dates.

Jan.: 10, 11, 19; Feb.: 6, 7, 16; Mar.: 15; Apr.: 11, 12; May: 9, 17; Jun.: 5, 14; Jul.: 11; Aug.: 7; Sep.: 3, 13; Oct.: 1, 10, 11, 28; Nov.: 4; Dec.: 1, 2, 11, 31.

HAIR: EXTENSIONS, WEAVING

These are favorable dates to have hair extensions. If you're interested in hair weaving try the underlined dates. See Buying: Wigs, Toupees, or Hair Pieces, page 134.

Jan.: 1-5, 6, 8, 12, 13, 14, 15, 16, 18-21, 22, 23, 24-28, 29, 30; Feb.: 1, 2, 3, 4, 6-9, 11, 14, 15, 16-22, 23, 24, 25-28; Mar.: 1-7, 8, 9, 10, 11, 12, 13-15, 16-22, 24, 25-28, 29; Apr.: 1, 2, 3, 4, 5, 6, 7, 8-11, 12, 18-21, 22, 23-25, 26, 27, 28, 29, 30; May: 2, 4, 9-13, 14, 15-17, 18, 19-26, 27, 28-30, 31; Jun.: 1, 2, 3, 4, 5, 6, 7-11, 12, 13, 14, 15-19, 20, 24, 25, 26, 27, 28, 29, 30; Jul.: 1, 2, 3, 4, 5, 6, 7-9, 10, 11-20, 21, 22-25, 26, 27, 28, 29, 30, 31; Aug.: 1-4, 5, 6, 7, 8, 9, 10, 12, 13, 14, 15, 16-19, 20, 21-24, 25, 26, 27, 28, 29, 30, 31; Sep.: 5, 6, 7, 9, 12-14, 16, 20, 23-25, 27, 28, 29, 30; Oct.: 1, 3, 4, 6-8, 9, 10-17, 18, 19, 20, 21, 22, 23-26, 27, 29, 31; Nov.: 2, 3, 5-7, 8, 9, 10-12, 13-15, 17, 18, 19, 20, 21, 22, 23, 24, 25-27, 28-30; Dec.: 1, 2, 3-7, 8-10, 11, 12, 17, 18, 19, 21, 23, 24, 26-28, 29, 30, 31.

HAIR: PERMANENT

All types of perms will last longer and you will like the results better if the perms are given on any of the following dates:

Jan.: 1, 8, 15, 28; Feb.: 11, 12, 18, 24; Mar.: 3, 4, 11, 17, 23, 24, 30, 31; Apr.: 7, 14, 20, 27; May: 11, 17, 24, 25, 31; Jun.: 1, 7, 14, 20, 21, 28; Jul.: 4, 5, 11, 18, 25, 26; Aug.: 1, 7, 14, 21, 22, 28; Sep.: 3, 10, 11, 18, 25; Oct.: 1, 7, 8, 15, 22, 28; Nov.: 4, 11, 18, 24, 25; Dec.: 1, 9, 15, 16, 22, 29.

HAIR: STRAIGHTENING

It is easiest to straighten hair on these dates. To hasten the procedure, try the underlined dates.

Jan.: 3, <u>10</u>, <u>11</u>, <u>17</u>, 23, 30; Feb.: <u>6</u>, <u>7</u>, <u>14</u>, 20, 26, 27; Mar.: <u>13</u>, <u>19</u>, 26; Apr.: 2, <u>9</u>, <u>15</u>, <u>16</u>, 22, 29, 30; May: <u>6</u>, <u>7</u>, <u>13</u>, 19, 20, 27; Jun.: <u>9</u>, <u>16</u>, 23, 30; Jul.: <u>7</u>, <u>13</u>, 20, 21, 28; Aug.: <u>3</u>, <u>9</u>, <u>10</u>, 16, 17, 24; Sep.: <u>5</u>, <u>6</u>, 13, 20, 21, 27; Oct.: <u>3</u>, 10, 11, 17, 18, 24, <u>30</u>; Nov.: <u>6</u>, <u>7</u>, 14, 20, <u>26</u>, <u>27</u>; Dec.: <u>4</u>, <u>11</u>, 18, 24, <u>31</u>.

HAIR: TRANSPLANTS

Have hair transplanted on these dates and you'll love the results. The best days are underlined. See Avoid: Hair Transplants, page 112.

Jan.: 1, 6, <u>10</u>, <u>11</u>, 15, <u>19</u>, 25, 26, 28; Feb.: 1, 2, <u>6</u>, <u>7</u>, 11, 12, <u>16</u>, 22; Mar.: 1, 11, <u>15</u>, 16, 21, 24, 28; Apr.: 2, 7, <u>11</u>, <u>12</u>, 18, 20, 24, 25, 29, 30; May: <u>9</u>, 15, <u>17</u>, 22, 27; Jun.: 1, <u>5</u>, 11, 12, <u>14</u>, 18, 23, 28; Jul.: 9, <u>11</u>, 15, 20, 21, 25, 26, 30; Aug.: 5, <u>7</u>, 12, 16, 17, 22, 26; Sep.: 1, <u>3</u>, 8, <u>13</u>, 18, 23, 29; Oct.: <u>1</u>, 5, <u>10</u>, <u>11</u>, 15, 20, 26, <u>28</u>; Nov.: 1, 2, <u>6</u>, <u>7</u>,11, 16, 22-25, 29; Dec.: <u>4</u>, 9, 13, 20, 22, 27, <u>31</u>.

HAIR: TREATMENTS

Treatments to increase the growth of your hair should be started on any of the following dates:

Jan.: None; Feb.: None; Mar.: None; Apr.: None; May: 17; Jun.: 14; Jul.: 11; Aug.: 7; Sep.: 3; Oct.: 1, 28; Nov.: None; Dec.: None.

HAIR: SUBSEQUENT TREATMENTS

For treatments after the initial one (see preceding category) to increase the growth of your hair, follow up on one of these dates:

Jan.: 10, 11, 19; Feb.: 6, 7, 16; Mar.: 15; Apr.: 11, 12; May: 9, 17; Jun.: 5, 14; Jul.: 11; Aug.: 7; Sep.: 3, 13; Oct.: 1, 10, 11, 28; Nov.: 4; Dec.: 1, 2, 11, 30.

HARVESTING

Dig all root crops to be used for food on these dates. They will be firmer and will keep better when harvested. This particularly applies to the harvesting of potatoes, beets, carrots and parsnips, or to any root crops that are usually stored for future use without canning. That which is to be stored or used for seed should be harvested on the underlined dates. See Avoid: Harvesting, page 112; see Grain Harvesting, page 155.

Note: The season of the year when various crops are harvested varies greatly in different regions. The suggestions offered here are applicable to each variety whenever the most appropriate time comes to harvest. In northern latitudes, October is the harvest month for root crops. All root vegetables, with the exception of parsnips, should be harvested and stored before the freezing weather arrives. Parsnips seem to improve by the ground having frozen before they are lifted from the soil. The following dates will cover all latitudes, and by knowing your latitude and harvest season you can follow these days accordingly.

Jan.: 3, <u>21</u>, 30; Feb.: <u>19</u>, 26, 27; Mar.: <u>20</u>, 26; Apr.: <u>19</u>, 22; May: 2, <u>18</u>, 19, 20, 29, 30; Jun.: <u>17</u>, 25, 26; Jul.: <u>16</u>, 23; Aug.: <u>15</u>, 19, 20, 28; Sep.: <u>14</u>, 15, 16, 25; Oct.: <u>13</u>, 22; Nov.: <u>12</u>, 18; Dec.: <u>12</u>, 15, 16, 24.

HAY: CUTTING

Cut hay on the following dates. The leaves will shatter less when hay is cut on The underlined dates.

Jan.: 25, 26; Feb.: 22; Mar.: <u>3</u>, <u>4</u>, 21, <u>30</u>, <u>31</u>; Apr.: <u>27</u>; May: <u>24</u>, <u>25</u>; Jun.: <u>20</u>, <u>21</u>, 30; Jul.: <u>18</u>, 28; Aug.: 24; Sep.: 20, 21; Oct.: 17, 18, 26; Nov.: 14, 22, 23; Dec.: 20.

HEALING: MENTAL

Try healing by sending out positive mental thoughts on any of the following dates:
Jan.: 1, 3, 16, 20, 25-28; Feb.: 1-3, 7-9, 12, 20, 24, 25, 27; Mar.: 4-7, 11-14, 19, 20, 23, 24, 30, 31; Apr.: 3, 8-11, 13-16, 20, 27; May: 5, 12-14, 17, 18, 25, 27, 31; Jun.: 1-4, 10, 14, 21, 24, 29; Jul.: 11, 18, 21, 26; Aug.: 3, 7, 10, 14, 22, 31; Sep.: 9, 11-13, 18; Oct.: 1, 3, 11-26, 28-30; Nov.: 4, 7, 12-14, 21, 25-30; Dec.: 1-17, 22-25, 29, 31.

HEALING: PHYSICAL — REHABILITATION

Physical healing and rehabilitation are more readily accomplished on any of these dates. The best days are underlined.
Jan.: 6, 7, 8, 9, 10, 11, 12-15, 16, 17-20; Feb.: 5, 6, 7, 8, 9, 10, 11-13, 14, 15-18; Mar.: 7-10, 11, 12-14, 15, 16, 17-19; Apr.: 6, 7, 8, 9, 10, 11-13, 14, 15-18; May: 5-8, 9, 10-13, 14, 15-17; Jun.: 4, 5, 6, 7, 8-11, 12, 13-16; Jul.: 3-5, 6, 7-10, 11, 12-15; Aug.: 1-4, 5, 6-8, 9, 10-14, 31; Sep.: 1, 2, 3, 4-7, 8, 9-13, 29, 30; Oct.: 1-7, 8, 9-12, 28-31; Nov.: 1, 2-5, 6, 7-11, 27-30; Dec.: 1, 2-5, 6, 7-11, 27, 28, 29, 30, 31.

HEDGES

Hedges will grow best if trimmed on any of the following days. For beauty, neatness and luxurious growth, trim hedges on any of the underlined dates.
Jan.: 6, 7, 8, 9-11, 12, 13; Feb.: 5-7, 8, 9, 10, 11; Mar.: 7, 8, 9, 10-12, 13; Apr.: 6, 7, 8-11; May: 5, 6, 7, 8-10; Jun.: 4, 5, 6, 7, 8, 9; Jul.: 3, 4, 5, 6-8; Aug.: 1, 2-4, 5, 6; Sep.: 1, 2, 3, 4, 29, 30; Oct.: 1, 2, 3, 4, 28, 29, 30, 31; Nov.: 1, 2, 3, 27, 28, 29, 30; Dec.: 1, 2, 3, 27, 28, 29, 30, 31.

HELICOPTER: RIDE

Enjoy a quick trip by taking a helicopter ride on any of these dates. See Avoid: Travel by Air, page 118.
Jan.: 27-29, 31; Feb.: 3-5, 7, 19, 21, 22, 24, 25, 28; Mar.: 1, 2, 4-6, 23, 28, 31; Apr.: 12, 20; May: 8, 9, 17, 22-25; Jun.: None; Jul.: 2, 23, 26, 30; Aug.: 7, 12, 22, 26; Sep.: 30; Oct.: 1, 2, 23, 27-29; Nov.: 1-9, 11, 16-18; Dec.: 13, 22, 29.

HIDING

Seek isolation on these dates, if you're in the mood for solitude or want to flee from disturbances. Hide valuables and other objects on these dates. It's a great time for a secret romance or rendezvous.
Jan.: 1, 28; Feb.: 24; Mar.: 3, 4, 23, 24, 30, 31; Apr.: 20, 27; May: 24, 25, 31; Jun.: 1, 20, 21, 28; Jul.: 18, 25, 26; Aug.: 21, 22, 28; Sep.: 18, 25; Oct.: 15, 22; Nov.: 18, 24, 25; Dec.: 15, 16, 22.

HIRE: CONSULTANT
ELECTRICAL, ELECTRONIC, ENGINEER, MECHANICAL

Hire an Electrical or Electronic consultant on these dates. Also favored are Engineers and Mechanical consultants. See Jobs, pages 163, 164.
Jan.: 9, 15, 16; Feb.: 5-7, 16, 18, 20, 26-28; Mar.: 1, 4; Apr.: 2-4, 18; May: 5, 8, 9, 11-13, 15, 19, 20, 22, 24-26, 31; Jun.: 1-3, 5, 24, 29; Jul.: 2; Aug.: 2, 5, 10, 11, 21, 24, 25; Sep.: 17-20, 22, 23; Oct.: 3, 11, 14, 17, 19, 30; Nov.: 20, 27-30; Dec.: 2-6, 10, 11, 13, 14, 17, 24, 25, 27, 29, 31.

HIRE: CONSULTANT MARKETING, PUBLIC RELATIONS

Retain a Marketing or Public Relations consultant on these dates. See Jobs, pages 163, 164.

Jan.: 8, 30; Feb.: 6-8, 17, 18, 20, 21, 27, 28; Mar.: 3, 4; Apr.: 1-4, 13-17; May: 24, 25, 27, 31; Jun.: 1, 2, 4, 7-9, 20-24, 27-30; Jul.: 1, 6; Aug.: 1-4, 9, 10, 14, 18, 21, 22, 24, 25, 28, 29, 31; Sep.: 10, 11, 27; Oct.: 3, 11, 14-19; Nov.: 20-22, 27; Dec.: 2, 8-10, 17.

HIRE: CONSULTANT SECURITY SYSTEMS

Hire a Security Systems expert (consultant) on these dates. See Jobs, pages 163, 164.

Jan.: 6-10, 15, 16, 24, 27-31; Feb.: 3-8, 10-15, 17, 18, 20, 21, 23-28; Mar.: 2-5, 31; Apr.: 2, 3, 13, 14, 16; May: 24-28, 31; Jun.: 1-4, 7-10, 20-25, 27-30; Jul.: 1, 4, 5, 31; Aug.: 1-4, 6-10, 13, 14, 16-18, 21-25, 28-31; Sep.: 2-7, 9-11, 13, 18, 27; Oct.: 1, 3, 14-19, 21, 30; Nov.: 20, 21, 25, 27, 28, 30; Dec.: 9-11, 15-18.

HIRE: SECURITY (GUARDS, BODYGUARDS)

Do you need security, professionally? Or to guard you in your private life? Hire security guards on these dates. The underlined dates are the best for hiring a bodyguard. Also, see Jobs, pages 163, 164.

Jan.: 9, 10, 15, 16, 27; Feb.: 5, 6, 7, 18, 20, 21, 24-28; Mar.: 4, 5, 31; Apr.: 2, 3; May: 24, 25-27, 31; Jun.: 1, 2, 3, 7-10, 21-25, 28-30; Jul.: 1; Aug.: 2-4, 6, 7, 9, 10, 13, 14, 18, 21, 22, 24, 25; Sep.: 18; Oct.: 1, 3, 16-19, 21, 30; Nov.: 20, 21, 27, 28, 30; Dec.: 10, 11, 15, 17.

HOBBIES

If you want a hobby that will continue for a long period of time, start it on one of these dates.

Jan.: 8, 15; Feb.: 11, 12, 18; Mar.: 11, 17; Apr.: 7, 14; May: 11, 17; Jun.: 7, 14; Jul.: 4, 5, 11; Aug.: 1, 7, 14; Sep.: 3, 10, 11; Oct.: 1, 7, 8, 28; Nov.: 4, 11; Dec.: 1, 2, 9, 29.

HOUSE: REMODEL OR REPAIR

Are you thinking about remodeling? Does your house need any repair work done? If so, try these dates. All work will be finished quickly if commenced on any of the underlined days.

Jan.: 1-4, 6-10, 15, 16, 24, 28-31; Feb.: 3, 5-7, 17, 18, 20, 21, 23-25, 27, 28; Mar.: 2-5, 31; Apr.: 2, 3, 6-11, 13, 14, 16, 20; May: 5, 10, 13, 17, 20, 21, 23-25, 27, 28, 31; Jun.: 1, 2, 4, 7-9, 20-24, 27-30; Jul.: 1, 4, 5, 6; Aug.: 1-4, 6, 8-10, 13, 14, 16-18, 21, 22, 24, 25, 28, 29, 31; Sep.: 2-4, 6, 7, 18, 27; Oct.: 1, 3, 10, 14-19, 30; Nov.: 20, 21, 27, 28, 30; Dec.: 9-11, 15-17, 19, 22, 23, 29, 31.

HYPNOSIS

Hypnosis is best performed on one of these dates because the hypnotic suggestions will stay firmly rooted in the subconscious mind. The underlined dates are best.

Jan.: 1, 8, 15, 28; Feb.: 11, 12, 18, 24; Mar.: 3, 4, 30, 31; Apr.: 7, 14, 20, 27; May: 11, 17, 24, 25, 31; Jun.: 1, 7, 14, 20, 21, 28; Jul.: 4, 5; Aug.: 1, 7, 14, 21, 22, 28; Sep.: 3, 10, 11, 18, 25; Oct.: 1, 7, 8, 15, 22, 28; Nov.: 24, 25; Dec.: 1, 2, 9, 15, 16, 22, 29.

IDEA: EXPRESS

Oral or written ideas are easily expressed and readily understood by others on any of the following dates.

Jan.: 2-4, 10, 15, 25, 30; Feb.: 1-10, 15-18, 21-26; Mar.: 1-4, 31; Apr.: 5-9, 11, 12, 18, 21, 27, 29; May: 5, 8, 13, 15-17, 20-24; Jun.: 1, 6-9, 14, 24; Jul.: None; Aug.: 3, 8, 19-21, 24; Sep.: 9-13, 15, 24, 25, 30; Oct.: 1-4, 10, 12, 14, 16-21, 29, 30; Nov.: 20, 22, 26-30; Dec.: 1, 3, 4, 9, 15, 22-25, 29-31.

IDEAS: NEW OR RADICAL

People will be receptive to any unusual or way-out ideas that are expressed verbally or in writing on any of these dates.

Jan.: 2-4, 8, 9, 30, 31; Feb.: 1, 3, 5-7, 16, 18, 20; Mar.: 3, 4, 31; Apr.: 1-4, 15, 18, 21, 22, 24, 27, 29; May: 1, 8, 12, 16, 19-22, 24, 25; Jun.: 5, 7, 8, 12, 14, 21, 22, 26, 27; Jul.: 6; Aug.: 11, 14, 24-27, 29; Sep.: 1, 7, 11, 12, 15, 22, 26; Oct.: 4, 9, 17, 19; Nov.: 20, 27-29; Dec.: 3, 10, 17, 24, 29-31.

IDEAS: UTOPIAN

Idealistic ideas are favorably expressed verbally or in writing, or received on any of the following dates:

Jan.: 5, 9, 10, 15, 16, 19, 20, 25-29, 31; Feb.: 1-13, 15-19, 21-25, 28; Mar.: 1-4, 28, 31; Apr.: 2, 5-8, 11-13, 20, 25, 27, 29; May: 4-6, 8, 9, 15-17, 22-27, 31; Jun.: 1, 2, 4-8, 11-14, 21-29; Jul.: 2; Aug.: 7, 12, 22, 26; Sep.: 16, 18; Oct.: 1, 10, 11, 14-16, 19-23, 26-29; Nov.: 25, 26, 28, 29; Dec.: 4-9, 13, 22, 29, 31.

ILLUMINATION

Experience a mental or spiritual enlightenment by mediating on any of the following dates. The brightest illumination will appear on the underlined days.

Jan.: 7-10, 15, 16, 24, 27-31; Feb.: 3-8, 10-15, 17, 18, 19, 20, 21, 23-28; Mar.: 2-7, 10-14, 20, 23, 31; Apr.: 2, 19, 20, 27, 29; May: 4, 17, 18, 23-27, 30, 31; Jun.: 1-4, 7, 8, 10, 20-25, 27-30; Jul.: 1, 4, 5, 18-21, 26; Aug.: 7, 14, 15, 16, 17; Sep.: 3, 4, 13, 14, 18; Oct.: 1, 11, 14-19, 21, 30, 31; Nov.: 3, 4, 6-8, 10, 11, 12, 13, 14, 17-19, 25-28; Dec.: 4, 5, 8, 9, 11, 12, 13, 22, 29, 31.

INSTALLATION: ANSWERING AND FAX MACHINES, TELEPHONES

For best results, and to avoid confusion and error, install answering and fax machines and/or have telephones installed on these dates. If quick service is desired, make the appointment for installation on the underlined dates. For Buying: Fax Machines, see Buying: Electronic Equipment, page 124.

Jan.: 2-4, 10, 15, 25, 30; Feb.: 1-10, 15-18, 21-26; Mar.: 1-4, 31; Apr.: 5-9, 11, 12, 18, 21, 27, 29; May: 5, 8, 13, 15-17, 20-24; Jun.: 1, 6-9, 14, 24; Jul.: None;

Aug.: 3, 8, 19-21, 24; Sep.: 9-13, 15, 24, 25, 30; Oct.: 1-4, 10, 12, 14, 16-21, 29, 30; Nov.: 20, 22, 26-30; Dec.: 1, 3, 4, 9, 15, 22-25, 29-31.

INSTALLATION: ELEVATORS, CEILING FANS, SIGNS

These are great dates for installing elevators, ceiling fans or signs. For lasting results, try the dates with an asterisk. The underlined dates are best if you want the work to be done quickly. See Buying: Signs, page 131.

Jan.: *1, 2, 10; *15 Feb.: *5, 6, 7, *18, *24, 25-28; Mar.: *4, *10, *12-*14, *17, 19; *23, *30, *31 Apr.: 2-4, *6-*8, *10, *11, 13, *14 *20; May: 1, 5, *11, 12, *17, 19, 20, 23, *24, *25, 26, *31; Jun.: *1, *7, 9, 24, *28, 29; Jul.: *5, 24, 28; Aug.: *7, 10, *14, *21, *22, 25; Sep.: *6, *7, 17, *18, *25, 30; Oct.: *1, 2, 3, *7, *8, *14, *15, 17, *18, *19, *21, 30; Nov.: *11 14, *18, 19, 27, *28, *30; Dec.: *2, *3, 13, *15, *17-*19, 21, *23, 24, 25, *29.

INSTALLATION: FLOORING (CARPET, LINOLEUM, VINYL, TILE)

Try these dates to install flooring. For lasting results, the asterisk dates are best. For the work to be done quickly, the underlined dates are favored. See Buying: Flooring (carpet, linoleum, vinyl tile), page 125.

Jan.: *1, 2, 3, *6-*10, *15, *16, *27; Feb.: *5-*7, *18, *24-*28; Mar.: *2, *4-*6, *7, *10, *12-*14, *17, 19, 26, *31; Apr.: 2-4, 6, *7, 8, *10, *11, *13, *14; May: *13, *14, *24, *26, *31; Jun.: *1-*3, *7-*10, *22-*25, *28-*30; Jul.: *1, *5, *6, 19-22, 24, 27-29, 31; Aug.: 2-4, 6, *7, 9, 10, 13, *14, *21, *22, 24, 25, *28, 29, *31; Sep.: *2, *3, 4, 6, 7, 17, *18, 19, 30; Oct.: *1, 2, 3, 10, 11, 14, *15-*19, *21, *30, *31; Nov.: *11, *13-*15, *18, *19, 20, 21, 27, 28, 30; Dec.: 2-5, 10, 11, 13, *15, 17, 18.

INSTALLATION: FLOORING (STONE, TILE, WOOD)

Install stone (granite, flagstone, etc.), tile (brick, ceramic) or wood (cherry, parquet), flooring on these dates. For the work to be done quickly, the underlined dates are best. For lasting results, try the asterisk dates. See Buying: Flooring (stone, tile, wood), page 125.

Jan.: *1, 2, 3, 6, 7, *8, 9, 10, *15, 16, 24, 27; Feb.: 5-7, *18, *24, 25-28; Mar.: 2, *4, 5, 6, 7, *10, *12-*14, *17, 19, 26, *31; Apr.: 2-4, *6-*8, 10, 11, 13, *14, *20; May: 5, 8, 10, *11, 12, 13, *17, 19, 20, 23, *24, 26, *31; Jun.: *1, 2, 3, *7, 8-10, 22-25, *28, 29, 30; Jul.: 1, *5, 6, 19-22, 24, 27-29, 31; Aug.: 2-4, 6, *7, 9, 10, 13, *14, 16-18, *21, *22, 24, 25, *28, 29, 31; Sep.: 2, *3, *4. *6, *7, 17, *18, 19, 30; Oct.: *1, 2, 3, 10, 11, *14, *15, 16-19, 21, 30, 31; Nov.: *11, 13-15, *18, 19-21, 27, *28, *30; Dec.: *2, 3-5, 10, 11, 13, *15, *17-*19, *21, *23, 24, 25, *29, 31.

INSTALLATION: SURVEILLANCE SYSTEMS

These are favorable dates to install burglar alarms, locks, vaults, and hi-tech security equipment. The underlined dates are best to finish the job quickly. For lasting results try the asterisk dates. See Buying: Surveillance Systems, page 132; see Hire: Consultant, page 159; see Hire: Security (guards, bodyguards), page 159.

Jan.: 9, 10, *15, 16, 27; Feb.: 5-7, 17, *18, 20, 21, 23, *24, 25-28; Mar.: *3, *4; Apr.: 1-4; May: *24, *25, 26, 27, *31; Jun.: *1, 2, 3, 4, *7, 8-10, 22-25, 27, *28, 29, 30; Jul.: 1; Aug.: 2-4, 6, *7, 8, 9, *21, *22, 23-25, *28, 29, 30, 31; Sep.: *18;

Oct.: *1, 3, 11, 14, *15, 16-19, 21, 30; Nov.: 20, 21, 27, 28, 30; Dec.: *1, *2, 3, 4, 8, *9, 10, 11, 13, *15, *16, 17, 18.

INSURANCE

Take out boat, trailer, truck, van, motorcycle, car, health, life, theft or travel insurance on these dates. The underlined dates are best for sticking with making the payments.

Jan.: 6, 7, 8, 9,10, 15, 16-18, 28, 29-31; Feb.: 3, 5-8, 10, 11, 13, 14, 17, 18, 20, 23, 24, 25, 27, 28; Mar.: 2, 3, 4, 5, 31; Apr.: 2, 3, 13, 14, 16; May: 24, 25, 27, 31; Jun.: 1, 2, 4, 7, 8, 9, 13, 14, 21, 22-24, 27, 28, 29, 30; Jul.: 1; Aug.: 2-4, 6, 8-10, 13, 14, 18, 21, 22, 24, 25, 28, 29, 31; Sep.: 2, 3, 4, 9, 10, 11, 13, 18; Oct.: 1, 3, 14, 15, 16-19, 22, 23-25, 28, 29, 30; Nov.: 20, 21, 25, 27, 28, 30; Dec.: 9, 10, 11, 15, 16, 17.

INVENTING

Use these dates for inventing devices involving electricity or electronics. The underlined dates are favorable for inventions which deal with engineering, mechanical operation, manufacturing, explosives, or fire-arms. The dates in asterisks favor inventions which involves oil, chemicals, air (things involving aircraft or anything dealing with the air) and/or maritime improvements. See Inventions: Marketing, (the following category).

Jan.: 2-4, *5, *6, 8, 9, *10-*12, 14, 15, 18, *21, 24, *27, 30, *31; Feb.: 1, 3, *4, 5, 6, 7, *11-*13, 16, 18-20, *21, 24-26, *28; Mar.: 4, *5, *6, 7, 8, *9, 10, 12-14, *15, 20, 21, *23, 25-27, *28, 29, *31; Apr.: 1-4, *6, *7, *8, 11, *12, 13, 15, 18, *20, 21, 22, 24, 27, 29; May: 1, *4, *6, 8, *9, 10, 11, 12, 13, 15, 16, 18-21, *22, 25, *26, *27, *31; Jun.: *1, 2, 3, 5, 7, 8, 9, 10, *12, 14, *17-*20, 21, 22, 24, 25-27, *28, 29; Jul.: 2, 3, *5, 6, *10, *11, 15, *16, *17, 18, *19, 20, 22, *23, 24, *26, 28, *30; Aug.: 5, *7, 10, 11, *12, 14, 19-21, *22, 23-25, *26, 27, 29, 30; Sep.: 1, 6, 7, 11, 12, 15, 17, *18, 19, 20, 22, *23, 26, 30; Oct.: *1, 2, 3, 4, *5, *8, 9, 10, 11, 13, 14, *15, *16, 17, 19, *20, *21, *23, *27, 28, *29, 30, *31; Nov.: 1, *2, *3, 4, *5, 6, 8, *10, 11, 12, 13, 14, 15, *16-*18, 19, 20, *22, *25, 27, 28, *29, 30; Dec.: 2, 3, 4, 5, 10, 11, 12, *13, 14, 15, 17, 18-21, *22, 24, 25, 27, *29, 30, 31.

INVENTIONS: MARKETING

For favorable results, an invention or any new product should first be placed on the market on one of the following dates. If a quick outcome is desired, bring the invention out on one of the underlined dates.

Jan.: 2-4, 8-11, 30, 31; Feb.: 1, 3, 5-7, 16, 18, 20; Mar.: 3, 4, 31; Apr.: 1-4, 15, 18, 21, 22, 24, 27, 29; May: 1, 2, 8, 12, 16, 19-22, 24, 25, 27; Jun.: 5, 7, 8, 12, 14, 21, 22, 26, 27; Jul.: 6; Aug.: 9-11, 14, 19, 20, 24, 29; Sep.: 1, 7, 11, 12, 15, 20, 22, 26; Oct.: 3, 4, 9, 10, 17, 19; Nov.: 20, 27-29; Dec.: 3, 10, 17, 24, 29-31.

INVESTIGATIONS

Be another Sherlock Holmes by starting an investigation on any of the following dates.

Jan.: 1, 3, 5, 8, 11, 16, 22-25, 27; Feb.: 7-9, 12, 20, 24, 25, 27; Mar.: 4; Apr.: 3, 8, 9, 26, 30; May: 5, 12-14, 17, 18, 25, 27, 31; Jun.: 1-4, 9, 10, 21, 24, 29; Jul.: None; Aug.: 3, 7, 10, 17, 22, 31; Sep.: 3-14, 18; Oct.: 1, 3, 8, 16-19, 21-25, 28-30; Nov.: 20, 21, 25-30; Dec.: 1-4, 6, 8, 9, 12, 13, 18, 22, 29, 31.

IRRIGATION

For satisfactory results, irrigate crops and fields on these dates.

Jan.: 1, 10, 11, 19, 28; Feb.: 6, 7, 16, 24; Mar.: 15, 23, 24; Apr.: 2, 11, 12, 20, 29, 30; May: 9, 17, 27; Jun.: 6, 14, 20; Jul.: 11, 20, 21, 30; Aug.: 7, 16, 17, 26; Sep.: 5, 13, 23; Oct.: 1, 10, 11, 20, 28; Nov.: 6, 7, 16, 24, 25; Dec.: 4, 13, 22, 31.

JOB: APPLY FOR WORK

Send in your resume for employment, or submit it and/or an application for a position, on these dates. The underlined dates are for quick results. See Employment Agency, page 146; see Job: Interview, below.

Jan.: 10, 11, 15, 25; Feb.: 1-3, 5-10, 14-18, 21-25; Mar.: 1-4, 30; Apr.: 18, 20-22, 27, 29; May: 5, 7-9, 13-17, 20-25, 31; Jun.: 1, 5, 12, 22, 24, 26; Jul.: None; Aug.: 3, 5, 8-12, 14, 19-21, 24; Sep.: 12, 15, 19, 24, 30; Oct.: 1-4, 16-20, 29, 30; Nov.: 20, 22, 27-30; Dec.: 1, 13-16, 22-25, 27-31.

JOB: HIRING EMPLOYEES

On one of these dates, hire a serious, efficient and stable employee. See Avoid: Hiring Employees, page 113.

Jan.: 3, 4, 6-13, 15-20, 22-26, 30, 31; Feb.: 1-3, 5-11, 13-18, 20-22, 27, 28; Mar.: 1-4, 31; Apr.: 2, 3, 6-11, 13, 14, 16, 30; May: 5, 9, 10, 13, 20-25, 27-31; Jun.: 1, 2, 4-9, 11, 12, 16, 18-24, 26-30; Jul.: 1, 3-6; Aug.: 1-5, 9-14, 16-22, 24-29, 31; Sep.: 1, 6-11, 13, 18, 27; Oct.: 3, 10, 12, 14-20, 22-27, 30; Nov.: 20, 21, 27-30; Dec.: 9-11, 14-17, 19, 20, 29, 31.

JOB: HIRING EMPLOYEES FOR PERMANENCY

For an employee to stay a long time on the job, do the hiring on any of these dates.

Jan.: 8, 15; Feb.: 11, 18; Mar.: 3, 4, 30, 31; Apr.: 7, 14, 27; May: 24, 25, 31; Jun.: 1, 7, 20, 21, 28; Jul.: 4, 5; Aug.: 1, 14, 21, 22, 28; Sep.: 10, 11, 18, 25; Oct.: 7, 8, 15, 22; Nov.: None; Dec.: 1, 2, 9, 15, 16, 29.

JOB: INTERVIEWS

Make an appointment for a job interview on any of the following days if quick results are desired. However, the underlined dates are when you make the best impression. See Employment Agency, see page 146; see Job: Apply For Work, above.

Jan.: 9, 10, 15, 16, 17-19; Feb.: 5-10, 11, 14-18; Mar.: None; Apr.: 6-9, 11, 13-15, 16, 18; May: 5, 6, 7-9, 12-17; Jun.: 4, 5-9, 12, 13, 14; Jul.: None; Aug.: 2, 3, 4, 5, 8-12, 14, 31; Sep.: 1, 9-13, 29, 30; Oct.: 1-4, 9, 10-12, 28, 29, 30; Nov.: None; Dec.: 1, 3, 5-9, 11, 27-31.

JOB: PROMOTIONS

Seek a job promotion on any of these dates. For quick action the underlined dates are best. See Favors, page 149.

Jan.: 8, 11, 28, 30; Feb.: 3, 6-8, 10, 14, 17, 18, 20, 21, 23-25, 27, 28; Mar.: 2-4, 30; Apr.: 1-4, 17, 20-22; May: 10, 12-14, 17, 19-21, 23-25, 27, 31; Jun.: 1, 2, 4, 20-24, 27-30; Jul.: 1; Aug.: 1-4, 6, 8-10, 13, 14, 18, 21, 22, 24, 25, 28, 29, 31; Sep.: 2-4, 19, 27, 30; Oct.: 1, 3, 16-19; Nov.: 20-22, 24, 25, 27, 28, 30; Dec.: 1-3, 10, 11, 13, 16, 17, 23, 24, 28, 30, 31.

JOB: TEMPORARY

Part-time, temporary or free-lance work is best sought on any of these dates.
Jan.: 3, 4, 9-11, 17, 18, 23, 30, 31; Feb.: 1, 2, 6, 7, 9, 14, 16, 20, 27; Mar.: 1; Apr.: 2-4, 9,16, 18, 22, 24, 30; May: 1, 6-8, 13, 19-22, 27; Jun.: 5, 9, 12, 16, 23, 26, 27, 30; Jul.: None; Aug.: 3, 9-11, 16, 17, 24-26; Sep.: 1, 6, 7, 13, 15, 20, 22, 27; Oct.: 3, 4, 10-12, 17, 19, 24, 30; Nov.: 20, 27-29; Dec.: 11, 24, 31.

KNITTING

Try the following dates for neat and beautiful knitting, crocheting, tatting (making lace) and needlepoint. If you want to complete it quickly, commence on the underlined dates.
Jan.: 1, 6, 12, 15, 17-20, 21-28, 30, 31; Feb.: 1-3, 11, 12, 14-18, 19-28; Mar.: 2, 8, 11-14, 16-19, 20-22, 25-28; Apr.: 1-4, 7-15, 17, 18,19-22, 26, 29; May: 2, 4, 5-17, 18-21, 27-31; Jun.: 1-3, 4, 6, 12-14, 20, 26, 29; Jul.: 1, 3, 4, 6-10, 16-19, 21, 26, 29; Aug.: 5, 6, 8, 9, 16, 20-26, 31; Sep.: 1-7, 9-13, 14, 15, 18, 20, 25, 27, 28, 29, 30; Oct.: 1-4, 9-12,13, 14, 18-27, 29; Nov.: 3, 8, 9, 11, 13-15, 19, 21-26, 27-30; Dec.: 1-11, 12, 18, 23, 24, 28-31.

LAND: DEVELOP PROPERTIES

These are favorable dates to convert a tract of land and build a group of dwellings (by the same contractor) extensively on the land. For speedy work, start the first step of the job on the underlined dates. See Building, page 120, see Land: Subdivide, below; see Selling, page 191.
Jan.: 10, 11, 15, 16, 24; Feb.: 5-7, 20, 24, 25, 27, 28; Mar.: 4, 31; Apr.: 2, 3; May: 24, 25, 27, 31; Jun.: 1, 2, 7-9, 24, 28, 29; Jul.: None; Aug.: 3, 9, 10, 14, 17, 21, 22, 25, 28, 29, 31; Sep.: 6, 7, 17-19, 30; Oct.: 1-3, 16-19, 30; Nov.: 20, 21, 27, 28, 30; Dec.: 2, 3, 5, 6, 8, 10, 11, 13, 15, 17.

LANDSCAPING

Would you like to (or hire a professional) adorn or improve a section of ground contouring the land and planting flowers, shrubs or trees? These dates are favorable to arrange and alter grounds artistically and functionally. Start on the underlined dates and the job will be done quickly. See Designing, page 143; see Planting, pages 179, 180.
Jan.: 1, 6, 12, 15, 25-28, 30, 31; Feb.: 1-3, 11, 12, 14, 15, 17, 18, 19-21, 23-25; Mar.: 8, 12-14, 26, 29; Apr.: 1-4, 7, 8, 10-15, 17, 18, 19-22, 26, 29; May: 2, 4, 12-15, 17, 18-21, 27-31; Jun.: 1-3, 4, 6, 12-14, 20, 26, 29; Jul.: 1, 3, 4, 6, 7, 9, 10, 17, 26, 29; Aug.: 5, 6, 9, 16, 20-22, 24-26, 31; Sep.: 1, 7, 9-13, 15, 18, 20, 27, 28; Oct.: 3, 4, 9, 10, 18-21, 23-27, 29; Nov.: 3, 8, 9, 11, 19, 22-26, 27-30; Dec.: 1-5, 7-11, 12, 18, 24, 28-31.

LAND: SUBDIVIDE

Subdivide on any of these dates because people will be favorably disposed to make property purchases. If fast results are desired, subdivide the land on the underlined days. See Building, page 120; see Land: Develop Properties, above; see Selling, page 191.

Jan.: 3, <u>8</u>, <u>16</u>; Feb.: <u>7-9</u>, 20, 24, 25, 27; Mar.: 4; Apr.: 3, <u>8</u>, <u>9</u>; May: <u>5</u>, <u>12-14</u>, <u>17</u>, 25, 27, 31; Jun.: 1, 2, <u>4</u>, 21, 24, 29; Jul.: None; Aug.: <u>3</u>, <u>10</u>, 22, 31; Sep.: <u>4</u>, <u>9</u>, <u>11-13</u>, 18; Oct.: <u>1</u>, <u>3</u>,16, 18, 19, 22-25, <u>29</u>; Nov.: 21, 25, <u>30</u>; Dec.: <u>1-3</u>, <u>6</u>, <u>8</u>, <u>9</u>, 13, 22, <u>29</u>, <u>31</u>.

LECTURING: CONFIDENCE

Speeches are best received on these days as well as you are confident, inspired and outgoing. If you want a large attendance, lecture on the <u>underlined</u> dates. Jan.: 30; Feb.: 3, <u>8</u>, <u>17</u>, <u>18</u>, 21, 25, 27; Mar.: 2-4; Apr.: 4, <u>13</u>, <u>14</u>,<u>17</u>; May: 24, 25; Jun.: 1, 2, 7, 8, 20, 21, 24, 27-30; Jul.: 1, 31; Aug.: <u>1</u>, <u>4</u>, <u>6</u>, <u>8-10</u>, <u>13</u>, <u>14</u>, 18, 21, 22, 24, 25, 28, 29, <u>31</u>; Sep.: <u>11</u>; Oct.: <u>3</u>, 14-19; Nov.: <u>27</u>; Dec.: <u>2</u>, <u>8-10</u>.

LECTURING: FAVORABLE IMPRESSION

Make a favorable impression by lecturing on any of the following dates. If you want a large attendance, lecture on the <u>underlined</u> dates. Jan.: 1, 3, 4, <u>10</u>, <u>15</u>, <u>16</u>; Feb.: <u>5-8</u>, <u>15</u>, <u>17</u>, <u>18</u>, 20, 21, 23-25, 27, 28; Mar.: 4; Apr.: 3, <u>7-9</u>, 21, 23, 27, 28; May: <u>5</u>, <u>12-14</u>, <u>17</u>, 20, 24, 25, 27, 31; Jun.: 1-3, <u>4</u>, <u>7</u>, <u>9</u>, 24, 29; Jul.: None; Aug.: <u>3</u>, <u>8-10</u>, <u>14</u>, 21, 22, 24, <u>31</u>; Sep.: <u>9-13</u>, 18, 24; Oct.: <u>3</u>, <u>4</u>, 16, 18, 19, 22-25, <u>29</u>, <u>30</u>; Nov.: 20-22, 25, <u>29</u>, <u>30</u>; Dec.: <u>1-3</u>, <u>6</u>, <u>8-10</u>, 13, 15, 17, 22, 24, <u>28-31</u>.

LEGAL ACTION: COMMENCE

These are good days for starting a legal action. Therefore, be at your lawyer's office to initiate a legal matter on any one of these dates. Retain an attorney on these dates; also, file contracts, legal papers or documents. If you want fast or slow results, or to force the issue to quick maturity, refer to the following categories. Jan.: 1-4, 8, 13, 18-20, 22-26, 28, 30; Feb.: 2, 3, 6-9, 16-18, 20-25, 27, 28; Mar.: 1-4; Apr.: 1-4, 6-11, 13-18, 20-25, 27-30; May: 1-3, 5-10, 12-17, 19-25, 27-31; Jun.: 1, 2, 4-9, 11-16, 18-24, 26-30; Jul.: 1, 3-6; Aug.: 1-6, 8-14, 16-22, 24-29, 31; Sep.: 1-4, 6-11, 15, 16, 23-25, 27, 29, 30; Oct.: 1, 3, 6-12, 14-20, 22-26; Nov.: 20-25, 27; Dec.: 2, 8-10, 17, 19, 21, 23, 24, 27, 28, 30.

LEGAL ACTION: COMMENCE (FOR FAST RESULTS)

For quick results, start legal proceedings by making an appointment with an attorney on one of the following dates. Also, retain a lawyer, or file contracts, legal papers or documents, on the same dates. Jan.: 8, 13, 18-20; Feb.: 6-9, 16-18; Mar.: None; Apr.: 6-11, 13-18; May: 5-10, 12-17; Jun.: 4-9, 11-16; Jul.: 3-6; Aug.: 1-6, 8-14, 31; Sep.: 1-4, 6-11, 29, 30; Oct.: 1, 3, 6-12; Nov.: 20-25, 27; Dec.: 2, 8-10, 27-30.

LEGAL ACTION: COMMENCE (FOR SLOW RESULTS)

If delays, postponements, stalls and passages of time are desired, be at the lawyer's office on any of the following dates to start legal proceedings. Retain an attorney or file contracts, legal papers or documents on these same dates. Jan.: 1-4, 22-28, 30; Feb.: 2, 3, 20-28; Mar.: 1-4; Apr.: 1-4, 20-30; May: 1-3, 19-31; Jun.: 1, 2, 18-30; Jul.: 1; Aug.: 16-29; Sep.: 15, 16, 23-25, 27; Oct.: 14-26; Nov.: 20-25; Dec.: 17, 19, 21, 23, 24.

LEGAL ACTION: COMMENCE (TO FORCE TO QUICK MATURITY)

To force any legal action to quick maturity, start the proceedings (file contracts, legal papers or documents) on one of these dates.

Jan.: 20; Feb.: 18; Mar.: 19; Apr.: 18; May: 17; Jun.: 16; Jul.: 15; Aug.: 14; Sep.: 13; Oct.: 12, Nov.: 11; Dec.: 11.

LESSONS: ACTING

Have you been yearning to be a Thespian? Here are some favorable dates to take private or class lessons in acting.

Jan.: 3-10, 15-20, 25-31; Feb.: 1-7, 16-28; Mar.: 1-4, 28, 31; Apr.: 2, 5-14, 20; May: 4-9, 15-17, 22-27, 31; Jun.: 1-5, 11-14, 18-30; Jul.: 1, 2, 6; Aug.: 7, 12, 20-22, 26, 28; Sep.: 3, 4, 18, 25; Oct.: 1, 10, 11, 14-30; Nov.: 27-29; Dec.: 4, 13, 15, 22, 29, 31.

LESSONS: AVIATION — FLYING

Take to the skies and learn how to fly on any of these dates. See Avoid: Travel by Air, page 118.

Jan.: 27-29, 31; Feb.: 3-5, 7, 19, 21, 22, 24, 25, 28; Mar.: 1, 2, 4-6, 23, 28, 31; Apr.: 12, 20; May: 8, 9, 17, 22-25; Jun.: None; Jul.: 2, 23, 26, 30; Aug.: 7, 12, 22, 26; Sep.: 30; Oct.: 1, 2, 23, 27-29; Nov.: 1-9, 11, 16-18; Dec.: 13, 22, 29.

LESSONS: CLOWNING

Go to clown camp or school and become a clown, professionally, or as a hobby or just for fun. It's therapeutic to laugh and make others laugh.

Jan.: 8, 27, 28, 30; Feb.: 4, 6-8, 17, 18, 23-27; Mar.: 3-7, 13, 14, 17, 24; Apr.: 1-4, 13, 14; May: 4, 24-28; Jun.: 3, 4, 7, 20-25, 30; Jul.: 1, 4, 5, 13, 18-22, 27-29, 31; Aug.: 1, 6-10, 14-18, 24, 25, 28; Sep.: 2-6, 10, 11, 30; Oct.: 1, 3, 11, 17-19, 21; Nov.: 5-8, 14, 15, 17, 18, 22, 24-27; Dec.: 2, 15.

LESSONS: DANCING

Take private or class dancing lessons on these dates; this includes ballroom, tap, modern, Hawaiian and any other form of dance.

Jan.: 1, 2, 6, 25-27; Feb.: 6, 7, 17-21, 23-25; Mar.: 8, 12-15, 25-28; Apr.: 1-8, 10-15, 17-22, 30; May: 1, 2, 4, 12-15, 17-21, 23, 27-31; Jun.: 1-4, 6, 26, 29; Jul.: 1, 3, 4, 6, 26, 29; Aug.: 5, 6, 9, 16, 20, 24-26, 31; Sep.: 1, 7, 20, 27, 28; Oct.: 3, 4, 9, 10, 18-21; Nov.: 9, 19, 27-30; Dec.: 1-5, 7-12, 15-18, 24, 25, 28-31.

LESSONS: DRIVING — CAREFUL, RETAIN

These dates are when you'll be careful, cautious, observant and do defensive driving. Also, you'll retain what you learn on these dates. You'll learn quickly, if you start the driving lessons on the underlined dates.

Jan.: 1-3, 9, 10, 15-18; Feb.: 5-7, 18, 20, 21, 24, 25, 27, 28; Mar.: 4, 5, 31; Apr.: 2, 3, 6-8, 10, 11, 14; May: 24, 25, 27, 31; Jun.: 1, 2, 7-9, 22-24, 28-30; Jul.: 1; Aug.: 2-4, 9, 10, 14, 18, 21, 22, 24, 25; Sep.: 18; Oct.: 1, 3, 10, 14-19, 23-25, 29, 30; Nov.: 20, 21, 27, 28, 30; Dec.: 11, 17.

LESSONS: DRIVING — COURAGE

Do you need courage to take driving lessons? On these dates, you'll be inclined to be courageous. If you start the driving lessons on any of the underlined dates, you'll learn quickly.

Jan.: 15, 16; Feb.: 5-7, 24, 25, 27, 28; Mar.: 1; Apr.: 2-4, 13, 18; May: 5, 8-10, 12, 13, 15-17, 19, 20, 22-24, 31; Jun.: 1, 2, 5-9, 24, 29; Jul.: None; Aug.: 5, 10,

21, 25; Sep.: 17-19, <u>30</u>; Oct.: <u>1-3</u>, <u>11</u>, 14, 17, <u>30</u>; Nov.: <u>27-30</u>; Dec.: <u>2</u>, <u>3</u>, <u>5</u>, <u>6</u>, <u>10</u>, <u>11</u>, 13-15, 17, 23-25, <u>27</u>.

LESSONS: HORSEBACK RIDING

Learn how to ride a horse on these dates.

Jan.: 1-3, 5; Feb.: 5-7, 19, 22, 24; Mar.: 7-10, 12, 13, 15-17, 19, 21, 22; Apr.: 2-8, 11, 13, 14, 18, 19; May: 9, 11, 16, 17, 19, 20, 22-25, 31; Jun.: 1-3, 5-10, 22-25, 28-30; Jul.: 1, 2, 6, 19-23, 27-30; Aug.: 2-5, 7, 9-12, 14, 18-21, 24, 25; Sep.: 17-19, 24, 30; Oct.: 1-3, 11, 13, 14, 16-19, 21; Nov.: 9, 11, 13-15, 19, 20, 27-30; Dec.: 3, 11-15, 23-27.

LESSONS: MUSICAL INSTRUMENTS — FEELING

These are favorable dates when you'll express feeling (and play with emotion) for a musical instrument. Also, you'll be alert on these days. The <u>underlined</u> dates are best if the musical instrument requires blowing, a good set of lungs and the mouth is used on the instrument.

Jan.: 2, <u>3</u>, <u>4</u>, 8, 10-13, 15, <u>25</u>, 28, <u>30</u>, 31; Feb.: <u>2-5</u>, 6, 7, <u>8</u>, 9, <u>10</u>, 11, <u>15</u>, 16, <u>17-19</u>, 20, <u>21-23</u>, 24, 25, <u>26</u>; Mar.: 2, <u>3</u>, <u>4</u>, 8, 11, 13, 15, 22, 23, 27, <u>31</u>; Apr.: 1, 2, <u>3</u>, 4, <u>5</u>, <u>6</u>, 7, <u>8</u>, <u>9</u>, 11, 12, <u>18</u>, <u>19</u>, 20, 21; May: 2, <u>5</u>, 9, <u>11</u>, 12, <u>13-15</u>, 17, 21, <u>22</u>, <u>24</u>, <u>25</u>, 27, <u>31</u>; Jun.: 1, 5, 6, <u>12</u>, <u>13</u>, 14, 20, 26, 29; Jul.: 1, 3, 10, 11, 18, 20, 21, 23, 26, 29, 30; Aug.: <u>3</u>, 5, 7, <u>8</u>, 9, 16, 17, <u>19</u>, 20, <u>21</u>, 22, 26; Sep.: 1, <u>9-13</u>, <u>15</u>, 18, 20, 23, <u>24</u>, 25, 29, <u>30</u>; Oct.: 1, <u>2</u>, 3, 4, 8-11, <u>12-14</u>, 15, <u>16</u>, <u>17</u>, <u>19</u>, 20, <u>21</u>, 24, <u>25</u>, 28, 29, <u>30</u>; Nov.: 3, 4, 6, 8, 9, 16, 19, <u>20</u>, <u>22</u>, 23, 25, <u>26</u>, <u>27</u>, 28, <u>29</u>; Dec.: <u>1</u>, 3, 4, 9, 13, <u>15</u>, 22, 23, <u>24</u>, <u>25</u>, 28, 29, <u>30</u>, 31.

LESSONS: MUSICAL INSTRUMENTS — PRACTICE

These are favorable dates for sticking with the learning, practicing and rehearsing. You'll retain what you learn on these dates. The <u>underlined</u> dates are best if the musical instrument requires blowing, a good set of lungs, and your mouth is used to play the instrument.

Jan.: 1, <u>2-4</u>, 6-10, 15, 16, 27-31; Feb.: 3, 4, <u>5-7</u>, 17, 18, <u>24</u>; Mar.: <u>3</u>, <u>4</u>, 5-7, 10-12, <u>13</u>, 14, 17-19, 23, 24, 26, 30, 31; Apr.: <u>2</u>, <u>3</u>, <u>6-11</u>, 13, 14, 16, 20, 27; May: <u>11</u>, <u>17</u>, <u>20</u>, <u>24</u>, <u>25</u>, <u>31</u>; Jun.: <u>1</u>, 2-4, <u>7</u>, <u>8</u>, 9, 10, 20-25, 27-30; Jul.: 1, 6, 18-22, 24-29, 31; Aug.: 1-4, 6-10, 13, 14, 18, 21-25, 28-31; Sep.: 2, <u>3</u>, <u>4</u>, <u>9</u>, 10, 11, 13, 18, 27; Oct.: <u>1</u>, <u>3</u>, 10, <u>14</u>, <u>15</u>, 16, <u>17-19</u>, <u>21</u>, 30, 31; Nov.: 3-8, 10-15, 17-21, 27, <u>28</u>, <u>30</u>; Dec.: <u>1</u>, <u>2</u>, 9-12, 15-17, <u>22</u>, <u>23</u>, <u>29</u>, <u>31</u>.

LESSONS: SINGING

Have you longed to be a singer or just wanted to improve your singing talents? Try these dates to take private lessons from pop to opera.

Jan.: 1-4, 10, 15, 16, 25, 28; Feb.: 1-12, 15-19, 21-26; Mar.: 1-4, 31; Apr.: 5-9, 11, 12, 18, 19, 21, 27, 29; May: 5, 8, 13, 15-17, 20-24, 31; Jun.: 1, 6-9, 14, 24, 28, 29; Jul.: None; Aug.: 3, 8, 19-21, 24; Sep.: 9-13, 15, 18, 19, 30; Oct.: 1-4, 10, 12-14, 16-21, 25, 28-30; Nov.: 20, 22, 25-30; Dec.: 1, 3, 4, 9, 15, 22-25, 29-31.

LESSONS: SKIING

Get ready to take to the ski slopes; take lessons on these dates. See Buying: Sports Equipment, page 131.

Jan.: 2, 15, 16, 27; Feb.: 5-7, 19, 22, 24-28; Mar.: 1, 10, 12-17, 19-22; Apr.: 2-8, 10, 11, 18; May: 5, 8-13, 15-20, 22-24, 26, 31; Jun.: 1-3, 5-10, 24, 29; Jul.: 22-

24, 28, 30; Aug.: 5, 10, 20, 21, 25-29; Sep.: 1, 17-19, 24, 30; Oct.: 1-3, 10-15, 17-19, 30; Nov.: 9, 11-15, 19, 28-30; Dec.: 2-6, 10-15, 23-25, 27.

LESSONS: SWIMMING

Learn to swim on these dates. The best dates are underlined.

Jan.: 5, 9, 10, 11, 13-16, 27; Feb.: 5, 6, 7, 16, 18, 19, 21, 22, 24, 25, 28; Mar.: 1, 2, 4, 5, 6, 7-9, 10, 12, 14, 15, 23, 28, 31; Apr.: 5-8, 11, 12, 20, 21; May: 1, 2, 4-6, 8, 9, 15, 16, 17, 22-24, 25, 26, 27, 31; Jun.: 1, 2, 5, 25, 28, 29; Jul.: 2, 3, 5, 16, 19, 23, 30; Aug.: 7, 12, 19, 22; Sep.: 18, 23, 25, 30; Oct.: 1, 2, 5, 8, 10, 13-16, 19, 21, 31; Nov.: 9, 11, 16, 18, 19, 28-30; Dec.: 2-4, 13, 15, 23, 25, 29.

LESSONS: TENNIS

Learn to play tennis on any of these dates. See Buying: Sports Equipment, page 131.

Jan.: 1, 2, 13-16, 27; Feb.: 5-7, 24-28; Mar.: 1, 8, 10, 12-15; Apr.: 2-4, 6, 11, 18; May: 1-3, 5, 8-13, 15-20, 22-26, 31; Jun.: 1-3, 5-10, 24, 29; Jul.: 22-24, 28, 30; Aug.: 5, 10, 19-21, 25; Sep.: 17-20, 23-25, 30; Oct.: 1-3, 10, 11, 13, 14, 17, 19, 21, 30; Nov.: 9, 11-15, 19, 28, 30; Dec.: 2-6, 10-15, 17, 23-25, 27.

LESSONS: TRAPEZE

Do you want to be daring and fly through the air with the greatest of ease? Why not take trapeze lessons? Start or get on a trapeze, on any of these dates.

Jan.: 7, 15, 16, 27; Feb.: 18, 24-28; Mar.: 8, 10, 12-14, 17; Apr.: 4, 14; May: 5, 10, 11, 17-20, 23-26, 31; Jun.: 1-3, 7, 8, 29; Jul.: 22, 24, 28; Aug.: 9, 10, 25; Sep.: 17-19, 25, 30; Oct.: 1-3, 14, 17, 30; Nov.: 11-15, 19, 27, 28, 30; Dec.: 2, 10-12, 15, 17, 23-25.

LICENSES: APPLY — BROKER, BUSINESS

Apply for a Broker or Business license on these dates. For quick results, the underlined dates are best.

Jan.: 1, 3-5, 10, 15, 16, 25; Feb.: 7-9, 19, 24, 25; Mar.: 4; Apr.: 3, 6-9, 21, 27; May: 5, 8, 12-14, 17, 24, 25, 31; Jun.: 1, 2, 4, 9, 24, 29; Jul.: None; Aug.: 3, 8, 10, 19, 21, 24; Sep.: 9, 11-13, 18, 24; Oct.: 1, 3, 4, 16, 18, 19, 22, 24, 25, 29; Nov.: 20-22, 25, 28-30; Dec.: 1, 3, 6, 8, 9, 13, 15, 22-24, 29-31.

LICENSES: APPLY — DRIVER'S

Apply for a Driver's license on these dates. For quick results, the underlined dates are best. For photo for license, see Photography, page 178.

Jan.: 1-5, 10, 15, 16, 25; Feb.: 5-9, 15, 17, 18, 21, 23-25; Mar.: 3, 4; Apr.: 3, 6-9; May: 24, 25, 27, 31; Jun.: 1, 2, 4, 7-9, 21, 24, 29; Jul.: 6; Aug.: 3, 8, 10, 19, 21, 24, 31; Sep.: 9-13, 15, 18, 24; Oct.: 3, 4, 16-19, 22, 24, 25, 29-31; Nov.: 20-22, 25, 27-30; Dec.: 1, 3, 6, 8, 9, 13.

LIMOUSINE SERVICE

For good service make reservations on any of these dates. Enjoy riding in a Limo on any of the underlined dates.

Jan.: 1-3, 4, 10, 15, 25; Feb.: 1-5, 6, 7, 8-10, 16, 17, 18, 19, 21, 22, 23-25, 26; Mar.: 1-4, 31; Apr.: 5-9, 11, 12, 16, 18, 19, 21, 27, 29; May: 5, 8, 13, 15-17, 20, 21-24; Jun.: 1, 6, 7, 8, 9, 14, 24; Jul.: None; Aug.: 3, 8, 19, 20, 21, 24; Sep.: 9-15,

30; Oct.: 1, 2, 3, 4, 10, 12-14, 16-18, 19-21, 24, 25, 28, 29, 30; Nov.: 20, 22, 26, 27, 28-30; Dec.: 1, 3, 4, 9, 15, 22, 23, 24, 25, 27, 29, 30, 31.

LIVESTOCK: BREED

Livestock (domestic animals such as cattle, horses, goats, hogs, sheep) breeding should be timed so the young are born on any of the following dates. The livestock is for home or for profit. See Animals: Birth, page 106.

Jan.: None; Feb.: 6; Mar.: None; Apr.: None: May: None; Jun.: 5; Jul.: None; Aug.: None; Sep.: 3; Oct.: 1, 28; Nov.: None; Dec.: 4.

LOBBYING

Favors are easily granted on these dates. The social scene and radical views are at their height. Take advantage of them by lobbying for your favorite cause.

Jan.: 9, 15, 25, 30, 31; Feb.: 3, 5-7, 18, 21, 22, 25; Mar.: 3, 4; Apr.: 1-4, 17, 18, 21-23, 27-29; May: 12, 14-16, 19-21, 24, 25, 27, 31; Jun.: 1, 2, 4, 11, 12, 26-30; Jul.: 1; Aug.: 4, 5, 8-11, 14, 18-22, 24, 25, 27, 29, 31; Sep.: 1, 12, 13, 15, 16; Oct.: 3, 4, 16-19, 29; Nov.: 21, 27, 28, 30; Dec.: 2, 3, 10, 17, 24, 29-31.

MAGIC

Perform white magic for healing, finances, business, love, sex, etc. on any of these dates. Also see the following category, Magnetizing Objects.

Jan.: 4; Feb.: 3; Mar.: 5; Apr.: 4; May: 3; Jun.: 2; Jul.: 1, 30; Aug.: 29; Sep.: 27; Oct.: 26; Nov.: 25, Dec.: 25.

MAGNETIZING OBJECTS

The Magic Ceremony which follows can be used to magnetize objects (for dates to magnetize objects, see below). You can also create your own ceremony or use parts of this one.

Use sandalwood incense because it purifies the air, gemstone, candle, etc. and a beeswax or white candle. Perform the ceremony alone. You do not want anyone else's vibrations on your gemstone or whatever it is that your are magnetizing.

• Light the candle.
• Light the incense.
• You should start by saying a protection prayer, such as, "I'm resting in the center of the pure white light of truth, forming a wall of protection through which no undesirable or evil thought, force or condition, on any plane astral or physical, can penetrate. My aura is sealed by the divine aura of the Godhead, shutting out all that does not vibrate harmoniously with divine love. So shall it be!"
• Say, "I empower this pendant with love, money, success, happiness and protection. And every time I look at it, I want these things to manifest. I want what is for my highest good. Love from my heart is imparted to this gemstone. So shall it be!" The preceding ceremony is to be used for a new gemstone or if you have purified the gemstone already in your possession. A cleansing ceremony should be performed

to erase the vibrations of others. It is best not to let others touch your charm because they may put negative vibrations on it.

There are several ways to purify a gemstone:

• Burn sandalwood incense, hold the gemstone over the smoke emanating from the incense so the incense will saturate the gemstone. At the same time, recite the Lord's Prayer and ask that your gemstone be purified.

• Burn a white candle and move the gemstone back and forth over the flame (without hurting it) and say, "I now purify this gemstone by fire. So shall it be!"

DATES TO MAGNETIZE OBJECTS

Magnetize an object, letter, wand, mirror, charm or gem by casting a spell on it through magic means on any of these dates at the bewitching hour of midnight (do it at the zero hour on dates listed). The best dates are underlined.

Jan.: 1, 6, 10, 11, 15, 19, 20, 21, 23, 28; Feb.: 1, 2, 6, 7, 11, 12, 16, 18, 19, 20, 24; Mar.: 1, 11, 15, 19, 20, 23, 24, 28; Apr.: 2, 7, 11, 12, 16, 18, 19, 20, 24, 25, 29, 30; May: 9, 13, 17, 18, 22, 27, 31; Jun.: 1, 5, 9, 14, 15, 16, 17, 18, 23, 28; Jul.: 7, 11, 15, 16, 20, 21, 25, 26, 30; Aug.: 3, 7, 12, 14, 15, 16, 17, 21, 22, 26; Sep.: 3, 8, 13, 14, 18, 23, 27; Oct.: 1, 5, 10, 11, 12, 13, 15, 20, 24, 28; Nov.: 1, 2, 6, 7, 11, 12, 16, 20, 24, 25, 29; Dec.: 4, 9, 11, 12, 13, 18, 22, 27, 31.

MAIL: BULK, CONTRACTS, DOCUMENTS, FLIERS, LETTERS, MAIL ORDER, SORTED

Send mail on these dates. For the mail to be quickly received send on the underlined dates. See Computer: E-mail, page 139; see Writing: Correspondence, page 208.

Jan.: 2-4, 10, 15, 25, 30; Feb.: 1-10, 15-18, 21-26; Mar.: 1-4, 31; Apr.: 5-9, 11, 12, 18, 21, 27, 29; May: 5, 8, 13, 15-17, 20-24; Jun.: 1, 6-9, 14, 24; Jul.: None; Aug.: 3, 8, 19-21, 24; Sep.: 9-13, 15, 24, 25, 30; Oct.: 1-4, 10, 12, 14, 16-21, 29, 30; Nov.: 20, 22, 26-30; Dec.: 1, 3, 4, 9, 15, 22-25, 29-31.

MAKE-UP: PERMANENT (TATTOO)

Get permanent make-up (tattoo) on eyebrows, eyeliner (upper and lower lids), mouth enlargement and/or color mouth with lipstick and/or face and cheeks with blush on any of these dates. The underlined dates are for quick healing. If you want to remove a tattoo, see Tattoo: Body and Removal, page 203.

Jan.: 1, 2, 14-16, 27; Feb.: 5-7, 18, 20, 21, 24, 25; Mar.: 4, 31; Apr.: 2-4, 6-8, 10-14, 17, 18, 20, 21; May: 12, 13, 15, 17, 19, 20, 22, 23, 25-28, 31; Jun.: 1, 2, 5-7, 9, 10, 29; Jul.: 1, 3, 5; Aug.: 5, 6, 9, 10, 16, 20, 21, 24, 25; Sep.: 7, 17-20; Oct.: 3, 8-11, 14, 17-19, 21, 30, 31; Nov.: 27-30; Dec.: 2-5, 8, 10, 11, 13, 15, 17, 18, 24, 25, 27-29, 31.

MANICURES AND PEDICURES

The best time for cutting nails follow; however the underlined dates are favorable for a beautiful, and lasting, manicure or pedicure. See Avoid: Manicures, page 113; see Avoid: Pedicures, page 113.

Jan.: 8, 15-17; Feb.: 11-14; Mar.: 11-13; Apr.: 7-9, 18; May: 6, 7, 15; Jun.: 11, 12; Jul.: 9; Aug.: 5, 14; Sep.: 1, 10, 11, 29; Oct.: 7, 8; Nov.: 4, 11; Dec.: 1, 2, 9-11, 29.

MANUSCRIPTS, OUTLINES AND PROPOSALS

Send or take a manuscript, proposal or book outline to an editor, literary agent, or publisher on any of these dates. But if quick results are desired, take action on the underlined dates. Note: See Projects and Propositions, pages 181, 182; see Writing: Commence, page 208.

Jan.: 2-4, 10, 15, 25, 30; Feb.: 1-10, 15-18, 21-26; Mar.: 1-4, 31; Apr.: 5-9, 11, 12, 18, 21, 27, 29; May: 5, 8, 13, 15-17, 20-24; Jun.: 1, 6-9, 14, 24; Jul.: None; Aug.: 3, 8, 19-21, 24; Sep.: 9-13, 15, 24, 25, 30; Oct.: 1-4, 10, 12, 14, 16-21, 29, 30; Nov.: 20, 22, 26-30; Dec.: 1, 3, 4, 9, 15, 22-25, 29-31.

MARRIAGE

Set your wedding date on one of these days to ensure a happy marriage.

Jan.: 1, 6, 12, 13, 15, 16, 25, 26, 28, 30, 31; Feb.: 1-3, 11, 14, 15, 17, 18, 20, 21, 23-25; Mar.: None; Apr.: 1, 4, 7, 8, 10, 11, 13-15, 17, 18, 20-22, 29; May: 2, 12-15, 17, 19-21, 27-31; Jun.: 1, 2, 4, 6, 12-14, 20, 26, 29; Jul.: 1, 3, 4, 6; Aug.: 5, 6, 9, 16, 20-22, 24-26, 31; Sep.: 1, 7, 9-13, 15, 18, 20, 27; Oct.: 3, 4, 9, 10, 18-20, 23-26, 29; Nov.: 22-25, 27-30; Dec.: 1-3, 5, 7-11, 24, 28-31.

MARRIAGE PROPOSALS

Marriage proposals are favored on any of the following dates. However, the answer can be hastened by proposing on one of the underlined days. See Engagements, page 146.

Jan.: 1, 6, 12, 13, 15, 16, 25, 26, 28, 30, 31; Feb.: 1-3, 11, 14, 15, 17, 18, 20, 21, 23-25; Mar.: None; Apr.: 1, 4, 7, 8, 10, 11, 13-15, 17, 18, 20-22, 29; May: 2, 12-15, 17, 19-21, 27-31; Jun.: 1, 2, 4, 6, 12-14, 20, 26, 29; Jul.: 1, 3, 4, 6; Aug.: 5, 6, 9, 16, 20-22, 24-26, 31; Sep.: 1, 7, 9-13, 15, 18, 20, 27; Oct.: 3, 4, 9, 10, 18-20, 23-26, 29; Nov.: 22-25, 27-30; Dec.: 1-3, 5, 7-11, 18, 24, 28-31.

MASSAGE

Pamper yourself and be delighted with the healthful results by getting a massage on any of these dates.

Jan.: 1, 2, 5, 9-11, 14-16, 18, 27; Feb.: 1, 3, 5-7, 16, 18-22, 24, 25, 28; Mar.: 1, 10, 12, 14-16, 19-22, 25, 27, 28; Apr.: 2, 3, 7, 8, 10-12, 14, 17, 18, 20, 21, 29; May: 1, 4, 5, 8, 9, 11-13, 15, 16, 18, 22, 26-28, 31; Jun.: 1-3, 5, 7-10, 24, 29; Jul.: 1, 16, 19-22, 24, 29, 30; Aug.: 5, 21, 22, 25-27, 29, 31; Sep.: 1, 7-9, 12, 14, 17-19, 23, 25, 28, 29; Oct.: 1, 2, 9-11, 13, 14, 19, 21, 23-25, 27, 29; Nov.: 11-13, 15, 19, 21, 28-30; Dec.: 3-5, 8, 10, 12-14, 17-20, 23, 25, 27, 31.

MEDIATION

Mediate on the following days for best results. People are inclined to be adaptable and differences are thus easier to settle, especially labor disputes (strikes). For quick results, try the underlined dates.

Jan.: 2, 3, 10-12, 16-19, 22-25, 30; Feb.: 6-9, 14, 15, 17, 18, 20, 21, 23, 25, 27, 28; Mar.: None; Apr.: 2, 3, 6, 8, 9, 22, 29, 30; May: 5, 7, 8, 10, 12-14, 19, 20, 27-29; Jun.: 2, 4, 9, 10, 23, 24, 29, 30; Jul.: 6; Aug.: 3, 6, 8, 9, 16, 17, 24, 31; Sep.: 4, 6-9, 12, 13, 20, 21, 24; Oct.: 3, 11, 12, 14, 16-19, 23-25, 29, 30; Nov.: 20-22, 27-30; Dec.: 3, 6, 8, 10, 11, 13, 23, 24, 27, 31.

MEDITATION

Become lost in another world and transcend into other realms by tuning in or out of any one of these dates.

Jan.: 5, 10, 11, 15, 27-29; Feb.: 1, 6, 7, 16, 18, 19, 21, 22, 24; Mar.: 1, 6, 15, 23, 28; Apr.: 2, 7, 8, 11, 12, 20; May: 4, 9, 15-17, 22, 27, 31; Jun.: 1, 5, 14, 18, 28; Jul.: 2, 16, 20, 21, 30; Aug.: 7, 12, 22, 26; Sep.: 18, 23; Oct.: 1, 10, 11, 21, 23, 27; Nov.: 1, 6, 7, 11, 16, 19, 29, 30; Dec.: 4, 13, 31.

MEN

Dealing with the male sex progresses best on the dates that follow. Quick results may be obtained on the underlined dates.

Jan.: 1-5, 8, 11, 16, 25; Feb.: 1-4, 6-10, 16-18, 23-28; Mar.: 3; Apr.: 6, 7, 10, 13-15, 17, 18, 20-22, 29; May: 7-9, 12-14, 23-26, 29-31; Jun.: 1, 5, 7, 12, 22, 25-27; Jul.: 5; Aug.: 1, 5-14, 16, 20, 28-30; Sep.: 1, 3-6, 8, 11-13, 19, 24, 25, 30; Oct.: 8, 11, 12, 14, 18, 22, 23; Nov.: 20, 21, 25-30; Dec.: 1-11, 13-16, 21, 23, 24, 26-28, 31.

MENTAL DEDUCTIONS

Make mental deductions through the use of analysis or logic on one of these days.

Jan.: 1-4, 9, 10, 15-18, 28-31; Feb.: 3-7, 17-19, 21, 23-26; Mar.: 2-5, 31; Apr.: 2, 3, 6-9, 11, 13, 14, 16, 20; May: 5, 11, 13, 17, 20, 21, 23-25, 31; Jun.: 1-4, 7-10, 13, 14, 21-25, 28-30; Jul.: 1; Aug.: 2-4, 7-10, 14, 18, 21, 23-25, 28-31; Sep.: 9-13, 18; Oct.: 1, 3, 10, 14, 16-19, 21, 22, 24, 25, 27-30; Nov.: 20, 21, 27, 28, 30; Dec.: 1, 3, 9, 11, 12, 15, 16, 22, 23, 29-31.

MENUS: PLAN

It is easy to plan a good menu on any of the following days:

Jan.: 1-4, 9, 10, 15, 16, 28-31; Feb.: 3, 5-8, 10, 11, 13-15, 17, 18, 20, 21, 23-25, 27, 28; Mar.: 2-5, 31; Apr.: 2, 3, 6-11, 13, 14, 16, 20; May: 5, 10, 13, 17, 20, 21, 23-25, 27, 31; Jun.: 1, 2, 4, 7-9, 21-24, 27-30; Jul.: 1; Aug.: 2-4, 6, 8-10, 13, 14, 18, 21, 22, 24, 25, 28, 29, 31; Sep.: 9-11, 13, 18, 27; Oct.: 1, 3, 10, 14-19, 30; Nov.: 20, 21, 25, 27, 28, 30; Dec.: 9-11, 15-17, 22, 23, 29, 31.

MERCURY RETROGRADE

These are the dates that Mercury goes Retrograde this year. Communication problems usually occur during these dates. It's a confusing time. It's best not to sign legal documents unless it's a necessity. Problems with travel can occur. Mistakes are easy to make. See page 101; also see Avoid: Making Important Decisions, page 113.

Jan.: None; Feb.: None; Mar.: 5-27; Apr.: None; May: None; Jun.: None; Jul.: 7-30; Aug.: None; Sep.: None; Oct.: 31; Nov.: 1-19; Dec.: None.

MERGERS

Discuss or commence a merger, especially when it involves a union of two or more commercial interests or corporations on any of these dates. Quick results will be obtained if action is taken on the underlined dates. See Acquisitions, page 105.

Jan.: 3, 8, 16, 25; Feb.: 7-9, 20, 24, 25, 27; Mar.: 4; Apr.: 3, 8, 9; May: 5, 12-14, 17, 25, 27, 31; Jun.: 1, 2, 4, 21, 24, 29; Jul.: None; Aug.: 3, 10, 22, 31; Sep.: 4, 9, 11-13, 18; Oct.: 1, 3, 16, 18, 19, 22-25, 29; Nov.: 21, 25, 30; Dec.: 1-3, 6, 8, 9, 13, 22, 29, 31.

MILITARY: ENLIST

Enlist on any of these dates, if a long term is desired. Enlist on any of the <u>un-derlined</u> dates, if a short term is desired.

Jan.: 1, <u>10</u>, <u>11</u>, <u>17</u>, <u>20</u>, 22-24, 27; Feb.: <u>6</u>, <u>7</u>, 24-28; Mar.: 4; Apr.: 20; May: 1, 2, <u>6</u>, <u>13</u>, <u>17</u>, 22-25, 31; Jun.: 1, <u>9</u>, 28; Jul.: None; Aug.: <u>3</u>, <u>9</u>, <u>10</u>, 21, 22, 28; Sep.: <u>6</u>, <u>7</u>, 17-20, 25; Oct.: <u>1-3</u>, <u>10</u>, <u>11</u>, 15, 22, <u>30</u>; Nov.: <u>27</u>; Dec.: <u>4</u>, <u>11</u>, 14, 15, 17-21, 23-25, <u>27-29</u>, <u>31</u>.

MINING

Excavate or dig for metal and ores from the earth's surface on any of these dates. For quick results, dig on the <u>underlined</u> dates.

Jan.: 1-4, <u>6-11</u>, <u>14-16</u>, 24, 27; Feb.: <u>5-7</u>, <u>17</u>, <u>18</u>; Mar.: 2-6, <u>7</u>, <u>10-14</u>, <u>17-19</u>, 24, 26, 31; Apr.: 2, 3, <u>6-11</u>, <u>13</u>, <u>14</u>, <u>16</u>, 20, 30; May: <u>5</u>, <u>10</u>, <u>11</u>,<u>13</u>, <u>17</u>, 20; Jun.: 1-3, <u>4</u>, <u>7-10</u>, 22-25, 27-30; Jul.: 1, <u>4-6</u>, 17-22, 24-29, 31; Aug.: <u>1-4</u>, <u>6-10</u>, <u>13</u>, <u>14</u>, 16-18, 21-25, 28-30, <u>31</u>; Sep.: <u>2-7</u>, 18, 27; Oct.: <u>1</u>, <u>3</u>, <u>10</u>, 14-19, 21, <u>30</u>, <u>31</u>; Nov.: <u>10</u>, <u>11</u>, 13-15, 17-21, <u>27</u>, <u>28</u>, <u>30</u>; Dec.: <u>9-11</u>, 15-19, 22, 23, <u>29</u>, <u>31</u>.

MIRRORS: CEMENT, HANG

Hang or cement the mirror or mirror-shaped pieces/sections on walls, doors, etc. on these dates.

Jan.: 9-11, 14-16, 27; Feb.: 5-7, 17-19, 21, 23-25, 28; Mar.: 2-7, 10-12, 14, 17, 18; Apr.: 6-8, 11, 13, 14; May: 4-6, 17, 23-27, 31; Jun.: 1, 2, 4, 7, 8, 22-25, 27-29; Jul.: 17-19; Aug.: 21, 22, 31; Sep.: None; Oct.: 14-16, 19, 21, 27-29, 31; Nov.: 10-13, 15, 17-19, 28, 30; Dec.: 5, 8-10, 12, 13, 15-17, 22, 23.

MOLES: REMOVAL

Rid yourself of moles on these auspicious dates. The preferred dates are <u>underlined</u>. However, if surgery is to be performed see Avoid: Surgery, pages 114-117; also see Surgery, pages 198-202.

Jan.: 23, <u>30</u>; Feb.: 20, 26, <u>27</u>; Mar.: <u>3</u>, <u>4</u>, 26, <u>30</u>, <u>31</u>; Apr.: <u>4</u>, 22, <u>27</u>; May: <u>2</u>, 19, 20, 24, 25, <u>29</u>, <u>30</u>; Jun.: 20, 21, 25, <u>26</u>, <u>30</u>; Jul.: 18, 23, <u>28</u>; Aug.: 19, 20, <u>24</u>, <u>28</u>; Sep.: 15, 16, 20, 21, <u>25-27</u>; Oct.: 17, 18, <u>22-24</u>; Nov.: 14, 18, 19, <u>20</u>; Dec.: 15-18, <u>24</u>.

MONEY: BORROWING OR LENDING

Borrow money so you will be able to repay the lender fast. Lend money or personal property and have it quickly returned, or obtain a mortgage by starting action on any of the following dates. See Avoid: Debts, page 111; see Credit Applications and Purchases, page 142.

Jan.: 6-13, 15-20; Feb.: 5-11, 13-18; Mar.: None; Apr.: 6-11, 13-18; May: 5-12, 14-17; Jun.: 4-9, 11-16; Jul.: 3-6; Aug.: 1-6, 8-14, 31; Sep.: 1-4, 6-13, 29, 30; Oct.: 1-4, 6-12, 28-30; Nov.: 27-30; Dec.: 1-3, 5-11, 27-31.

MONEY: ECONOMIZE

Be thrifty and go on a budget on any of these dates:

Jan.: 1-4, 9, 10, 15, 16, 28-31; Feb.: 3, 5-8, 10, 11, 13-15, 17, 18, 20, 21, 23-25, 27, 28; Mar.: 2-5, 31; Apr.: 2, 3, 6-11, 13, 14, 16, 20; May: 5, 10, 13, 17, 20, 21, 23-25, 27, 31; Jun.: 1, 2, 4, 7-9, 21-24, 27-30; Jul.: 1; Aug.: 2-4, 6, 8-10, 13, 14, 18, 21, 22, 24, 25, 28, 29, 31; Sep.: 9-11, 13, 18, 27; Oct.: 1, 3, 10, 14-19, 30; Nov.: 20, 21, 25, 27, 28, 30; Dec.: 9-11, 15-17, 22, 23, 29, 31.

MONEY: SAVING

Accumulate money easily by starting a piggy bank or savings account on any one of the dates which follow:

Jan.: 8, 15; Feb.: 11, 12, 18; Mar.: 11, 17; Apr.: 7, 14; May: 11, 17; Jun.: 7, 14; Jul.: 4, 5, 11; Aug.: 1, 7, 14; Sep.: 3, 10, 11; Oct.: 1, 7, 8, 28; Nov.: 4, 11; Dec.: 1, 2, 9, 29.

MOVIES

Film a movie or go to a screen show on any of the following dates. When filming is begun on any of the underlined days, the movie will be finished quickly.

Jan.: 4, 6-13, 15, 16, 23, 25, 26, 28, 29, 31; Feb.: 1-3, 5-11, 13, 15-18, 21-25, 28; Mar.: 1-4, 28, 31; Apr.: 2, 6-8, 11, 13, 20, 30; May: 2, 5, 6, 8, 9, 15-17, 22-25, 27, 31; Jun.: 1, 2, 4, 5, 11-15, 18-20, 26-29; Jul.: 3-5; Aug.: 12, 16, 17, 22, 26; Sep.: 16, 18, 23; Oct.: 1, 8, 10, 11, 14-16, 19, 20, 22, 23, 26, 28, 29; Nov.: 25, 28, 29; Dec.: 13, 22, 29, 31.

MOVING: A LONG STAY

To ensure a long stay in a new location, move on any of these dates. Also, moving will be done quickly on these days. See Avoid: Moving, page 113.

Jan.: 8, 15; Feb.: 11, 12, 18; Mar.: 3, 4, 30, 31; Apr.: 7, 14, 27; May: 11, 24, 25, 31; Jun.: 1, 7, 20, 21, 28; Jul.: 4, 5; Aug.: 1, 14, 21, 22, 28; Sep.: 10, 11, 18, 25; Oct.: 7, 8, 15, 22; Nov.: None; Dec.: 1, 2, 9, 15, 16, 29.

MOVING: A SHORT STAY

Move to a temporary location on any of these dates. Moving is done quickest on the underlined days. See Avoid: Moving, page 113.

Jan.: 3, 10, 11, 17, 23, 30; Feb.: 6, 7, 14, 20, 26, 27; Mar.: None; Apr.: 2, 9, 16, 22, 29, 30; May: 6, 7, 13, 19, 20, 27; Jun.: 9, 16, 23, 30; Jul.: None; Aug.: 3, 9, 10, 16, 17, 24; Sep.: 5, 6, 13, 20, 21, 27; Oct.: 3, 10, 11, 17, 18, 24, 30; Nov.: 20, 27; Dec.: 4, 11, 18, 24, 31.

MUSCLE DEVELOPMENT

Do you want to improve your physical body by having big muscles? If so, try these dates. By starting the muscle development on the underlined days, you will be more inclined to stick with it and get fast results.

Jan.: 2, 3, 13, 14, 15, 16, 24, 27; Feb.: 5-7, 15, 18, 24-28; Mar.: 1, 8, 10, 12-16, 17, 19-22; Apr.: 2-4, 6, 11, 14, 18; May: 1, 2, 5, 8-10, 11, 12, 13, 15, 16, 17, 18-20, 22-24, 26, 30, 31; Jun.: 1-3, 5, 6, 7, 8-10, 24, 29; Jul.: 3, 5, 22-24, 28, 30; Aug.: 5, 9, 10, 19-21, 25; Sep.: 6, 7, 17-20, 23, 25, 30; Oct.: 1-3, 10, 11, 13, 14, 17, 28, 30; Nov.: 9, 11, 12-15, 19, 27, 28, 30; Dec.: 2, 3-6, 10-15, 17-21, 23-25, 27.

MUSEUM

Learn some knowledge about art, history, science and other cultures. You'll absorb plenty on these dates.

Jan.: 4, 7, 10, 15, 16, 27; Feb.: 5-7, 17-21, 23-25; Mar.: 11, 14, 25-27, 31; Apr.: 2, 3, 6-11, 13-16, 20-22; May: 4, 12-14, 17-20, 23, 24, 27, 31; Jun.: 1, 3, 4, 9, 10, 28; Jul.: 6, 24-26; Aug.: 7-9, 14, 22-25, 30, 31; Sep.: 18, 27; Oct.: 3, 4, 10, 15, 18, 19, 21, 22, 24, 25, 28-30; Nov.: 11, 20, 21, 27, 28, 30; Dec.: 1-5, 8, 9, 15, 24, 25, 29-31.

MUSHROOMS

Gather mushrooms on any of these dates because they are more plentiful.
Jan.: 21; Feb.: 19; Mar.: 20; Apr.: 19; May: 18; Jun.: 17; Jul.: 16; Aug.: 15; Sep.:
14; Oct.: 13; Nov.: 12; Dec.: 12.

NETWORKING

These are favorable dates to make new contacts; therefore, socialize, exchange
business cards and have fun as you network. If you network on the underlined
dates, the results are quick.

Jan.: 2, 3, 5, 6, 8, 11, 12, 14-16, 24, 25, 27; Feb.: 6-9, 11, 12, 14, 15, 17, 18, 19,
21, 23, 25; Mar.: 4; Apr.: 1, 3, 4, 7-9, 17; May: 25, 27-29, 31; Jun.: 1-3, 4, 7, 10,
29; Jul.: 1, 4; Aug.: 6, 9, 10, 16, 17, 21-25, 28, 31; Sep.: 1, 6-13, 14, 15, 18, 20,
24; Oct.: 3, 4, 8, 9, 16-19, 21-23, 25, 29; Nov.: 21, 22, 26, 27-30; Dec.: 1-6, 8-11,
12, 15.

OIL DRILLING

Drill for oil on any of these dates because they are the best days to strike it rich.
If you want quick results, start the drilling on the underlined dates.

Jan.: 4, 6-13, 15, 16, 23, 25, 26, 28, 29, 31; Feb.: 1-3, 5-11, 13, 15-18, 21-25, 28;
Mar.: 1-4, 28, 31; Apr.: 2, 6-8, 11, 13, 20, 30; May: 2, 5, 6, 8, 9, 15-17, 22-25,
27, 31; Jun.: 1, 2, 4, 5, 11-15, 18-20, 26-29; Jul.: 3-5; Aug.: 12, 16, 17, 21, 22,
26; Sep.: 18, 23; Oct.: 1, 8, 10, 11, 14-16, 19, 20, 22, 23, 26, 28, 29; Nov.: 20,
25, 28, 29; Dec.: 13, 22, 27, 29, 31.

OIL: LUBRICANTS

Do you want soft and silky skin? Rub your body with body oils on these dates.
If the oil is to be used on furniture, machines, engines, etc. the underlined dates
are best. See Skin Care, page 194.

Jan.: 4-6, 7, 8-10-16, 23, 25-29, 31; Feb.: 1-4, 5, 6-13, 15, 16-19, 21-25, 28;
Mar.: 1, 2-6, 7-12, 14, 15, 23, 28, 31; Apr.: 6, 7, 8, 11, 12, 20, 30; May: 2, 4, 5, 6,
8, 9, 15-17, 22-25, 26, 27, 31; Jun.: 1, 2, 4, 5, 11-15, 17-20, 25-28, 29; Jul.: 2-5,
8-12, 16-19, 23, 26, 30; Aug.: 5, 7, 12, 22, 26; Sep.: 1, 18, 23, 29; Oct.: 1, 5, 8,
14, 15, 16, 19-21, 22, 23, 26, 27, 28, 29, 31; Nov.: 1-6, 7-11, 16-18, 19, 23, 25,
26, 28, 29; Dec.: 13, 22, 29.

ORIGINALITY

Originality in artistic areas such as decorating, designing, painting, writing or
sculpting is best expressed when the activity commences on any of these dates.
Jan.: 2-4, 8, 9, 30, 31; Feb.: 1, 3, 5, 16, 18-20; Mar.: 3, 4, 7, 11-14, 16, 18-22, 25-
28, 31; Apr.: 1-4, 15, 18, 21, 22, 24, 27, 29; May: 1, 8, 12, 16, 18-22, 24-26;
Jun.: 5, 7, 8, 12, 14, 21, 22, 25-27; Jul.: 2, 6, 15, 18, 20; Aug.: 11, 14, 23-27, 29,
30; Sep.: 1, 7, 11, 12, 15, 22, 26; Oct.: 4, 9, 17, 19; Nov.: 1, 6, 8, 13, 15, 20, 27-
29; Dec.: 3, 10, 17, 24, 29-31.

PACKING

Packing will be neat and organized on these dates. If you're in a hurry (especially if you are going on a trip or moving), the underlined dates are best.

Jan.: 8, 10, 13, 14, 15, 16, 17, 19, 20, 28; Feb.: 4, 7, 9, 14, 24; Mar.: 3, 4, 8, 9, 11, 13, 16-18, 24, 30, 31; Apr.: 2-4, 7-9, 11-14, 20, 27, 30; May: 2, 5, 6, 7, 15, 16-18, 24, 25, 27, 31; Jun.: 1, 14, 20, 21, 23, 25, 26, 28, 30; Jul.: 18, 20, 21, 23, 25, 26, 28; Aug.: 7, 14, 19, 20, 21, 22, 24, 30, 31; Sep.: 1, 15, 16, 18, 20, 21; Oct.: 1, 7, 8, 10, 12, 15, 17, 19-21, 28; Nov.: 1, 4, 6, 7, 9, 11, 13, 15; Dec.: 1, 2, 4, 6, 7, 9, 11, 22, 27, 29-31.

PAINTING

Commence painting a room, house, building or object such as pottery, ceramics or furniture on any of these dates and the paint will stay on for a long time without needing a touch-up or repainting. The underlined dates are best.

Jan.: 1, 28; Feb.: 24; Mar.: 3, 4, 30, 31; Apr.: 20, 27; May: 24, 25, 31; Jun.: 1, 20, 21, 28; Jul.: None; Aug.: 21, 22, 28; Sep.: 18, 25; Oct.: 15, 22; Nov.: 24, 25; Dec.: 15, 16, 22.

PARTIES: ATTENDANCE

People seem to flock in droves to parties thrown on the following dates. The underlined dates are best.

Jan.: 6-14, 15, 16; Feb.: 5-10, 11, 12, 13, 14, 15-18; Mar.: 7-10, 11, 12, 13, 14, 15; Apr.: 6, 7, 8, 9, 10-17, 18; May: 12-14, 15, 16, 17; Jun.: 4-10, 11, 12, 13-15, 16; Jul.: 3-8, 9, 10-12, 13; Aug.: 4, 5, 6-8, 9, 10, 11-14, 31; Sep.: 1, 6, 7-13; Oct.: 3, 4-10, 28, 29, 30, 31; Nov.: 1-10, 11, 27, 28-30; Dec.: 1-8, 9, 10, 11, 27-31.

PARTIES: COSTUME

Dramatic, exotic and bizarre costumes are seen at their best when worn on the following dates:

Jan.: 8, 10, 11, 13, 15, 17-22, 28; Feb.: 1, 6, 7, 9, 11, 14-18, 24; Mar.: 1, 11, 14, 15, 23, 28, 31; Apr.: 2, 7-12, 20, 25, 27, 29, 30; May: 2, 4, 9, 17, 22, 27-31; Jun.: 1, 5, 14, 18, 21-24, 26, 28; Jul.: 3, 11, 18-21, 23, 26, 30; Aug.: 7, 12, 16, 17, 22, 26; Sep.: 2-5, 13; Oct.: 1, 5, 8, 10, 11, 15, 19-22, 28; Nov.: 1, 4, 6, 7, 9, 12-16, 25, 29; Dec.: 2, 4-9, 18, 22, 29, 31.

PARTIES: FORMAL

Elegance and dignity are best displayed on any one of the following dates; thus, give a formal party on one of these days.

Jan.: 1, 15, 28; Feb.: 12, 15-25; Mar.: 11; Apr.: 7, 13-20; May: 13, 16-18, 28, 31; Jun.: 1-4, 7, 9, 14, 28; Jul.: 5, 7, 11, 26; Aug.: 6, 7, 11-13, 21-23, 25, 26, 28, 31; Sep.: 1, 2, 4, 7, 13, 14, 18, 27-30; Oct.: 19-28; Nov.: 1, 11, 20, 22, 23, 25, 26, 28-30; Dec.: 3, 5, 8-10, 12, 15, 18, 27.

PARTIES: FUN

For laughter and lavishness, throw a shindig or attend one on any of these dates:

Jan.: 8, 15, 16, 27, 28, 30; Feb.: 3, 4, 6-8, 14, 15, 17, 18, 23-25; Mar.: 3-7, 10-14, 25, 26; Apr.: 1-4, 13, 14; May: 24-28, 31; Jun.: 1-4, 7, 20, 25, 27-30; Jul.: 1, 4, 5, 13, 22, 24-29; Aug.: 9, 10, 14-18, 21-25, 28; Sep.: 6, 10-14; Oct.: 3, 15-19, 21; Nov.: 5-8, 10, 11, 17, 18, 22, 27; Dec.: 1-5, 8-12.

PARTIES: INFORMAL

Comfortable and informal parties are favored because people can relax and be themselves.

Jan.: 8-11, 13, 14, 16, 24, 27, 30, 31; Feb.: 3; Mar.: 4, 12-15, 25-27, 30, 31; Apr.: 2, 4, 8-12, 21, 22, 27, 29; May: 4, 14, 20, 25-27; Jun.: 16; Jul.: 3, 8, 13, 22; Aug.: 8-10, 14-17; Sep.: 11, 12; Oct.: 3, 8-10, 17; Nov.: 4-6, 21, 27; Dec.: 4, 13, 24-26, 29-31.

PARTIES: INTELLECTUAL

Give or attend a party that has informative and intellectual conversation as its main theme on any one of these dates. The best dates are underlined.

Jan.: 2-4, 7, 8, 10, 15, 24, 25, 30; Feb.: 1-10, 15-19, 21-26; Mar.: 1-4, 11-13, 17-19, 21, 22, 30, 31; Apr.: 5-9, 11, 12, 16, 18, 19, 21, 27, 29; May: 3, 13, 15-17, 20-25, 28, 29; Jun.: 1, 6-10, 12-14, 21, 24; Jul.: 6, 7, 8; Aug.: 3, 8, 14, 19-21, 23-26, 31; Sep.: 3, 4, 7-9, 10-13, 15, 16-19, 29, 30; Oct.: 1-4, 8, 10,12-14, 16-21, 24, 25, 29, 30; Nov.: 4, 20, 22, 23, 26-30; Dec.: 1, 3, 4, 9, 15, 20, 22-25, 29-31.

PARTIES: SURPRISE

Pleasant surprises in the form of gifts, events or people are in store for those giving or attending a party on any of these dates.

Jan.: 8, 9, 16, 30, 31; Feb.: 3, 5, 10, 17, 18, 20; Mar.: 3, 4, 7, 11-14, 17-19, 25-27, 30, 31; Apr.: 1-4, 15, 21, 22, 27, 29; May: 12, 17, 19-21, 23-26; Jun.: 7, 8, 21, 22, 25, 27; Jul.: 13, 18, 20, 27, 29; Aug.: 9, 10, 14, 23-25, 28-30; Sep.: 7, 11, 12; Oct.: 3, 4, 17, 19; Nov.: 4, 6, 8, 13, 15, 20, 27, 28; Dec.: 3, 10, 17, 24, 29-31.

PAWNING

To receive the most cash for anything, pawn it on one of these dates. Get it out of hock quickly by pawning the object on one of the underlined days.

Jan.: 8, 24, 27, 30, 31; Feb.: 3, 4, 6-8, 14, 15, 17, 18, 19, 21, 23, 25-28; Mar.: 2-6, 7, 12-14, 17, 18, 20 26, 27; Apr.: 1-4, 13-15, 17; May: 24-28; Jun.: 2, 3, 4, 20, 21, 29; Jul.: 1, 4-6, 8, 10, 13, 18, 19, 21, 22, 24, 29; Aug.: 1, 6, 9, 14, 16, 23-25, 28, 31; Sep.: 2, 4-7, 9-13, 14; Oct.: 2-4, 11, 14, 16-19, 21, 31; Nov.: 3-8, 10, 12-15, 17-19, 21, 22, 26, 27, 28, 30; Dec.: 1-5, 8, 10, 11, 12,17.

PET GROOMING

The following dates are when your pet (includes horses and large animals) will sparkle the most. The best dates are underlined. For hair clipping (cutting or trimming), refer to Hair: Cutting or Trimming, pages 155-157.

Jan.: 1, 6, 15, 27; Feb.: 18-20, 21, 24, 25; Mar.: 8, 12-14, 26, 27, 29; Apr.: 2-6, 7, 8, 10-13, 14, 17-19, 20, 21; May: 2, 4, 12, 13, 15, 17, 18-20, 27, 28, 30, 31; Jun.: 1, 2, 3, 6, 7, 9, 13, 14, 28, 29; Jul.: 1, 3, 5, 6, 29; Aug.: 5, 6, 9, 16, 20, 21, 22, 24-26, 28, 31; Sep.: 1, 18, 20; Oct.: 3, 9, 10, 18, 19, 21, 23, 24, 25, 27, 28, 29; Nov.: 9, 11, 19, 20, 27, 28, 29, 30; Dec.: 2-5, 7, 8, 10-12, 15, 17, 18, 24, 27, 28, 29, 31.

PETITIONS

Get a petition signed easily on any of the following dates. For quick action and results, start the petition on one of the underlined days.

Jan.: 2-4, 10, 15, 25, 30; Feb.: 1-10, 15-18, 21-26; Mar.: 1-4, 31; Apr.: 5-9, 11, 12, 18, 21, 27, 29; May: 5, 8, 13, 15-17, 20-24; Jun.: 1, 6-9, 14, 24; Jul.: None; Aug.: 3, 8, 19-21, 24; Sep.: 9-13, 15, 24, 25, 30; Oct.: 1-4, 10, 12, 14, 16-21, 29, 30; Nov.: 20, 22, 26-30; Dec.: 1, 3, 4, 9, 15, 22-25, 29-31.

PETS: KENNELS

If you need to put a pet in a kennel, try these dates.

Jan.: 1-5, 15, 25-27; Feb.: 19-24; Mar.: 10-22; Apr.: 5-8, 10-16; May: 24-27, 31; Jun.: 1-10, 22-30; Jul.: 1, 2, 15-30; Aug.: 2-14, 18-31; Sep.: 1, 18, 24, 29, 30; Oct.: 12-15, 18-21; Nov.: 11, 13-15, 20, 21, 28-30; Dec.: 6-10, 14-17.

PHOTOGRAPHY

Snap or pose for extra good pictures on these dates. This includes your photo taken for a passport, driver's license or as an I.D. card (identification) or underwater photography and film processing. The underlined dates are best for the film processing (personal/professional, movies) to be completed fast. See Applications: Passport, page 107; see Movies, page 174; see Photography, Kirlian (the following category).

Jan.: 4, 5, 6-16, 23, 25-29, 31; Feb.: 1-4, 5-13, 15-18, 21-25, 28; Mar.: 1-6, 7-12, 14, 15, 23, 28, 31; Apr.: 2, 6-8, 11, 12, 20, 30; May: 2, 4, 5, 6, 8, 9, 15-17, 22-27, 31; Jun.: 1, 2, 4, 5, 11-15, 18-20, 25-29; Jul.: 2, 3-5, 8-12, 17-21, 23, 26, 30; Aug.: 7, 12,16, 17, 22, 26; Sep.: 18, 23; Oct.: 1, 5, 8, 10, 11, 14-16, 19-23, 26, 27, 28, 29, 31; Nov.: 1-11, 16-19, 25, 26, 28, 29; Dec.: 4, 13, 22, 29, 31.

PHOTOGRAPHY: KIRLIAN

If you want to have a clearer view of your aura maybe Kirlian photography will do it. (Kirlian photography is to enhance the images of the aura of a plant, animal or living person. The field of the electromagnetic body is pictured by Kirlian photography.)

Jan.: 4, 8, 9, 13, 15, 16, 19; Feb.: 5, 16, 18, 19, 21, 22, 24, 25, 28; Mar.: 1, 3, 4, 7, 11, 15, 23, 27, 28, 31; Apr.: 1, 5-8, 11, 12, 15, 20; May: 1, 2, 8, 9, 12, 21, 22, 26; Jun.: 1, 5, 22, 25, 26; Jul.: 2, 15, 18, 20, 23, 26, 27, 29, 30; Aug.: 2, 7, 11, 12, 22, 26; Sep.: 4, 18, 22, 23, 26; Oct.: 1, 4, 9, 12, 15, 19, 20; Nov.: 9, 13, 15, 16, 28, 29; Dec.: 3, 9, 10, 13, 17, 22, 29, 30.

PHYSICAL THERAPY

Have a disability treated by a physical therapist on these dates.

Jan.: 2, 3, 13-16, 27; Feb.: 5-7, 16, 18-20, 22, 24-28; Mar.: 1, 2, 4, 10, 12-16, 19-22; Apr.: 2-4, 6, 10, 11, 18, 19; May: 1, 2, 5, 8-10, 12, 13, 15-20, 22-26, 30, 31; Jun.: 1-3, 5-10, 24, 25, 29; Jul.: 22-24, 28, 30; Aug.: 5, 10, 21, 25-29; Sep.: 1, 6, 7, 17-20, 23, 30; Oct.: 1-3, 10, 11, 13, 14, 17-19, 21, 30; Nov.: 9, 11-15, 19, 28, 30; Dec.: 2-6, 10-15, 17-21, 23-25, 27, 29, 31.

PICKLING: BEETS, CUCUMBERS, HERRING, ETC.

Spend time pickling your favorite foods on these favorable dates.

Jan.: 1, 2-4, 22-27, 28, 29-31; Feb.: 1-3, 20-23, 24, 25-28; Mar.: 1-5; Apr.: None; May: 20-26, 27, 28-31; Jun.: 1, 2, 18-22, 23, 24-30; Jul.: 1, 17-19, 20, 21, 22-29, 30; Aug.: 16, 17, 18-25, 26, 27-29; Sep.: None; Oct.: 14-19, 20, 21-26; Nov.: 13-15, 16, 17-19; Dec.: 13, 14-20, 22, 23.

PLANS

These dates are favorable if you want to be very serious and exacting when making plans. For special event plans, such as award ceremonies, make the plans on the underlined dates. See Architectural Plans, page 107; see Menus: Plan, page 172; see Travel Plans, page 205.

Jan.: 1, 2-4, 6, 7-10, 15-17, 18, 27, 28, 29-31; Feb.: 3, 4, 5-7, 17, 18, 20, 21, 23, 24, 25-28; Mar.: 2-5, 31; Apr.: 2, 3, 6-8, 9-11, 13, 14, 16, 20; May: 5, 10, 11, 13, 17, 20, 21, 23-27, 31; Jun.: 1-4, 7, 8, 9, 10, 13, 14, 20-25, 27-30; Jul.: 1, 6, 31; Aug.: 1, 2, 3, 4, 6-9, 10, 13, 14, 18, 21, 22-25, 28-31; Sep.: 2, 3, 4, 18, 27; Oct.: 1, 3, 10, 12, 14, 15, 16-18, 19, 21, 22, 23-25, 27, 28, 29, 30; Nov.: 20, 21, 27, 28, 30; Dec.: 9-11, 15-17, 22, 23, 29, 31.

PLANTING: BULBS

The best dates on which to plant bulbs for seeds are as follows. See Landscaping, page 164.

Jan.: 1, 28; Feb.: 24; Mar.: 23, 24; Apr.: 2, 20, 29, 30; May: 27; Jun.: 20; Jul.: 20, 21, 30; Aug.: 16, 17, 26; Sep.: 23; Oct.: 20; Nov.: 24, 25; Dec.: 13, 22.

PLANTING: FLOWERS FOR ABUNDANCE OF BLOOM

Plant flowers on the following dates and notice how others will admire them as they bloom in abundance. See Landscaping, page 164.

Jan.: 10, 11, 19; Feb.: 6, 7, 16; Mar.: 15; Apr.: 11, 12; May: 9, 17; Jun.: 5, 14; Jul.: 11; Aug.: 7; Sep.: 2, 13; Oct.: 1, 10, 11, 28; Nov.: 4; Dec.: 1, 2, 11, 31.

PLANTING: FLOWERS FOR BEAUTY AND FRAGRANCE

Plant flowers on any of the following dates and they will be gorgeous and smell divine. See Landscaping, page 164.

Jan.: 15; Feb.: 11, 12; Mar.: 11; Apr.: 7, 18; May: 15; Jun.: 11, 12; Jul.: 9; Aug.: 5; Sep.: 1, 29; Oct.: None; Nov.: 11; Dec.: 9.

PLANTING: LAWNS, SHRUBS, EVERGREENS, PLANTS

Plant on these dates and enjoy the results. The best days are underlined. See Landscaping, Page 164.

Jan.: 10, 11, 15, 19; Feb.: 6, 7, 11, 12, 16; Mar.: 11, 15; Apr.: 7, 11, 12, 18; May: 9, 15, 16, 17; Jun.: 5, 11, 12, 14; Jul.: 9, 11; Aug.: 5, 7; Sep.: 1, 3, 13, 29; Oct.: 1, 10, 11, 28; Nov.: 4, 11; Dec.: 1, 2, 9, 11, 31.

PLANTING: TREES AND VEGETABLES
(ABOVE THE GROUND CROPS)

If trees are planted on the following dates, they will live longer and grow better than when planted on other days. Plant vegetables which make their crops above the ground (asparagus, cabbage, celery, corn, endive, peas, peppers, spinach, squash, string beans, tomatoes, etc.) on the following dates.

Jan.: 10, 11, 19; Feb.: 6, 7, 16; Mar.: 15; Apr.: 11, 12; May: 9, 17; Jun.: 5, 14; Jul.: 11; Aug.: 7; Sep.: 2, 13; Oct.: 1, 10, 11, 28; Nov.: 4; Dec.: 1, 2, 11, 31.

PLANTING: VEGETABLE FOR RANK GROWTH
(ABOVE THE GROUND CROPS)

For large growth of vegetables which make their crops above the ground, plant them on the following dates. The best dates are <u>underlined</u>.

Jan.: 6-9, <u>10</u>, <u>11</u>, 12, 13; Feb.: 5, <u>6</u>, <u>7</u>, 8-11; Mar.: 7-13; Apr.: 6-10, <u>11</u>; May: 5-8, <u>9</u>, 10; Jun.: 4, <u>5</u>, 6-9; Jul.: 3-8; Aug.: 1-4, <u>5</u>, 6; Sep.: <u>1</u>, 2-4, <u>29</u>, 30; Oct.: 1-4, 28-31; Nov.: 1-3, 27-30; Dec.: <u>1</u>, <u>2</u>, 3, 27, 28, <u>29</u>, 30, 31.

PLANTING: VEGETABLES FOR TENDERNESS
(ABOVE THE GROUND CROPS)

For tenderness of vegetables which make their crops above the ground, plant them on any of the following dates. The best dates are <u>underlined</u>.

Jan.: 15-18, <u>19</u>, 20; Feb.: 13-15, <u>16</u>, 17, 18; Mar.: <u>15</u>, 16-19; Apr.: 13-18; May: 12-16, <u>17</u>; Jun.: 11-13, <u>14</u>, 15, 16; Jul.: 10, <u>11</u>, 12-15; Aug.: 8-14; Sep.: 6-12, <u>13</u>; Oct.: 6-9, <u>10</u>, <u>11</u>, 12; Nov.: 5, <u>6</u>, <u>7</u>, 8-11; Dec.: 5-11.

PLANTING VEGETABLES (BELOW THE GROUND CROPS)

Plant vegetables which make their crops below the ground (beets, carrots, onions, parsnips, potatoes, radishes, turnips, etc.) on the following dates.

Jan.: 1, 28; Feb.: 24; Mar.: 23, 24; Apr.: 2, 20, 29, 30; May: 27; Jun.: 20; Jul.: 20, 21, 30; Aug.: 16, 17, 26; Sep.: 23; Oct.: 20; Nov.: 24, 25; Dec.: 13, 22.

PLANTING: VEGETABLES FOR RANK GROWTH
(BELOW THE GROUND CROPS)

For large growth of vegetables which make their crops below the ground, plant them on the following dates.

Jan.: None; Feb.: None; Mar.: 23, 24; Apr.: 20; May: None; Jun.: None; Jul.: 20, 21; Aug.: 16, 17; Sep.: None; Oct.: None; Nov.: 16; Dec.: 13.

PLANTING: VEGETABLES FOR TENDERNESS
(BELOW THE GROUND CROPS)

For tenderness of vegetables which make their crops below the ground, plant them on the following dates. The best dates are <u>underlined</u>.

Jan.: <u>1</u>, 2-4, <u>28</u>, 29-31; Feb.: 1-3, 27, 28; Mar.: 1-5, 29-31; Apr.: 1, <u>2</u>, 3, 4, 27, 28, <u>29</u>, <u>30</u>; May: 1-3, <u>27</u>, 28-31; Jun.: 1, 2, 26-30; Jul.: 1, 25-29, <u>30</u>; Aug.: 24, 25, <u>26</u>, 27-29; Sep.: 22, <u>23</u>, 24-27; Oct.: 22, 23, <u>24</u>, <u>25</u>, 26; Nov.: 20-23, <u>24</u>, <u>25</u>; Dec.: 19-21, <u>22</u>, 23-25.

POLES AND POSTS

Set posts (including fences or poles) on these dates so they will stay in place longer.

Jan.: 1, 28; Feb.: 24; Mar.: 3, 4, 23, 24, 30, 31; Apr.: 20, 27; May: 24, 25, 31; Jun.: 1, 20, 21, 28; Jul.: 18, 25, 26; Aug.: 21, 22, 28; Sep.: 18, 25; Oct.: 15, 22; Nov.: 18, 24, 25; Dec.: 13, 16, 22.

POTATOES

Potatoes dug on the following dates will keep a long time. However, they will keep longest if removed on the <u>underlined</u> days. For planting potatoes, see Planting: Vegetables (Below the Ground Crops), above.

Jan.: 3, 30; Feb.: 26, 27; Mar.: 26; Apr.: 4, 22; May: 2, 19, 20, 29, 30; Jun.: 25, 26; Jul.: 23; Aug.: 19, 20, <u>28</u>; Sep.: 15, 16, <u>25</u>; Oct.: <u>22</u>; Nov.: 18; Dec.: 15, 16, 24.

POTTERY

These dates are great for making the mold for pottery. The <u>underlined</u> dates are favorable for glazing the pottery. See Painting, page 176.

Jan.: 2, <u>3-5</u>, <u>8-12</u>, 13-16, 24, 27, <u>29</u>, <u>31</u>; Feb.: <u>1</u>, <u>3</u>, <u>4</u>, 5-7, <u>10-14</u>, <u>16</u>, <u>18-22</u>, 24-28; Mar.: 1, <u>3-9</u>, 10, 12-15, <u>23</u>, <u>28</u>, <u>31</u>; Apr.: 2-4, 6, <u>7-10</u>, 11, <u>12</u>, 18, <u>20</u>; May: 1, 2, <u>4</u>, 5, <u>6</u>, 8-13, <u>15</u>, 16, <u>17</u>, 18-20, <u>22</u>, 23, 24, <u>25</u>, 26, <u>27</u>, 30, 31; Jun.: 1-3, 5-10, <u>16-19</u>, 24, <u>26-28</u>, 29, <u>30</u>; Jul.: <u>1</u>, <u>2</u>, 3, <u>5-7</u>, <u>9</u>, <u>11</u>, <u>16</u>, <u>18</u>, <u>19</u>, 22-24, 28, <u>29</u>, 30; Aug.: 5, <u>7</u>, 10, <u>12</u>, 21, <u>22</u>, 25, <u>26</u>; Sep.: 6-8, 17, 18, <u>23</u>, 30; Oct.: 1-3, <u>5</u>, <u>8</u>, 10, 11, 13, 14, <u>15</u>, <u>16</u>, 17, <u>18-21</u>, <u>23-27</u>, <u>29</u>, 30, <u>31</u>; Nov.: <u>1</u>, <u>2</u>, <u>5</u>, 9, <u>10</u>, 11-15, <u>16</u>, 19, <u>25-27</u>, 28, <u>29</u>, 30; Dec.: 2-6, 10-12, <u>13</u>, 14, 15, 17-21, <u>22</u>, 23-25, 27, <u>29</u>.

PREGNANCY

A woman's most fertile time to become pregnant is on the following dates.

Jan.: 10, 11, 19; Feb.: 6, 7, 16; Mar.: 15; Apr.: 11, 12; May: 9, 17; Jun.: 5, 14; Jul.: 11; Aug.: 7; Sep.: 3, 13; Oct.: 1, 10, 11, 28; Nov.: 4; Dec.: 1, 2, 11, 31.

PRINTING

Printing is favored on the following dates. This include ads, articles, books, brochures, fliers, magazines, manuals, manuscripts, newsletters, newspapers, tickets, etc. For quick results, be at the printer on any of the <u>underlined</u> days.

Jan.: 2-4, 10, 15, 25, 30; Feb.: 1-10, 15-18, 21-26; Mar.: 1-4, 31; Apr.: 5-9, 11, 12, 18, 21, 27, 29; May: 5, 8, 13, 15-17, 20-24; Jun.: 1, 6-9, 14, 24; Jul.: None; Aug.: 3, 8, 19-21, 24; Sep.: 9-13, 15, 24, 25, 30; Oct.: 1-4, 10, 12, 14, 16-21, 29, 30; Nov.: 20, 22, 26-30; Dec.: 1, 3, 4, 9, 15, 22-25, 29-31.

PROJECTS: PITCH (SELL) — CABLE, RADIO, RECORDS, TV

Start to pitch a project that involves Cable, Records, Television or anything that is recorded or televised including Commercials and Infomercials for radio and television. If quick results are desired, pitch the project on the <u>underlined</u> dates. See Projects and Propositions: Quick Maturity, page 182 and use those dates if they also appear below.

Jan.: 3, 5, <u>10</u>, <u>16</u>, 25, 27; Feb.: <u>6-9</u>, <u>12</u>, 25, 27; Mar.: 4; Apr.: 2, 3, <u>8</u>, <u>9</u>; May: 25, 27, 31; Jun.: 1-3, <u>4</u>, <u>10</u>, 24, 29; Jul.: None; Aug.: <u>9</u>, <u>10</u>, 22, <u>31</u>; Sep.: <u>9</u>, <u>11-13</u>, 18; Oct.: <u>3</u>, 16-19, 21-23, 25, <u>29</u>; Nov.: 21, <u>27</u>, <u>30</u>; Dec.: <u>1-4</u>, <u>6</u>, <u>8</u>, <u>9</u>, 13.

PROJECTS: PITCH (SELL) — FILM, PLAY, MUSICAL

Start to pitch a new project such as a film, play or musical on these dates. If quick results are desired, pitch the project on the <u>underlined</u> dates. See Projects and Propositions: Quick Maturity, page 182 and use those dates if they also appear below.

Jan.: 5, <u>7-10</u>, <u>15</u>, <u>16</u>, 25-27, 29, 31; Feb.: 3, 4, <u>5-13</u>, <u>15-18</u>, 21-23, 25, 28; Mar.: 2-4, 31; Apr.: 2, <u>13-15</u>; May: 24-27, 31; Jun.: 1, 2, <u>4</u>, <u>5</u>, 19, 20, 25-29; Jul.: 2, <u>3-5</u>; Aug.: <u>5</u>, <u>6</u>, <u>8</u>, 16, 17, 20-22, 26; Sep.: <u>1</u>, 18, 24, 25, 28, <u>29</u>, <u>30</u>; Oct.: <u>11</u>, <u>12</u>, 14-16, 19-21; Nov.: 22, 23, 26, <u>28</u>; Dec.: <u>4</u>, <u>10</u>, 13.

PROJECTS: PITCH (SELL) — PRODUCTS, REAL ESTATE

Start to pitch a new project that involves a product (for merchandising) or real estate development. If quick results are desired, pitch the project on the underlined dates. See Projects and Propositions: Quick Maturity, below and use those dates if they also appear below.

Jan.: 10, 12, 27; Feb.: 6-8, 18, 20, 21, 24-28; Mar.: 3, 4; Apr.: 1-4, 17; May: 24-27, 31; Jun.: 1-3, 4, 25, 27-30; Jul.: 1; Aug.: 2-4, 7-10, 14, 18, 21-25, 29, 30, 31; Sep.: None; Oct.: 1, 3, 16-19, 21; Nov.: 20-22, 25, 26, 27; Dec.: 2, 4, 10, 17.

PROJECTS AND PROPOSITIONS: QUICK MATURITY

Force a project or proposition to quick maturity on any of the following dates. Also see Manuscripts, Outlines and Proposals, page 171.

Jan.: 20; Feb.: 18; Mar.: 19; Apr.: 18; May: 17; Jun.: 16; Jul.: 15; Aug.: 14; Sep.: 13; Oct.: 12; Nov.: 11; Dec.: 11.

PROMOTING

Promote a person, product or business on any of the following dates. If quick action is desired, do the promoting on the underlined dates.

Jan.: 4, 6-13, 15, 16, 23, 25, 26, 28, 29, 31; Feb.: 1-3, 5-11, 13, 15-18, 21-25, 28; Mar.: 1-4, 28, 31; Apr.: 2, 6-8, 11, 13, 20, 30; May: 2, 5, 6, 8, 9, 15-17, 22-25, 27, 31; Jun.: 1, 2, 4, 5, 11-15, 18-20, 26-29; Jul.: 3-5; Aug.: 12, 16, 17, 22, 26; Sep.: 18, 23; Oct.: 1, 8, 10, 11, 14-16, 19, 20, 22, 23, 26, 28, 29; Nov.: 25, 28, 29; Dec.: 13, 22, 29, 31.

PROSTHESIS: ARTIFICIAL LIMBS

To wear artificial limbs for the first time, try these dates. To wear for the second time, and subsequent times, the underlined dates are best.

Jan.: 2, 3, 5, 9-11, 13, 14, 15, 16, 24; Feb.: 5-7, 16, 18, 19-22, 24-28; Mar.: 1, 4, 5-10, 12-15, 28; Apr.: 2-4, 6, 7, 11, 18; May: 1, 2, 5, 8, 9, 11, 12, 13, 15, 16, 18-20, 22, 24-27, 31; Jun.: 1-3, 5, 25 28-30; Jul.: 1-3, 5, 22-24, 28, 30; Aug.: 5, 10, 12, 21, 25; Sep.: 17-20, 23; Oct.: 1, 2, 3, 5, 10, 11, 13-19, 21, 30, 31; Nov.: 9, 11, 16, 19, 27, 28, 29, 30; Dec.: 2, 3, 4, 10-14, 17, 23-25, 27.

PRUNING

Trees with superfluous branches should be cut or trimmed on any of these dates.

Jan.: 1, 28; Feb.: 24; Mar.: 23, 24; Apr.: 2, 20, 29, 30; May: 27; Jun.: 20; Jul.: 20, 21, 30; Aug.: 16, 17, 26; Sep.: 23; Oct.: 20; Nov.: 24, 25; Dec.: 13, 22.

PSYCHIC ENDEAVORS

On the following dates ESP or other psychic endeavors are facilitated and bring concrete results. However, the underlined dates are the best days for tuning in and experiencing psychic impressions, thus get a psychic reading from a medium or clairvoyant and/or take classes in psychic development on these dates. See Illumination, page 160.

Jan.: 15, 16, 19; Feb.: 16; Mar.: 15; Apr.: 16; May: 14, 17; Jun.: 14; Jul.: 11; Aug.: 10, 12; Sep.: 6, 8, 11, 13; Oct.: 8, 11; Nov.: 7, 9; Dec.: 9.

PSYCHOANALYSIS AND PSYCHOTHERAPY

These dates are good for evaluation treatment.

Jan.: 1-4, 9, 25, 28, 30, 31; Feb.: 1, 3-10, 16, 18, 20, 24, 27; Mar.: 1, 3, 4, 31; Apr.: 1-8, 15, 16, 18, 21, 22, 24, 27, 29; May: 8, 12, 13, 16, 19-22, 24-26; Jun.: 5, 12, 14, 21, 22, 25-27; Jul.: 2, 6; Aug.: 2, 11, 14, 23-27, 29, 30; Sep.: 1, 12, 15, 22; Oct.: 1, 4, 9, 12, 14, 15, 17, 19, 24; Nov.: 20, 25, 27-30; Dec.: 3, 10, 17, 22-24, 29-31.

PUBLICITY

For quick and favorable results, arrange for publicity to appear on any of these dates. See Promoting, page 182.

Jan.: 6-13, 15-20; Feb.: 5-11, 13-18; Mar.: None; Apr.: 6-11, 13-18; May: 5-10, 12-17; Jun.: 4-9, 11-16; Jul.: 3-6; Aug.: 1-6, 8-14, 31; Sep.: 1-4, 6-13, 29, 30; Oct.: 1-4, 6-12, 28-30; Nov.: 27-30; Dec.: 1-3, 5-11, 27-31.

PUBLIC RELATIONS

Go to school to learn public relations work, sign up and/or take a special course, on these dates. Or if a public relations firm wants to train you in the field, start on the underlined dates. To open a Public Relations Firm, see Business: Commence, page 121; to Hire a Consultant, see page 159.

Jan.: 1-4, 10, 15, 25, 28, 30; Feb.: 1-3, 4, 5, 6, 7-10, 11, 12, 15-18, 21-23, 24, 25, 26; Mar.: 1-4, 31; Apr.: 2, 3, 5-7, 8, 9, 11, 12, 14, 15, 16, 18, 19, 20, 21, 27, 29; May: 5, 8, 11, 13, 15, 16, 17, 20, 21-24, 27; Jun.: 1, 6-9, 10, 21, 23, 24, 28; Jul.: None; Aug.: 3, 7, 8, 9, 14, 19-21, 22, 24, 28, 30; Sep.: 9, 10, 11, 12, 13, 15, 18, 30; Oct.: 1, 2-4, 10, 12, 14, 16-22, 24, 25, 29, 30; Nov.: 20, 22, 25, 26, 27, 28, 29, 30; Dec.: 1, 3, 4, 9, 11, 15, 22, 23-25, 29, 30, 31.

PUBLISHING

A magazine, newspaper, periodical or book should appear to the public for the first time on one of these dates because it will sell fast and be widely discussed.

Jan.: 6-13, 15-20; Feb.: 5-11, 13-18; Mar.: None; Apr.: 6-11, 13-18; May: 5-12, 14-17; Jun.: 4-9, 11-16; Jul.: 3-6; Aug.: 1-6, 8-14; Sep.: 1-4, 6-13, 29, 30; Oct.: 1-4, 6-12, 28-30; Nov.: 27-30; Dec.: 1-3, 5-11, 27-31.

PUZZLES: CROSSWORD, JIGSAW

Your mind is extra sharp on these dates, so have fun solving the puzzle.

Jan.: 1, 2, 4, 10, 14, 15, 25, 28; Feb.: 1-10, 15-19, 21-25; Mar.: 1-4, 31; Apr.: 5-8, 11, 12, 18, 19, 21, 27, 29, 30; May: 5, 8, 15-17, 21-24; Jun.: 1, 6-8, 14, 24; Jul.: None; Aug.: 8, 19-21; Sep.: 9-13, 15, 30; Oct.: 1, 2, 4, 10, 12-14, 16, 19-21, 29; Nov.: 22, 25, 26, 28-30; Dec.: 1, 3, 4, 9, 15, 20, 22, 23, 25, 29-31.

RECONCILIATIONS

Revive a broken friendship, love affair or marriage on one of these dates:

Jan.: None, Feb.: 6, 7, 20, 21, 25; Mar.: None; Apr.: 2-4, 17, 23, 24, 29; May: 13, 14, 19-21, 27; Jun.: 4, 9, 30; Jul.: 1; Aug.: 4, 9, 10, 18, 24, 25; Sep.: 13; Oct.: 3, 4, 17-19, 24; Nov.: 20, 21, 27, 28; Dec.: 3, 5, 11, 17, 24, 31.

RECORDINGS: PHONOGRAPH, CASSETTE, COMPACT DISC OR VIDEO TAPE/DISCS

Record or tape on these dates for great results. Bring out the disc or tape recording on any of the underlined dates, and it will catch on quickly and have a better chance of being a hit. See Selling, page 191.

Jan.: 3, 8, 16; Feb.: 7-9, 20, 24, 25, 27; Mar.: 4; Apr.: 3, 8, 9; May: 5, 12-14, 17, 25, 27, 31; Jun.: 1, 2, 4, 21, 24, 29; Jul.: None; Aug.: 3, 10, 22, 31; Sep.: 4, 9, 11-13, 18; Oct.: 1, 3, 16, 18, 19, 22-25, 29; Nov.: 21, 25, 30; Dec.: 1-3, 6, 8, 9, 13, 22, 29, 31.

RECREATION

Would you like to refresh your mind or body after laborious tasks through diverting activity? If so these dates are great to play, relax, be lazy and take life easy. See Spa, page 195.

Jan.: 3, 5, 7-11, 13-15, 27-31; Feb.: 1, 3-7, 16, 18-22, 24, 25; Mar.: 4-10, 12-15, 20, 23, 27, 28, 31; Apr.: 2, 5-8, 10-12, 14, 17, 18, 20, 21; May: 2, 4-6, 8, 9, 15, 16, 18-20, 22, 24-28, 30, 31; Jun.: 1-3, 5, 7-10, 14-18, 21-25, 28-30; Jul.: 1, 2, 6, 16, 19-21, 23; Aug.: 7, 12, 21, 22, 26; Sep.: 4, 18, 23, 25, 28, 29; Oct.: 1, 2, 15-19, 21, 23, 24, 29-31; Nov.: 1, 4-9, 11-16, 19, 27-29; Dec.: 4-8, 13, 29, 31.

REFORMS: COMMENCE

Start reform proceedings on any of the following dates because groups and the public will welcome the change. Also, quick results are indicated. See Crusades, page 142.

Jan.: 8, 9, 11; Feb.: 5, 7, 18; Mar.: None; Apr.: 8, 9; May: 5, 8, 12-14; Jun.: 4, 7, 8; Jul.: 6; Aug.: 2, 3, 10, 11, 14, 31; Sep.: 1, 4, 6-9, 11-13; Oct.: 1, 3, 4, 9, 29; Nov.: 27-30; Dec.: 1-3, 6, 8-10, 29-31.

REGULATIONS

Post rules or regulations on these dates because people will be inclined to accept and follow them.

Jan.: 7-19; Feb.: 5-16, 18; Mar.: None; Apr.: 5-12, 14, 16; May: 5, 9, 11, 13, 16; Jun.: 4, 5, 7-12, 14-16; Jul.: 1-3, 5, 6; Aug.: 1-5, 7-12, 14, 31; Sep.: 1, 2, 4-9, 11-13; Oct.: 1, 3, 10, 12, 29, 30; Nov.: 27-30; Dec.: 9-11, 29, 31.

REHEARSALS

To repeat routines until they are perfect, practice on any of these dates. The routines will stay firmly entrenched in your subconscious mind if you rehearse on the underlined days. Note: Rehearsals include music, dancing, singing, acting and any other area where memory or a routine is involved.

Jan.: 7, 8, 9, 10, 15, 27, 28, 29-31; Feb.: 3-7, 18, 19-21, 24, 25-28; Mar.: 3, 4, 5, 31; Apr.: 2, 3, 14, 16; May: 24, 25, 26-28, 31; Jun.: 1, 2-4, 7, 8-10, 21, 22-25, 27, 28, 29, 30; Jul.: 1; Aug.: 1, 2-4, 7, 8-10, 14, 18, 21, 22, 23-25, 29-31; Sep.: 2, 4-7, 9, 11, 13, 18, 27; Oct.: 1, 3, 14, 15, 16-19, 21; Nov.: 20, 21, 27, 28, 30; Dec.: 9, 10-12, 16, 17, 18.

RENOVATING

Renovations will be completed quickly if started on the following dates. The building will best resist destruction if renovation is begun on any of the <u>underlined</u> days.

Jan.: 7, <u>8</u>, 9-11, 14, <u>15</u>, 16-18; Feb.: 5-8, 10, <u>11</u>, <u>12</u>, 13-15, 18; Mar.: None; Apr.: 6, <u>7</u>, 8-11, <u>14</u>, 16; May: <u>11</u>, 13, 16, 17; Jun.: 4, <u>7</u>, 8-10, 16; Jul.: <u>5</u>, 6; Aug.: <u>1</u>, 2-4, 9, 10, <u>14</u>, 31; Sep.: 2, 4, 9, <u>11</u>, 13; Oct.: 3, 10, 30, 31; Nov.: 27, 28, 30; Dec.: <u>9</u>, 10, 11, <u>29</u>, 30, 31.

RENTING: BEAUTY AND NEATNESS

Rent a beautiful and neat apartment, cottage, house, office or RV (recreational van) room on any of these dates. If quick results are desired, look for, and rent on any of the <u>underlined</u> dates.

Jan.: <u>15</u>; Feb.: 22; Mar.: 21; Apr.: <u>7</u>, 18; May: 15, <u>31</u>; Jun.: 1, 28; Jul.: None; Aug.: 5, <u>21</u>, <u>22</u>; Sep.: 1, <u>18</u>, 29; Oct.: <u>15</u>; Nov.: <u>11</u>; Dec.: None.

RENTING: BOAT, WATERCRAFT, THEATRE, YACHT

If you want to produce a play, concert, musical or stage show, rent a hall or theatre on these dates. These dates are also favorable for renting a boat, schooner or other watercraft. However, if you want to splurge and rent a yacht, the <u>underlined</u> dates are best.

Jan.: 1, <u>2</u>, 4, 6-9, <u>10</u>, 15, 16, 23, 27, <u>28</u>, 29, 31; Feb.: <u>3</u>, <u>4</u>, 5, <u>6-8</u>, 10-13, 15, 17, <u>18</u>, 21, 23-25, 28; Mar.: 2, 3, <u>4</u>, 5-7, 10-12, 14, <u>18</u>, 23, <u>24</u>, 31; Apr.: <u>2</u>, 6-8, 11, 20; May: 4-6, 8, <u>10-12</u>, 17, 23, 24, <u>25</u>, 26, 27, 31; Jun.: 1, 2, 4, 13, <u>14</u>, 20, 25, 27-29; Jul.: <u>4</u>, <u>5</u>, 8, 10, <u>11</u>, 12, 17, <u>18</u>, 19, <u>20</u>, <u>21</u>, 26; Aug.: <u>1</u>, <u>6</u>, 7, <u>8</u>, <u>14</u>, <u>17</u>, 21, 22, <u>28</u>; Sep.: 18, <u>24</u>, <u>25</u>, <u>28</u>, <u>30</u>; Oct.: <u>1</u>, 8, <u>10</u>, <u>11</u>, 14-16, <u>19</u>, <u>21</u>, 22, <u>23</u>, <u>27</u>, 28, 29, <u>31</u>; Nov.: 3, 4, <u>5</u>, 6-8, 10, 11, 17, 18, <u>19</u>, <u>22</u>, <u>24-26</u>, 28, 30; Dec.: <u>2</u>, <u>4</u>, <u>10</u>, 13, <u>15</u>, <u>17</u>, 22, <u>23</u>, <u>28</u>, 29, <u>30</u>, <u>31</u>.

RENTING: COMFORT

Rent a comfortable apartment, car, cottage, house, land vehicle, office, room or RV (recreational van) on any of these dates. If quick results are desired, look for and rent a place on any of the <u>underlined</u> days.

Jan.: None; Feb.: <u>18</u>; Mar.: None; Apr.: <u>14</u>; May: <u>11</u>; Jun.: <u>7</u>; Jul.: <u>4</u>, <u>5</u>; Aug.: <u>1</u>, 28; Sep.: 25; Oct.: 22; Nov.: None; Dec.: 15, 16.

RENTING: COSTUMES, EQUIPMENT, FURNITURE

Rent costumes, equipment or furniture on one of these dates. For quick service, rent on any of the <u>underlined</u> dates.

Jan.: 1, 2, 4, <u>6-10</u>, <u>15</u>, <u>16</u>, 27-29, 31; Feb.: 3, 4, <u>5-7</u>, <u>17</u>, 18, 19, 21, 23-25, 28; Mar.: 2-6, <u>7</u>, <u>10-12</u>, <u>14</u>, <u>17</u>, <u>18</u>, 23, 24, 31; Apr.: 2, 3, <u>6-8</u>, <u>11</u>, <u>13</u>, <u>14</u>, 20; May: 4, <u>10</u>, <u>11</u>, <u>17</u>, 23-28, 31; Jun.: 1, 2, <u>4</u>, <u>7</u>, <u>8</u>, 20, 25, 27-29; Jul.: <u>4</u>, <u>5</u>, 18-22, 24-27, 29, 31; Aug.: <u>1</u>, <u>2</u>, <u>4</u>, <u>6-8</u>, <u>13</u>, <u>14</u>, 15-18, 21-23, 25, 28, 29, <u>31</u>; Sep.: <u>7</u>, 18; Oct.: <u>1</u>, <u>8</u>, <u>10</u>, 14-16, 19, 21, <u>31</u>; Nov.: <u>3-8</u>, <u>10</u>, <u>11</u>, 17-19, <u>28</u>, <u>30</u>; Dec.: <u>5</u>, <u>8-10</u>, 12, 13, 15-17, 19, 22, 23, <u>29</u>, <u>31</u>.

RENTING: FAST RESULTS

If you are in a hurry, rent anything on any of the following dates:
Jan.: 5-20; Feb.: 4-18; Mar.: None; Apr.: 5-18; May: 4-19; Jun.: 1-16; Jul.: 2-6; Aug.: 1-14, 30, 31; Sep.: 1-13, 28-30; Oct.: 1-12, 27-30; Nov.: 26-30; Dec.: 1-11, 26-31.

RENTING: HORSES

Do you want to go horseback riding? Rent a horse on any of these dates and enjoy your ride. See Avoid: Accidents, page 109; see Buying: Horse, page 127; see Lessons: Horseback Riding, page 167.
Jan.: 15, 16, 24, 27; Feb.: 6, 7, 18-21, 24-28; Mar.: 2, 4-7, 10, 12-14, 17-20; Apr.: 2-4, 13, 14, 17; May: 24-28, 31; Jun.: 1-3, 7-10, 22-25, 28-30; Jul.: 1, 5, 19-22, 24, 27-29, 31; Aug.: 2-4, 6, 7, 9, 10, 13, 14, 16-18, 21, 22, 24, 25; Sep.: 6, 7, 24, 25, 28, 30; Oct.: 3, 11, 14-19, 21; Nov.: 11-15, 18-21, 28, 30; Dec.: 2-5, 8, 10-13, 15, 17, 18.

RENTING: INEXPENSIVE

Look for and rent a bargain place or inexpensive item, object, land vehicle or watercraft on one of these dates:
Jan.: 9, 10, 15, 16, 30, 31; Feb.: 3-8, 10-15, 17-19, 26-28; Mar.: 1-5, 31; Apr.: 2, 3; May: 24-27; Jun.: 1-4, 20, 24, 25, 27-30; Jul.: 1, 31; Aug.: 1-4, 9, 10, 13, 14, 18, 21-25, 28-30; Sep.: 11, 13, 18, 27; Oct.: 3, 14-19, 21, 30; Nov.: 20, 21, 27, 28, 30; Dec.: 9-12, 15-17.

RENTING: PERMANENT

Rent a permanent place on one of these dates. For quick results, look for and rent an apartment, or a cottage, house, office, store or room on any of the underlined days.
Jan.: 15, 27, 28; Feb.: 3, 10-12, 17, 18; Mar.: 2-4, 31; Apr.: 6, 7, 11, 13, 14, 27; May: 10, 11, 23-25, 31; Jun.: 1, 7, 20, 21, 25, 27, 28; Jul.: None; Aug.: 1, 13, 14, 21, 22, 28; Sep.: 9-11, 18, 25; Oct.: 14, 15, 21, 22; Nov.: 30; Dec.: 9, 15, 16, 29.

RENTING: TEMPORARY

Rent a temporary place on one of these dates. For quick results, look for and rent an apartment, cottage, house, office, store, room, land vehicle or watercraft on any of the underlined days.
Jan.: 3, 4, 10, 17, 18, 30, 31; Feb.: 6-8, 17, 18, 26-28; Mar.: None; Apr.: 2-4, 9, 10, 16, 17, 22-24, 29; May: 5-8, 13, 14, 19-21, 27; Jun.: 4, 9, 10, 23-25, 30; Jul.: None; Aug.: 3, 4, 9, 10, 18, 24, 25, 31; Sep.: 13, 27; Oct.: 3, 4, 10, 11, 17-19, 24, 25, 30; Nov.: 20, 21, 27, 28; Dec.: 4, 5, 11, 24, 25, 31.

RENTING AND LEASING: TO OTHERS

Tenants will remain for a long time if the place is rented and/or leasing terms are arranged on the following dates. The underlined dates are best if renting/leasing is for a long term. For signing, see Contracts, page 141.
Jan.: 3, 4, 9, 10, 15, 16-18, 30, 31; Feb.: 3-8, 10, 11, 12, 14, 15, 17, 18, 21, 26; Mar.: 2, 3, 4, 5, 31; Apr.: 2, 3, 6, 7, 8, 9, 11, 13, 14, 16; May: 5, 11, 13, 20, 21, 23, 24, 25, 31; Jun.: 1, 2-4, 7, 8-10, 21, 22-25, 28, 29, 30; Jul.: None; Aug.: 2-4, 9, 10, 14, 18, 21, 23-25, 28, 29-31; Sep.: 9, 10, 11, 13, 18; Oct.: 3, 10, 14, 16-19, 21, 22, 24, 25, 30; Nov.: 20, 21, 27, 28, 30; Dec.: 9, 11, 15, 16, 29, 31.

RENTING: TUXEDO
Rent a tuxedo on any of these dates. See Buying: Tuxedo, page 133.
Jan.: 1, 6, 27, 28, 30, 31; Feb.: 3, 11, 14, 15, 17-21, 23-25; Mar.: 12-14, 17, 19-22, 25-28; Apr.: 1-4, 7, 8, 10, 11, 13-15, 17, 19, 20, 26; May: 2, 4, 12-14, 17-21, 27, 28, 31; Jun.: 1-4, 7, 13, 14, 20, 29; Jul.: 1, 4-7, 10, 26, 29; Aug.: 6, 9, 16, 24, 25, 28, 31; Sep.: 7, 9-13, 20, 27, 28; Oct.: 3, 4, 9, 10, 18, 19, 21, 23-25, 27, 29; Nov.: 3, 8, 19, 22, 24-28, 30; Dec.: 1-5, 8-12, 15, 18, 24, 28-31.

RENTING: WHEELCHAIRS
Rent a manual wheelchair on any of these dates. However, rent an electric wheelchair on the underlined dates.
Jan.: 2, 3, 4, 8, 13-15, 16, 24, 27, 30, 31; Feb.: 1, 3, 5-7, 9, 16, 18-20, 24-28; Mar.:1, 3, 4; Apr.: 2, 3, 4, 6, 11, 13, 15, 18, 21, 22, 24, 27, 29; May: 1, 2, 5, 8, 9-11, 12, 13, 15, 16, 17-20, 22, 23, 24, 25, 26, 30, 31; Jun.: 1-3, 5, 6, 7, 8, 9, 10, 21, 22, 24, 25-27, 29; Jul.: 2, 3, 6; Aug.: 5, 10, 11, 14, 19-21, 23, 24, 25, 30; Sep.: 1, 6, 7, 11, 12, 15, 17-19, 22, 23, 26, 30; Oct.: 1-3, 4, 9, 10, 11, 13, 14, 17, 19, 30; Nov.: 27, 28, 29, 30; Dec.: 2, 3, 4-6, 10, 11-15, 17, 18-21, 23, 24-27, 29-31.

REORGANIZING
Organize or reorganize your office, personal belongings, drawers, house, apartment or plans on these dates.
Jan.: 1, 5, 6, 13-15, 19-28; Feb.: 1, 2, 9-12, 16-24; Mar.: 1; Apr.: 5-7, 11-14, 16, 20, 24, 25; May: 5, 9-11, 16, 17, 29-31; Jun.: 1-18, 25, 26; Jul.: 1-6, 31; Aug.: 1-7, 12, 19-22, 26-31; Sep.: 1-3, 8, 18, 27; Oct.: 1, 5, 12-15, 20-28; Nov.: 20, 21, 25, 29, 30; Dec.: 9, 14-20, 22, 27.

REPAIRS: AUTOMOBILES, ELECTRICAL PRODUCTS/ APPLIANCES AND ELECTRONIC EQUIPMENT
For satisfactory service, take a car, motorcycle, trailer, truck or van to be repaired on any of the following dates. Call an electrician for repair work or take in or have picked up, anything that uses electricity and needs to be repaired (dishwasher, heater, lawn mower, refrigerator, stove, typewriter, vacuum, washing machine/dryer or wheelchair). Also electronic equipment (computers, printers, word processors, etc.). If quick service is desired, the underlined days bring good results.
Jan.: 7-10, 15, 28-31; Feb.: 3, 4, 5-7, 18, 20, 21, 24-28; Mar.: 3-5, 31; Apr.: 1-4, 14-16; May: 24-28, 31; Jun.: 1-3, 4, 7-10, 21-25, 27-30; Jul.: 1; Aug.: 1-4, 7-10, 14, 18, 21-25, 29, 30, 31; Sep.: 2, 4-7, 9, 11-13, 18, 26, 27; Oct.: 1, 4, 14-19, 21, 30; Nov.: 20, 21, 27, 28, 30; Dec.: 3, 9-11, 16-18.

REPAIRS: BOOTS, SHOES
Repair boots and shoes on these dates.
Jan.: 1, 2, 8, 10, 15, 28, 30; Feb.: 4, 7, 11, 12, 20, 24; Mar.: 10-14, 17-19, 23, 24, 26, 31; Apr.: 2, 3, 6-8, 10, 11, 13, 14, 16, 20, 27, 29; May: 13, 17, 20, 27, 31; Jun.: 1, 9, 10, 18, 21, 23, 28; Jul.: 6, 7, 11, 18, 20, 21, 25, 26; Aug.: 3, 7, 9, 14, 16, 17, 22, 30, 31; Sep.: 2-7, 9, 10, 13, 18, 27; Oct.: 1, 3, 8, 10, 11, 14, 15, 18, 19, 21; Nov.: 4, 6, 7, 11, 13-15, 20, 21, 25, 27, 28, 30; Dec.: 4, 9, 13, 15-19, 22, 23, 29, 31.

REPAIRS: CLOCKS, WATCHES

Clocks and watches should be repaired on any of these dates. Work done on the underlined dates will last the longest; thus, the items should be repaired on one of these dates if possible.

Jan.: 1, 2-4, 9, 10, 15, 16, 27; Feb.: 5-7, 17, 18, 20, 24; Mar.: 2, 3, 4, 5-7, 10, 11, 12-14, 17, 18, 19, 23, 24, 26, 31; Apr.: 2, 3, 6, 7, 8-11, 13, 14, 16, 20; May: 5, 10, 11, 13, 17, 20; Jun.: 1, 2-4, 7, 8-10, 22-25, 27, 28, 29, 30; Jul.: 1, 17, 18, 19-22, 24, 25, 26, 27-29, 31; Aug.: 1, 2-4, 6, 7, 8-10, 13, 14, 18, 21, 22, 23-25, 28, 29-31; Sep.: 18, 27; Oct.: 1, 3, 10, 14, 15, 16-19, 30, 31; Nov.: 10, 11, 12-15, 17, 18, 19-21, 27, 28, 30; Dec.: 9, 10-12, 15, 16, 17, 22, 23, 29, 31.

REPAIRS: FURNITURE

These are favorable dates to have furniture repaired. Work done on the underlined days will last the longest; thus, the furniture should be repaired on one of these dates. For Furniture: Refinish, see page 152.

Jan.: 1, 2-4, 9, 10, 15, 16, 27, 28, 29-31; Feb.: 3-7, 17, 18, 20, 24; Mar.; 2, 3, 4, 5-7, 10, 11, 12-14, 17, 18, 19, 24, 26, 30, 31; Apr.: 2, 3, 6, 7, 8-11, 13, 14, 16; May: 31; Jun.: 1, 2-4, 7, 8-10, 20, 21, 22-25, 27, 28, 29, 30; Jul.: 1, 18, 19-22, 24, 25, 26, 27-29, 31; Aug.: 1, 2-4, 6, 7, 8-10, 13, 14, 18, 21, 22, 23-25, 28, 29-31; Sep.: 9, 10, 11, 13, 18, 27; Oct.: 1, 3, 10, 14, 15, 16-19, 21, 30, 31; Nov.: 3, 4, 5-8, 10, 11, 12-15, 17, 18, 19-21, 27, 28, 30; Dec.: 9, 10-12, 15, 16, 17.

REPAIRS: JEWELRY, SILVER

Jewelry or silver should be taken or picked up for repair on one of these dates. Work done on the underlined days will last the longest; thus, these items should be repaired on one of these dates.

Jan.: 1, 2-4, 6, 7, 8, 10, 15, 16, 27; Feb.: 5-7, 17, 18, 19-21, 23, 24, 25; Mar.: 3, 4, 5-7, 12-14, 25-27, 31; Apr.: 1-4, 6, 7, 8, 11-13, 14, 15, 17, 19, 20, 21, 22; May: 4, 12-14, 17, 18-21, 27, 28, 31; Jun.: 1, 2-4, 7, 9, 10, 25, 27, 28, 29, 30; Jul.: 1, 4, 5, 6, 22, 25, 26, 27-29; Aug.: 4, 6, 8-10, 13, 16-18, 21, 22, 24, 25, 28, 29-31; Sep.: 7, 18, 27, 28; Oct.: 3, 4, 9-11, 14, 16-19, 21, 30, 31; Nov.: 10, 11, 17, 18, 19, 20, 27, 28, 30; Dec.: 1, 2, 3-5, 8, 9, 10-12, 15, 16, 17, 18, 24, 28, 29, 30, 31.

REPAIRS: MACHINERY, MECHANICAL DEVICES, TOOLS

Machinery, mechanical devices or tools should be repaired on any of the following days. For quick service, take the item in on any of the underlined dates.

Jan.: 1-3, 9-11, 14-16, 27; Feb.: 5-7, 18, 24-28; Mar.: 2, 4-7, 10, 12-15, 17, 19, 20, 26, 31; Apr.: 2-4, 6-8, 10, 11, 13, 14, 20; May: 1, 2, 5, 8, 10-13, 17-20, 23, 24, 26, 31; Jun.: 1-3, 7-10, 22-25, 28-30; Jul.: 1, 19-22, 24, 27-29, 31; Aug.: 2-4, 6, 7, 9, 10, 13, 14, 18, 21, 22, 24, 25, 28, 29, 31; Sep.: 17-20, 30; Oct.: 1-3, 10, 11, 14-19, 21, 30, 31; Nov.: 11-15, 18-21, 27, 28, 30; Dec.: 2-5, 10-13, 15, 17, 23-25, 29, 31.

REPAIRS: PLUMBING — SINKS

Call the plumber to come on one of these dates. The underlined dates are best for sinks.

Jan.: 1, 2, 3, 9, 10, 15, 16, 24, 27; Feb.: 5-7, 18, 24-28; Mar.: 2, 4-7, 10, 12-14, 17, 19, 26, 31; Apr.: 2, 3, 4, 6-8, 10, 11, 13, 14, 20; May: 5, 8, 10-13, 17, 19, 20, 23, 24, 26, 31; Jun.: 1-3, 7-10, 22-25, 28-30; Jul.: 1, 5, 19, 20, 21, 22, 24, 28-30;

Aug.: 2-4, 6, <u>7</u>, 9, 10, 13, 14, <u>16</u>, <u>17</u>, 18, 21, 22, 24, 25, 28, 29, 31; Sep.: 6, 7, 18, 19, 30; Oct.: <u>1</u>, 2, 3, <u>10</u>, <u>11</u>, 14, 15, <u>16-19</u>, <u>21</u>, <u>30</u>, <u>31</u>; Nov.: <u>11-15</u>, <u>18</u>, <u>19</u>, 20, 21, 27, 28, 30; Dec.: 2, 3, <u>4</u>, 5, <u>10-13</u>, <u>15</u>, 17-19, 21, 23-25, 29, <u>31</u>.

REPAIRS: PLUMBING — TOILETS

Call the plumber to come on one of these dates. The <u>underlined</u> dates are best for toilets.

Jan.: <u>1</u>, 2, 3, 6-10, 15, 16, 24, 27; Feb.: 5-7, 18, 20, <u>24</u>, 25, 27; Mar.: 4-8, 10, 12-14, 17, 19, 20, 26, 31; Apr.: 2, 3, 6-8, 10, 11, 13, 14, 20; May: 5, 11-13, <u>17</u>, 18, 20, 23-25, 27, 31; Jun.: 1-3, 7-10, 22-25, 28-30; Jul.: 1, 5, 6, 19-22, 27-29; Aug.: 2-4, 6, 7, 9, 10, 13, 14, 16-18, 21, 22, 24, 25, 28, 29, 31; Sep.: 3, 4, 6, 7, 18, 30; Oct.: <u>1</u>, 2, 3, 8, 10, 11, 14-19, 21, 30, 31; Nov.: 11-15,18-21, 27, 28, 30; Dec.: 2-4, 8, 10-13, 15, 17-19, 23-25, 29, 31.

REPAIRS: STEREOS, COMPACT DISC PLAYERS, DVD's, RADIOS, RECORDERS, TAPE PLAYERS,
TELEVISION SETS, TRANSISTORS, VCR'S, VIDEO CASSETTES AND VIDEO GAMES

Repair work on these dates should give satisfaction. The <u>underlined</u> days are for quick results; therefore, take the item in, or have it serviced, on one of these dates.

Jan.: 1-4, <u>6-10</u>, <u>15</u>, <u>16</u>, 27; Feb.: <u>5-8</u>, <u>11-15</u>, <u>17</u>, <u>18</u>, 20, 24, 25, 27; Mar.: 3-6, <u>7</u>, <u>10-14</u>, <u>17-19</u>, 20, 23, 24, 26, 31; Apr.: 2, 3, <u>6-11</u>, <u>13-16</u>, 20; May: <u>5</u>, <u>13</u>, <u>14</u>, <u>17</u>, 20, 25, 27; Jun.: 1-3, <u>4</u>, <u>7</u>, <u>8</u>, <u>10</u>, 22-25, 27-30; Jul.: 1, <u>6</u>, 17, 22, 25-29; Aug.: <u>2-4</u>, <u>6-10</u>, <u>13</u>, <u>14</u>, 18, 21-25, 28-30, <u>31</u>; Sep.: <u>3</u>, <u>4</u>, 18; Oct.: <u>3</u>, <u>10</u>, <u>11</u>, 14-19, 21, <u>30</u>, <u>31</u>; Nov.: <u>11</u>, 12-15, 18-21, <u>27</u>, <u>28</u>, <u>30</u>; Dec.: <u>1-4</u>, <u>8-11</u>, 12, 13, 15-17, 22, 23, <u>29</u>, <u>31</u>.

RESEARCH:
LAW, MEDICAL, SCIENTIFIC AND FOR WRITING

On these dates you'll do excellent research work. The ability to concentrate is best done on the dates with an asterisk. The <u>underlined</u> dates are best for quick results. See Chemistry Experiments, page 136.

Jan.: *1, *2, <u>6-10</u>, *<u>14</u>, *<u>15</u>, <u>16</u>, 24, 27, *28; Feb.: *1, <u>5-8</u>, <u>11-15</u>, <u>17</u>, *<u>18</u>, 19-21, 23, *24, 25-28; Mar.: *1, 2-5, 31; Apr.: 2, 3, *5, *<u>6</u>-*<u>8</u>, *<u>14</u>, *20; May: *<u>11</u>, <u>15</u>, *<u>16</u>, *18, *22, 24-29, 31; Jun.: *1, 2, 3, <u>4</u>, <u>7-10</u>, *<u>14</u>, 22-25, 27, *28, 29, 30; Jul.: 1, <u>4</u>, <u>5</u>; Aug.: *<u>1</u>, <u>2-4</u>, <u>6</u>, *<u>7</u>, <u>8-10</u>, *<u>11</u>, *<u>12</u>, <u>13</u>, <u>14</u>, 15-18, *20-*22, 23-25, 28-30, <u>31</u>; Sep.: *<u>4</u>, <u>5</u>, <u>6</u>, 7, <u>9-13</u>, *18; Oct.: *<u>1</u>, <u>3</u>, *<u>12</u>, *13-*16, 17, 18, *19-*21, *<u>29</u>, <u>30</u>; Nov.: 20, 21, 25, <u>27</u>, *<u>28</u>-*<u>30</u>; Dec.: <u>1</u>, *<u>2</u>, *<u>3</u>, <u>4</u>, <u>8-11</u>, 12, 13, 15, *16, 17, 18, *22, *23, *<u>29</u>, *<u>31</u>.

RESERVATIONS: HOTEL, MOTEL, INN, LODGE, RESORT
TRAIN, AIRPLANE, CRUISE SHIP

Make reservations on these dates; thus, avoid misunderstandings and confusions:

Jan.: 1-4, 10, 15, 25, 28, 30; Feb.: 1-12, 15-18, 21-26; Mar.: 1-4, 31; Apr.: 5-9, 11, 12, 14, 16, 18, 21, 27, 29; May: 5, 8, 13, 15-17, 20-24, 31; Jun.: 1, 6-9, 14, 24, 28; Jul.: None; Aug.: 3, 8, 19-21, 24, 28; Sep.: 9-13, 15, 18, 30; Oct.: 1-4, 10, 12, 14, 16-22, 24, 25, 28-30; Nov.: 20, 22, 25-30; Dec.: 1, 3, 4, 9, 15, 22-25, 27, 29-31.

RETURNING: GIFTS, PURCHASES

Return a defective or unwanted gift or purchase to the shop where it was bought on one of these dates. People will be inclined to be helpful and sympathetic.

Jan.: 2, 3, 10, 18, 30; Feb.: 3, 4, 6, 7, 20, 21, 26, 27; Mar.: 3, 4; Apr.: 1, 2, 7-11, 16, 17, 22, 27-29; May: 4-8, 13, 14, 19, 24-27, 31; Jun.: 1-4, 9, 10, 20-23, 28-30; Jul.: 1, 6; Aug.: 3, 4, 9, 10, 14, 21-25, 30, 31; Sep.: 10, 11, 27, 28; Oct.: 3, 9-11, 15-19, 24, 25; Nov.: 20-22, 27; Dec.: 2, 4, 8-10, 13, 17, 24, 28, 30, 31.

REUNIONS

These are favorable dates for reunions — school, college, fraternity, sorority, club, friend, lover, partner, mate, etc.

Jan.: 2-4, 8, 9, 16; Feb.: 5-7, 18, 21, 25; Mar.: 3, 4; Apr.: 1-4, 6-11, 14, 15, 17, 21-23, 27-29; May: 12, 19-21, 24-26; Jun.: 7, 8, 25, 27; Jul.: 6; Aug.: 8-10, 14, 21, 23-25, 29, 30; Sep.: 12; Oct.: 3, 4, 9, 10, 15-19, 21, 23, 25, 27; Nov.: 21, 27, 28; Dec.: 2, 3, 8-10, 17, 24, 29-31.

RODEO: PERFORM

Perform on these dates; you'll be courageous and able to show off your skills. The underlined dates are best for persistence.

Jan.: 2, 3, 13-15, 16, 24, 27; Feb.: 5, 18, 24-28; Mar.: 1, 8, 10, 12-14, 16, 17, 19, 22; Apr.: 3, 4, 6, 14; May: 10, 11, 12, 13, 16, 17, 19, 20, 22, 23, 24, 26, 30, 31; Jun.: 1, 2, 3, 6, 7, 8-10, 24, 29; Jul.: 3, 5, 22-24, 28; Aug.: 9, 10, 19, 20, 21, 25; Sep.: 6, 7, 18, 19, 20, 25, 30; Oct.: 1, 2, 3, 14, 17, 28, 30; Nov.: 9, 11, 13-15, 19, 27, 28, 30; Dec.: 2, 3, 5, 6, 10, 11, 14, 15, 17-19, 21, 23-25, 27.

ROMANCE

The night is young and lovers everywhere will be in the mood for spooning. Enjoy yourself on these dates by courting someone or starting a love affair. See Affectional Interest, page 105; see Avoid: Blind Dates, page 109; see Dating, page 142.

Jan.: 1, 6, 15, 25-28, 30, 31; Feb.: 1-3, 11, 12, 14, 15, 17-21, 23-25; Mar.: 8, 12-14, 25-28; Apr.: 1-4, 7, 8, 10-15, 17-22, 26, 29; May: 2, 4,, 10-15, 17-21, 27-31; Jun.: 1-4, 6, 12-14, 20, 26, 29; Jul.: 1, 3, 4, 6, 7, 9, 10, 19, 21, 26; Aug.: 5, 6, 9, 16, 20, 21, 31; Sep.: 1, 2, 7, 9-13, 15,18, 20, 25, 27-30; Oct.: 1-4, 9, 10, 18-21, 23-27, 29; Nov.: 3, 8, 9, 11, 19, 22-30; Dec.: 1-5, 7-12, 18, 24, 28-31.

ROOF: INSTALLATION AND REPAIR

Install a new roof or repair an old one on any of these dates. All work commenced on the underlined days will be finished quickly. See Shingle, page 193.

Jan.: 1-5, 6-16, 24-31; Feb.: 1-4, 5-7, 16-18, 20-28; Mar.: 1-5, 31; Apr.: 2, 3, 5, 6-14, 16, 20, 30; May: 5, 9-11, 13, 16, 17, 20-31; Jun.: 1-3, 4-10, 18-30; Jul.: 1, 2, 3-6, 31; Aug.: 1-14, 16-30, 31; Sep.: 1-7, 18, 27; Oct.: 1, 3, 5, 10, 12, 14-21, 30; Nov.: 20, 21, 27-30; Dec.: 9-11, 14-20, 22, 23, 27, 29, 31.

SAUERKRAUT

Sauerkraut tastes best when made on these dates.
Jan.: None; Feb.: None; Mar.: 23, 24; Apr.: 20; May: None; Jun.: None; Jul.: 20, 21; Aug.: 16, 17; Sep.: None; Oct.: None; Nov.: 16; Dec.: 13.

SCULPTING

Artistic abilities are favored on the following dates. Also, physical energy to create a piece of sculpture is at its height. See Art, page 107; see Designing, page 143.
Jan.: 1, 2, 13-16, 27; Feb.: 5-7, 18-21, 24, 25; Mar.: 8, 12-15, 25-28; Apr.: 2-4, 6-8, 10-14, 18, 21; May: 1, 2, 4,12, 13, 15, 17-20, 22, 23, 26, 27, 31; Jun.: 1-3, 5-7, 9, 10, 29; Jul.: 1, 22, 23, 28-30; Aug.: 5, 6, 9, 10, 20, 21, 24-29, 31; Sep.: 1, 17-20, 28; Oct.: 3, 9, 10, 17-19, 21, 30; Nov.: 9, 19, 28-30; Dec.: 2-5, 7, 8, 10-13, 15, 17, 24, 25, 27, 28, 31.

SECRETS

Favored on these dates are secret alliances, having meetings, joining clubs, fraternities, societies or anything you want to keep a secret such as computer codes. To ensure that something you want is kept secret — tell it (or program the code on a computer) on any of the underlined days. See Hiding, page 158.
Jan.: 1, 2, 22, 23-26, 27, 28; Feb.: 1, 2, 3, 20-22, 23, 24; Mar.: 1, 2-5, 28, 29-31; Apr.: 1, 2, 20, 24, 25, 26-30; May: 22, 23-27, 31; Jun.: 1, 18, 19-23, 28; Jul.: None; Aug.: 16, 17, 21, 22, 28, 29; Sep.: 18, 25, 26, 27; Oct.: 14, 15, 22, 23-26; Nov.: 20-24, 25; Dec.: 15, 16, 17-21, 22.

SELF-DISCIPLINE

Start projects which require self-discipline on these dates. If you want to finish the project quickly, start it on any of the underlined days.
Jan.: 1, 5, 6-8, 15, 19, 27, 28; Feb.: 1-4, 16-18, 19-22; Mar.: 1-4, 31; Apr.: 7, 11-14, 16, 20, 27; May: 9-11, 13, 17, 22-25, 31; Jun.: 5-9, 13, 14, 18-21, 28; Jul.: 2, 6, 31; Aug.: 1-3, 7, 11-14, 21, 22, 26-30; Sep.: 3, 4, 9-11, 18, 25, 27; Oct.: 1, 15, 20-24, 28; Nov.: 20, 29, 30; Dec.: 1, 2, 9, 14-17, 22, 29.

SELLING

Sell on these dates because the customers are willing to pay high prices for purchases. If a fast sale is desired, place the object for sale on any of the underlined days. Selling includes antiques, boats, clothes, computers, furniture, games, horses, jewelry, jingles, land, real estate, recordings, religious items, sailboat, tickets (to events — charity, movies, shows, sports), toys, yachts, writing (articles, books, etc.). Note: For franchise selling, see the following category.
Jan.: 8, 10, 27, 28; Feb.: 4, 6-8, 17, 18, 23-27; Mar.: 2-6, 7, 13, 17, 24; Apr.: 1-4, 13, 14; May: 24-27; Jun.: 3, 7, 20-25, 30; Jul.: 13, 18-22, 27, 28; Aug.: 1, 4, 6-10, 14, 18, 24, 25, 28; Sep.: 2-4, 10, 11, 28, 30; Oct.: 1, 3, 11, 17-19, 21, 31; Nov.: 5-8, 13-15, 17, 18, 22, 24-26, 27; Dec.: 2, 4.

SELLING: FRANCHISE

Sell a franchise on any of these dates because people are favorably disposed to pay a higher price.

Jan.: 1-4, 16, 18; Feb.: 6-8, 17, 18, 20, 21, 23-25, 27, 28; Mar.: 3, 4; Apr.: 1-4, 6-9, 17; May: 24, 25, 27, 31; Jun.: 1, 2, 4, 7-9, 22-24, 27-30; Jul.: 1; Aug.: 2-4, 6, 8-10, 13, 14, 18, 21, ,22, 24, 25, 28, 29, 31; Sep.: 9-13, 18, 24, 30; Oct.: 1, 3, 9, 16-19, 22-25, 29; Nov.: 20-22, 24, 25, 27, 30; Dec.: 1-3, 8-10, 13, 17.

SEWING

These dates are favored for dressmaking (including bridal and evening gowns), embroidery, mending (socks, fish nets, etc.), making fishing nets or sewing on a button, etc. The sewing will be more permanent if sewn on any of the underlined days. See Avoid: Cutting Cloth, page 110; see Cloth: Cut, page 138.

Jan.: 15, 25, 26; Feb.: 11, 12, 22; Mar.: None; Apr.: 7, 18; May: 15, 31; Jun.: 1, 11, 12, 28; Jul.: None; Aug.: 5, 21, 22; Sep.: 1, 18, 29; Oct.: 15, 26; Nov.: 22, 23; Dec.: 9, 20.

SEX: BOLDNESS

Throw away shyness and be bold. Conquer the person desired on any of the following dates. The underlined days are for obtaining quick results.

Jan.: 1-3, 7, 13, 17, 21, 27, 28, 30; Feb.: 9, 15, 18, 24-27; Mar.: 8, 13, 23; Apr.: 3, 4, 14, 27; May: 1, 2, 7, 10, 11, 17, 18-20, 24, 30; Jun.: 2, 3, 6, 7, 13-16; Jul.: 4, 5, 11-13, 22, 23, 28; Aug.: 9, 10, 19, 20, 28; Sep.: 3-6, 10, 15, 16, 20, 25, 30; Oct.: 1-3, 12, 13, 17, 22, 28, 30; Nov.: 4, 8, 9, 13, 14, 19, 25, 27; Dec.: 1, 2, 6, 10, 11, 15, 16, 21-24.

SEX: ENDURANCE

A man's endurance in the sex act is best expressed on these dates.

Jan.: 1, 8-11, 15, 19, 28; Feb.: 6, 7, 11, 12, 16-18, 24; Mar.: 3, 4, 11, 15-17, 23, 24, 30, 31; Apr.: 2, 7, 11-14, 20, 27-30; May: 9, 11, 17, 24-27, 31; Jun.: 1, 5-7, 14, 20, 21, 28; Jul.: 4, 5, 11, 18, 19-21, 25, 26, 30; Aug.: 1, 7, 14-17, 21, 26-28; Sep.: 3, 10-13, 18, 23-25; Oct.: 1, 7-11, 15, 20-22, 28; Nov.: 4-7, 16-18, 24, 25; Dec.: 1-4, 9, 13-16, 22, 29, 31.

SEX: PASSION

Passion reigns during these dates; thus, ardent and fiery states of sexual passion can be easily reached. The best dates are underlined.

Jan.: 10, 15, 16, 27, 28; Feb.: 5-8, 11, 12, 15, 18, 24, 25; Mar.: 10, 11, 14, 17, 20, 23; Apr.: 1-4, 14, 29; May: 10, 11, 14, 17, 18, 26, 27, 31; Jun.: 1-4, 7, 24, 25, 28; Jul.: 4, 20-22, 24, 25, 26; Aug.: 16, 17, 21, 22, 25; Sep.: 3, 4, 13, 14, 17, 18, 30; Oct.: 1, 11, 14; Nov.: 6-8, 10, 11, 12, 15, 17, 19, 25; Dec.: 3-5, 9, 12, 13, 15, 16, 19, 21, 22, 31.

SHEEP

Shear sheep on the following dates if you want to be assured of a better growth for the next shearing. The best dates are underlined.

Jan.: 10, 11, 19; Feb.: 6, 7, 16; Mar.: 15; Apr.: 11, _12_; May: 9, 17; Jun.: 5, 14; Jul.: 11; Aug.: 7; Sep.: _3_, 13; Oct.: _1_, 10, 11, 28; Nov.: 6, 7; Dec.: 4, _31_.

SHINGLE

Shingle a roof on any of these dates and it will resist destruction and last longer. See Roof: Installation and Repair, page 190.

Jan.: 1, 28; Feb.: 24; Mar.: 3, 4, 23, 24, 30, 31; Apr.: 20, 27; May: 24, 25, 31; Jun.: 1, 20, 21, 28; Jul.: 18, 25, 26; Aug.: 21, 22, 28; Sep.: 18, 25; Oct.: 15, 22; Nov.: 18, 24, 25; Dec.: 15, 16, 22.

SHIPPING

Cargo and other items will arrive quickly if they are shipped on the following dates. There is less chance of them being damaged if they are shipped on the underlined days, and also these are favorable dates to unload cargo.

Jan.: 6, 7, _8_, 9-13, _15_, 16-20; Feb.: 6-10, _11_, 13-17; Mar.: None; Apr.: 6, _7_, 8-11, 13, _14_, 15-18; May: 5-10, 12-15; Jun.: 4-6, _7_, 8, 9, 11-13, _14_, 15, 16; Jul.: _4_, _5_, 6; Aug.: _1_, 2-6, 8-13, _14_, 31; Sep.: 1, 2, _3_, 4, 6-9, _10_, _11_, 12, 13, 29, 30; Oct.: 1-4, 6, _7_, _8_, 9-12, _28_, 29, 30; Oct.: 1-4, 6, _7_, _8_, 9-12, _28_, 29, 30; Nov.: 27-30; Dec.: _1_, _2_, 3, 5-8, _9_, 10, 11, 27, 28, _29_, 30, 31.

SHOES, BOOTS, SNEAKERS, SLIPPERS: WEAR FOR THE FIRST TIME

New shoes, boots, sneakers, slippers, or other footwear will be comfortable if worn for the first time on any of the following dates. See Avoid: Buying or Wearing Shoes, Boots, Sneakers, Slippers, page 110; see Buying Shoes, Boots, etc., page 131; see Shoes: Custom Made, the following category; see Shoes: Dying, below.

Jan.: 3, 4, 7-11, 14-18, 21-24, 27-31; Feb.: 3-8, 10-15, 17-21, 23-28; Mar.: 2-7, 10-14, 23, 31; Apr.: 2, 6-11, 20, 27, 29, 30; May: 4-8, 17, 23-28, 31; Jun.: 1-4, 7-10, 13-17, 20-25, 27-30; Jul.: 1, 4-8, 10-12, 17-21, 26; Aug.: 7, 16, 17, 22; Sep.: 3, 4, 18; Oct.: 1, 8, 10, 11, 14-19, 21-25, 27-31; Nov.: 3-8, 10-15, 17-19, 25-28; Dec.: 4, 5, 8, 9, 13, 22, 29, 31.

SHOES: CUSTOM MADE

These dates are favorable to go for measurements for custom made shoes; thus, a mold can be cast. For quick results, the underlined dates are best. See Avoid: Buying or Wearing Shoes, page 110; see Buying Shoes, page 131; see Shoes, Boots (the preceding category)

Jan.: _8_, _10_, _11_, _15_, _18_, 21-24, 28, 30; Feb.: _6-8_, _11_, _14_, _15_, _17_, _18_, 19, 24; Mar.: _7_, _10-12_,_14_, _17-19_, 23, 25, 26, 31; Apr.: 1-4, _6-11_, _13_, _14_, _17_, 19-22, 27, 29, 30; May: 1, 4, _5_, _6_, _17_, 18-20, 24, 27, 28, 31; Jun.: 1, _13-15_, 21; Jul.: _6-8_, _11_, 18-21, 23, 26; Aug.: _7_, 16, 17, 22-25, 28-30, _31_; Sep.: _2-6_, 18, _30_; Oct.: _1-3_, _8_, _10_, _11_, 14, 15, 18, 19, 21, 22, _28_; Nov.: _4_, 6, _9_, 13-15, 25, _27_; Dec.: _4_, _5_, _8-11_, 12, 13, 15, 22-25, _29_, _31_.

SHOES: DYING

These are the best dates to dye shoes.

Jan.: 4-16, 23, 25-29, 31; Feb.: 1-19, 21-25, 28; Mar.: 1-12, 14, 15, 23, 28, 31; Apr.: 2, 5-8, 11-15, 17-20, 30; May: 2, 4-6, 8, 9, 15-17, 22-27, 31; Jun.: 1, 2, 4, 5, 11-15, 17-20, 25-29; Jul.: 2-5, 8-12, 16-21, 23, 26, 30; Aug.: 7, 12, 16, 17, 22, 26; Sep.: 18, 23; Oct.: 1, 5, 8, 10, 11, 14-16, 19-23, 26-29, 31; Nov.: 1-11, 16-19, 25, 26, 28, 29; Dec.: 4, 13, 22, 29, 31.

SHOWS

Open a show (animal, backers, ballet, Broadway, off-Broadway, cabaret, cable, car, charity, circus, concert, convention, dance, exposition, fashion, flower, folk, fund raising, hypnosis, jewelry, ice, industrial, movie, musicals, night club act, opera, pageant, play, poetry reading, radio, revue, stage, television, theater, theater-in-the round, theatre-restaurant or trade) on any of these dates. This includes previews. Attendance will be higher if the show opens on any of these dates because during this time the public goes out more. The best dates are underlined. Also see Entertainment, page 147.

Jan.: 6, 7, 8, 9-12, 13, 15-17, 18-20; Feb.: 5, 6-9, 10, 11, 13-15, 16-18; Mar.: None; Apr.: 7-11, 13-18; May: 5-10, 12-17; Jun.: 4-9, 11-16; Jul.: 3-6; Aug.: 1-6, 8-14; Sep.: 2-4, 6-11, 12, 13, 29, 30; Oct.: 1, 2, 3, 4, 6-12, 28-30; Nov.: 27, 28-30; Dec.: 1, 2, 3, 5-7, 8-10, 11, 27, 28, 29, 30, 31.

SKIN CARE

Beautify and feel great by having a facial, herbal wrap or other form of skin care on any of these dates.

Jan.: 1, 6, 12-16, 25-28, 30, 31; Feb.: 1-3, 11, 12, 14, 15, 17-21, 23-25; Mar.: 28; Apr.: 1, 4, 7, 8, 10-15, 17-22, 26, 29; May: 2, 4, 12-15, 17-21, 27-31; Jun.: 1-4, 6, 12-14, 20, 26, 29; Jul.: 1, 3, 4, 6; Aug.: 5, 6, 9, 16, 20-22, 24-26, 31; Sep.: 1, 7, 9-13, 15, 18, 20, 27, 28; Oct.: 3, 4, 9, 10, 18-21, 23-27, 29; Nov.: 22-30; Dec.: 1-5, 7-12, 18, 24, 28-31.

SKYDIVING OR SKY SAILING, HANG GLIDING, PARAGLIDING, BUNGEE JUMPING

Do you find it exciting to fly through the air? If so, these are favorable dates to hang glide, paraglide, sky dive (indoor/outdoor), or sky sail above canyons, or be thrilled by bungee jumping. See Avoid: Travel by Air, page 118.

Jan.: 27-29, 31; Feb.: 3-5, 19, 21, 22, 24, 25, 28; Mar.: 1, 2, 4-6, 23, 28, 31; Apr.: 12, 20; May: 8, 9, 17, 22-25; Jun.: None; Jul.: 2, 23, 26, 30; Aug.: 7, 12, 22, 26; Sep.: 30; Oct.: 1, 2, 23, 27-29; Nov.: 1-9, 11, 16-18; Dec.: 13, 22, 29.

SOCIALIZING: ENJOYMENT

Warmth and friendliness abound; greet and welcome others at social functions on any of these dates. See Parties, pages 176, 177; also see the following category.

Jan.: 8, 10, 15, 24, 27, 30, 31; Feb.: 3, 4, 6, 7, 11, 12, 14, 15, 17-19, 21, 23, 25; Mar.: 4, 11-14, 17, 18, 20, 25-27, 30, 31; Apr.: 1-4, 13-15, 17, 19, 21, 22, 26, 27, 29; May: 4, 12, 18-21, 25, 27, 28, 31; Jun.: 1-4, 7, 13, 20, 29; Jul.: 1, 4-6, 8, 10, 13, 26, 29; Aug.: 6, 9, 10, 14, 16, 17, 21-25, 28, 31; Sep.: 6, 7, 9-14, 18, 28; Oct.: 3, 4, 17-19, 21-23, 25, 27, 29; Nov.: 3, 4, 6, 8, 11, 19, 21, 22, 26-28, 30; Dec.: 1-5, 8-12, 15, 24, 28-31.

SOCIALIZING: MEETING NEW PEOPLE

Friendships are easily formed on these dates. Make new acquaintances on any of the following dates because a pleasant and friendly atmosphere prevails. Those who are shy will be gregarious, and who knows what new contacts will bring? Give the singles scene a try: you will find it interesting.

Jan.: 15, 16, 25, 30, 31; Feb.: 3, 5, 9-11, 14, 15, 18, 21, 25; Mar.: 3, 4; Apr.: 1-4, 14, 15, 17, 18, 21, 22, 29; May: 12, 14, 15, 19-21, 25, 27, 31; Jun.: 1, 2, 4, 7, 12, 26, 27, 29; Jul.: 1; Aug.: 5, 9, 11, 20, 24, 25, 27, 29, 31; Sep.: 1, 9, 11-13, 15; Oct.: 3, 4, 17-19, 23, 25, 26, 29; Nov.: 22, 23, 27, 28, 30; Dec.: 2, 3, 5, 7-11, 17, 24, 29-31.

SOCIAL SECURITY

Apply for social security on these dates. For quick results, contact social security on the underlined dates.

Jan.: 2-4, 10, 15, 25, 30; Feb.: 1-3, 5-10, 15-18, 21-25; Mar.: 1-4, 31; Apr.: 6-9, 11, 18, 21, 27, 29; May: 5, 8, 13, 15-17, 20-24; Jun.: 1, 6-9, 24; Jul.: None; Aug.: 3, 8, 19-21, 24; Sep.: 9-13, 15, 30; Oct.: 1-4, 10, 12, 14, 16-20, 25, 29, 30; Nov.: 20, 22, 27-30; Dec.: 1, 3, 9, 15, 22-25, 29-31.

SODDING

These dates are best for cultivating or turning sod. The underlined dates are the most favorable.

Jan.: 23, 30; Feb.: 20, 26, 27; Mar.: 3, 4, 26, 30, 31; Apr.: 4, 22, 27; May: 2, 19, 20, 24, 25, 29, 30; Jun.: 20, 21, 25, 26, 30; Jul.: 18, 23, 28; Aug.: 19, 20, 24, 28; Sep.: 15, 16, 20, 21, 25-27; Oct.: 17, 18, 22-24; Nov.: 14, 18, 19, 20; Dec.: 15-18, 24.

SPA

These are great dates to go to a spa and be pampered with a facial, herbal wrap, body waxing, etc. The underlined dates are for relaxing at a resort and taking the waters — mineral spring, sauna, Jacuzzi, hot tub or mud bath. See Massage, page 171; see Recreation, page 184; see Skin Care, page 194.

Jan.: 1, 10, 11, 15, 19, 20, 25-28; Feb.: 1, 2, 6, 7, 16-18, 19-24, 28; Mar.: 11, 16-22; Apr.: 2, 7, 11, 12, 13-15, 17-20, 30; May: 4, 5, 8, 9, 10-14, 15-17, 18, 21, 27, 31; Jun.: 1, 6, 7, 11, 12, 23, 28; Jul.: 16, 20, 21, 25, 26; Aug.: 1, 5, 6, 21, 22, 26, 28, 31; Sep.: 1, 18, 25, 29; Oct.: 1, 10, 11, 15, 19-27; Nov.: 6, 7, 11, 18, 19, 21, 29; Dec.: 3, 4, 8, 9, 15, 16, 18, 20, 31.

SPECULATING

Speculate on these dates for your greatest luck. Also see Gambling, pages 152, 153.

Jan.: 27, 28, 30; Feb.: 3, 4, 6, 7, 17-19, 24-28; Mar.: 2-4; Apr.: 1-4; May: 24-27; Jun.: 27-30; Jul.: 1; Aug.: 1-4, 6-10, 13, 14, 18, 21-25, 28, 29; Sep.: 30; Oct.: 1, 3, 11, 14-19, 21; Nov.: 20, 21, 27; Dec.: 2, 4, 10, 17.

SPIRITUALITY

Clear your mind, transcend high mental realms and tap your spirituality on these dates. Start a religious training course, such as Zen Buddhism, on the underlined dates. See Classes: Meditation, page 137; see Illumination, page 160; see Meditation, page 171.

Jan.: <u>1-5</u>, 6, 7, <u>8</u>, 10-12, <u>13</u>, <u>14</u>, 15, 16, <u>18</u>, <u>22</u>, 23, <u>25</u>, 27, <u>28</u>, 30; Feb.: <u>2-4</u>, 5, <u>6-9</u>, <u>11</u>, 12, 13, <u>14</u>, <u>15</u>, 17, <u>18</u>, 19, 24, 25, <u>26</u>, <u>28</u>; Mar.: <u>1-3</u>, 4, 5, <u>6-9</u>, 10, 11, 15, <u>19-22</u>, 23, <u>24</u>, 28, <u>29</u>, 31; Apr.: <u>1</u>, <u>2</u>, 3, <u>4</u>, <u>5</u>, 6-8, <u>16-19</u>, 20, <u>21-24</u>, <u>26</u>, <u>28</u>, 30; May: 5, 6, <u>9-11</u>, 12, <u>14</u>, 15, 17, <u>18-21</u>, 22, 23, <u>24</u>, 25, 26, <u>27</u>, 28; Jun.: <u>1-3</u>, 4, 11, <u>14</u>, 15, <u>16-18</u>, <u>22-24</u>, 25, <u>27-29</u>. Jul.: <u>1-3</u>, 4, 5, <u>8-10</u>, 11, <u>13-15</u>, 17, <u>20</u>, <u>22</u>, <u>24</u>, <u>25</u>, 26, <u>27-29</u>; Aug.: <u>1</u>, <u>2</u>, <u>4-6</u>, 7, <u>8</u>, <u>9</u>, <u>11</u>, 12, <u>13-16</u>, 17, <u>18-21</u>, 22, <u>23-25</u>, 26, <u>27-30</u>, 31; Sep.: <u>1</u>, <u>2</u>, <u>16</u>, 18, <u>24</u>, <u>25</u>, <u>28-30</u>; Oct.: <u>1</u>, 5, <u>6</u>, <u>7</u>, 8, <u>9</u>, <u>10</u>, <u>12</u>, <u>13</u>, <u>16</u>, <u>17</u>, 19, <u>21</u>, <u>22</u>, 23, <u>26</u>, <u>27</u>, 28, 29, <u>31</u>; Nov.: <u>2</u>, 3, 4, <u>5</u>, 6, 7, <u>8</u>, <u>9</u>, 11, <u>12</u>, <u>13</u>, <u>17</u>, <u>18</u>, 19, <u>20</u>, <u>22-24</u>, 25, 26, <u>27</u>, 28-30; Dec.: 1, <u>2</u>, 3, 4, <u>8-10</u>, 12, 13, <u>17</u>, <u>19</u>, <u>21</u>, 22, <u>23</u>, <u>24</u>, <u>26-28</u>, 29, <u>30</u>, 31.

SPORTS ACTIVITIES: COMPETITIVE

Be daring, gusty, courageous and have a winning spirit on these dates. Compete in such sports as: basketball, baseball, fencing, football, golf, gymnastics, ice skating, polo (on horseback), racing (car, horse, track, motorcycle), racquetball, rollerblading, rollerskating, skiing, sledding, tennis or volleyball. See Buying: Headgear, Helmets, page 127; see Rodeo, page 190; see Sports Training, below; see Sports: Water, below.

Jan.: 15, 16, 27; Feb.: 5, 18, 24-28; Mar.: 1, 8, 10, 12, 13, 17, 23; Apr.: 3, 4, 14; May: 5, 18-20, 22-24, 31; Jun.: 1-3, 5-8, 29; Jul.: 22-24, 28, 30; Aug.: 9, 10, 19-21, 25; Sep.: 6, 7, 17-19, 25, 30; Oct.: 1-3, 13, 14, 17, 30; Nov.: 9, 11-15, 19, 27, 28, 30; Dec.: 2,6, 10, 11, 23-25, 27.

SPORTS ACTIVITIES: NON-COMPETITIVE

Your zest, skill and enthusiasm will be great on these dates. Have fun! Go camping, backpacking, caving, hiking, horseback riding, ice skating, mountain-biking, rock-climbing, rollerblading, rollerskating, scooter, skateboarding, sledding, skiing, snowmobiling, snowshoeing, biking, or do gymnastics. See Buying: Horse, 127; see Fishing, pages 150, 151; see Sky Diving, Hang Gliding, Paragliding, Bungee Jumping, page 194; see Sports: Training, the following category; see Sports Water, below.

Jan.: 2, 3, 15, 16, 24, 27; Feb.: 5-7, 15, 18, 24-28; Mar.: 1, 8, 10, 12-17, 19, 20, 22; Apr.: 3, 4, 6, 11, 14, 18; May: 5, 8-13, 16-20, 22-25, 30, 31; Jun.: 1-3, 5-9, 29; Jul.: 3, 5, 22-24, 28, 30; Aug.: 9, 10, 19-21, 25; Sep.: 6, 7, 17-19, 25, 30; Oct.: 1-3, 13, 14, 17, 30; Nov.: 9, 11-15, 19, 27-30; Dec.: 2, 5-8, 10-15, 17, 18, 21, 23-25, 27.

SPORTS: TRAINING

Train on these dates when persistence and hard work can make you a winner. The <u>underlined</u> dates are best.

Jan.: <u>1</u>, 3, 14, <u>15</u>, 16, <u>28</u>, 30; Feb.: 4, <u>18</u>, 19, 20, <u>24</u>, 25-28; Mar.: 2, <u>4</u>, 10, 12-14, <u>17</u>, 19, 26, <u>31</u>; Apr.: 6, <u>7</u>, 8, <u>20</u>; May: 5, 13, <u>17</u>, 18, 20, <u>25</u>; Jun.: <u>1</u>, 9, <u>28</u>, 29; Jul.: 22, 24; Aug.: 3, <u>7</u>, 9, 10, <u>14</u>, <u>21</u>, <u>22</u>; Sep.: 17-20; Oct.: <u>1</u>, 3, 14, <u>15</u>, 16, 17, <u>18</u>, 19, 21, 30; Nov.: <u>11</u>, 20, 21, 27, 28, 30; Dec.: <u>2</u>, 10-13, <u>15</u>, 17, 23-25, <u>29</u>.

SPORTS: WATER

These are great dates to indulge in water sports, such as jet skiing, sailing, snorkeling, surfing, swimming: play polo, go sea kayaking, enjoy driving your PWC (personal water craft), try a jet- boat ride or white water rafting.

Jan.: 1-3, 5, 7-10, 15, 16, 24, 27, 29-31; Feb.: 1, 3-7, 16, 18-22, 24-28; Mar.: 1, 4-10, 12-16, 19-22, 27, 28, 31; Apr.: 2-8, 10-12, 14, 17, 18, 20; May: 4, 9, 11-13,

15, 16, 18-20, 22, 24-27, 31; Jun.: 1-3, 5, 18, 25, 28-30; Jul.: 1-3, 5, 6, 19-24, 28, 30; Aug.: 5, 7, 10, 12, 16, 17, 21, 22, 25-27, 29; Sep.: 1, 17-19; Oct.: 1-3, 5, 8, 10, 11, 13-19, 21, 30, 31; Nov.: 1, 4-9, 11, 16, 19, 27-30; Dec.: 2-4, 10-14, 17, 23-25, 27, 29, 31.

SPRAYING

Spray insecticides on garden pests, bugs, roaches, flies, etc., or use other types of spray for objects such as hair, throat, house, art objects, etc. on these dates and you will obtain good results.

Jan.: None; Feb.: 1, 2; Mar.: 1, 28; Apr.: 4, 24, 25; May: 2, 22, 29, 30; Jun.: 18, 25, 26; Jul.: 23; Aug.: 19, 20, 28; Sep.: 15, 16, 25; Oct.: 22; Nov.: 18; Dec.: 15, 16.

STONE: CUT, POLISH — ABRASION

Cut stones (diamonds, gems, granite, marble or other stones from a mine or quarry) on these dates. Make stones smooth and shiny by polishing them through abrasion (rubbing) on the underlined dates.

Jan.: 2, 3-5, 7, 8-12, 13-20, 22-27, 29, 31; Feb.: 1, 3, 4, 5-9, 10-14, 15, 16, 18, 20-22, 23-28; Mar.: 1, 3, 4, 31; Apr.: 2-4, 6, 7-10, 11, 12, 13, 18, 20, 30; May: 1, 2, 4, 5, 6, 7, 8, 9, 10-14, 15, 16, 17, 19-21, 22, 23, 24, 25, 26, 27, 30, 31; Jun.: 1-12, 16, 18, 19, 24, 25-28, 29, 30; Jul.: 1, 2, 3, 4, 5, 6; Aug.: 5, 7, 10, 12, 21, 22, 25, 26, 27-30; Sep.: 1, 3-7, 16, 17-20, 23, 30; Oct.: 1, 2, 3, 5, 8, 10-12, 14, 15, 16, 17, 18-21, 22, 23-27, 28, 29, 31; Nov.: 25, 26-28, 29, 30; Dec.: 1-6, 9-11, 13, 14-21, 22, 23-25, 27, 29.

STONE: CUT, POLISH — CHEMICAL ACTION

Cut stones (diamonds, gems, granite, marble or other stones from a mine or quarry) on these dates. Polish stones by using chemical action on the underlined dates.

Jan.: 2, 5, 8, 11, 13-15, 16, 22, 24, 27; Feb.: 5, 6, 7, 12, 20, 24, 25, 26, 27, 28; Mar.: 1, 4; Apr.: 2-4, 6, 8, 9, 11, 13, 18, 26, 30; May: 5, 9-11, 12, 13, 15-17, 18, 19, 20, 22-24, 25, 27, 30, 31; Jun.: 1, 2, 3, 5-9, 10, 24, 29; Jul.: 3; Aug.: 3, 5, 7, 10, 17, 21, 22, 25, 31; Sep.: 4, 6, 7, 11, 12, 17, 18, 19, 20, 23, 30; Oct.: 1, 2, 3, 8, 10, 11, 13, 14, 16, 17, 19, 21, 23-25, 29, 30; Nov.: 21, 25, 27-29, 30; Dec.: 1, 2-6, 8, 10-15, 17, 18, 19-21, 22, 23-25, 27, 29, 31.

STORAGE

Do you need to save space at home or in an office? Keep your possessions safe, put them in storage on these dates. The best dates are underlined.

Jan.: 1, 2-4, 9, 10, 15, 16, 27; Feb.: 5-7, 17, 18, 20, 24; Mar.: 2, 3, 4, 11, 17, 18, 19, 23, 24, 26, 31; Apr.: 2, 3, 6, 7, 8-11, 13, 14, 16, 20; May: 5, 10, 11, 13, 17, 20; Jun.: 1, 2-4, 7, 8-10, 22-25, 27, 28, 29, 30; Jul.: 1, 17, 18, 19-22, 24, 25, 26, 27-29, 31; Aug.: 1, 2-4, 6, 7, 8-10, 13, 14, 18, 21, 22, 23-25, 28, 29-31; Sep.: 18, 27; Oct.: 1, 3, 10, 14, 15, 16-19, 30, 31; Nov.: 10, 11, 12-15, 17, 18, 19-21, 27, 28, 30; Dec.: 9, 10-12, 15, 16, 17, 22, 23, 29, 31.

STRIKES

For fast results, start a strike on any of the following dates. See Avoid: Strikes, page 114.

Jan.: 9, 16, 18; Feb.: 5, 9, 10, 16, 17; Mar.: None; Apr.: 15, 18; May: 8, 12, 16; Jun.: 5-8, 12-14; Jul.: 6; Aug.: 2, 11; Sep.: 1, 7, 12; Oct.: 4, 9, 12; Nov.: 27-29; Dec.: 3, 10, 30, 31.

SUBSCRIPTIONS: MAGAZINE, NEWSPAPER, NEWSLETTER, PERIODICAL, TABLOID

If personal or professional subscriptions are important to you, send (subscribe) on any of these dates. This includes the opera, ballet, sports events, theatre and concerts.

Jan.: 2-4, 10, 15, 25, 30; Feb.: 1-10, 15-18, 21-26; Mar.: 1-4, 31; Apr.: 5-9, 11, 12, 18, 21, 27, 29; May: 5, 8, 13, 15-17, 20-24; Jun.: 1, 6-9, 14, 24; Jul.: None; Aug.: 3, 8, 19-21, 24; Sep.: 9-13, 15, 24, 25, 30; Oct.: 1-4, 10, 12, 14, 16-21, 29, 30; Nov.: 20, 22, 26-30; Dec.: 1, 3, 4, 9, 15, 22-25, 29-31.

SURGERY

Have an operation on any of the following dates if surgery is to be performed on any of the following regions of the body: The brain (upper hemisphere); brow, cerebrum, cheeks, eyelids, eyes, face, forehead, gums, head, jaw (upper), lips, mouth, nose, teeth (upper). For dates to avoid surgery on these areas, see page 114. The best days to heal quickly from operations performed on these bodily areas are underlined. The dates listed with asterisks afford the best chances for the operation to be permanent so it does not have to be repeated.

Jan.: *1, 2-4, 6-8, 17-20, 22-27, *28, 29-31; Feb.: 1-3, 14-17, *18, 20-23, *24, 25-28; Mar.: 1-4, 13-16, *17, 18, 19, 21, 22, *23, *24, 25-31; Apr.: 9-13, *14, 15-18, *20, 21-27; May: 6-10, *11, 12-16, *17, 19-25; Jun.: 4-6, *7, 8-12, *13, *14, 15, 16, 18-21, 30; Jul.: 1, 3, *4, *5, 6-10, *11, 12-15, 17, 18, 28-30; Aug.: *1, 2-6, *7, 8-14, 24-27, *28, 29, 31; Sep.: 1, 2, *3, 4-11, 20-24, *25, 26, 27, 29, 30; Oct.: *1, 2-8, 17-21, *22, 23-26, *28, 29, 30, 31; Nov.: 1-4, 14-17, *18, 19-24, *25, 27-30; Dec.: 1, 2, 11, 13, 14, *15, *16, 17-21, *22, 23-25, 27-31.

SURGERY

Have an operation on any of the following dates if surgery is to be performed on any of the following regions of the body: The blood vessels of the carotid arteries, brain (base, lower lobes), cerebellum, ears, jaw (lower), larynx, neck (and its bony structure), occipital region (bone), palate, pharynx, teeth (lower), throat, thyroid gland, tonsils, vein (jugular), vocal cords. For dates to avoid surgery on these areas, see page 114. The best days to heal quickly from operations performed on these bodily areas are underlined. The dates listed with asterisks afford the best chances for the operation to be permanent so it does not have to be repeated.

Jan.: *1, 2-4, 6, 7, *8, 9, 10, 19, 20, 22-27, *28, 29-31; Feb.: 1-3, 5-7, 16, 17, *18, 20-23, *24, 25-28; Mar.: 1, 2, *3, *4, 5, 15, 16, *17, 18, 19, 21, 22, *23, *24, 25-29, *30, *31; Apr.: 1, 2, 11-13, *14, 15-18, *20, 21-26, *27, 28-30; May: 9, *10, 11-16, *17, 19-23, *24, *25, 26, 27; Jun.: 5, 6, *7, 8-13, *14, 15, 16, 18, 19, *20, *21, 22, 23; Jul.: 3, *4, *5, 6-10, *11, 12-15, 17, *18, 19-21, 30;

Aug.: *1, 2-6, *7, 8-13, *14, 16, 17, 26, 27, *28, 29, 31; Sep.: 1, 2, *3, 4-9, *10, *11, 12, 13, 23, 24, *25, 26, 27, 29, 30; Oct.: *1, 2-6, *7, *8, 9-11, 20, 21, *22, 23-26, *28, 29-31; Nov.: 1-3, *4, 5-7, 16, 17, *18, 19-24, *25, 27-30; Dec.: *1, *2, 3, 4, 13, 14, *15, *16, 17-21, *22, 23-25, 27, 28, *29, 30, 31.

SURGERY

Have an operation on any of the following dates if surgery is to be performed on any of the following regions of the body: The arms, bronchi (bronchial tubes), clavicle (collarbone), fingers, hands, lungs (upper lobes), nervous system (central), respiratory system (upper), ribs, shoulders and shoulder blades, windpipe, wrists. For dates to avoid surgery on these areas, see page 115. The best days to heal quickly from operations performed on these bodily areas are underlined. The dates listed with asterisks afford the best chances for the operation to be permanent so it does not have to be repeated.

Jan.: *1, 2-4, 6, 7, *8, 9-13, 22-27, *28, 29-31; Feb.: 1-3, 5-9, *18, 20-23, *24, 25-28; Mar.: 1, 2,*3, *4, 5, 7, 8, *17, 18, 19, 21, 22, *23, *24, 25-29, *30, *31; Apr.: 1-4, *14, 15-18, *20, 21-26, *27, 28-30; May: 1, 2, *11, 12-16, *17, 19-23, *24, *25, 26-30; Jun.: *7, 8-13, *14, 15, 16, 18, 19, *20, *21, 22-26; Jul.: *4, *5, 6-10, *11, 12-15, 17, *18, 19-23; Aug.: *1, 2-6, *7, 8-13,*14, 16-19, *28, 29, 31; Sep.: 1, 2, *3, 4-9, *10, *11, 12, 13, 15, *25, 26, 27, 29, 30; Oct.: *1, 2-6, *7, *8, 9-12, *22, 23-26, *28, 29-31; Nov.: 1-3, *4, 5-9, *18, 19-24, *25, 27-30; Dec.: *1, *2, 3-6, *15, *16, 17-21, *22, 23-25, 27, 28, *29, 30, 31.

SURGERY

Have an operation on any of the following dates if surgery is to be performed on any of the following regions of the body: The breasts, diaphragm, digestive organs, lacteals (lymph carrying vessels), lungs (lower lobes), respiratory system (lower), stomach, womb (belly). For dates to avoid surgery on these areas, see page 115. The best days to heal quickly from operations performed on these bodily areas are underlined. The dates listed with asterisks afford the best chances for the operation to be permanent so it does not have to be repeated.

Jan.: *1, 2-4, 6, 7, *8, 9-15, 23-27, *28, 29-31; Feb.: 1-3, 5-11, 20-23, *24, 25-28; Mar.: 1, 2, *3, *4, 5, 7-10, 19, 21, 22, *23, *24, 25-29, *30, *31; Apr.: 1-4, 6, 7, 16-18, *20, 21-26, *27, 28-30; May: 1-3, 13-16,*17, 19-23, *24, *25, 26-31; Jun.: 9-13, *14, 15, 16, 18, 19, *20,*21, 22-26; Jul.: 7-10, *11, 12-15, 17, *18, 19-25; Aug.: 3-6, *7, 8-13, *14, 16-21, 31; Sep.: 1, 2, *3, 4-9, *10, *11, 12, 13, 15-18, 27, 29, 30; Oct.: *1, 2-6, *7, *8, 9-12,14, 24-26, *28, 29-31; Nov.: 1-3, *4, 5-10, 20-24, *25, 27-30; Dec.: *1, *2, 3-8, 18-21, *22, 23-25, 27, 28, *29, 30, 31.

SURGERY

Have an operation on any of the following dates if surgery is to be performed on any of the following regions of the body: The aorta, back, heart, spine (and the marrow and nerves of the spine), spleen. For dates to avoid surgery on these areas, see page 115. The best days to heal quickly from operations performed on these bodily areas are <u>underlined</u>. The dates listed with asterisks afford the best chances for the operation to be permanent so it does not have to be repeated.

Jan.: *1, 2-4, <u>6</u>, <u>7</u>, *<u>8</u>, <u>9-14</u>, *<u>15</u>, <u>16</u>, 25-27, *28, 29-31; Feb.: 1-3, <u>5-10</u>, *<u>11</u>, *<u>12</u>, <u>13</u>, 22, 23, *24, 25-28; Mar.: 1, 2, *3, *4, 5, <u>7-10</u>, *<u>11</u>, <u>12</u>, <u>13</u>, 21, 22, *23, *24, 25-29, *30, *31; Apr.: 1-4, <u>6</u>, *<u>7</u>, 8, <u>18</u>, *20, 21-26, *27, 28-30; May: 1-3, <u>5</u>, <u>6</u>, <u>15</u>, <u>16</u>, *17, 19-23, *24, *25, 26-31; Jun.: *1, <u>11-13</u>, *<u>14</u>, <u>15</u>, <u>16</u>, 18, 19, *20, *21, 22-27, *28, 29; Jul.: <u>9</u>, <u>10</u>, *<u>11</u>, <u>12-15</u>, 17, *18, 19-24, *25, *26, 27; Aug.: <u>5</u>, <u>6</u>, *<u>7</u>, <u>8-13</u>, *<u>14</u>, 16-21, *22, 23, <u>31</u>; Sep.: <u>1</u>, <u>2</u>, *<u>3</u>, <u>4-9</u>, *<u>10</u>, *<u>11</u>, <u>12</u>, <u>13</u>, 15-17, *18, 19, 20, <u>29</u>, <u>30</u>; Oct.: *<u>1</u>, <u>2-6</u>, *<u>7</u>, *<u>8</u>, <u>9-12</u>, 14,*15, 16, 17, 26, *<u>28</u>, <u>29-31</u>; Nov.: <u>1-3</u>, *<u>4</u>, <u>5-10</u>, *<u>11</u>, 13, 22-24, *25, <u>27-30</u>; Dec.: *<u>1</u>, *<u>2</u>, <u>3-8</u>, *<u>9</u>, <u>10</u>, 20, 21, *22, 23-25, <u>27</u>, <u>28</u>, *<u>29</u>, <u>30</u>, <u>31</u>.

SURGERY

Have an operation on any of the following dates if surgery is to be performed on any of the following regions of the body: The abdominal region, appendix, bowels, chylification, colon, duodenum, gastro-intestinal system, intestinal canal tract, mesenteric glands, navel, peristaltic action of the bowels, pyloris glands, small intestines, umbilical cord. For dates to avoid surgery on these areas, see page 116. The best days to heal quickly from operations performed on these bodily areas are <u>underlined</u>. The dates listed with asterisks afford the best chances for the operation to be permanent so it does not have to be repeated.

Jan.: *1, 2-4, <u>6</u>, <u>7</u>, *<u>8</u>, <u>9-14</u>, *<u>15</u>, <u>16-19</u>, *28, 29-31; Feb.: 1-3, <u>5-10</u>, *<u>11</u>, *<u>12</u>, <u>13-15</u>, *24, 25-28; Mar.: 1, 2, *3, *4, 5, <u>7-10</u>, *<u>11</u>, <u>12-14</u>, *23, *24, 25-29, *30, *31; Apr.: 1-4, <u>6</u>, *<u>7</u>, <u>8-12</u>, *20, 21-26, *27, *28, 29, 30; May: 1-3, <u>5-8</u>, *17, 19-23, *24, *25, 26-31; Jun.: *1, 2, <u>4</u>, *<u>14</u>, <u>15</u>, <u>16</u>, 18, 19, *20, *21, 22-27, *28, 29, 30; Jul.: 1, *<u>11</u>, <u>12-15</u>, 17, *18, 19-24, *25, *26, 27-30; Aug.: *<u>7</u>, <u>8-13</u>, *<u>14</u>, 16-21, *22, 23-25; Sep.: *<u>3</u>, <u>4-9</u>, *<u>10</u>, *<u>11</u>, <u>12</u>, <u>13</u>, 15-17, *18, 19-22; Oct.: *<u>1</u>, <u>2-6</u>, *<u>7</u>, *<u>8</u>, <u>9-12</u>, 14, *15, 16-19, *<u>28</u>, <u>29-31</u>; Nov.: <u>1-3</u>,*<u>4</u>, <u>5-10</u>, *<u>11</u>, 13-15, *25, <u>27-30</u>; Dec.: *<u>1</u>, *<u>2</u>, <u>3-8</u>, *<u>9</u>, <u>10</u>, <u>11</u>, 13, *22, 23-25, <u>27</u>, <u>28</u>, *<u>29</u>, <u>30</u>, <u>31</u>.

SURGERY

Have an operation on any of the following dates if surgery is to be performed on any of the following regions of the body: The fallopian tubes, internal generative (reproductive) organs, kidneys, lumbar area, ovaries, suprarenals, veins. For dates to avoid surgery on these areas, see page 116. The best days to heal quickly from operations performed on these bodily areas are <u>underlined.</u> The dates listed with asterisks afford the best chances for the operation to be permanent so it does not have to be repeated.

Jan.: 3, 4, <u>6</u>, <u>7</u>, *<u>8</u>, <u>9-14</u>, *<u>15</u>, <u>16-20</u>, 30, 31; Feb.: 1-3, <u>5-9</u>, *<u>10</u>, *<u>11</u>, <u>12-17</u>, 26-28; Mar.: 1, 2, *3, *4, 5, <u>7-10</u>, *<u>11</u>, <u>12-16</u>, 26-29, *30, *31; Apr.: 1-4, <u>6</u>, *<u>7</u>, <u>8-13</u>, 22-26, *27, 28-30; May: 1-3, <u>5-10</u>, 19-23, *24, *25, 26-31; Jun.: *1, 2, <u>4-6</u>, <u>16</u>, 18, 19, *20, *21, 22-27, *28, 29, 30; Jul.: 1, <u>3</u>, <u>4</u>, <u>13-15</u>, 17, *18, 19-24, *25, *26, 27-30; Aug.: <u>9-13</u>, *<u>14</u>, 16-21, *22, 23-27; Sep.: <u>5-9</u>, *<u>10</u>, *<u>11</u>, <u>12</u>, <u>13</u>, 15-17, *18, 19-24; Oct.: 3-6, *<u>7</u>, *<u>8</u>, <u>9-12</u>, 14, *15, 16-21, <u>30</u>, <u>31</u>; Nov.: <u>1-3</u>, *<u>4</u>, <u>5-10</u>, *<u>11</u>, 13-17, <u>27-30</u>; Dec.: *<u>1</u>, *<u>2</u>, <u>3-8</u>, *<u>9</u>, 10, 11, 13, 14, 24, 25, <u>27</u>, <u>28</u>, *<u>29</u>, <u>30</u>, <u>31</u>.

SURGERY

Have an operation on any of the following dates if surgery is to be performed on any of the following regions of the body: The bladder and gall bladder, excretory organs, external generative (reproductive) glands (penis, testicle, vagina), groin, inguinal region, kidneys (sinus or pelvic areas), nose and nasal bones, pelvis, perineum, prostrate gland, rectum, sigmoid flexure, spermatic cord, sphincter, ureter, uterus, urogenital orifice. For dates to avoid surgery on these areas, see page 116. The best days to heal quickly from operations performed on these bodily areas are underlined. The dates listed with asterisks afford the best chances for the operation to be permanent so it does not have to be repeated.

Jan.: 6, 7, *8, 9-14, *15, 16-20, 22; Feb.: 1-3, 6-10, *11, 12-17, *18; Mar.: 1, 2, *3, *4, 5, 7-10, *11, 12-16, *17, 18, 28, 29, *30, *31; Apr.: 1-4, 6, 7, *8, 9-13, *14, 15, 24-26, *27, *28, 29, 30; May: 1-3, 5-10, *11, 12, 22, 23, *24, *25, 26-31; Jun.: *1, 2, 4-6, *7, 8, 18, 19, *20, *21, 22-27, *28, 29, 30; Jul.: 1, 3, *4, *5, 6, 15, 17, *18, 19-24, *25, 26-30; Aug.: *1, 2, 12, 13, *14, 16-21, *22, 23-27, *28, 29; Sep.: 8, 9, *10, *11, 12, 13, 15-17, *18, 19-24, *25, 26; Oct.: 5, 6, *7, *8, 9-12, 14, *15, 16-21,*22, 23; Nov.: 1-3 *4, 5-10, *11, 13-17, *18, 19, 29, 30; Dec.: *1, *2, 3-8, *9, 10, 11, 13, 14,*15, *16, 17, 27, 28, *29, 30, 31.

SURGERY

Have an operation on any of the following dates if surgery is to be performed on any of the following regions of the body: The buttocks, femur, gluteus, hips (locomotor muscles of the hips and thighs), ischium, legs (above the knees), liver, pancreas,, sciatic nerve, sartorius, thighs, lumbar. For dates to avoid surgery on these areas, see page 117. The best days to heal quickly from operations performed on these bodily areas are underlined. The dates listed with asterisks afford the best chances for the operation to be permanent so it does not have to be repeated.

Jan.: *8, 9-14, *15, 16-20, 22-24; Feb.: 5-10, *11, *12, 13-17, *18, 20, 21; Mar.: *3, *4, 5, 7-10,*11, 12-16, *17, 18, 19, *30,*31; Apr.: 1-4, 6, *7, 8-13, *14, 15-17, *27, 28-30; May: 1-3, 5-10, *11, 12-14, *24, *25, 26-31; Jun.: *1, 2, 4-6, *7, 8-10, *20, *21, 22-27, *28, 29, 30; Jul.: 1, 3, *4, *5, 6-8, *18, 19-24, *25, *26, 27-30; Aug.: *1, 2-4, *14, 16-21, *22, 23-27, *28, 29, 31; Sep.: *10, *11, 12, 13, 15-17, *18, 19-24, *25, 26, 27; Oct.: *7, *8, 9-12, 14, *15, 16-21, *22, 23-25; Nov.: *4, 5-10, *11, 13-17, *18, 19-21; Dec.: *1, 2, *3, 4-8, *9, 10, 11, 13, 14, *15, *16, 17-19, *29, 30, 31.

SURGERY

Have an operation on any of the following dates if surgery is to be performed on the bones, bony-skeleton-framework of the body, cartilages, joints, kneecaps, knees, teeth (bone and bone-like structure part of the teeth). For dates to avoid surgery on these areas, see page 117. The best days to heal quickly from operations performed on these bodily areas are underlined. The dates listed with asterisks, afford the best chances for the operation to be permanent so it does not have to be repeated.

Jan.: 10-14, *15, 16-20, 22-27; Feb.: 6-10, *11, *12, 13-17, *18, 20-23; Mar.: 7-10, *11, 12-16,*17, 18, 19, 21, 22; Apr.: 2-4, 6, *7, 8-13, *14, 15-18, 29, 30; May: 1-3, 5-10, *11, 12-16, 27-31; Jun.: *1, 2, 4-6, *7, 8-13, 23-27, *28, 29, 30; Jul.: 1, 3, *4, *5, 6-10, 20-24, *25, *26, 27-30; Aug.: *1, 2-6, 16-21, *22, 23-29,

31; Sep.: 1, 2, 13, 15-17, *18, 19-24, *25, 26, 27, 29; Oct.: 10-12, 14, *15, 16-21, *22, 23-26; Nov.: 6-10, *11, 13-17, *18, 19-24; Dec.: 4-8, *9, 10, 11, 13, 14, *15, *16, 17-21, 31.

SURGERY

Have an operation on any of the following dates if surgery is to be performed on the Achilles tendon, ankles, calves, circulation, legs (below the knees), shins. For dates to avoid surgery on these areas, see page 117. The best days to heal quickly from operations performed on these areas are underlined. The dates listed with asterisks afford the best chances for the operation to be permanent so it does not have to be repeated.

Jan.: *1, 2, 3, 13, 14, *15, 16-20, 22-27, *28, 29; Feb.: 9, 10, *11, *12, 13-17, *18, 20-23, *24, 25; Mar.: 8-10, *11, 12-16, *17, 18, 19, 21, 22, *23, *24, 25; Apr.: 4, 6, *7, 8-13, *14, 15-18, *20, 21; May: 2, 3, 5-10, *11, 12-16, *17, 29-31; Jun.: *1, 2, 4-6, *7, 8-13, *14, 15, 25-27, *28, 29, 30; Jul.: 1, 3, *4, *5, 6-10, *11, 12, 23, 24, *25, *26, 27-30; Aug.: *1, 2-6, *7, 8, 19-21, *22, 23-27, *28, 29, 31; Sep.: 1, 2, *3, 4, 15-17, *18, 19-24, *25, 26, 27, 29, 30; Oct.: *1, 2, 14, *15, 16-21, *22, 23-26, *28, 29; Nov.: 9, 10, *11, 13-17, *18, 19-24, *25; Dec.: 6-8, *9, 10, 11, 13, 14, *15, *16, 17-21, *22, 23.

SURGERY

Have an operation on any of the following dates if surgery is to be performed on the feet, metatarsus, phalanges, plantaris, tarsus, toes. For dates to avoid surgery in these areas, see page 117. The best days to heal quickly from operations performed on the foot or the toe area are underlined. The dates listed with asterisks afford the best chances for the operation to be permanent so it does not have to be repeated.

Jan.: *1, 2-4, *15, 16-20, 22-27, *28, 29-31; Feb.: *11, 12-17, *18, 20-23, *24, 25-28; Mar.: *11, 12-16, *17, 18, 19, 21, 22, *23, *24, 25-27; Apr.: *7, 8-13, *14, 15-18, *20, 21-23; May: 5-10, *11, 12-16, *17, 19-21; Jun.: *1, 2, 4-6, *7, 8-13, *14, 15, 16, *28, 29, 30; Jul.: 1, 3, *4, *5, 6-10, *11, 12-14, *25, *26, 27-30; Aug.: *1, 2-6, *7, 8-11, *22, 23-27, *28, 29, 31; Sep.: 1, 2, *3, 4-7, *18, 19-24, *25, 26, 27, 29, 30; Oct.: *1, 2-4, *15, 16-21, *22, 23-26, *28, 29-31; Nov.: *11, 13-17, *18, 19-24, *25, 27, 28; Dec.: *9, 10, 11, 13, 14, *15, *16, 17-21, *22, 23-25.

SWEETS: COOK, MAKE

Do you want to satisfy your sweet tooth by making your own sugary goodies? Make candy, cookies and pastries on these dates. To make ice cream the underlined dates are best. See Avoid: Eating Sugar, page 112.

Jan.: 1, 6, 12, 13-15, 17, 18-26, 27, 28, 30, 31; Feb.: 1-3, 11, 12, 14-19, 20-22, 23-25, 26, 27, 28; Mar.: 2, 8, 11-18, 19-22, 25, 26, 27-29; Apr.: 1-4, 7-15, 17, 18, 19-21, 22, 26, 29; May: 2, 4, 9, 10, 11-14, 15, 16-18, 19, 20, 21, 27-31; Jun.: 1-4, 6, 12, 13, 14, 20, 26, 29; Jul.: 1, 3, 4, 6-8, 9, 10, 18, 19, 21, 26, 29; Aug.: 21-26; Sep.: 1, 2-4, 5, 6, 7, 9-15, 18, 20, 27-30; Oct.: 1, 2, 3, 4, 9-14, 18-22, 23-27, 29; Nov.: 3, 8, 9, 11, 13-15, 19, 21-26, 27-30; Dec.: 1-12, 18, 23, 24, 28-31.

TAILORING

See a tailor or dressmaker on any one of these dates to have custom clothing made. For fittings, the underlined dates are best.

Jan.: 1, 6, 12, 23-27, 28, 30, 31; Feb.: 1-3, 11, 14-18, 20, 21-23, 24, 25; Mar.: 8, 11, 12-14, 26, 27, 29; Apr.: 1-4, 7, 8-15, 17, 18, 20-22, 26, 29; May: 2, 4, 12, 13, 14, 15-17, 19, 20, 21, 27-30, 31; Jun.: 1-4, 6, 12, 13, 14, 20, 26, 29; Jul.: 1, 3, 4, 6, 7, 8-10, 26, 29; Aug.: 5, 6, 9, 16, 20, 23-26, 31; Sep.: 1, 6, 9, 10, 15, 20; Oct.: 3, 4, 9-11, 12, 14, 18-21, 22, 23, 24, 25-27, 29; Nov.: 3, 8, 9, 19, 21-24, 25-30; Dec.: 1-3, 4-8, 9, 10, 11, 18, 24, 28-31.

TATTOO: BODY

1. See the category Avoid: Surgery. Find the part of the body to be tattooed and do not have a tattoo on those dates listed (for that part of body you want tattooed).

2. If the date you want to be tattooed is not listed under Avoid: Surgery, then see the category Surgery. Find part of the body to be tattooed and have the tattoo done on any of those dates listed (for that part of the body you want tattooed).

TATTOO: REMOVAL

If you want to remove a tattoo do so on any of the dates listed below in this category if these dates do not appear under Avoid: Surgery (for that part of the body that the tattoo is to be removed).

Jan.: 3, 8, 16; Feb.: 7-9, 20, 24, 25, 27; Mar.: 4; Apr.: 3, 8, 9; May: 5, 12-14, 17, 25, 27, 31; Jun.: 1, 2, 4, 24, 29; Jul.: None; Aug.: 3, 10, 22, 31; Sep.: 4, 9, 11-13, 18; Oct.: 1, 3, 16, 18, 19, 22-25, 29; Nov.: 21, 25, 30; Dec.: 1-3, 6, 8, 9, 13, 22, 29, 31.

TAXES: AUDIT, INSTALLMENT AGREEMENT

These are favorable dates if you need to appear in person for an audit or to get an installment agreement. If you want quick action, try the underlined dates.

Jan.: 10, 15, 25, 26, 28, 30; Feb.: 1-3, 5-10, 15-18, 24, 25; Mar.: 1-4, 31; Apr.: 1-4, 18, 20-23, 25, 27-29; May: 5-9, 12-17, 19-25; Jun.: 1, 2, 4, 5, 14, 21-24, 26, 28-30; Jul.: None; Aug.: 2-5, 8-12, 14, 18-21, 24-29, 31; Sep.: 1, 12, 13, 15, 16, 24, 29, 30; Oct.: 1-4, 9, 16-20, 22, 24, 29, 30; Nov.: 20-25, 27-30; Dec.: 1, 3, 11, 15, 22-25, 27-31.

TAXES: CALCULATE, QUICK ACTION

Calculate your City, State or Federal taxes on these dates or have your accountant or tax preparer calculate them on these same dates. If you want quick action (in case a refund is due), file your tax form in person or by mail on the underlined dates.

Jan.: 2-4, 10, 15, 25, 30; Feb.: 1-10, 15-18, 21-26; Mar.: 1-4, 31; Apr.: 5-9, 11, 12, 18, 21, 27, 29; May: 5, 8, 13, 15-17, 20-24; Jun.: 1, 6-9, 14, 24; Jul.: None; Aug.: 3, 8, 19-21, 24; Sep.: 9-13, 15, 24, 25, 30; Oct.: 1-4, 10, 12, 14, 16-21, 29, 30; Nov.: 20, 22, 26-30; Dec.: 1, 3, 4, 9, 15, 22-25, 29-31.

TEACHING

Start teaching on any of the following dates because people will be inclined to attend classes. If a class commences on any of the underlined days, the students will try their best to continue and the lessons will remain firmly entrenched in their subconscious minds.

Jan.: 6, 7, 8, 9-13, 15, 16-20; Feb.: 6-10, 11, 13-17; Mar.: None; Apr.: 6, 7, 8-11, 13, 14, 15-18; May: 5-10, 12-15; Jun.: 4-6, 7, 8, 9, 11-13, 14, 15, 16; Jul.: 4, 5, 6; Aug.: 1, 2-6, 8-13, 14, 31; Sep.: 1, 2, 3, 4, 6-9, 10, 11, 12, 13, 29, 30; Oct.: 1-4, 6, 7, 8, 9-12, 28, 29, 30; Nov.: 27-30; Dec.: 1, 2, 3, 5-8, 9, 10, 11, 27, 28, 29, 30, 31.

TIMBER: CUTTING

Timber seasons best if cut on any of the following dates. See Avoid: Cutting Timber, page 110.

Jan.: 2-4, 22-27, 29, 30, 31; Feb.: 1-3, 20-23, 25, 26, 27, 28; Mar.: 1-5, 21, 22, 25, 26, 27-31; Apr.: 1, 3, 4, 21, 22, 23-28; May: 1, 2, 3, 19, 20, 21-26, 28, 29, 30, 31; Jun.: 1, 2, 18, 19, 21-24, 25, 26, 27-30; Jul.: 1, 17-19, 22, 23, 24-29; Aug.: 18, 19, 20, 21-25, 27, 28, 29; Sep.: 15, 16, 17-22, 24, 25, 26, 27; Oct.: 14-19, 21, 22, 23-26; Nov.: 13-15, 17, 18, 19-23; Dec.: 14, 15, 16, 17-21, 23, 24, 25.

TINTING: CAR WINDOWS

These are favorable dates to have car windows tinted; thus, reducing the sun's glare. See Fabric: Tinting, page 149; see Hair: Coloring, page 155.

Jan.: 4-16, 23, 25-29, 31; Feb.: 1-13, 15-19, 21-25, 28; Mar.: 1-12, 14, 15, 23, 28, 31; Apr.: 6-8, 11, 12, 20, 30; May: 2, 4-6, 8, 9, 15-17, 22-27, 31; Jun.: 1, 2, 4, 5, 11-15, 17, 18; Jul.: 2-5, 8-12, 16-19, 23, 26, 30; Aug.: 7, 12, 22, 26; Sep.: 18, 23; Oct.: 1, 5, 8, 14-16, 19-23, 26-29, 31; Nov.: 1-11, 25, 26, 28, 29; Dec.: 23, 22, 29.

TRADING

Bargain, barter, negotiate and trade on any of these dates because they're more economical; shrewdness and cleverness are favored. This includes gold, bonds, stocks, commodities, collectibles, real estate, treasury notes and foreign currency. Jan.: 6-10, 15, 16, 27-31; Feb.: 3-8, 10-15, 17-21, 23-28; Mar.: 2-5, 31; Apr.: 2, 3, 13, 14, 16, 20; May: 5, 10, 11, 13, 17, 20, 21,23-27, 31; Jun.: 1-4, 7-10, 20-25, 27-30; Jul.: 1, 31; Aug.: 1-4, 6-10, 13, 14, 18, 21-25, 28-31; Sep.: 2-4, 9-11, 13, 18, 27; Oct.: 1, 3, 14-19, 21, 30; Nov.: 20, 21, 25, 27, 28, 30; Dec.: 9-12, 15-17, 22, 23, 29, 31.

TRAINING: DISCIPLINE

Potty and other types of training are best done on these dates, because your conscious mind is disciplined and retains learning. For Sports Training, see page 196.

Jan.: 9, 15, 27-29, 31; Feb.: 3-5, 18-21, 24-28; Mar.: 3-5, 31; Apr.: 3, 14, 16, 20; May: 5, 11, 13, 21, 24-26, 31; Jun.: 1-4, 7-10, 22-25, 27-29; Jul.: 1; Aug.: 1-4, 7, 8, 14, 18, 21-23, 25, 29-31; Sep.: 18, 27; Oct.: 1, 14, 15, 16, 19, 21; Nov.: 20, 21, 28, 30; Dec.: 9, 10, 12, 16, 17, 22, 23, 29.

TRAVEL: BY LAND

Take a bus, train or travel by cable car, car, street car, train, truck, van, RV (recreational van), motorcycle on any of these auspicious dates. See Avoid: Accidents, page 109; see Avoid: Travel by Land, page 118; see Travel: City, Country or Island Hop, below: see Travel: Enjoyment, below: see Travel: Plans, below.

Jan.: 2, 3, 9, 10, 15, 16; Feb.: 5-7, 16, 18, 19, 24, 27, 28; Mar.: 1, 4, 7, 25-29, 31; Apr.: 2-4, 6-8, 18, 20, 21; May: 5, 8, 12, 13, 16, 18-20, 22, 24-27, 31; Jun.: 1, 5, 7-10, 22-25, 28, 29; Jul.: 2, 15, 20, 21, 24; Aug.: 2, 3, 5, 7, 9-11, 14, 21, 22, 24, 25; Sep.: 18; Oct.: 1-3, 9, 10, 15, 17, 19, 30; Nov.: 11, 13-15, 19-21, 27-29; Dec.: 3, 4, 10, 13, 17, 23-25, 27, 29, 31.

TRAVEL: BY WATER

Travel on a boat, ship or yacht or go sailing on any of these favorable dates. See Avoid: Travel by Water, page 118; see Travel: City, Country or Island Hop, (the following category); see Travel: Enjoyment, below; see Travel: Plans, below. The best dates are underlined.

Jan.: 23, 25-27; Feb.: 5-7, 16-19, 21-25, 28; Mar.: 2, 5-7, 8, 9, 10, 11, 12, 14, 15, 23, 28, 31; Apr.: 6, 7, 8, 11, 12, 20, 30; May: 2, 4-6, 8, 9, 15-17, 22-26, 27; Jun.: 26, 27, 28, 29; Jul.: 2, 3, 4, 5, 16-19, 23, 26, 30; Aug.: 7, 12, 22, 26; Sep.: None; Oct.: 1, 5, 8, 14, 15, 16, 19-23, 26, 27, 28, 29, 31; Nov.: 9, 10, 11, 16-18, 19, 28, 29; Dec.: 13, 22, 29.

TRAVEL: CITY, COUNTRY OR ISLAND HOP

These are favorable dates to go island hopping by boat or yacht. Do you want to city or country hop? Do you like seeing things as fast as you can? If so, try these dates to hop-on and hop-off of a train. See Avoid: Accidents, page 109; see Avoid: Travel by Land, page 118; see Avoid: Travel by Water, page 118; see Travel by Land, page 204; see Travel by Water, above: see Travel: Enjoyment, (the following category); see Travel: Plans, below.

Jan.: None; Feb.: 5, 7, 18, 19; Mar.: 4, 25-27-29; Apr.: 2, 3, 6, 18, 21; May: 8, 11, 18, 22, 24-26; Jun.: 29; Jul.: 2, 15, 20, 24; Aug.: 11, 21, 25; Sep.: None; Oct.: 1, 2, 9, 10; Nov.: 30; Dec.: 2-4, 17, 25, 27, 29, 31.

TRAVEL: ENJOYMENT

A pleasant time will be had if you travel on any of the following dates: however, see Avoid: Accidents, page 109; see Avoid: Travel by Air, page 118; see Avoid: Travel by Land, Water, page 118; see Travel: by Land, Water, page 204; see Travel: by Water, above; see Travel: City, Country or Island Hop, (preceding category); see Travel: Plans, which follows.

Jan.: 27; Feb.: 7, 19, 21, 24, 25; Mar.: 4-6, 25, 27, 31; Apr.: 2, 3, 17, 19-21; May: 10, 11, 17, 18, 23-26; Jun.: 28, 29; Jul.: 20-22, 24, 27, 29; Aug.: 4, 7, 18, 21, 22, 25; Sep.: 30; Oct.: 1, 2, 21; Nov.: 11, 18, 30; Dec.: 2-4, 17, 25, 28, 29, 31.

TRAVEL: PLANS

These dates are good for making detailed and thorough plans for any traveling you are contemplating for the future. See Avoid: Accidents, page 109; see Avoid: Travel by Air, page 118; see Avoid: Travel by Land, page 118; see Avoid: Travel by Water, page 118; see Travel: City, Country or Island Hop, above; see Travel: Enjoyment, preceding category; see Travel: by Water, above; see Travel by Land, page 204.

Jan.: 1-4, 9, 10, 15-18, 28-31; Feb.: 3, 5-8, 10, 11, 13-15, 17, 18, 20, 21, 23-25, 27, 28; Mar.: 2-5, 31; Apr.: 2, 3, 6-11, 13, 14, 16, 20; May: 5, 10, 13, 17, 20, 21, 23-25, 27, 31; Jun.: 1, 2, 4, 7-9, 21-24, 27-30; Jul.: 1; Aug.: 2-4, 6, 8-10, 13, 14,

18, 21, 22, 24, 25, 28, 29, 31; Sep.: 9-11, 13, 18, 27; Oct.: 1, 3, 10, 14-19, 30; Nov.: 20, 21, 25, 27, 28, 30; Dec.: 9-11, 15-17, 22, 23, 29, 31.

UPHOLSTERY

These are favorable dates to have an upholsterer work on your furniture. If you want the job done quickly, call the upholsterer on any of the underlined dates.
Jan.: 1, 6, 25-27; Feb.: 6, 7, 17, 18, 19-21, 23-25; Mar.: 8, 12-14, 26, 27, 29; Apr.: 1-5, 6-8, 10-15, 17, 18-22; May: 4, 12-15, 17, 18-21, 23, 27, 31; Jun.: 1-3, 4, 6, 26, 29; Jul.: 1, 6, 26, 29; Aug.: 5, 6, 8, 9, 20, 24-26, 31; Sep.: 1; Oct.: 3, 4, 9, 10, 18-21; Nov.: 9, 19, 27-30; Dec.: 1-5, 7-11, 12, 24, 25, 28-31.

VACCINATION: IMMUNIZATION

Flu shots, and other shots for immunization, are best on these dates.
Jan.: 2, 13-16, 27; Feb.: 5-7, 24-28; Mar.: 1; Apr.: 2-4, 6, 18; May: 5, 8-13, 15-20, 22-24, 26, 31; Jun.: 1-3, 5, 29; Jul.: 3; Aug.: 5, 10, 21, 25-29; Sep.: 1, 17-20, 23, 30; Oct.: 1-3, 17, 30; Nov.: 27-30; Dec.: 2-4, 10-15, 17, 21, 23-25, 27.

VOICE MAIL

Start voice mail on any of these dates.
Jan.: 1-4, 9, 10, 15, 16, 18, 25, 28, 30, 31; Feb.: 1, 3-7, 18, 21, 24-26; Mar.: 3, 4, 31; Apr.: 1-4, 6-9, 11, 15, 16, 20-22, 27, 29; May: 5, 8, 12-15, 19-22, 24, 25; Jun.: 1, 7-10, 14, 21, 22, 24, 25, 29; Jul.: 2; Aug.: 2, 3, 7, 8, 10, 11, 19, 21, 23-26, 29-31; Sep.: 1, 9, 11-13, 15, 18, 26, 27; Oct.: 1-4, 9-12, 14, 16-19, 21, 24, 29, 30; Nov.: 20, 21, 27-30; Dec.: 3, 4, 9, 22-25, 29-31.

VOLUNTEER WORK

These dates are favorable to volunteer your services and do some volunteer work for charities, hospitals, foundations or help build homes for the needy. See Charity: Donations, Fundraising, page 135.
Jan.: 8, 10, 27; Feb.: 6-8, 17-21, 23-28; Mar.: 2-7, 10-14, 17-20, 24; Apr.: 1-4, 13-17; May: 24-27, 31; Jun.: 1-4, 7-10, 22-25, 27-30; Jul.: 1, 13, 22, 24-29; Aug.: 2-4, 6-10, 13, 14, 18, 21-25, 28-31; Sep.: 2-4, 9-11; Oct.: 3, 11, 14-19, 21, 31; Nov.: 10-15, 17-22, 24-27; Dec.: 2, 4, 8-10, 13, 17.

WARTS: REMOVAL

These are the best days on which to have warts removed. The preferred dates are underlined. However, if surgery is to be performed, see Avoid Surgery, pages 114-117; also, see Surgery, pages 198-202.
Jan.: 23, 30; Feb.: 20, 26, 27; Mar.: 3, 4, 26, 30, 31; Apr.: 4, 22, 27; May: 2, 19, 20, 24, 25, 29, 30; Jun.: 20, 21, 25, 26, 30; Jul.: 18, 23, 28; Aug.: 19, 20, 24, 28; Sep.: 15, 16, 20, 21, 25-27; Oct.: 17, 18, 22-24; Nov.: 14, 18, 19, 20; Dec.: 15-18, 24.

WEANING: ANIMALS OR HUMAN BABIES

Commence the weaning of an animal or human baby on any one of these dates. The best days are underlined.
Jan.: 4, 5-9, 30, 31; Feb.: 1-3, 4, 26-28; Mar.: 26-31; Apr.: 22-27; May: 19-25; Jun.: 16-18, 19-21; Jul.: 13-16, 17, 18; Aug.: 9-14; Sep.: 5-11; Oct.: 3-8, 30, 31; Nov.: 1-4, 27-30; Dec.: 1, 2, 24, 25, 26-29.

WEAVING: BASKET

These are good dates to weave a basket; your hands and brain work well together on these days. For finishing it quickly, the underlined dates are best. See Knitting, page 164.

Jan.: 1-3, 7, 10, 15, 16, 28, 30; Feb.: 1, 3, 4, 5-7, 16, 18, 19, 21, 22, 24, 25; Mar.: 4, 10, 12, 13, 15, 29, 31; Apr.: 2-5, 6-8, 11-13, 18, 19, 21; May: 12, 13, 15-17, 19, 20, 22-24, 31; Jun.: 1-3, 5-10, 13, 14, 28, 29; Jul.: 6, 22, 23, 27, 28, 30; Aug.: 5, 7, 10, 19-21, 24-29; Sep.: 1, 17-19; Oct.: 3, 10, 16-19, 21, 22, 24, 25, 28-30; Nov.: 4, 6-9, 11, 19, 20, 27-30; Dec.: 3-6, 11, 12-15, 24, 25, 27, 29, 31.

WEAVING: CLOTH

These are favorable dates to make cloth (interlace yarn, the threads of the weft and the warp on a loom). For finishing it quickly, the underlined dates are best. See Knitting, page 164.

Jan.: 1-4, 6, 7, 10, 14, 15, 18, 19, 21, 22, 25, 26, 28, 30, 31; Feb.: 1-4, 5-7, 17, 18, 19, 21, 23-26; Mar.: 1-4, 8, 12, 13, 16, 17, 19, 21, 22, 27, 29, 31; Apr.: 1-5, 6-8, 11-15, 18, 19-22, 30; May: 1-4, 5, 6, 15, 17, 19-23, 28-31; Jun.: 1-3, 4, 6, 7, 9, 12-14, 16, 17, 20, 24, 26, 29; Jul.: 1, 3, 4, 6, 7, 9, 18, 19, 21, 26, 29; Aug.: 3, 5, 8, 9, 16, 19-21, 24-26, 31; Sep.: 1-4, 7, 20, 24, 25, 29, 30; Oct.: 1-4, 9-12, 13, 14, 16-21, 24-27, 29, 30; Nov.: 3, 8, 9, 13, 15, 19, 20, 27-30; Dec.: 1, 3-5, 7-9, 11, 12, 15, 20, 22-25, 28-31.

WEEDS

Cut weeds on the following dates so they will grow back more slowly.

Jan.: None; Feb.: 1, 2; Mar.: 1, 28; Apr.: 4, 24, 25; May: 2, 22, 29, 30; Jun.: 25, 26; Jul.: 23; Aug.: 19, 20, 28; Sep.: 15, 16, 25; Oct.: 22; Nov.: 18; Dec.: 15, 16.

WELLS: TO DIG OR DRILL

For best results, dig or drill wells on any of these dates.

Jan.: 1, 28; Feb.: 24; Mar.: 23, 24; Apr.: 2, 20, 29, 30; May: 27; Jun.: 20; Jul.: 20, 21, 30; Aug.: 16, 17, 23; Sep.: 23; Oct.: 20; Nov.: 24, 25; Dec.: 13, 22.

WHEAT

If winter wheat is sown (seeds scattered over the ground for growing) on the following dates, it will have a good root system. See Avoid: Harvesting, page 112; see Grain Harvesting, page 155; see Grain Planting, page 155.

Jan.: None; Feb.: None; Mar.: 23, 24; Apr.: 20; May: None; Jun.: None; Jul.: 20, 21; Aug.: 16, 17; Sep.: None; Oct.: None; Nov.: 16; Dec.: 13.

WINE: MAKE

Wine made on these dates will taste excellent and age well.

Jan.: None; Feb.: None; Mar.: 23, 24; Apr.: 20; May: None; Jun.: None; Jul.: 20, 21; Aug.: 16, 17; Sep.: None; Oct.: None; Nov.: 16; Dec.: 13.

WIRE

For wire to stay in good shape, stretch it on any of the following dates.

Jan.: 8, 15; Feb.: 11, 12, 18; Mar.: 11, 17; Apr.: 7, 14; May: 11, 17; Jun.: 7, 14; Jul.: 4, 5, 11; Aug.: 1, 7, 14; Sep.: 3, 10, 11; Oct.: 1, 7, 8, 28; Nov.: 4, 11; Dec.: 1, 2, 9, 29.

WOMEN

Dealings with the female sex progress best on the dates that follow. The underlined dates bring quick results.

Jan.: 1-3, <u>8-11</u>, <u>15</u>, <u>16</u>, <u>18</u>, <u>22</u>, <u>24</u>, 27, 28; Feb.: 4, <u>5-7</u>, <u>11</u>, <u>12</u>, <u>15</u>, <u>18</u>, 20, 24, 25, 27, 28; Mar.: 4, 31; Apr.: 2, 4, <u>6-8</u>, <u>11</u>, <u>14</u>, 21, 27, 28, 29; May: 1, <u>5</u>, <u>8</u>, <u>12</u>, <u>13</u>, 20, 25-27, 31; Jun.: <u>7</u>, <u>9</u>, <u>10</u>, <u>14-16</u>, 21, 22, 24, 28, 29; Jul.: 1, <u>5</u>; Aug.: <u>2</u>, <u>9</u>, <u>10</u>, <u>14</u>, 16, 17, 21, 22, <u>31</u>; Sep.: <u>4</u>, <u>7</u>, <u>9</u>, <u>11</u>, <u>12</u>, 18, 19, 25, 26; Oct.: <u>1</u>, <u>3</u>, <u>8-11</u>, 16, 17, 19, 23-25, <u>29</u>; Nov.: 20, 22, 25, <u>27</u>, <u>28</u>; Dec.: <u>3</u>, <u>4</u>, <u>8</u>, 13, 17, 18, 23, <u>29</u>, <u>31</u>.

WRITING: COMMENCE

Commence writing an ad, article or a book, brochure, commercial, dissertation, flyer, greeting card, jingle, legal brief, manual, medical narrative, musical score, screen (movie, television), stage play or technical report on any of the following dates because you will finish it quickly. The <u>underlined</u> dates are when you will steadfastly stick with the writing until it is completed.

Jan.: 10, 15; Feb.: 5-10, 15-17, <u>18</u>; Mar.: None; Apr.: 6, <u>7</u>, 8, 9, 11, 18; May: 5, 8, 13, 15, 16, <u>17</u>; Jun.: 6, <u>7</u>, 8, 9, <u>14</u>; Jul.: None; Aug.: 3, 8; Sep.: <u>3</u>, 4, 9, <u>10</u>, <u>11</u>, 12, 13, 30; Oct.: <u>1</u>, 2-4, 10, 12, 29, 30; Nov.: 27-30; Dec.: <u>1</u>, 3, <u>9</u>, 10, <u>29</u>, 30, 31.

WRITING: CORRESPONDENCE

Fax, e-mail, or write documents, letters, messages, notes or reports on any of the following dates because your ideas could be readily and favorably expressed. For quick results, write, fax, e-mail or send by mail correspondence on any of the <u>underlined</u> days. See Computer: E-mail, page 139; see Mail, page 170.

Jan.: 2-4, 10, 15, 25, 30; Feb.: 1-10, 15-18, 21-26; Mar.: 1-4, 31; Apr.: 5-9, 11, 12, 18, 21, 27, 29; May: 5, 8, 13, 15-17, 20-24; Jun.: 1, 6-9, 14, 24; Jul.: None; Aug.: 3, 8, 19-21, 24; Sep.: 9-13, 15, 24, 25, 30; Oct.: 1-4, 10, 12, 14, 16-21, 29, 30; Nov.: 20, 22, 26-30; Dec.: 1, 3, 4, 9, 15, 22-25, 29-31.

X-RAYS

These are good days for X-Rays or any form of Radiology, including MRI's. For Avoid: Dental X-Rays, see page 111; for Dental X-Rays, see page 143.

Jan.: 1, 3, 5, 8, 16, 21-25, 27; Feb.: 7-9, 12, 20, 24, 25, 27; Mar.: 4-7, 11-14, 19, 20, 24; Apr.: 3, 8, 9; May: 17, 18, 25, 27, 31; Jun.: 1-4, 10, 24, 29; Jul.: 7, 11, 21, 26; Aug.: 3, 7, 10, 17, 22, 31; Sep.: 4-9, 11-13, 18; Oct.: 1, 3, 8, 16, 18, 19, 21-25, 29; Nov.: 12-14, 30; Dec.: 1-4, 6, 8, 9, 12, 13, 18.

YOGA: LEARN

Do you want to train your conscious mind to achieve a state of perfect insight and tranquility? These are favorable dates to learn Yoga. The <u>underlined</u> dates are when you can stick to the Yoga techniques of exercises, produced as a part of this discipline, to promote control of your body and mind.

Jan.: <u>1</u>, 3-5, 9-12, <u>13-15</u>, 25; Feb.: 5-7, 16, <u>18</u>, 19, <u>24</u>, 25-28; Mar.: 3-10, <u>11</u>, 12, 13, 19, 20, <u>23</u>, <u>28</u>, 31; Apr.: 2, 3, <u>5-8</u>, <u>14</u>, 15, 16, <u>20</u>, <u>25</u>, 27, 29, 30; May: 2, 4-9, 12-14, <u>15</u>, <u>16</u>, <u>18</u>, <u>22</u>, 24-29; Jun.: <u>1</u>, 2-5, <u>7</u>, 8-12, 21-27, <u>28</u>, 29; Jul.: 1, 2, 16, 18-21, 23; Aug.: <u>7</u>, 10, <u>12</u>, <u>22</u>; Sep.: 7, <u>8</u>, 9, 11-13, 16, <u>18</u>, 23, 27; Oct.: <u>1</u>, 3, 10, <u>15-21</u>, 23, 24, <u>29</u>, <u>30</u>, 31; Nov.: 9, 10, <u>11</u>, 12-17, 19, 21, <u>27-30</u>; Dec.: <u>2-9</u>, 12-14, 18, <u>29</u>, <u>31</u>.

47796389R00115

Made in the USA
Columbia, SC
04 January 2019